PRAISE FOR *ENLIGHTENED POWER*

"*Enlightened Power* offers a design for competitive advantage and success. But it does more than guide. It inspires."
—Sharon L. Allen, chairman of the board,
Deloitte & Touche USA LLP

"Without question, the best set of essays on women and leadership around. Every leader will need to have this one on their bookshelf."
—Warren Bennis, University Professor,
University of Southern California, and author,
On Becoming a Leader and *Geeks and Geezers*

"This remarkable new book documents how leaders who are women are changing the old concepts of leadership and redefining future leadership. This timely book is for leaders of the future."
—Frances Hesselbein, chairman, Leader to Leader Institute

"*Enlightened Power* is a book that all women from all walks of life can embrace. The personal stories and lessons contained in this book can teach us all how to become better leaders and, more important, better people."
—Sue Myrick, United States Congresswoman,
Charlotte, North Carolina

"The men and women who contributed to *Enlightened Power* generously share their personal journeys and observations. Readers will come away feeling that they've been privy to a unique and important dialogue; they will also be inspired to exercise their own personal power—and to nurture the best that resides in all of us."
—Ruth G. Shaw, president and chief executive officer,
Duke Power Company

"No doubt, this book will engender spirited discussions among both men and women. Hopefully, one of the key ideas that will get attention is how important it is for all of us to keep thinking more creatively about leadership in organizations."
—Kenneth T. Stevens, CEO, Express

Enlightened Power

Linda Coughlin
Ellen Wingard
Keith Hollihan
Editors

Enlightened Power

How Women Are Transforming the Practice of Leadership

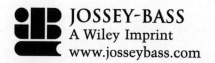

JOSSEY-BASS
A Wiley Imprint
www.josseybass.com

Published by Jossey-Bass
A Wiley Imprint
989 Market Street, San Francisco, CA 94103-1741 www.josseybass.com

Jossey-Bass books and products are available through most bookstores. To contact Jossey-Bass directly call our Customer Care Department within the U.S. at 800-956-7739, outside the U.S. at 317-572-3986, or fax 317-572-4002.

Jossey-Bass also publishes its books in a variety of electronic formats. Some content that appears in print may not be available in electronic books.

Library of Congress Cataloging-in-Publication Data

Coughlin, Linda, 1952–
  Enlightened power : how women are transforming the practice of leadership / by Linda Coughlin, Ellen Wingard, Keith Hollihan, editors—1st ed.
    p. cm.
  Includes bibliographical references and index.
  ISBN 0-7879-7787-X (alk. paper)
  1. Leadership. 2. Women executives. I. Wingard, Ellen, 1952– II. Hollihan, Keith
HD57.7 .E55 2005
658.4'092'082—dc 22

                                                            2005002449

Printed in the United States of America
FIRST EDITION
HB Printing 10 9 8 7 6 5 4 3 2 1

For our children

Contents

David Gergen is a leader who has earned widespread respect and international acclaim for his impartiality, insight, and wisdom. Commentator, editor, teacher, public servant, best-selling author, leadership expert, and adviser to four presidents, David Gergen has been an active participant in American national life for thirty years. He served as director of communications for President Reagan and held positions in the administrations of Presidents Nixon and Ford. In 1993, he put his country before politics when he agreed to counsel President Clinton on both foreign policy and domestic affairs and serve as a special international adviser to the president and to Secretary of State Warren Christopher. He is currently the director of the Center for Public Leadership at the John F. Kennedy School of Government. Also the author of *Eyewitness to Power: The Essence of Leadership*, David is a bipartisan, inclusive leader of global scale and a voice for enlightened power.

In this Foreword, David extols those leaders and thinkers who have challenged our basic assumptions around gender and leadership and makes a passionate call for further progress in balancing the inner and outer facets of the leadership-gender equation so that we may see tangible results and profound change in our lifetimes.

Foreword

WOMEN LEADING IN THE TWENTY-FIRST CENTURY

David Gergen

For more than two centuries, conventional wisdom held that women were incapable of climbing mountains. As he prepared an expedition to climb Mount Everest, for example, Sir Edmund Hillary refused a request to include women. He allegedly gave three reasons: women didn't have the qualities of leadership that were required, they weren't strong enough to carry the packs, and (that most ancient of all prejudices) they would become hysterical at high altitudes.

Fortunately, some women were bold enough to challenge conventional wisdom. Arlene Blum began experimenting with mountain climbs in Oregon and Washington. Lo and behold, she found that she had the leadership, strength, and temperament to make it. Soon she organized a team of ten American women to prepare a quest in which no woman and no American male had ever succeeded: scaling Annapurna, at 26,545 feet the world's tenth highest mountain. In 1978, they succeeded—magnificently—and Blum eventually wrote a book titled *Annapurna: A Woman's Place*.

As a white male, I am not sure I can ever fully appreciate how challenging it has been—and remains—for women to shatter old barriers. But I can say that as a participant in American public life for more than three decades, I am convinced that women are the equals of men in all fields of endeavor, starting with leadership. I can say that as a father, I want to be damned sure that my daughter, just like my son, has an untrammeled opportunity to become all she wants to be. And as a citizen, I can say that it's long past time to be asking women to shatter old barriers: the twenty-first century should become the century of women's equality.

Over the past few years, I have been privileged to teach at the John F. Kennedy School of Government at Harvard University, where we have launched the Center for Public Leadership with a generous grant from the Wexner Foundation. There we are trying to put our money where our mouth is. Barbara Kellerman, a respected scholar in leadership studies, became our first executive director; Betsy Myers, who ran the women's outreach effort at the Clinton White House, has recently succeeded her. Our first academic hire was a woman, Hannah Riley Bowles, and several women have been visiting scholars. One of them, Deborah Rhode, published an edited volume partly as a result, *The Difference "Difference" Makes*, and it has been an important contribution to the field. In partnership with Swanee Hunt, who runs the Women and Public Policy Program, we have begun an annual leadership training program for women, and in the coming academic year we will devote our annual leadership conference to the advancement of women. The school itself, through Holly Taylor Sargent, has created a Women's Leadership Board that is increasingly vibrant. Are we doing enough? Not yet, but we are trying.

These experiences, as well as those stretching back to politics in Washington, have led me to three inescapable conclusions.

The Summit: A Woman's Place

First, women make great leaders. For a long while, that issue was a matter of debate, similar to the mountain climbing nonsense. But the argument is now over. The evidence is in, and it's overwhelming: in one community after another, women are proving to be capable, effective, and—yes—tough leaders who get the job done.

Look at the largest state in the union, California. Carly Fiorina embarked on a high adventure when she took the reins at Hewlett-Packard and moved to a merger with Compaq. Many thought she would never make it; her judgment and acumen were attacked, and it was whispered that her womanhood would be her undoing. No CEO lasts long these days, but to be sure Fiorina was a bold and visionary leader in her near six years at HP. She beat the odds that some of her critics gave her, and the merger worked out better than some of the spectacular failures engineered by male CEOs in recent years. Consider, too, the politics of California, a state that has often been a bellwether for others. Arnold Schwarzenegger got off to an excellent start as governor, but he is matched in popularity by Senator Dianne Feinstein. And from that soil has sprung many other women leaders: Senator Barbara Boxer; Nancy Pelosi, the first woman to become minority leader in the House of Representatives; Jane Harman, a major voice in the House as well. When George W. Bush was looking for a national security adviser, his first choice was Condoleezza Rice, then the provost at Stanford. Some Republicans believe she could one day change places and sit behind the desk in the Oval Office herself.

Many of these women have gravitated to Washington, D.C., and there they find themselves in the company of many other leaders who happen to be women—Sandra Day O'Connor, Ruth Bader Ginsburg, Madeleine Albright, and Pat Mitchell among them. The spirit of Kay Graham continues to inspire there, as does that of her good friend, Meg Greenfield.

If you turn south to my native North Carolina, you will find equally impressive leaders. Elizabeth Dole is now serving the state well in the Senate. Until recently, the three major universities at the corners of the Research Triangle—Duke, the University of North Carolina, and North Carolina State—simultaneously had women at their helms, and all three were highly successful. When Nan Keohane became president of Duke, the university was undertaking the biggest fundraising drive in its history, shooting for $750 million. She quickly raised the goal to $1 billion, then higher, then higher again. At the end, Nan and her team pulled in $2.3 billion, and she retired in a blaze of glory.

Women are racking up successes all over the country. Further south, Donna Shalala is not only maintaining football prowess at the University of Miami but also guiding the school toward an intellectual renaissance. A little further north, Christie Todd Whitman commands widespread respect for years as governor of New Jersey and as head of the U.S. Environmental Protection Agency. Shirley Tilghman is quickly making her mark as the new president of Princeton, recruiting other women to serve in top administrative positions and bringing in more women to the faculty. Together, they will make Princeton a magnet for promising young women going to college. At the University of Pennsylvania, Judith Rodin succeeded so well that when she stepped down as president, they recruited another woman to replace her.

In New York, of course, Hillary Clinton has become a powerful member of the Senate in her first term and could be heading toward the White House in her own right. When she went to the Senate, some worried that she would be a show horse; instead, she has become a workhorse, winning respect from unexpected quarters. I recently had dinner with the officers of a major corporation headquartered in upstate New York. Most of them were Republicans, and their company is in a place where there aren't many Democratic votes. But they said Senator Clinton had represented them more effectively than any other senator of either party.

In my adopted state of Massachusetts, a woman heads the Supreme Judicial Court and wrote the opinion recognizing gay marriages. While controversial, the decision is also pathbreaking and, in my modest judgment, will likely be embraced by more and more Americans in the decades ahead. When people are pioneers, they often take heat at first—but many of them also wind up on pedestals. We have a long record of women pathbreakers in Massachusetts, stretching back to Abigail Adams and Mercy Otis Warren. Today these pioneers are officially recognized.

Overseas, we see the same pioneering leadership. I've had the experience in recent years of coming to know Mary Robinson. After her success as president of Ireland, she went on to head up the Human Rights Commission at the United Nations. Some criticized her for her handling of a human rights summit in South Africa where Israel was unfairly targeted, but she struck me as brave for going forward with the enterprise at all. Coming from Japan, which has had trouble fielding strong diplomats, Sadaka Ogata served with distinction at the United Nations. So did Gro Brundtland, who headed the World Health Organization and who earlier, as prime minister of Norway, pulled the world forward toward sustainable development. All over the world, then, women have proven themselves to be good leaders. The argument is over!

Circles of Influence: The New Leadership Style

Second, we have learned that women seem ideally suited to the new leadership style that has been widely embraced. The old style was top-down, command and control, and directional. If you see the movie *Patton* with George C. Scott, you will spot it instantaneously. There are many other examples: Lyndon Johnson as president, "Chainsaw Al" Dunlap as CEO, Bobby Knight on the basketball court, Herbert von Karajan conducting an orchestra.

Today that kind of command-and-control leadership has given way to a new approach, often called an influence model of leadership. Instead of picturing a leader at the top of a pyramid, we envision her in the middle of a circle with spokes extending outward. Instead of hurling thunderbolts from atop Mount Olympus, the new leader persuades, empowers, collaborates, and partners. The best leader, we are finding, is one who identifies top talent and nurtures them to become leaders in their own right—a leader of leaders. Serving on the board at Yale University, I was extremely impressed by how effective Rick Levin, its president, became by recruiting and then empowering such strong talent around him. He built such a great team that no less than three of his appointees—two of them women—have now been tapped to run major universities on their own. That is the mark of a good leader.

Adapting to this new world, the way we teach leadership has changed considerably. If you ask an expert like Rosabeth Moss Kanter at the Harvard Business School, sign up for an executive session with the Center for Creative Leadership, or attend one of the training programs for our Women in Power series at the Kennedy School, you will find that leadership is viewed as a series of concentric circles. In the innermost circle is the individual leader—you. To be a leader—regardless of gender—you must first know thyself and then achieve self-mastery. Leadership is a journey that starts from within, as I have found in working with and studying U.S. presidents: those who have been most effective over the years have first made their own journey. Franklin Roosevelt was transformed as a leader by his struggle with polio, for example. The second, larger concentric circle—containing the first—is the organization of which you are a part. After learning self-leadership, one must learn to lead this larger group. In the framework of emotional intelligence popularized by Daniel Goleman, the essence of leading others is to develop empathy with them and to develop the social skills that will persuade them to work toward shared goals. Much of the literature about leadership is devoted to this second circle. Increasingly, leaders within organizations discover there is yet a third circle just beyond, which also must be mastered: the multitude of other organizations with which yours must cooperate, coordinate, and partner. Whether you are running eBay, the Red Cross, or the Centers for Disease Control—all now headed by women—you must learn to work across silos, collaborating with others in order to move your own work forward.

Recognizing these concentric rings, it is easier to understand the value of what I call 360-degree leadership—that is, leadership that requires you to listen and learn from others all around your outer circles. In days gone by, a CEO might pay attention only to those directly beneath him in the pyramid. A president might pay attention only to those who form his political base or share his ideology. But that approach is no longer sufficient: it means that a leader is making decisions with only a fraction of the information and insight that she needs. We live in such interconnected environments that to be effective, a leader today must seek out information from a wide array of people, especially those who *don't* share his or her biases.

Whatever his personal flaws, I found that Bill Clinton often made excellent decisions in the Oval Office because he was insatiably curious about the views of everyone around him. As president, he not only wanted to talk to his fellow Democratic chieftains but also wanted to hear from those have usually been in the shadows of national power—African Americans, Hispanics, and women seeking a place at the table. Overseas, he wanted to hear from Europeans, of course, but he also wanted to know the perspectives of people in Africa and India. To this day, Nelson Mandela remains a staunch friend, and Clinton is hailed in India. John F. Kennedy showed a similar approach during the Cuban missile crisis when he assembled a team around him that represented not just his cabinet secretaries but men who had diverse views and personal knowledge of Nikita Khrushchev. Both Clinton and Kennedy were practicing 360-degree leadership.

Women leaders, as it turns out, seem perfectly tailored for this new style. Think about the words we use to describe the old-style leadership: *aggressive, assertive, autocratic, muscular, closed*. When we describe the new leadership, we employ terms like *consensual, relational, web-based, caring, inclusive, open, transparent*—all qualities that we associate with the "feminine" style of leadership. One can argue whether this feminine style is in women's genes or is created by socialization. It doesn't matter much. The key point, as Sally Helgesen points out in her book *The Female Advantage*, is that women are knocking on the door of leadership at the very moment when their talents are especially well matched with the requirements of the day.[1]

Before setting down this argument, however, we should recognize that there are times when a leader must be decisive, aggressive, and autocratic. In a crisis, for example, a president or a CEO does not have time to roundtable a question for several days, hammering out a consensus. If someone in your organization chronically underperforms, you must first ask him to do better, but sooner rather than later you must put him off the bus. Effective leaders, in other words, must mix together masculine as well as feminine qualities. The psychologist Carl Jung argued that each of us is born with a feminine as well as masculine side—an anima and animus. Typically, one side dominates and the other is more hidden. In Jung's view, an individual achieves a healthy personality when he or she fully recognizes both sides and integrates them into a balanced whole. The best leaders are those who achieve that balance in their approach to others. One of the reasons Rudy Giuliani was so inspiring on September 11 was that we saw his caring side as well as his decisive qualities. Of all our presidents, Lincoln demonstrated the greatest balance of masculine and feminine traits, and he remains today a beloved leader.

In the same way, women who have the qualities that we associate with the new style of leadership need to have a masculine side that they integrate as an authentic part of their personalities. Carly Fiorina certainly has a steely edge—one that helped her during her long run at HP. In her early days as First Lady, Hillary Clinton struck many as so overly aggressive that she was off-putting, especially for older men, but in more recent years she has matured into a more balanced and more appealing leader. Madeleine Albright turned her many hats into a trademark, and everyone knew she had a softer side, but she could also be tough as a boot. If anything, the Defense Department thought she wanted to send troops into too many countries. Donna Shalala, one of my favorite leaders, once told me a story that illustrates the importance of this masculine integration for women who aspire to the top. When she was president of Hunter College in New York, the trustees at the University of Wisconsin were seeking a new head. Donna soon found herself on the short list and was the only female candidate. She had a reputation then as a liberal and a keen feminist. That didn't drive off the trustees at Wisconsin, but they did have one concern. During their interview with her, very gingerly one said in effect, "As you know, our football team hasn't been doing so well lately, and we want to know how you would feel about building a good team." Donna seemed to confirm their fears when she said, "No, that would not make me happy." Then she continued, "If your ambition is only to build a good team, I'm not your person. I want a great team, and if you're willing to do that, I'm willing to do the job!" As it turned out, Donna may have been the only candidate who showed a keen interest in football. The trustees hired her, of course, and she built one of the best football programs in the country. Eventually, the University of Wisconsin went to the Rose Bowl, and Shalala rode on a float down the streets of Pasadena. There's even better news to the story. So happy were the regents and the state legislature with her successes in football that they supported her financially on nearly all the academic programs she wanted! She was a memorable president—one of the best. The masculine and the feminine sides, coming together, form a powerful whole.

The Gap: Our National Shame

Third, we know that our commitment to equal opportunity for rising women leaders is riddled with hypocrisy. In my view, we should be ashamed as a nation that we have so few women in positions of power, authority, and influence in our national organizations despite knowing that women can lead and, in fact, are well suited to the new leadership style. In February 2004, the magazine *Fast Company* looked at this matter of leadership, and its headline asked, "Where Are the Women?"[2] Where are they, indeed. Women constitute 47 percent of our workforce and 63 percent of all workers earning the minimum wage or less.[3] Yet they represent only 13.6 percent of the Fortune 500 boards,[4] and as of this writing only eight Fortune 500 companies have women as their CEOs.[5] The Bush White House has made a public commitment to equality, but tellingly, the prestigious White House Fellows program in recent years has hovered around 20 percent or less in female selections. In every major university of which I am aware, more than 50 percent of the student body is now female, but not a single one of the big universities comes close to having women represent half of their top faculty; rare is the university whose recruits to junior faculty positions are half female. In other words, when female students sit down in college classrooms across the country, they almost always have a man standing in front of them. The United States today is the world's number one economic, military, political, and cultural power—yet it is 60th in the world when it comes to women in positions of political leadership.[6] All of this needs to change. We must deal with the gap by confronting it head-on.

Some point insistently to the progress we have made—and to be sure, it's there—but we are moving at a perilously slow rate. Marie Wilson, who was at the Ms. Foundation and then started the White House Project to elect a woman president by the year 2008, has just written a book titled *Closing the Leadership Gap*. She argues that at the rate we are going, the percentage of women on Fortune 500 boards won't reach 25 percent for another twenty-five years.[7] In politics, the progress is even slower: we won't see parity for several hundred years.

To repeat: we now know that women make good leaders. We know they are well suited to the new leadership style. More and more women are knocking on the door, seeking positions of leadership. Yet we are still saddled with this tremendous hypocrisy. To me, that points to an inescapable conclusion about where we should be headed.

Setting Goals, Measuring Progress

The United Nations has set admirable goals for the world in this new millennium. One is to cut the rate of world poverty in half by 2015. Many people are working hard to achieve that objective. We may not be making as much progress as we should, but we have a specific goal that helps keep us on track. Within the United States, we often set social goals for America, too, as President George H. W. Bush and the nation's governors did a decade-and-a-half ago on advancing children in school.

It's long past time that we set goals for advancing women in our midst. If the United Nations can cut the rate of world poverty in half by 2015, surely the United States can cut its leadership gap for women within the same time frame! If we have performance and accountability measures in our schools, surely we can measure the rate at which women move forward as leaders. We ought to cut the leadership gap in half by 2015 as a first step and then move beyond to close it altogether. Before we leave this earth, we should be able to look back and say, "We did it."

The reasons for closing the gap are both simple and compelling. The first is economic. We all want to build a more prosperous society. If you have read the 2004 Catalyst study, *The Bottom Line: Connecting Corporate Performance and Gender Diversity,* you know that corporations with large percentages of women on their executive leadership teams gain returns that are 35 percent higher than those with few women in positions of leadership.[8] In other words, having women at the top is smart business.

The rise of more women to leadership will also make us a more caring society. Recent experience shows that once women occupy about 20 percent or so of top positions in an organization, the organization's agenda begins to change. If only one or two women are at a table, men may seek to smother their voices, but if they are there in sizable numbers, they will speak up and be heard. Although we are still far behind Scandinavia in percentages of women serving in our national legislature, we have already seen a shift in the congressional agenda as more women are elected. In the Senate, women of both parties have tried to get together for a dinner once a month. It's a bipartisan group. Not coincidentally, the women in that caucus have helped usher many critical bills to enactment, such as the Family and Medical Leave Act, the Pregnancy Discrimination Act, the Child Support Enforcement Act, the Women's Health Equity Act, and the initiative for the Office of Women's Health Research at the National Institutes for Health.

Even more fundamentally, the advancement of women into positions of leadership will help make this a more just society. It took many long years of suffering and struggle before the country finally woke up to the fact that extending freedom to black Americans would enhance the freedom of white Americans, too. We are still far from achieving equal opportunity, but at least we understand. Not so with regard to women. It is still too easy for men to pay lip service to equal opportunity for women but not really believe it. Until men know that full freedom for women enriches their own freedom, they will drag their heels and find excuses. And it is increasingly easy for women to become discouraged, too. Indeed, we see some signs of backlash occurring among both men and women as the excruciating challenges of finding a balance between work and family are encouraging growing numbers of professional women to curtail their careers—and level off their incomes—after children are born.

Women scholars like Deborah Rhode, Kathleen Hall Jamieson, and Alice Eagly have written persuasively that we must first dismantle the emotional and physical barriers that exist for women seeking leadership roles. As Kathleen Hall Jamieson has pointed out, women still find themselves in a double bind in which aggressive, male-like leadership will prompt others to call them a witch, while nonaggressive, female-like behavior will brand them as weaklings.[9] Young, caring fathers are experiencing a similar bind. If they take time off to look after a baby, their superiors may regard them as soft; if they stay on the job, their peers may regard them as insensitive. Getting rid of gender stereotypes should be at the top of the agenda for today's CEOs.

Clearly, we also need to work hard at creating equal access to mentors and networks. Every white male I know, including me, would not have achieved his success were it not for the mentors he met early in his career. In my case, older white males went out of their way to open doors for me, give me recommendations, and introduce me to others who helped me move up. If not for the five or six men who had been there for me along the way, I would not have enjoyed the privileges I have had as a citizen, and I am immensely grateful to each of them. But as I look back and also look around today, it is blindingly obvious that rising young women lack the same degree of help from mentors and networks, especially in corporate and political America. *What* you know these days is important, but, for better or worse, *who* you know can be crucial.

Friends make a big difference, too. I once asked David Herbert Donald, author of the best single-volume biography of Lincoln, "What's the most important asset of a president?" He replied that the most important asset for any leader is a friend. In order to reach the summits of life, you need people with whom you can talk candidly and to whom you can pour out your troubles. I was blessed to know both Katherine Graham and Meg Greenfield of the *Washington Post* and could see that their close friendship inspired each of them to become the best in their field. At our Women and Power seminar at the Kennedy School, the attendees prize their breakfasts together. All the participants are women, and they are divided into groups of five. Each morning at breakfast, one woman plays CEO and the others serve as her board. The CEO describes the challenges she faces as leader of her organization (usually drawn from real-life issues back home), and the others provide their frank, candid counsel. Together, they work through the challenges, and the next morning someone else sits in the CEO's chair. Over the course of the week, those women bond and develop a safe place to talk.

As we know, women don't have many safe places to talk in a male-dominated society. There is little opportunity to speak openly, to say, "I'm not sure I can handle this. Do you have any advice?" Men do have those places, group settings in which friends can help each other. Sometimes the issues lurking beneath the surface are family related, sometimes work related: "How can I be more present at home?" "How do I fire this person?" "What if I fail at my new assignment?" As I have grown older, more men are concerned about their health, and they don't like to talk about their issues in mixed company. I believe in the creation of "all-women" groups, just as I have come to believe that "all-men" groups are worthwhile, so long as the men are committed to equality of opportunity for both genders. I happen to belong to such a group, and the bonding process with other men has been enormously helpful, allowing me to form new friendships and to become more open and honest with others because I have a safe place to talk. Women deserve those places, too.

It is increasingly urgent that we make work more family-friendly as well. Americans have not come close to what Europeans have accomplished in balancing work and family life. If you are a professional woman and you enter a competitive track in a law firm, university, or other institution, your organization should stop the clock when you take time out for a new child. And after you return to work, special provisions should be made so that both you and your spouse can achieve both professional and family success. A decade ago, we patted ourselves on the back as a nation when the Congress and the Clinton White House enacted the Family and Medical Leave Act, providing twelve weeks of *unpaid* leave. But in truth, as the Europeans show us, the leave should be fully paid and at least six months.

I've recently joined the board of Bright Horizons, a for-profit corporation that provides high-quality child care, especially in corporate and university settings. What makes Bright Horizons successful is that it pays child-care workers much more than the industry average, and because of that, many of their child-care workers are college graduates who are dedicated to helping their charges grow. The service costs more, but the difference is worth it. Serving on the board—and thinking, too, of grandchildren on the way—has opened my eyes to issues of child care. We know high-class attention works better for children than custodial care; we simply haven't mustered the will yet to make it affordable to families nationwide.

Finally, may I suggest that it is important for women in America to reach out to women around the world. On a global scale, women are taking a real beating. Two-thirds of the world's poor are women and children. Massive numbers are dying because of malnutrition, HIV-AIDS, deprivation, and violence. The sex traffic in women is increasing, not decreasing. Yet women are clearly the solution to many of the world's problems. We know, for example, that one of the most productive investments of foreign assistance is in the education of young women. We know that microfinancing in places like India and Bangladesh empowers women and lifts the quality of life. We know that empowering women with the vote deepens the roots of democracy.

No nation on earth treats women with full equality yet—though some are coming close. If we are going to change the nature of the world in which we live, women here must form partnerships with women beyond our shores. At a time when the United States is seen as exercising command-and-control, autocratic leadership in the world, alliances that come through caring and networking with people in other countries would be good not only for the world but for the United States, too. In fact, it would open more doors for women here at home than we can possibly imagine. I have learned firsthand from women leaders like Swanee Hunt, Pat Mitchell, Elizabeth Dole, Glenn Close, and Sally Field how much can be accomplished.

In short, the leadership gap today is daunting, but as Tom Paine wrote at the time of the American Revolution, we have it within our power to turn the world upside down. It's time again. Back in the early 1990s, we had the Year of the Woman. It wasn't enough. Some writers like Tom Peters called the 1990s the Decade of the Woman, but that wasn't enough, either. Now it's critical that we truly show our commitment to justice by making this the Century of the Woman. Before we leave this world, it's imperative that we be able to look back and say that we closed the gap here at home. We need to create a new definition of power in our organizations and communities and recognize new and different ways to exercise that power. This book provides urgent and helpful steps toward that worthy goal.

Enlightened Power

Lin Coughlin is chief administrative officer of Cendant Corporation, a Fortune 150 provider of travel and real estate services serving businesses and consumers in more than one hundred countries. A seasoned leader with more than twenty-seven years of experience in corporate America, she has spent most of her career in the financial services industry at American Express Company, Citibank, and Scudder Investments, a global investment management company serving institutions, high net worth individuals, and retail investors. At Scudder, Lin was a managing director, chairman of the board of three families of mutual funds, and president of the Americas Mutual Funds Group where she was responsible for businesses with combined assets under management of more than $100 billion and annual revenues in excess of $750 million. Prior to assuming her current position at Cendant, Lin was the vice chair of the board of directors and president of Linkage, Inc., an organizational development company specializing in leadership. She continues to serve as chair of Linkage's annual Women in Leadership Summit. She is also a member of several prominent groups focused on women in leadership, including The Committee of 200 and The Women's Leadership Board at the John F. Kennedy School of Government at Harvard University.

In this Introduction, Lin defines enlightened power and uses her own values-based journey through corporate America to make a compelling case for inclusive leadership styles and organizations.

PHOTO CREDIT: Linda Coughlin by Bachrach Photos

Introduction

THE TIME IS NOW

A Leader's Personal Journey

Linda Coughlin

Belonging is a powerful phenomenon. When we feel accepted and validated by others, we reconnect to our inner selves and to the world around us. This is why leaders find the company of other leaders reinforcing and emboldening. The "permission" we are granted to safely share defining experiences and complex, confusing emotions stimulates us to look inward. In turn, the realization of that inner awareness—that powerful reflection point, that ability to awaken an internal voice of authority, that quiet of deep resolve, that "still point" that my colleague and coeditor Ellen Wingard refers to—catalyzes, defines, and solidifies belonging. The result: the bold, confident expression of an outward-directed passion and vision can be manifest.

For women leaders, the affirmation and support of a larger community are still uncommon. Women leaders can feel alone in the most crowded of rooms. Whether in the ranks of middle management, in the high echelons of the executive suite, at the helm of entrepreneurial or philanthropic ventures, or in a political arena, we are constantly reminded—subtly and not so subtly—that we are not truly welcome as we attempt to impart perspective or advocate a point of view. This type of repeated rejection has a profound effect. We doubt our own ideas, intuition, and knowledge. We lose our self-esteem, confidence, and desire to contribute. We do not feel valued or resilient. Although every woman leader knows the personal costs of such marginalization, it is hard to imagine the losses we have incurred in organizations as a result.

This book, a room of our own, is more than just a collection of essays on leadership experiences and learnings. It is the manifesto of an impassioned, liberated, life-loving community of leaders who belong. That community has emerged and grown up around the Women in Leadership Summit, an event that Linkage has presented each year since 1999. The community includes hundreds of thought leaders and practitioners who have presented at the summit. It also includes the more than 5,000 business and community leaders who have attended the summit—women and a small but growing number of men from the middle and upper ranks of corporations, entrepreneurs, and leaders from the public sector and not-for-profit organizations—individuals who are making a difference and who are committed to achieving a powerful sense of belonging. The volume in your hands represents our ambitious attempt to tap the richness of the Women in Leadership Summit experience and extend that experience to a wider audience via the written page.

What binds this vibrant, dynamic, and growing community? Shared experiences and challenges, and a singular desire: to recast leadership from the confines of traditional models. Our resounding vision is one of organizations that invoke the full participation of men and women leaders toward transformative contribution to the social and economic well-being of the organizations they represent, their communities, and our world.

As individual family members, leaders of organizations, and members of society, we are changing the nature and use of power through our practice of *enlightened power*—that which is manifest as we:

- Enact inclusive leadership models that bring to bear the full and equal partnership of men and women leaders
- Link productive, economically rewarding work with positive, personally fulfilling, and sustainable change that benefits all

stakeholders—customers, employees, shareholders, suppliers, and the "community" at large

The "we" includes a preponderance of women. However, the message of this book is emphatically not about exclusion. We in fact encourage and applaud the participation of our male colleagues as partners in the dialogue that is the heart and spirit of our community. It is in fact our "enlightened" and impassioned male colleagues who are willing to champion the collaborative, solution-focused discovery process that will catapult us in the quest to achieve the full partnership of men and women leaders. The realization of this partnership is a passion of mine—one that I, like many others, bring to my role as a leader in business and to the dialogue now taking place on a global scale regarding the roles of women in leadership. Therefore, I focus this Introduction on the topic of inclusive leadership, one of the two primary manifestations of enlightened power.

As our contributors show, women, in ever greater numbers, are truly leading the way in challenging the status quo and demanding a more inclusive, *enlightened* approach to the use of power. In fact, our contributors—men and women alike, representing a synthesis and symphony of many voices—share the belief that thriving, wealth-producing organizations and societies are ones that promote the full and equal partnership of men and women leaders.

Together, we are doing our part to celebrate and coax a shift from a hierarchical privilege for a few to an inclusive empowerment of all. We are emboldened by the potential of this tectonic shift, not only for moral reasons but because we have experienced its social and economic benefit: greater personal fulfillment, extraordinary business results, and more humane organizations and societies.

Reaching Forward: What If . . . ? How Can . . . ?

"The collective energy of possibility unleashed" characterizes the tone of our community's exploration of enlightened power. Our shared understanding is the scaffolding on which we are building an expansive, solution-focused dialogue—one that includes men and women, extends beyond the confines of traditional discussions of gender, and centers on authenticity and the celebration of uniqueness as defining qualities of twenty-first-century leaders. In the generative space of this dialogue, we find ourselves addressing compelling questions:

- How can leaders bring their whole selves to the practice of leadership? In this regard, how can the development of a new type of power—one that is internally generated and derived from a way of *being*—be hastened?

- To what extent could the practice of this enlightened power be accelerated if it were recognized that women and men are gifted in a variety of ways and that we need the feminine and masculine perspectives to be represented in balanced and complementary ways for society to thrive?

- How can each of us locate, develop, and express the values of authenticity and the celebration of uniqueness in our leadership roles?

- How can these attributes of authenticity and uniqueness be assessed as legitimate performance criteria of results-oriented leadership in our organizations, communities, and the world?

- How can the practice of "social entrepreneurship" be advanced, focusing on the realization of "value to the third power"—that which involves leaders' development of themselves and others, leaders' delivery of breakthrough results at high-performing organizations, and leaders' support of the communities their organizations operate in, locally and globally?

- What could be expected in the way of enhanced organizational performance if appointments to positions with the greatest power, responsibility, and influence were truly a function of measurement against clearly articulated performance standards, instead of gendered perceptions of leadership potential?

- To what extent might rising levels of social, political, and economic uncertainty be abated if power and its consequences, in terms of influence and financial reward, were shared equally by women and men?

Our contributors offer perspective and answers to these questions and more. The book's exploration of enlightened power—its focus on a willingness and ability to shift to new contexts in a fast-changing world, its recognition of paradoxes and polarities that must be reckoned with along the way, its assessment of the ways in which inclusive organizations and their leaders are redefining the workplace, and its emphasis on linking productive work outcomes with positive and sustainable change benefitting *all* stakeholders—offers extraordinary stories, learnings, and messages that reveal what can be done.

A Revolution Stalled

As David Gergen says in the Foreword, "Our commitment to equal opportunity for rising women leaders is riddled with hypocrisy." He declares, "We should be ashamed as a nation that we have so few women in positions of power, authority, and influence. . . ." Pat Mitchell eloquently states in her Afterword that there has never been a more urgent imperative for inclusive leadership in our increasingly polarized political climate.

Global uncertainty has affected our sense of security about the future. On the one hand, the corporate scandals of recent years feel like the shedding of outdated and exclusionary modes of hierarchy, privilege, and power. That said, our post-9/11 era has been marked by a retreat and return to more conservative times. This confluence of paradoxes has changed the debate involving women leaders. The dialogue has shifted away from *how* women leaders can compete with their male counterparts to *whether* women leaders even want to be in "the game."

Fortune recently asked the question, "Power: Do Women Really Want It?"[1] Many of the women leaders quoted in the article expressed discomfort with the traditional demands of power and little inclination for seizing it for its own sake. Likewise, a cover story in *Fast Company* not long ago asked, "Where Are the Women?" and answered its own question: "Not in the corner office, even after all these years. Not now. Maybe not ever. So what happened?"[2] A widely cited article from the *New York Times Magazine*, written by Lisa Belkin and entitled "The Opt-Out Revolution," struck a similar chord. Women, the article noted, are less likely than men to pay the price over the long haul in the corporate setting and are increasingly likely to "opt out" for more fulfilling or family-focused roles. According to the author, "Measured against the way things once were, this [the increasing number of women assuming positions of power and leadership] is certainly progress. But measured against the way things were expected to be, this is a revolution stalled."[3]

No one in our community regards "opting out" as an act of surrender or a sign of failure. Indeed, for many women, opting out is a courageous choice. Yet for women who choose to climb the leadership ladder, the stories of those who are opting out ring a distressing note. Without women in positions of leadership, the likelihood of advancing cultures of inclusion declines. Formal and informal barriers will continue to perpetuate an unequal playing field that will lead, over time, to physical, emotional, and psychological fatigue. The time is now to confront the looming specter of institutional disenfranchisement.

The Performance Impact of Inclusive Leadership: Possibility Unleashed

What is the impact of the fully enabled partnership of men and women leaders on organizational performance? Recent research affirms a strong correlation. For example, a study conducted by the Glass Ceiling Research Center collected data for an average of 215

Fortune 500 companies for every year from 1980 to 1998.[4] The results were calculated using several different measures of profitability. They show a clear pattern: Fortune 500 companies with the best track record of developing and promoting women outperformed their respective industry medians by 18 to 69 percent. The results were deemed highly conservative, in that focusing on a smaller set of only the most friendly organizations for women would have resulted in even more dramatic differences in profitability.

A recently published study by Catalyst (a leading research and advisory organization working to advance women in business) draws the correlation between inclusivity at the leadership level and financial performance even more starkly.[5] Examining 353 Fortune 500 companies and evaluating return on equity and total return to shareholders, the study showed that companies in which women have the highest representation in the top management teams outperform by a significant margin those companies with the lowest levels of representation.

What accounts for this organizational performance boost when proportionate numbers of women are developed, promoted, and positioned at the tables where key strategic and operational decisions are made? Multiple factors are at work. Surely innovative output is one, because, as never before, the ability to gain and *sustain* competitive advantage depends on an organization's ability to continually learn and innovate. Without an emphasis on generating ideas and applying knowledge, businesses fall farther and farther behind. Innovation requires unlearning old ways and learning new ways. It requires expanding and multiplying perspectives and actively challenging the status quo; and, contrary to popular thinking, innovation requires the presence of diverse, highly collaborative, generative teams operating in knowledge-rich learning environments.

Over the past three decades, women have established several thousand thriving small and medium-size businesses—proof of their strong entrepreneurial skills and tendencies. Every day, an average of 1400 to 1600 women leaders are leaving Fortune 500 companies to start their own businesses or work for competitors—twice the rate of their male counterparts.[6] They do so usually after exhausting efforts to make a difference within their company. Thus organizational commitment to developing and retaining women leaders as part of an inclusive leadership model delivers dual benefits: it increases innovative output, and it drives down attrition costs. Deloitte Consulting, for example, discovered the significant bottom-line benefit when it saved $250 million in turnover costs—in large part as a result of implementing a comprehensive professional development system to retain and advance women.[7]

The conclusion is not that women are better suited to leadership roles than men, but rather that women, like men, do in fact possess innate leadership qualities and the potential to lead in support of breakthrough results. The performance gap will continue to grow between those organizations that recognize this truth and actively work to create more inclusive organizational systems and those that do not. Indeed, the organizational and personal costs of failing to make this work a strategic priority are climbing steeply.

The Harsh Reality

Our examination of women in leadership is grounded in certain sobering facts about the large, paradoxical gap between the numbers of men and women leaders. A review of a few of the most salient and germane are worth noting. Women make up

- 47 percent of the U.S. labor force[8]
- 50 percent of managerial and professional specialty positions[9] but only 13.6 percent of Fortune 500 board members (with additional data further suggesting that equal representation of women on the boards of America's biggest companies could take another fifty years)[10]
- Less than 8 percent of the Fortune 500 highest titles (with the pace of women moving into such high-level roles slowing considerably)[11]

- A disproportionately small number of leadership roles in the public sector (following the 2004 elections, women represent just 65 of the 435 members of the United States House of Representatives, 14 of the 100 members of the United States Senate, and 8 of the 50 governors in the nation)[12]

What accounts for the significant gap between the numbers of men and women leaders? One explanation is that continued institutional barriers—formal and informal, overt and subtle—create an unequal playing field that over time leads to physical, emotional, and psychological fatigue. Thus, in time, even capable, well-conditioned leaders give up the game.

Several excellent studies support this explanation. Presenters and participants at Linkage events over the years suggest that the impediments to the advancement of women in business and public life are rooted in a variety of social, psychological, and organizational dynamics.

Four particularly stubborn perceptions are most toxic. Deborah M. Merrill-Sands and Deborah M. Kolb, formerly codirectors at the Center for Gender in Organizations (CGO) at Simmons Graduate School of Management, provide an excellent discussion of the first three in their article "Women as Leaders: The Paradox for Success."[13] Each of the four perceptions acts as a significant derailer for many promising women leaders.

1. *The perception of leadership potential.* Even when organizations' leadership models espouse more balanced and inclusive skill sets, promotions are not based solely or even largely on candidates' evaluations against these formal standards. Advancement is often based on informal, subtle, traditionally masculine assumptions about the requirements of leadership—assumptions developed and reinforced by popular culture images of the take-charge, heroically autonomous, "buck stops here" leader. Men are perceived as "natural" carriers of these

leadership essentials, possessing greater potential. A recent study of 2,800 managers bears this out: whereas supervisors rated women somewhat higher than men on their current leadership and managerial competencies, they rated men significantly higher with respect to their perceived potential as leaders in the long run.[14]

2. *The perception of willingness to lead.* As Merrill-Sands and Kolb note, studies confirm the existence of the widely held and gendered belief that women are not interested in taking on leadership roles. Acting on this belief, decision makers often pass over women for selection into leadership positions. Yet the belief is untested and unfounded. Indeed, Merrill-Sands and Kolb's research shows that women are just as likely as men to accept leadership positions if offered.[15]

3. *The perception of valuable leadership skills.* Critical leadership skills may be valued differently when men or women enact them. For example, a study by Robert Kabacoff found that supervisors, of whom 81 percent were male, saw the following behaviors as positively related to leadership effectiveness when demonstrated by men, but as negatively related to leadership effectiveness when demonstrated by women: focusing on results, taking charge and directing others, striving for high levels of achievement, and seeking out positions of influence.[16]

4. *The perception of tokenism.* Particularly in those organizations with a scarcity of women or minority leaders at the top, conflict occurs when women and minorities are appointed to top positions because they represent a solution to the problem of "optics" in organizations. As perceived tokens, their "differences" make them subject to stereotyping. They are also subjected to expectations—explicit and tacit—that their performance must meet higher standards than other leaders in the organization. This can lead to higher stress levels, which in turn can affect productivity, motivation, and effectiveness.

Even in the absence of overtly discriminatory practices and in the presence of laudable policies promoting equity and diversity, these four pervasive dynamics combine to derail disproportionate numbers of qualified women, preventing them from reaching levels that are commensurate with their potential.

In short, the full valuing and expression of leadership, in all its necessarily multifaceted aspects and attributes, continues to be stifled. Although women have traditionally been more silenced, men may increasingly be victimized as well—their styles, actions, and behaviors bounded by narrowly defined notions of leadership and power. Forced to accept this narrow range of conventionally gendered options for acceptable behavior, both men and women may suffer from arrested and diminished personal development, which can render them less capable of functioning effectively in a gender-integrated workforce. All of this leads to costly consequences over time. Consistently acting out of balance with our core selves has its price—for the individual and, in turn, for any results-driven organization.

My Own Crossroad

In my own life and leadership journey I stand now at a point at which my values and passions direct me to forcefully engage with these compelling questions—as a mother of three beautiful and high-achieving young adults, an aspiring contributor to the greater good, and a change-oriented leader. Having spent my twenty-seven-year career in corporate America, I have been fortunate to have ascended the leadership ranks. My rise has, however, been punctuated by some difficult but defining life learnings and experiences. I have achieved a deep understanding of the cost to organizations and society when women and other minority groups are excluded from leadership and policymaking roles.

Working throughout my career in primarily male environments, I have become convinced that feminine values—whether expressed by women *or* men—are too often trivialized or ignored.

Further, when the full potential and qualities of men and women leaders are synergistically and harmoniously unleashed, ground-breaking, model-shattering change can and does occur. I say this confidently, having personally experienced a defining "rite of passage" while leading a successful but complex and far-reaching change management initiative for a $1 billion business at a large financial services institution.

I had learned that a critical success factor for thriving twenty-first-century organizations requires moving from hierarchical, secretive, and change-averse cultures to open, collaborative, and risk-tolerant ones. I had also learned that people and organizations achieve stretch goals when those goals are rooted in a shared purpose and vision characterized by the presence of authentic, inclusive relationships where personal agendas are not tolerated and where agendas for change that put the interests of the enterprise first are championed. Our leadership team therefore committed to the development of "trusting" and "trusted" working relationships. The investment in this culture change was the single biggest contributing factor to brilliant execution of a groundbreaking, model-shattering change initiative. The outcome: a strategically rationalized operating model, breakthrough financial results, and the presence of a highly emboldened team of leaders who trusted in the possibility and supported each other as they ultimately ran through walls "to get the job done."

At the ground level, I have learned that the development of inclusive leadership teams requires, first and foremost, the belief that trusting relationships are possible and achievable. I have also learned that it is the leader's responsibility to create that environment of trust that enables such relationships to flourish. It is more important than the presence of well-honed technical skills. It is more important than "résumé management." It is more important than the cultivation of our network of supporters and influencers.

"Trusting" and "trusted" relationships with stakeholders—customers, employees, shareholders, suppliers, and the larger "community"—are grounded in a deep and crystal-clear understanding of and conviction around a leader's own values. I have found that the more consistently I practice my values, the more emboldened and effective I am at solving complex problems; being decisive when the stakes are high; and anticipating, managing, and overcoming the onset of situations in which I may be undermined or feel compromised.

It is hard work to locate, clarify, articulate, and reflect our values, and it is harder still to consistently practice those values as we grapple with life's demands, paradoxes, and polarities. Yet doing so is absolutely necessary work—work that fosters courage, fortitude, and resilience to lead with conviction and impact, especially when our resolve may be tested. This volume's collection of moving and instructional essays is offered to inspire and embolden you to locate, define, and hold your own values, like a sturdy, dependable walking stick you can more firmly grasp in hand for the long, challenging journey ahead.

I am heartened by the call for leadership models that break the status quo and invoke the equal partnership of men and women leaders. I ask, What must the work of leaders be in shaping corporate culture (the "software" of the organization) to unleash the full performance potential of inclusive leadership models? What must we do to cultivate environments that nurture, honor, and value the full and productive partnership of men and women leaders?

No leader can implement sustainable, model-shattering change that is not rooted in the practice of enlightened power. Toward this end, high-performing, inclusive organizations

- Align their mission, vision, values, operating principles (ways of making decisions, working through conflicts, managing dependencies, and so on), and strategies with stakeholders' urgent needs for meaning, fairness, authentic relationships, integrated self-expression, and, in the private sector, wealth creation

- Encourage the expression of flexible, gender-integrated leadership behaviors and styles in individual leaders and in leadership teams

- Extend the concept of wealth creation and its distribution to the social and economic well-being of the communities in which they operate, if not the world
- Strategically invest in the development of their human and social capital in good times *and* in bad to build trusting—and, in turn, innovative, forward-moving, risk-tolerant, individually supportive—environments
- Understand the power of belonging—at the individual, organizational, community, and societal levels—as critically important to effecting groundbreaking, model-shattering change

Progress cannot happen overnight, but the seeds can be sowed and cultivated by readers of this volume—leaders who, as part of our growing community, have the conviction, power, and influence to envision the possibilities, to trust in the achievability of those possibilities, and to support each other as we individually and collectively drive for changes that will spawn high levels of personal fulfillment, extraordinary business results, and more humane organizations and societies. To realize this more enlightened expression of power we must

- Raise awareness and create a sense of the urgency for the case for developing the full partnership of men and women leaders in order to achieve and sustain economic and social well-being for all on a global scale.
- Coax the mind-sets and behaviors of current and emerging leaders and policymakers—and, in turn, policies and reward systems—away from the confines of traditional hierarchically focused uses of power toward an inclusive empowerment of all.
- Commit to finding the "power within" that is required to master the practice of enlightened power. Such mastery is the most important step to enabling us to cope with, if not rise above, the confidence-deflating challenges we face from those who consciously or unconsciously, subtly or not so subtly, manifest demeaning and hurtful behavior because they per-

ceive women as "weak" or insufficiently committed or trust-
worthy, or because they are threatened by the leadership
potential of their female counterparts. For most women,
power is derived from a "power within" or a "power with" as
opposed to a "power over"—a hierarchical paradigm. Nonetheless, the achievement of a form of "positional power" by more
women is essential as a matter of economic and social equity.

To help leaders address these priorities, the authors of this volume present multiple methods and hard-won lessons for unleashing
the wealth-creating, socially responsible potential of inclusive
workplaces. At the same time, they remind us repeatedly that we
cannot underestimate the effort required and the necessity of whole-
hearted personal engagement. For this work is, after all, highly personal and will take time to effect in full.

Let the Drums Roll . . .

The honor of introducing this volume's special literary gathering
would not be complete without saying a few words about our distinguished contributors, 40 extraordinary men and women who
individually and collectively represent the most powerful voices in
the emerging field of women in leadership. Because they represent
a variety of disciplines, backgrounds, and life experiences, they offer
diverse perspectives relating to the subject at hand, enlightened
power. Many of our contributing authors have made their mark and
built their legacy as business leaders or leaders in other arenas. Others are best-selling authors in their own right who have written
landmark books and articles on the role of women leaders. Still others are distinguished professors who have advanced the subject from
an academic perspective.

The chapters that follow—many offered by some of the most accomplished, compelling, and innovative participants at Linkage's
Women in Leadership Summit—represent a recasting of traditional
ideas of leadership and the practices, uses, and misuses of power.

Their stories demonstrate the extent to which women can effect sustainable change through the use of enlightened power. As you read their stories, you will discern authentic and inclusive voices. You will notice the extent to which they reject the status quo. In so doing, they not only reconcile with but also embrace the many paradoxes and polarities of our fast-changing world—a world that is marked by high levels of technology-enabled access to and transparency of information as well as rising levels of uncertainty (if not upheaval) at the individual, organizational, community, and societal levels.

Finally, you will be inspired by the stories that speak to the authors' capacities to link productive, personally fulfilling, economically rewarding work with positive and sustainable change that benefits all. Our contributors, formidable leaders in their own right, are indeed models of the practice of enlightened power.

Together with my coeditors, Ellen Wingard and Keith Hollihan, I welcome you to our community.

Part One

REIMAGINING POWER

If we don't disturb the mind's familiar concepts of power, we can hardly be smart when using it.
—*James Hillman*, Kinds of Power: A Guide to Its Intelligence Uses, *1995*

In Part One, our contributors emphasize the importance of enlarging our understanding of power beyond traditional forms of control to embrace a new type of power—one that is internally generated and derived from a way of *being*.

For today's women leaders, focusing on *being* may present a considerable hurdle. Despite all the progress that has been made, succeeding in the workplace and the world still requires, in the words of one of our contributors, Stacy Blake-Beard, the donning of a suit of armor and a mask. As women leaders, we become accustomed to the tension between overcommitment and undersupport, as well as to the reality of being overlooked and underpaid. Not surprisingly, we become compliant—even from the corner office and other positions of power—hiding our true emotions, withholding our whole selves, and seeking to fit into systems that do not truly reflect our aspirations.

Today we are finally acknowledging and understanding the impact of that "self" sacrifice. What does it take for the individual to transcend obstacles and create a personal expression of power and leadership? Skills, tactics, and a supportive work environment can all help. There is, however, no substitute for the power that comes from self-awareness and the ability to shift one's context (and that of others) to achieve something new.

At a time when women leaders are struggling just to remain whole, creative, energized, and motivated in their organizations, a simple truth emerges: we must learn to lead ourselves before we can presume to lead others.

 Riane Eisler, an eminent social scientist, attorney, and futurist, is best known as author of the international best-seller *The Chalice and the Blade*, translated into twenty languages, and the award-winning *The Power of Partnership*, a guide to personal and cultural transformation. Riane is also renowned for her pioneering work in human rights, integrating the rights of women and children into mainstream theory and practice. She has taught at UCLA and is the cofounder of the Spiritual Alliance to Stop Intimate Violence as well as the Alliance for a Caring Economy. She is also president of the Center for Partnership Studies, dedicated to research and education on the partnership model introduced by her work.

Riane's chapter revolves around this partnership model—and how it is increasingly guiding the way that women (and men) are defining and exercising power. Along the way, she also shows us how this new model calls for further transformation of gender roles and relations as well as for new economic rules that no longer devalue women and stereotypically feminine traits and activities. In so doing, Riane provides us with a platform for reimagining power.

PHOTO CREDIT: Riane Eisler by David Loye

1

THE ECONOMICS OF THE ENLIGHTENED USE OF POWER

Riane Eisler

Ours is an exciting and challenging time. It is a turbulent time of major problems but also of major opportunities: a period of rapidly changing consciousness when, for the first time in recorded history, women can be leaders in shaping our future.

Technological and economic changes over the last centuries opened the door for questioning much that was once taken for granted—from the "divinely ordained" right of kings and princes to absolute authority over their "subjects," to the "divinely ordained" right of men to absolute control over women and children. These challenges to traditions of domination are part of a shift from authoritarian family and social structures to structures that support more democratic and egalitarian relations. And an integral part of this shift has been a view of leadership no longer based on control, coercion, and disempowerment but on inspiration, facilitation, and empowerment.

This chapter examines these two different ways of defining and exercising power from the perspective of two models of social organization: the domination model and the partnership model. It shows that changes in our concepts of leadership are directly related to changes in gender roles and relations. It also shows why the entry of women into positions of leadership is an index of fundamental change in social structures and values—and why raising women's status and bringing traits and activities stereotypically associated with femininity into the workplace and society at large are fiercely resisted by those who believe that top-down rankings of domination are natural and moral.

The Domination and Partnership Models

Examining human societies cross-culturally and historically, I became aware that to better understand and more effectively solve our global problems, we have to go beyond conventional conceptual frameworks—as in today's mantra of "thinking outside the box." Old social categories, such as right or left, religious or secular, Eastern or Western, and industrial or pre- or postindustrial, do not describe whole social systems. None of them describes the totality of a society's family, educational, religious, political, and economic institutions and its guiding system of values. And all fail to recognize the enormous impact of gender roles and relations on both women's and men's lives, as well as on our beliefs, families, education, religion, economics, and politics.

When I began to examine societies from a perspective that takes all this into account, I saw that underneath the great surface diversity of human societies—transcending differences of time, place, technological development, ethnic origin, and religious orientation—are two underlying configurations. I call them the *domination model* and *partnership model* of social organization.

Societies such as Khomeini's Iran, Hitler's Germany, Stalin's Soviet Union, and the Masai of nineteenth- and early twentieth-century Africa are very different. But they all have striking commonalities. They are characterized by strong-man rule in both the family and the state or tribe, rigid male dominance, and a high degree of institutionalized violence, from child and wife beating to chronic warfare. They are also societies where so-called masculine values, such as toughness, strength, conquest, and domination are given high social and economic priority, as in the emphasis on weapons and wars. So-called feminine values, such as caring, compassion, empathy, and nonviolence, are, along with women, relegated to a secondary, subservient sphere cut off from the "real world" of politics and economics. These four characteristics—strong-man rule, rigid male dominance, institutionalized violence, and the devaluation of women and the "feminine"—are the core configuration of the domination model.

This model is marked by well-defined in-groups and out-groups. Social differences—beginning with the most fundamental difference in our species, that between women and men—are equated with superiority or inferiority, with dominating or being dominated. In the partnership model, by contrast, difference is valued, as in the ideal of the more pluralistic society now gaining currency.

In partnership-oriented societies, whether in the family, workplace, or society at large, so-called feminine qualities and behaviors are not only held in high esteem but also incorporated into the operational guidance system. There is equal partnership between women and men, a more democratic and egalitarian social structure, and less built-in violence, as it is not needed to maintain rigid rankings of domination.

The partnership configuration also transcends differences of time, place, and level of technological development. It can be found in technologically primitive tribal societies, such as the Teduray of the Philippines; agrarian societies, such as the Minangkabau of Sumatra; and technologically advanced industrial societies, such as the Nordic nations. In the Nordic countries, attempts to create a more equitable economic system resulted not in a dominator form of communism ruled from the top (as found in the former Soviet Union) but rather in a democratic society with a mix of free enterprise and welfare state. Here we also see a strong interest in nonviolent means of conflict resolution, as well as systemic attempts to create a more gender-balanced society—one where women, along with stereotypically feminine values, are not relegated to an inferior status and excluded from the public world.

If we reexamine modern history from this new perspective, we see that underneath its many complex currents and crosscurrents lies a powerful movement toward a partnership social organization, countered by strong resistance. We see that all the modern progressive movements have challenged different forms of domination backed by force and fear. This challenge is the common thread in the eighteenth- and nineteenth-century rights of man, antislavery, antimonarchist, socialist, pacifist, and feminist movements. The twentieth-century anticolonial, antiwar, participatory democracy, women's rights, and economic justice movements are also not isolated phenomena. They are all part of a much larger movement: the movement to create a world in which principles of partnership rather than domination and submission are primary. And a key aspect of this movement is the transformation of gender roles and relations—and with this shift, a redefinition of power and leadership in more stereotypically feminine ways.

Women, Men, and Power

I want to emphasize that when I say "stereotypically," I mean just that. There are obvious differences between women and men. But much that is considered masculine and feminine is our heritage from earlier times when women were strictly barred from positions of leadership and power.

Another part of this dominator heritage is the belief that a fear-based, institutionally insensitive, and all too often abusive and dehumanizing leadership and management style is a requisite for social order and economic productivity. The good news is that this leadership and management style is increasingly recognized as an impediment rather than a spur to social order and economic productivity.

Today's management and organizational development literature proposes that, particularly in the postindustrial knowledge economy, a new leadership and management style based on respect, accountability, and empowerment is needed. We are told that effective leaders and managers are not cops or controllers whose commands must be unquestioningly obeyed, but rather are people who facilitate, inspire, and elicit from others their highest productivity and creativity.

Such a leadership and management style models caring rather than coercion. Although some leaders—male and female—have always recognized the effectiveness of this leadership style, it is becoming more prevalent today because of the rising status of women, and thus of qualities and behaviors associated with femininity, such as nurturance and empathy.

Studies show that precisely because women's socialization was not designed for them to function in the "men's world," women today bring to the workplace some of the very skills needed if it is to be fundamentally transformed. For example, Leonard Greenhalgh conducted a study of women and men in simulated negotiations sessions at the Dartmouth School of Business Administration and found that women tend to be more flexible, more empathic, and more likely to reach agreement.[1] When a man visualizes a negotiating situation, he sees it as a one-shot deal to win or lose, like a sport or game, Greenhalgh states. A woman sees it as part of a long-term relationship. And because most business situations involve long-term relationships, the "female" approach is more productive, he concludes. Or, as John Naisbitt and Patricia Aburdene put it in their book *Re-Inventing the Corporation*, as the manager's role shifts to that of a teacher, mentor, and nurturer of human potential in the information society, there is even more reason for corporations to take advantage of women's managerial abilities, because these people-oriented traits are the ones women are socialized to possess.[2]

The problem, however, is that if women are forced to operate in domination-style structures, they are under tremendous external and internal pressure to "be more like men." As noted by Alice Sargent and Ronald Stupak, women—particularly as middle managers, but sometimes even when they reach the top—will have to "step into the shoes of men."[3]

This dynamic too is our heritage from earlier times, when the occasional female leader such as a Queen Elizabeth or Catherine the Great by and large stepped into leadership positions as the widows, daughters, or mothers of men. In business, too, management was a male preserve, with the occasional female top executive figuratively stepping into the shoes of men. In other words, power was synonymous with characteristics (such as strength, toughness, control, and decisiveness) that are stereotypically considered masculine.

This view of power as a male's power to control people, be it for ill or good, is appropriate for a dominator social organization, which orders human relations primarily in terms of rigid rankings—man over man, man over woman, nation over nation, and man over nature. Economic relations in this model of society also follow this pattern. Just as women's and children's labor was by law and custom the property of the male head of household, the labor of slaves (and later of serfs) was said to be due their owners or lords. Even later, in the early stages of the Industrial Revolution, with the shift from a primarily agrarian to a manufacturing economy, the relations of workers and bosses tended to follow this mold. Sweatshops, where women, men, and children worked from dawn to dusk in unsafe and oppressive conditions, were accepted as "just the way things are." The use of force by industrialists against those who sought to organize workers was often condoned, and at times supported by government leaders.

As we move toward the partnership end of the partnership-domination continuum, these practices are no longer acceptable. But old habits and beliefs linger on—particularly when it comes to the roles and relations of women and men. Indeed, the movement toward partnership has been resisted every inch of the way. And this resistance is particularly fierce when it comes to "women's issues."

Those trying to push us back to the "good old days" when most men and all women still "knew their place" in rigid rankings of domination recognize the social importance of gender roles and relations. Be it Khomeini in Iran, the Taliban in Afghanistan, or the rightist-fundamentalist alliance in the United States, these people give top priority to "getting women back into their traditional place"—a code word for a subordinate place.

Yet many people who want democracy and equality still view "women's issues" as secondary—failing to recognize that gender equity is a core element of the shift to a more humane, productive, and prosperous way of life for all.

Raising Women's Status

A study using data compiled by the United Nations and other international agencies from eighty-nine countries compared measures of the status of women with quality-of-life measures such as infant mortality, human rights ratings, and percentage of the population with access to health care. This study, conducted by my colleagues and me for the Center for Partnership Studies, found that the status of women can be a better predictor of quality of life than gross domestic product (GDP), the conventional measure of a nation's economic development.[4]

For example, Kuwait and France had almost identical GDPs, but infant mortality, one of the most basic measures of quality of life, was *twice* as high in Kuwait. Similarly, the GDP of Finland and Singapore were almost identical. But the maternal mortality rate in Singapore, where the status of women is much lower than in Finland, was more than double that of Finland, a society where, as in other Nordic nations, women have made strong gains.

This study, "Men, Women, and the Global Quality of Life," statistically verifies that there is a strong correlation between, on the one hand, such indicators of gender inequity as a substantially lower literacy rate for females than for males, high maternal mortality, and low female participation in government and, on the other, indicators of a generally lower quality of life for all, such as high infant mortality, a high number of refugees fleeing the country, and a high ratio of GDP going to the wealthiest as opposed to the poorest 20 percent of the population.

This study illustrates the value of gender-specific research. It shows that economics cannot be understood, or effectively changed, without attention to other core cultural components—and that a central cultural component is the social construction of gender roles and relations.

Nordic nations such as Finland, Sweden, and Norway are particularly interesting in connection with what happens as women make strong gains. In a very short time during the twentieth century these nations changed from poor, famine-ridden countries to prosperous, creative economies.[5] Why? Because their policies give value and fiscal support to the stereotypically feminine work of caregiving. Such measures as universal health care, child-care allowances, elder care, and paid parental leave helped produce the higher-quality human capital that transformed them into prosperous nations. These nations always rank on the top of the U.N. *Human Development Reports*. Even beyond that, Finland was ahead of the much wealthier United States in the 2004 Global Competitiveness ratings.[6] And of course women in the Nordic nations occupy a far higher percentage of political leadership positions than anywhere else in the world: they make up approximately 40 percent of legislators.

These nations also pioneered the first peace studies courses. They pioneered laws against physical punishment of children in families. They pioneered a strong men's movement to disentangle male identity from violence. They also pioneered what we today call industrial democracy: using teamwork in factories rather than turning human beings into mere cogs in the industrial machine.

None of this is random or coincidental. It is part of the cultural configuration characteristic of the partnership rather than domination model: a configuration in which the higher status of women is central. What happens is that as the status of women rises, so too does the status of traits and activities stereotypically associated with the feminine: soft rather than hard values, empathy, caring, nonviolence—and men then find it more possible to embrace these values without feeling threatened in their status.

In short, how a society structures the relations between women and men is of profound personal, social, and economic significance. It is of key importance in how leadership and power are conceptualized and exercised. It is also an important factor in shifting the architecture of the workplace from top-down hierarchies of domination to what I call hierarchies of actualization.

From Hierarchies of Domination to Hierarchies of Actualization

Some people think that the new business and social structures should be completely flat. But every organization needs lines of responsibility. The difference between the partnership and domination models is *not* that the domination model is hierarchical and the partnership model is hierarchy-free. The difference is the distinction between *hierarchies of domination* and *hierarchies of actualization*.

Hierarchies of actualization are characteristic of partnership-oriented organizations, where the culture values and rewards relations based on mutual benefit, respect, caring, and accountability rather than relations in which there must be winners and losers. These actualization hierarchies are more flexible, allowing many people to be leaders in different contexts. They empower rather than disempower workers, and encourage rather than discourage creativity. They encourage collegial leadership styles, rather than the command-and-control style of a sole leader at the top making all important decisions. Actualization hierarchies do not rely on one-way orders from above; rather, they have open lines of communication, making it possible for organizations to use everyone's knowledge and input. In these ways, they promote relational practices that result in greater organizational capacity.

In hierarchies of domination, accountability and respect flow only from the bottom up. In hierarchies of actualization, they flow both ways. Hierarchies of domination are imposed and maintained by fear. Hierarchies of actualization are not based on power *over*. They are based on power *to*—creative power, the power to help and to nurture—as well as power *with*—the collective power to accomplish goals together, as in teamwork. And all this is directly related to changes in gender roles and relations.

Because most new jobs created today in the U.S. economy are being filled by women, women have been a major driving force behind corporate innovations such as flextime, day-care programs, elder-care programs, parental leave, and other workplace policies that, as Naisbitt and Aburdene observe, are forcing the humanization of the workplace.[7]

However, although women can make a special contribution to the creation of a more productive, creative, and humane workplace, this in no way means that men do not also have a very important role to play in the process. The domination model has been disempowering to both women and men. And it will require women and men working in full and equal partnership to transform that model.

Today, many men, even CEOs of major corporations, are rejecting dominator approaches and moving toward a more "feminine" or nurturing way of managing and organizing business. But, as noted earlier, if men are finding it possible to adopt such values and behaviors, it is because the status of women—and with this, the status of traits and activities stereotypically associated with women—has been rising. Another example of men rejecting the dominator role is the current trend among men of redefining the role of fathering to include some of the nurturing behaviors stereotypically associated with mothering.

As Susan G. Butruille writes in "Corporate Caretaking," the trends we are seeing today in the workplace go along with important trends in people's personal and family lives, particularly the trend toward shared roles by women and men in both work and the family. Butruille reports that, thanks largely to the massive entry of women into the workforce and the rise in dual-career couples, women and men are increasingly concerned about similar issues. In other words, as both work and family relations shift more to partnership, we are seeing a blurring of stereotypical gender-linked attitudes and roles. And we are also seeing the gradual emergence of what Butruille calls an ethos of corporate caretaking.[8]

An ethos of caretaking shared by both women and men is a key element in the transformation from a dominator to a partnership business culture. But this ethos of caretaking cannot take full root unless the status of women rises worldwide.

Toward a Partnership Economics

Business cultures are part of larger economic systems. And economic systems in turn are part of larger social systems—which, as we have seen, are radically different depending on the degree to which they orient to the domination model or the partnership model.

Change leaders need to raise public awareness of the benefits of partnership—and show that the traditional male-superior, female-inferior model of relations is an obstacle to a more generally prosperous, equitable, and peaceful world. The traditional model is a mental map children learn early on for equating difference—beginning with the basic difference between man and woman—with superiority and inferiority, with dominating or being dominated, with being served or serving. This mental map can then be applied on the basis of race, religion, ethnicity, or any other difference as the basis for the in-group versus out-group thinking that is the cause of so much suffering, injustice, and violence. And this map directly leads to a fundamentally distorted system of values that is yet another cause of chronic suffering, injustice, and violence worldwide.

Consider that even today the first thing that usually gets cut is government funding for health, education, and welfare—in other words, funding to care for people. The Structural Adjustment Policies of the International Monetary Fund even demanded such cuts, with disastrous human and economic results for debtor nations. But notice that even though we are told we don't have enough money for these purposes, there always is enough money for weapons, wars, and prisons—for controlling, hurting, and killing people, rather than for nurturing, empowering, and caring for people.

This distorted system of priorities is also directly related to the systemic devaluation of women and the work of caregiving. This devaluation has shaped our economic models and rules. And as long as these rules and models are in place, we women will remain on the periphery.

Already women in the United States are quitting high-paying corporate jobs because of their double burden: the difficulty, indeed almost impossibility, of balancing jobs with caregiving responsibilities at home. But returning to a dependent and subordinate place is *not* the answer. The answer is to develop rules, models, and measures that give visibility and value to the activities that nurture and support life—whether they are performed by women or men.

A first step toward this new partnership economics is to change how we measure productivity. The reason is simple: what is not counted is not considered in making economic policy. Change will not occur without the hard measures of costs and benefits.

Today the GDP counts activities that take life and destroy our natural habitat: coal burning and cleaning up the environmental damage it causes, selling cigarettes and the medical costs and funeral costs of the health damage they cause. These destructive activities are on the positive side of the GDP. But not only do GDP measures put negatives on the positive side: they do *not* include the unpaid caregiving work primarily performed by women in the "informal" economy, be it in their homes or in their communities as volunteers—even though these services contribute most to everyone's social well-being.

In the formal economy, in the labor market, professions that involve caring—such as child care and primary school teaching, professions until now largely composed of women—are paid significantly less than those that do not involve caregiving—such as plumbing and engineering. Thus people think nothing of paying plumbers, the people to whom we entrust our pipes, $50 to $60 per hour. But child-care workers, the people to whom we entrust our children, are paid only $10 or $15 an hour—and that's already considered a high rate. Moreover, we demand that plumbers have some training, but not that all child-care workers have training.

None of this is logical—it is actually pathological. We must change it—and we can change it. But to do so, we have to go beyond old economic models, whether capitalist or socialist, and develop new economic rules that give visibility and value to the stereotypically feminine work of caregiving.

Economic Inventions That Recognize the Value of Caregiving Work

Just about everything involved in our economic life is a human invention—from stock exchanges and sweatshops to banks and Social Security. We already have a few economic inventions that give monetary value to caring and caregiving, such as parental leave for both mothers and fathers, on-site child care, and flexible work options. But we need many more.

Companies that provide paid parental leave can be supported by public policy through matching local, state, and federal grants. Companies that provide employees with child care or parenting classes can be given tax rebates. These are all sound investments in a high-quality future workforce and a healthier, more secure world.

The issue is simply one of fiscal priorities. That these priorities can be changed is dramatically illustrated by what happened in Ontario, Canada, when government leaders were shown the benefits of investing in caring for children. Based on extensive cost-benefit analyses showing the economic and social benefits of supporting good caregiving during a child's early years—from before birth to age six—the Healthy Babies, Healthy Children program was launched in 1998 by a fiscally conservative government under Premier Mike Harris. This program offers information on parenting and child development to all families with new babies and delivers extra help and support, including home visits, to families who can benefit from it. When researchers compared families who received Healthy Babies, Healthy Children home visiting with similar families who did not receive home visiting, they found better child and family health among home visiting families. Specifically, their 2003 report found that among home visiting families, children scored higher on most infant development measures, including self-help, gross motor skills, fine motor skills, and language development—all important indicators of a higher level of human capital development, not to speak of prospects for a brighter future for the children receiving the better care supported by the program.[9]

The Canadian program is not alone in recognizing the importance of government investment in caring and caregiving. The French creche programs and the Nordic caregiving programs—which include parenting education in schools—are notable examples that also provide models for forward-thinking leaders.

These are all sound investments in our future. They are investments in a successful postindustrial information economy—an economy in which high-quality human capital is the most important capital. This economy requires people able to learn, relate, work in teams, and solve problems flexibly and creatively. This high-quality human capital is not just produced in universities or through job training. Findings from psychology, and more recently neurobiology, show that the quality of human capital is, to a much greater extent than has been recognized, shaped by the quality of child care and early childhood education.[10]

Meeting Our Global Challenges

The shift into the postindustrial era offers us a window of opportunity to reassess what is and what is not productive work. When it comes to social policies and funding, what matters is *not* money; what matters is what is or is not really valued. We must change current value systems if we are to find solutions to such seemingly intractable problems as poverty, social inequity, and chronic violence. What's generally missing from discussions of social change, however, is the recognition that our problems flow from the social and economic failure to support caring and caregiving. In short, an economic paradigm that hides and devalues the work of caring and caregiving is corrosive to our most basic life-support system.

We can change this paradigm by joining to envision and create a new partnership economics—and by providing the hard data that show how partnership rules, measures, and practices work better than the old dominator ones. This is why I want to bring together visionary leaders from academia, government, business, and civil society into an Alliance for a Caring Economy to collect information on what is already happening to give economic value to caregiving and provide a forum for new ideas, initiatives, and economic policies.[11]

Economic rules, measures, and policies that recognize the real value of the essential work of caring for children and the elderly, keeping our families healthy, and maintaining a clean and healthy environment will lead to the higher valuing of caring and caregiving in our homes, schools, and workplaces. These rules, measures, and policies will greatly accelerate the empowerment of women worldwide. And they will greatly benefit men and children of both genders because they will support the more caring economic, environmental, and social policies needed to move toward a more equitable, sustainable, and prosperous future.

Five Levers for Change

The recognition of the pivotal importance of so-called women's issues is urgent, because as long as women are devalued, so also are stereotypically feminine traits and activities, such as empathy, nonviolence, and caregiving. These are the traits and activities we need for a better future. Indeed, in our age of nuclear and biological weapons, they are urgently needed if we are to have a future at all.

As more women enter leadership positions, we can use our power to shape the future. As numerous studies have shown, the empowerment of women is key to economic development, to a sustainable global population, and to a less violent society. The challenge is to collectively transform policies to implement these findings into actions.

There are many actions we can take, but we can be most effective by focusing on these five levers for fundamental, systemic change:

1. Demonstrating to policymakers and the public at large the social and economic benefits of empowering women

2. Working to create a partnership economics that no longer devalues women and stereotypically feminine traits and activities, such as caregiving, nonviolence, and empathy

3. Changing economic measurements such as GDP to include the work of caregiving stereotypically relegated to women

4. Developing, supporting, and disseminating partnership economic inventions, such as paid parental leave, that give visibility and value to caregiving—whether it is performed by men or women

5. Forming alliances to work together with one another as well as with men—locally, nationally, and internationally—to bring women's issues to where they belong: from the back to the front of the political and economic agenda

Largely because of the continuing dislocation of patterns of work and thought caused by massive technological change, ours is a time of enormous opportunity. The shift to the postindustrial society offers an unprecedented chance to forge new economic models, rules, and practices.

We women must take leadership in this historic enterprise. We must do this for ourselves, so that we create economic models, rules, and measures that don't put us at a disadvantage and don't put caring men at a disadvantage. We must do this because assuming such a leadership role is really the only way to end the shameful fact that women and children are the mass of the poor and hungry worldwide. And we must do this to build solid foundations for the more sustainable and humane future we want and need—for ourselves, for our male partners and colleagues, and, above all, for our children and generations still to come.

 As the founder and president of the Institute for Women's Leadership, Rayona Sharpnack is a profoundly influential leadership teacher who has guided countless women leaders to achieve breakthrough results in all areas of their lives. The source of her success can be described in simple but powerful terms: whereas traditional leadership theory focuses primarily on the *doing* or functional aspects of leadership, Rayona urges leaders to create a new way of *being* by shifting their thinking, enlarging the context for new possibilities, and articulating a compelling and achievable vision. Her approach has had a major impact on women and men leaders in businesses and communities across the country.

In this chapter, Rayona discusses how we can adopt such an approach so that we move beyond the traditional leadership view to one that integrates core aspects of "contextual leadership" and creates power in the world of possibility.

2

THE POWER OF SHIFTING CONTEXT

Becoming a Contextual Leader

Rayona Sharpnack

The ability to define and create new and better possibilities is the mark of high-impact leadership, a capacity that is in high demand in our organizations and society today. As a leader, then, what view of the world are you making a case for? How can you bring others into partnership around that perspective? How do you define a coherent context for the changes you seek, and how do you cause those changes to happen? Every successful leader, from Madeleine Albright to Mother Teresa to Meg Whitman, has used the principles of "context shifting" to lead significant, sustainable change. In this chapter, I describe how context shifting occurs and what that does for us, as individuals and leaders. As you will come to see, the process, by definition, works from the inside out.

What is context? For now, let me define it simply as the deeply ingrained attitudes and beliefs that create our worldview and shape our lives. All individuals and all organizations have a prevailing context, whether recognized or not. Most individuals don't purposely design their belief contexts—they inherit them. In the same way, most organizations don't deliberately design their culture ("how we do things around here") but find that it evolves over time and is reinforced by rules, recognition, punishments, and rewards. Although we may think that we act freely based on a rational assessment of the objective evidence, this isn't the case. The real source of people's actions is not what they know but how they perceive the world around them and what conclusions they draw as a result. It is easy to confuse those conclusions with reality. It takes a kind of disciplined awareness to separate what we think to be true from the actual facts and to choose a different course instead. Contextual thinking—the foundation of contextual leadership—is about that discipline.

Nose to the Grindstone

Let me start with a very personal example to help illustrate. From a very young age, I've always had my "nose to the grindstone." You may know what that feels like. I felt that I would never get anywhere in life if I didn't work extremely hard. In some respects, this was a useful belief, and over the years I'd achieved a lot because of it. Certainly, building a flourishing leadership consulting firm from the ground up had some relationship to my willingness to work hard. Nevertheless, by the time I had reached the tender age of fifty-one, I discovered that this lifelong view—to which I attributed much of my success—was also an insidious hindrance. In recent years, I had come to believe not just that hard work was important, but that *everything* had to be hard work. I paid a heavy personal cost as a result, with many trade-offs and sacrifices and not enough compensation in terms of enjoyment, ease, and celebration to lighten the load and stir up my life.

Once I became aware that "nose to the grindstone" was a context in which I was *choosing* to operate, I could see that my destiny was not going to be what I wanted it to be if I remained there. So I embarked on a journey to discover a different context to which I would be willing to entrust my future. In other words, I decided to shift my context and create a greater opportunity to be the whole person I really wanted to be in the world. I knew that changing who I was, with respect to that one belief, would fundamentally change how I live and lead. I knew because that's what I coach leaders to do. For themselves, for the people around them, for their organiza-

tions, and for their industries, leaders are responsible for one important thing: they are in the context-shifting business.

Wait a minute. Isn't leadership about getting results? Yes, absolutely. But results stem from actions. And people's actions are determined by what they believe. So any result—whether it is doubling
sales for the year with a smaller sales force, inventing a new product that will take the market by storm, or restructuring a company
to save billions of dollars—begins with an ability to shift people's
beliefs, or their context. This means that as a leader, whether the
conundrum you face is how to help an employee unleash her true
potential or how to get great performance out of a multinational
company, you begin your job with a simple question: What is the
context here?

It Starts with You

When I work with leaders, one of the key concepts we strive to
understand is how context affects us on a personal level and within
our organizations. Real change, for a leader, needs to begin with
understanding what you believe, not what you do. Out of that
awareness comes the ability to inform how you act in the world.
The framework for what you believe on a personal level sets the
stage for everything else.

Take the example of Sarah, an executive at an information
technology company. Recently, she was placed on the executive
committee because of her past achievements and the organization's
confidence in her leadership. Sarah and I met to discuss some of the
challenges that she was experiencing in working with her peers and
getting change to occur in the organization from a more senior position. As we talked, we made an invaluable discovery. Sarah's prevailing context for herself was "local girl makes good." It framed
how she saw herself and colored her relationships with the other
members of the executive committee. It was a limiting context that
was getting in her way, and we felt that we had touched on something critical when we stumbled across it.

It wasn't easy to discover that context. It took a lot of questions and some analysis of things that had happened and how messages had been sent and received. We realized that there were some consistent patterns to those challenges. As we took a closer look, an underlying theme emerged. When we gave voice to that theme, it was as though we had uncovered something that was critically formative in who Sarah is and how she leads. Because she is "local girl makes good," she does not really feel as though she belongs at the management table. She's happy to be there, certainly, and has a great deal of pride in that accomplishment. But the context she is coming from limits how much credibility, visibility, power, and impact she can have going forward. It is too narrow to allow her to make the difference she wants to make.

Sarah was caught in a wasteful but self-generated situation. Because she was "local girl makes good," she was just happy to be there, hanging out with the big boys. Underneath, she felt anxious that she would one day be uncovered as a "fraud." Although there was no factual basis for this sentiment, it was nevertheless limiting her effectiveness as a leader. She had placed herself in a position where she felt satisfied to be merely acting on and executing what the "real leaders" were telling her to do. She was not supplying the vision herself, nor articulating that vision and evoking action on its behalf. She wasn't being the leader they had brought her to the table to be.

Identifying that context and becoming aware of it was a very profound awakening for Sarah. When she saw it and understood it, she was able to reject it and replace it. She immediately came up with language that described a context she was much more interested in coming from. Doing so, she changed everything. From "local girl makes good" she shifted to "my unique perspective always adds value." From that place, she was able to raise issues that the others at the executive committee hadn't been willing to talk about. Because she was now dealing with those executive committee members as peers, she was also committed to bringing those issues to the point of resolution rather than allowing them to be buried. She had the sense of authority and standing necessary to say, "Stop. Time out. What are we, as an executive committee, going to do about the following issue?" She was, both in effect and in practice, a different leader. Her new behavior led to a change in the way her peers treated her as well. She became an integral part of the team, not just a bystander.

It All Turns Out with Grace and Ease

How do you shift context? Identifying your prevailing context is step one. With that awareness, a leader can see the limits of that context in terms of what people can execute and accomplish. If those limits are too restrictive, the leader must shift the context to provide more space for innovation and possibility to emerge. I refer to that context-shifting act as the process of *trading up*.

When I discovered that "nose to the grindstone" was not a context from which I wanted to operate anymore, I engaged in an exercise to find language for a new context that would suit my future better. I knew that this would not mean simply swinging the pendulum to the opposite side. I couldn't shift from "nose to the grindstone" to "laid-back Rayona" any more than an organization that is antidiversity can suddenly declare itself to be prodiversity. Instead I had to find a way to widen the opening that already worked for me and trade up to something that worked even better.

Naturally, being a "nose to the grindstone" person, I labored over this idea. I searched long and hard for the words that—when I spoke them—would resonate in my body and describe the compelling future I could pledge myself to living. Suddenly it came to me, a very simple phrase that allowed me to trade up to a whole new universe.

"It all turns out with grace and ease," I said. That statement opened me up to the possibility that not *everything* had to be hard work. Perhaps my default mode could be something other than trying to work myself to death as a solution to every challenge. More important, I liked what the new phrase showed me about myself and what it was saying about my life. It allowed me to be driven, but it gave me the enjoyment and reward of the moment.

I started to work with that phrase in the back of my mind and began a process of being deliberately conscious of my new context. Every time I fell into my "nose to the grindstone" routine, I'd stop and think, "It all turns out with grace and ease." Sometimes I caught myself too late, and had to look back and say, "Rayona, you just spent two hours with your nose to the grindstone." Simply recognizing that fact relieved my burden a little bit, and I was able to think, "It all turns out with grace and ease." That realization let me relax, rejuvenate, and enjoy what I was doing.

Essentially, my new phrase for my new context allowed me to pause and reclaim my behavior and my power. But it wasn't sufficient to go it alone—I needed a web of support to be successful. I enlisted my staff at the Institute for Women's Leadership (IWL) and asked them to help me by calling out those times when I was in "nose to the grindstone" mode. When they saw me with my nose to the grindstone, they would say something like, "Rayona, you seem pretty stressed-out today," and act as my radar for identifying that behavior. I also asked them to identify when I or the company was doing something easily, seamlessly, and flawlessly. At those moments, we could enjoy saying, "It all turns out with grace and ease."

Little by little, my new context took hold, and I started seeing surprising results. Knowing that it all turns out with grace and ease, I was able to use the resources around me in a much more efficient way. I looked for elegant, simple solutions rather than assuming that any problem would take a twelve-hour day to fix. Suddenly I saw more opportunities to delegate to my staff. Their taking on additional responsibility was often a *better* solution than my adding three hours to my workload—not just for me or for my company overall but for them as well. They were being groomed to take on leadership roles within IWL. I also saw more opportunities to problem-solve, where I once would have jumped to the conclusion that I needed to churn out an additional report or take an additional meeting or make an additional trip to fix whatever "crisis" developed.

Does this sound mundane and simple? It should. The course of our leadership day is filled with mundane and simple moments that we ignore at our peril. It's rarely the gigantic things that get in our way, the strategic summit or the vision from the mountaintops. Instead, it's the frame of mind you are in when you walk into a room filled with senior executives and engage in the dance of personality, politics, and power. Are you able to be in that moment, or are you hampered and made awkward by the tightness of your contextual framework? To be present and at the same time to have a different attitude about what is possible allows you to be a much different resource to other people and the world.

Context and Organizational Change

Let's take a look at how that process of shifting context works inside an organization. In 1999, when Carly Fiorina became the first woman CEO in the Fortune 25, she took a hard look at Hewlett-Packard (HP), the company she was now leading. The company had logged a steady, single-digit percent growth rate every year for the past ten years. However, the company had missed its own and Wall Street's expectations ten quarters in a row. Those goals were modest to begin with, so it's fair to say the sights of the executive team were low.

Carly Fiorina's first senior leadership meeting was about "holding the mirror up to our company's performance." She featured customers talking about the great possibilities of working with HP that were continuously thwarted by HP's complexity and slow time to respond. She had channel and industry partners describe working with HP, and phrases like "slow, ponderous, complicated, unable to collaborate across your own internal organizations" peppered the conversation. She asked industry analysts for their views, and they reached consensus on HP's "unrealized potential" and "debilitating internal focus."

It was a sobering day, but it established a platform for change. HP could no longer be seventy-two brands with multiple profit and loss centers led by their own CEOs. It had to become an integrated

computer company that delivered the IT solutions current and future HP customers needed for business success. The goalpost was no
longer year over year growth. The goals were all externally based,
with a sharp eye on the competition. HP would reinvent itself to
compete and be a market leader, not just in printers but in every
market it served.

At the conclusion of her first senior leadership meeting, Carly
asked Susan Burnett, her corporate leader of global learning and a
long-time student of contextual leadership, "Do I have the most
competitive workforce in the world? Do we have leaders that can
outperform their peers in the industry? We need this to lead the IT
industry, so where do we stand?" Carly left Susan with the challenge
of answering these critical questions and coming to her executive
team with a proposal for the future.

HP training and development organizations were small and
large teams (from five to two hundred employees) who set priorities
based on the requirements of their individual units. There was no
galvanizing purpose for these organizations—they did not exist to
build the most competitive workforce in the world. Carly's question
could not be answered in the current context.

Susan and I began to design a large-scale change process that
would spur the training and development community toward a
shared purpose. Carly's question provided the answer. We invited
more than fifty HP training and development leaders to a three-day
session designed to explore what it would take to produce the most
competitive workforce and the most competitive leaders in the world.
Although everyone couldn't agree, especially on organizational structure, the meeting was designed to get great ideas heard and documented. Susan had created a forum for bringing to the executive
committee the best thinking of this group. All agreed it was a historic
moment for the training and development function at HP. Carly
Fiorina was asking them to build a core competency for the company!

HP's executive committee (EC) discussed the proposal for a
new Enterprise Workforce Development organization for ninety
minutes. The group had created a new context for this discussion and

subsequent action. No longer was this a training organization proposal; instead the focus was on the capabilities the company needed to lead the marketplace, reinvent itself, and compete to win. The EC approved the proposal and asked Susan to establish the organization by the next fiscal year—three months away. The CFO implemented Susan's proposal to create an "investment budget" at 2.5 percent of payroll (the ASTD industry average) and centralized training and development funding at the company level. In addition, the EC agreed to and appointed a "board of directors" to govern this new organization, ensuring that the development team was setting the right priorities and resourcing them at the appropriate level.

I worked with Susan's team for twelve months, to help them internalize what it meant to operate in a context of "enterprise" instead of "business unit," to define and lead company priorities as well as unit priorities, and collaborate across organizational boundaries.

All told, in the first year of the restructuring, HP saved $100 million on training and development expenditures. More important, the workforce initiative had begun to build a development capability directly tied to the business initiatives of the company and designed as an engine for change and reinvention. This was a capability Carly would turn to over and over as she needed to build individual and organizational capability to pull off the largest technology merger in history. Carly's tenure at HP may now be over, but her legacy (and a stronger company) endures. Today HP can ask the question "Do we have the most competitive workforce in the world?" and the answer on many fronts is *yes!*

Why Is Context So Powerful?

As a conceptual framework, context explains what's going on in the complex interactions that occur among ourselves and those around us. By becoming aware of context we can see how our views shape what happens to us, and we can learn how to separate conclusion from fact. This awareness leads us to understand the inflection points we can use to create change in how we act and how we lead.

Context is an idea from linguistics that applies to other disciplines, including systems theory. According to systems theory, all systems, from the smallest molecule to the universe itself, comprise three dimensions. There is the content, or "what," of the system—which is the knowledge, resources, and structure. There is the process, or "how," of the system—which is the activities and behaviors that emerge. And then there is the context of the system—which is the setting in which the content and processes exist.

For the individual, content might be what that person knows; process would be what he or she does. For the organization, content would be the company's structure, resources, and knowledge; process would be its activities and operations. Content and process are relatively easy to identify and manipulate. Individuals as well as organizations constantly change what they do and how they do it. Real, meaningful change will not occur, however, without addressing the underlying context.

All systems are context-sensitive. Context includes all the assumptions and norms, the unspoken rules of a given work culture, that are brought to the table. Those assumptions often masquerade as facts and can determine people's reality. Sarah thought that the reality of her situation at the executive committee was "local girl makes good." The executive committee brought her on board because she was "an innovative force for change." Which conclusion was reality? I suggest that Sarah's limited conclusion about reality was creating a situation in which she was bound to underperform and ultimately fail. By shifting that conclusion, she created a greater possibility for success.

Looking at the organizational level, imagine how difficult it would be to launch a successful new product, for example, if the contextual belief is that new products always fail or that the organization can never work across silos effectively or that the market is too unsettled to master. Consider how difficult it would be to bring more women to the senior management ranks if the organization's contextual belief were that women can't cut it and don't contribute value. No matter how many women were promoted or identified as high potential, the barriers to their success would be significant. To increase the odds of success, we need to identify the fabric of the organization's culture and belief system, its web of conclusions if you will, and shift them.

Leaders are in the context-shifting business. This is how they effect significant and lasting change. They are able, by instinct or training, to see that context drives process and structure. They know that if they want to change an individual or a system, the place to go is the contextual dimension. When a leader is successful at altering context, processes and structures change, too. Consider these examples of unprecedented business results brought about by shifting context.

Gretchen McCoy is the senior vice president of global technology management for Visa. In 2003, she was tasked with the project of revamping the billing system for Visa's twenty-one thousand member banks. The project was projected to cost about $40 million to implement over the course of two-and-a-half years. The system handles some five hundred million transactions per day, so the complexity of upgrading the computer coding and processes beneath that system was dizzying. Gretchen worked on shifting two contexts with her team of seventy (thirty of whom have gone through IWL training). First, she asked for their commitment in creating an environment in which the team constantly challenged "how things *have to* be done." None of the protocols governing computer coding or company procedures were to be accepted at face value. Further, she encouraged her team to shift from a mentality of "I work on my specific piece of the project" to "I work to optimize the system." As a result of these two shifts, the team was vigilant in communicating across department lines about particularly challenging aspects of the system; they were rigorous about asking, Is there a better way to do this?

Two specific innovations came out of these shifts: one project manager took a look at the time line for the project and wondered, do we *have to* do all these steps in a linear fashion? He and another technician from a different department figured out a way to assign work so that development on different stages could occur simultaneously. That insight shaved $2 to $3 million off the total cost of the project, Gretchen says.

Next, the core team of twenty leaders questioned whether meetings had to drag on for hours. They all made a commitment to fifteen-minute meetings, a goal they have kept throughout the duration of the project, easily racking up a cost savings in salary time of hundreds of thousands of dollars. Gretchen, who has worked at Visa for twenty-two years, says the energy of the team and their innovation are unprecedented in her experience: "It's all about spreading a high-performance culture, and shifting context was a very effective tool to make that happen," she says.

Kavita Ramdas, director of the Global Fund for Women (GFW), had just started in her position in 1999, and was trying to map out her goals and agenda for the nonprofit. The GFW, which supports women's human rights and development in 160 countries around the world, had a legacy of being a groundbreaking funder of important women's projects. But it had few internal resources and relied on annual foundation support to provide its budget. Although the agency's reputation as an innovative start-up had been key to its initial success, Ramdas was able to see that the context of "lean, innovative start-up" also carried some baggage. Because she wanted the work of the GFW ultimately to change the course of history for women around the world, the fund needed a new context, something more like "stable, long-term, big-change player." So she started asking herself what kind of action would flow from that context.

While participating in IWL's leadership class, she decided that one of the best ways to achieve that goal would be to raise enough money for an endowment for GFW, something that most foundations take many years to do. Ramdas decided that she would do it within five years. She began a campaign in October 2000 to raise $20 million for the agency for an endowment. Within months, she secured a grant to study the feasibility of establishing an endowment. By the end of 2003, she had already raised $10 million from corporate and foundation sponsors (in one of the most difficult economies of the last fifty years) and had begun a public campaign to raise the remaining $10 million.

Imagine how powerful context shifting could be when unleashed against some of the most common problems in business! For example, organizations these days are very concerned about attending to diversity. Many of those organizations will put together content-based approaches that involve awareness and sensitivity training. Or they may have people engaged in recruiting practices that are aimed at increasing diversity. The success or failure of those efforts, however, will depend very much on how compliant or committed the organization actually is to the idea of creating a diversity that will live and last.

Contextual leadership would start by asking, What is the prevailing context of the organization? What is the long-standing, embedded web of conclusions from which the organization is operating? What are the limits of the context in terms of the system's effectiveness? What kind of resources will be required to shift that context? It's the leader's job to figure out how to shift the existing context in a way that increases the possibilities for that change to be meaningful and successful.

Becoming a Contextual Leader

We think about the future as if there were one actually out there, waiting for us to reach it. If you think about futures as clusters of possibilities, then any future could happen. One of the leader's most critical jobs is to articulate a compelling future and enlist others in making it happen. She does this, in part, by shifting the prevailing context to allow for the future that is more advantageous.

Language is key because context lives inside language. Our culture, personally and organizationally, is transmitted through language. To the extent that conclusions influence reality, you can say that our ability to change our language changes that reality.

Of course, this shift in context has to be based in fact, experience, and discipline. You cannot create a possible future by declaring the outlandish and expecting it to happen merely because you have spoken the words. That's nothing more than positive thinking. "Possible thinking," in contrast, shifts what's already there to create room for something more desirable. At Visa, "what's possible" meant that two computer technicians could look at a different way of working—that saved $3 million. At HP, it meant reenvisioning the structure of the global training and development function—and saving $100 million. Those possibilities exist all around us. We just have to have the vision to see them.

For you to become a contextual leader, the place to start is within. By being more aware of who you are and how you act, you can shift how you lead and the impact you have on others. I believe that all leaders are on a journey of exploration. It starts with signing up and saying, "I must do this because . . ." A leader, by definition, makes something happen on her shift. But there is a great deal of searching that takes place to make that "something" meaningful. As I tell people all the time, don't enlist in the leadership army unless you've got a big appetite for creativity, paradox, and experimentation.

Any discussion of leadership should leave people with a self-generated conversation going forward. And so I ask you: What does this conversation open up? What can you do about it for yourself? If it's something that has value for you, what are you going to commit yourself to? I suggest that you seek out and find a prevailing context that has been limiting you or causing you some measure of suffering, and go about shifting it. Include others. Don't do it all alone, with just you and the committee in your head. See what happens when you examine what you think to be real and widen that opening to include other, more desirable possibilities. Make something happen on your shift.

Carol Anderson and Patricia Shafer have spent much of their professional lives examining the essence of personal and organizational power. They bring diverse experiences to the analysis. Carol is an organizational systems artist. Her innovative use of visual scrolls brings organizational images and assumptions literally into view. Besides her work with Fortune 500 firms, Carol is founder of Rebellious Dreamers, a nonprofit organization that helps women reclaim their dreams through financial and mentoring support. Like Carol, Patricia uses storytelling and narrative techniques to uncover assumptions about power in organizational settings. She does so as president of Compel Ltd., an organizational excellence alliance dedicated to evoking courageous leadership and guiding organizational change.

In this chapter, Carol and Patricia explain how we can use internally generated power to rise above restrictive organizational systems that would otherwise limit our leadership impact.

3

DEEPER POWER

Carol Anderson and Patricia Shafer

The emotional truth of our world is held in and revealed through stories. We are a collection of them.

We have stories about our upbringing, childhood, coming of age, first kisses, first jobs, first surprises, first disappointments, highest highs and lowest lows. We have stories about the meaning of life and our purpose in it.

We also have stories within us about power. They are mostly untold or not fully acknowledged. Power, like the scintillating and sometimes taboo topics of sex, money, religion, and politics, is maddeningly abstract and intangible. But it's always there, in our faces, in the air, and embedded in memories that begin in childhood and take us to the end of life.

Our stories about power—who has it, who doesn't, if we have it, if we don't—are woven into beliefs and mental models socialized by gender, ethnic group, culture, and family. They are a mélange of idiosyncratic elements, universal themes, and the granular experiences of daily living. They form a personal frame of reference affecting how we experience ourselves, others, and the world.

The degree to which we consider ourselves power-full or powerless has broad and lasting implications. Our perceptions of power—where we think it comes from, how much of it we think we have, whether or not we're willing to embrace it, and the choices we make about its appropriate use—are critical.

So, what is power? What makes it good or bad? What is the path to authentic power?

We tend to live in the illusion that power has an external source, stemming from privilege and fostered through force. In age-old practices of business and politics, power and influence reside in the hands of a small minority. The majority remains fearful of challenging the status quo for threat of being dismissed, ridiculed, or squashed. Organizational structures based on patriarchs and pyramids encourage us to show up as pallid silhouettes. Life force, which is the source of our deepest power and potential, is suppressed.

In this familiar schema, human attention focuses on gathering material possessions; measuring personal value by title, position, and paycheck; and imposing beliefs on one another. Typical aspects of power are reflected as (1) physical force or strength; (2) control or influence over other people and their actions; (3) political control of a country, exercised by its government or leader; and (4) authority to act or do something according to a law or rule. There is an underlying assumption in all of these definitions that our value comes from external evaluations of our worth.

Other definitions of power *are* available, however. Power, from the Old French word *poeir*, means "to be able."[1] This suggests that power arises out of our being, and our willingness to embrace it gives us the capacity to transform reality. This is what we would characterize as *authentic power*, where there is an alignment of personality with soul.

This is the type of power we explore in this chapter—a passionate force of energy, operating with crisp intention toward a clear objective. Each of our stories is about working to discover people's deeper sources of power. And each reflects our belief that all human beings are born with this fire of intention, which comes naturally to us as children. It's only over time that it is dampened, leaving embers atrophied beneath ashes, ever ready to be stirred and fanned. Societies and their organizations tend either to diminish or to develop the core within us.

Experiments with Authentic Power

Carol's Story

My inspiration to become a consultant emerged from a wish to guide and facilitate large systems toward being more humane. I had worked in organizations that cramped creativity and prevented passion from shining through. I knew what it was to be *dis*empowered—wedged in by restriction, hierarchy, and conformity.

My first major team-building assignment came in 1984 with an information technology group that was responsible for conceiving, designing, and delivering an integrated set of HR systems to serve more than 250,000 employees. In one-on-one interviews over three days, I listened to stories from passionate, intelligent, creative people blistering with rage and disappointment over the launch of this system. The stories were similar regardless of grade level, role, gender, or position. Supervisors felt that managers didn't support them. Employees experienced supervisors as aloof and uninterested in their concerns. The HR director felt that he had been set up to fail. Contract workers felt relegated to routine tasks that did not use their gifts.

After the interviews, I realized that there was no way to capture the boldness of my impressions on 8½-by-11-inch paper. The frustration and longing deserved a broader canvas on which to validate differing perspectives and help individuals see their places in a complex set of relationships, structures, and events. I struggled, searching to reveal a fuller truth that integrated fragments of each person's story. The knot in my stomach tightened each day that I failed to produce even a single sentence for my report.

The words *we need the big picture* kept returning to me as I pondered how to give voice to what was real and vital to people searching for clarity and meaning. My feedback needed to be bold, honest, poignant, large, compelling, and encompassing. The story had to reflect emotion as well as intellect, passion as well as thought. Forsaking conventional report making, I drew a picture of what I had heard in three days of interviews. The story emerged on large pieces of flip-chart paper taped end to end. It began, "Once upon a time, there was a dream . . ."

In simple, colorful artwork, I described the system, structure, roles, and relationships between individuals. I added events and their effects, fears of failure, and the anger at being shut down. Experiences of hope and excitement were laced with anxiety and despair, showing how everyone in the department was affected by each other's attitudes and actions. Technical problems and interpersonal conflicts received equal attention, reflecting a holistic perspective of multiple "truths."

The final document was sixty-four feet long and three feet wide. I rolled it up so I could reveal it inch by inch, the way it was told. I was both elated and terrified by my invention. My elation came from the burst of ingenuity that expressed complexity in a simple yet robust way. I felt I had captured something real, not abstract and removed. My fear was that this unusual presentation by a young and inexperienced consultant would be dismissed as unsophisticated and unprofessional. I remember standing in front of that group thinking this was either the most brilliant idea I had ever had—or the dumbest. Yet for me this was the most inspiring way I could share the data. To be authentic, I needed to risk personal discomfort to bring a new view into being.

There was total silence at the end of the presentation. Then one man in the front row began to speak: "I think we are all stunned at how well we have been heard." More people described the impact of seeing the whole, and a softer mood spread across the room. I organized the group into circles and invited people to ask questions rather than to blame. Seeing the individual parts woven together in a work of art allowed them to see how goodwill and right intentions were compromised by faulty structures, incomplete information, and lack of a clear project plan.

Something occurred in that room on that day that I could not have predicted, calculated, or measured. It was a shift in perspective, an opening of hearts, and the beginning of a willingness to learn together. The group moved from cynicism and belligerence toward tenderness and care. For a few hours, people became undefended, found a connection to their power within, spoke their truths with kindness, and changed their perceptions. The powerless thought of themselves as power-full.

I am not saying that this single event washed away all the woes of the department. But something real and genuine found its way through the usual defenses and ignited a spark of hope on which to build.

Patricia's Story

Through my mid-thirties, I believed wholeheartedly that university degrees and job titles were the most legitimate tools with which to gain power as a woman in America. No one in my family had gone to college. Scholarships and two graduate degrees later, I was a senior vice president and one of the top 250 executives at a major financial institution. I thought—and people around me reinforced the idea—that I had "made it," that I was powerful, that most people would "kill" for a similar opportunity.

Yet I was feeling deprived of power. I had been recruited by my employer to "lead change" from its headquarters city. I couldn't bear to leave another city and the home that I had spent nearly two years refurbishing. My husband had been transferred to yet a third city.

I also sensed that the company with which I signed on didn't really want to change. My budget was cut within a month after I walked in the door. The staff that I was promised remained segregated, distributed throughout various divisions for political reasons. When, after eighteen months, the team was integrated under my direction, they were suspicious of my intent. I was an enigma as a leader.

My first instinct was to do what I had been trained to do in three previous organizations. I knew from experience and education that I should move fast, talk tough, lay out strategies, and establish guidelines. But somewhere inside, I knew that my team would be dissatisfied with my approach and that I would fail. An overt attempt to assert power would certainly undermine it.

What to do? I went away for two days, vowing to disconnect the phones, speak to no one, and come back with a strategy. Instead, I returned with a new outlook. During my sojourn, I realized that what I really wanted was to be understood and appreciated for who I am, not for my ability to imitate a given boss or set of policies. I also imagined how I could evoke a similar desire in my team.

I recalled that during the dreamy days of high school I had fantasized about becoming a journalist, and in the previous year my mother-in-law Dr. Barbara Haight had introduced me to her work and techniques in life review, reminiscence, personal autobiography, and storytelling. I decided that my first job as a leader in this group was to do one of the things I most enjoy—ask questions. I wanted to know this team more intimately.

I set up "talk times" with everyone, individually, intent on sincerely inquiring into the nuances of their lives. I learned who did ministry work on weekends; who secretly aspired to be a landscaper, not a banker; whose father had recently died; whose husband was a chef; and what were the proudest and darkest moments of their lives. I shared some of my own. And I asked how we could take full advantage of the personal to more fully enjoy the professional.

It was the first time that I felt really close to people I worked with, and I was nervous most of the time. This was new—tearing down walls that I had spent nearly twenty years carefully constructing around my image and way of being. I was shaping a new me while not taking center stage to do it. What if, having stepped away from the limelight, I came to be viewed as "too soft"? A "pushover"? What if all my credibility was lost?

Something else occurred. Barriers eroded as stories took front and center. In my eyes, people were no longer managers of processes waiting for the next round of merger-related layoffs. Their power was transferred to the realm of personal identity. For the first time,

I saw how limited and limiting are old, established parameters. To empower meant giving people the space to be seen and daring to reveal more of myself. I had a glorious glimpse of what leadership and power—from a deeper place—can look like.

It's been several years since that life-changing event and my stint with the financial services company. I stay in touch with several members of the team. What I hold on to most tightly is the potential of stories to help people bring their authentic selves to the surface and regain their power by moving ego out of the way.

Learnings

Each of us learned firsthand from these experiences that people long to be seen, that they connect with what is real and genuine, and that a leader who creates an environment that illuminates passions and concerns redistributes power in a profound way. This view of leadership is in contrast with organizational norms and practices that narrow and homogenize experience through arbitrary standards of effectiveness and efficiency—that which can be counted, quantified, and easily resolved. Failure to incorporate the emotionally evocative leaves out what is ultimately significant. Only compliance, not commitment, can be achieved through the use of external power. Far more creative things unfold when we nurture internal sources of power instead.

We also learned that we cannot guide others toward authentic self-expression if we're not willing to face the anxiety raised by being genuine. We can only develop a sense of security in our own instincts by risking. We must shatter surface illusions, unearthing and caring about what matters to people, who they are, what concerns them, and what has their attention and energy. We also learned the art and positive consequence of connecting through stories. Revelation and collective sharing of individual truths create a bond from which community emerges.

As we discovered, people's deeper sense of power is best accessed in environments where the following characteristics are present:

- *Listening* that demonstrates care and respect for others' needs and our own
- *Integration* of personal stories that brings people together within a framework of logical meaning and emotional coherence
- *Reflection* that creates a space in which to cultivate community, goodwill, shared contribution, and connection
- *Dialogue* that fosters curiosity and wonder rather than judgment and blame
- *Nurturing the human spirit* through alternative forms of expression, such as drawing, storytelling, and movement
- *Creating space for healing* by defining organizations as human social systems formed from a spectrum of bodies, minds, and spirits—*not* a mere collection of tasks

Shifting Images of Organizations

In organizations, it is often understood that human qualities—especially frailties and tender mercies—should not be acknowledged on the job. The goal is to mask vulnerabilities through external control (power) and to produce an image of invincibility. Yet this superficial, control-oriented presentation of power undermines individual and group confidence. It leaves people and organizations unsatisfied and off balance. It is primarily for show and therefore inauthentic.

Accordingly, the much-needed shift to authentic power—that which draws on creative life force—does not begin with big, organized strategies and policies. Transformation originates in one's own ways of thinking, expressing, and acting.

If we think someone has power, then we give it to him or her. If we think we don't have power, then we give it away. We reinforce our own worth when we acknowledge our own truths. We draw on what is authentic each time we express ourselves honestly and thoughtfully to a boss, colleague, or client. Forming thoughts into words and displaying them for public or private consumption are simultaneously uncomfortable and courageous.

Of course, the outcomes of such expression are unpredictable. Initial satisfaction at taking a stand can be accompanied by social rejection, job loss, or the end of a relationship. But when we take action that is pure, right, simple, and sustainable, we defang the fears that would stop us. Think Rosa Parks. In 1955, this poor black seamstress unofficially launched the civil rights movement by refusing to give up her seat on a bus to a white passenger. This is a model of deeper power.

At times, we will be asked by "those in power" to do things that are questionable. When we dare not to be swayed, we explore greatness. Consider Sherron Watkins, the vice president at Enron who wrote a letter to chairman Kenneth Lay warning that the company's accounting methods were improper. This is a model of deeper power.

Self-Awareness as Source

At its core, deeper power is anchored in the commitment to gain self-knowledge and grow through a continuing journey toward self-acceptance. The work of Robert Tannenbaum suggests there are three key components that shape such an important endeavor: values, strengths and limitations, and unresolved personal issues.[2]

Values guide our behavior, determine the work we choose, and establish priorities for how we use our time. Living our values ignites pride in who we are, provides us with dignity, and gives us energy for life. An honest assessment of our *strengths and limitations* grounds us in reality, allowing us to act consciously and in ways that are self-aware. *Unresolved personal issues*—such as low self-esteem, the need to be accepted, fear of conflict, and lingering anger—limit our abilities to see, feel, and act from strength and wholeness.

Resolving personal issues moves us toward evolved consciousness and compassion.

If we are unaware of our values, strengths and limitations, or unresolved personal issues, then we will protect and defend rather than reveal and open. Greater strength is often gained through vulnerability. We come to see that living and leading with respect for people's total well-being enhances our capacity to be human and to strive for legacies that go beyond quarterly results, financial ranking, or military prowess. Instead, we can weave a tapestry reflecting universal principles of good living: selflessness, communion, and appreciation for each person's inborn drive to be unique.

No one can give us power, nor can anyone steal it away. The path to authentic power is to become relentless and undefended in seeking knowledge of ourselves—to understand our values and see that living them is essential to physical, spiritual, and emotional well-being.

In organizations, we have seen, heard, and understood what good comes when people are honored for who they are. Joy, enthusiasm, and productivity are unleashed in environments where—for hours or months—people experience communion. They don't have to be coerced to participate if they are truly invited to play.

New Style of Leadership

What does this mean for organizations and those who aspire to lead? Whether for-profit or nonprofit, private or public, organizations do not arise from the mist. They are compiled from a bundle of mental models, belief systems, and tacit assumptions. Unfortunately, most of today's organizations and their policies and practices derive from perspectives on power that emphasize force and control—views present for so long that we take them for granted. We are not fully cognizant of why we manage the way we do.

The result is corporations, universities, and governing bodies run on structures and systems that are generally hierarchical, regimented, nondiverse, exclusionary, and threatened by suggestions that there's a better way. They are encoded with overt and covert beliefs about the "right ways" to work: hard-charging and tough-minded approaches win the day, work is battle, leaders must think like warriors, and rank indicates intelligence and capacity to achieve, to name a few. Basic human needs—for dignity, connection, respect, and self-expression—are seen as ancillary, even counterproductive to getting the job done. Operating from these premises, most organizations and their leaders haven't begun to tap the full potential of human beings.

To "do it differently," we must begin to acknowledge and embrace individuals and their authentic selves—not jobs or titles. The linchpin is a new concept of power that

- Celebrates a wide range of individual traits and styles
- Responds with compassion, love, and generosity to everyday and multifaceted challenges
- Prompts change by openly inviting diverse opinions and approaches

As Margaret Mead said, "Every social institution which teaches human beings to cringe to those above and step on those below must be replaced by institutions which teach people to look each other straight in the face."[3]

Longing for Leaders

To create this kind of environment, we need leaders imbued with higher aims, willing to live in the uncertainty of self-exploration. Without such leadership we will remain mired in "business as usual."

Envisioning oneself as this kind of leader is, in a word, scary. It involves deconstructing and reconstructing, stepping out without ground beneath. But the rewards are more than worth the risks. As Audre Lorde said, "When I dare to be powerful—to use my strength in the service of my vision, then it becomes less and less important whether I am afraid."[4]

Leadership from this place is a gift that sparks new possibilities in the world. To encourage others to recognize their own power is to invite a wonderful paradox of independence and interdependence. No doubt these invitations will result in some false starts and culminate in both successes and failures. There are no guarantees as to who will meet the call or for how long. But one thing is sure. Real leaders exhibit great hope and the will to extend themselves before asking the same of others. That is authentic power, not just authority, and it attracts others.

Wonder of Women

Certainly, we need both sexes fully engaged in this endeavor. It is an assignment and opportunity that affects and benefits all humans. But someone has to get momentum moving in the right direction. If we are going to cultivate more authentic power in individuals and organizations, women are perfect candidates to jump-start the change, for three reasons.

First, we are still a nondominant group trying to function in systems dominated by male views and mental models. We've experienced trying to assimilate but still feel left out, on the fringes. Second, we represent a burgeoning force of untapped energy. Numerically, we comprise nearly half of the workforce. Our presence, alone, puts us in a position to make some noise and model new standards of behavior. Third, women have an enviable track record of challenging the system, believing that humans and the organizations we create are responsible for behaving in respectable ways.

As women, we need to look within ourselves, and around us, to know what needs to be done. Noticing means shining a light on what's really happening. We can decide to "get right" in our internal landscape on our way to changing the world. Every woman can *take a day off*. Go to a secure place. Turn off televisions, telephones, and other distractions to reflect on these questions:

What do I value most deeply?

Where and how do I compromise myself to belong?

What is my vision for myself, my family, my community, and
the planet?

What can I, personally, do differently?

How can I change the places where I work, participate, and
play?

With personal story in hand, we can then seek out other people's stories, one-on-one and in groups. Then we can partner—two,
three, four, fifty, five hundred people—to collaborate for a common
purpose. When we reach out for change, linkages form in unexpected places—across boundaries of age, gender, race, class, geogra-
phy, and culture. We become a force of creative problem solvers,
and we begin to see that, everywhere, there are men and women
waiting to be rejuvenated. We must keep our eyes and ears alert for
anyone eager to redirect attention from a myopic focus on the bottom line to a restoration of spirits.

In these changing times, we have choices to make. We can
awaken, find our courage, and act from authentic, internal power.
Or we can sleepwalk—accepting surface symbols of power and living in the illusion that we are separate from each other.

As we think of the work about which we care most deeply, it is
clear that we need to be in touch with our power to leverage what
we value. To own one's power is to be a creative contributor. To
inspire others to own their power is to invite the human community to shape its collective future.

 Barbara Corcoran rose to the top of her field against seemingly impossible odds. Her résumé includes straight D's in high school and college, as well as twenty jobs by the time she turned twenty-three years old. But then she borrowed $1,000 from her boyfriend to start a tiny real estate company in New York City. She subsequently parlayed that loan into a billion-dollar business. Today, The Corcoran Group is a premier New York real estate firm, and Barbara is considered one of the most powerful brokers in the country. In her new book, *If You Don't Have Big Breasts, Put Ribbons on Your Pigtails & Other Lessons I Learned from My Mom,* Barbara credits her success to fierce determination, creativity, and the steadfast application of her mother's kitchen table wisdom.

In this chapter, Barbara demonstrates how power and persistence often go hand in hand. She employs her distinctive "tell it like it is" style to remind us that no success story would be lasting without failure along the way—and that the difference between those who succeed and those who don't lies in the capacity for "failing well."

4

FAILING WELL

How to Be Vulnerable and Strong

Barbara Corcoran

If you're alive and playing the game, then dealing with setbacks is something you'll have to do time and again. Business schools may teach you to market and plan, but they don't teach you how to fail. Failure, however, is something about which I am highly qualified to speak. In fact, it's been one key to my success. Every fall back has inspired a spring forward. Everything I learned about failure and what to do about it, I learned from my mother.

Edgewater

I grew up in a small town called Edgewater, New Jersey. Picture it on the Hudson River, facing the skyline of New York City, exactly two miles long and two blocks wide. We lived in the ground-floor apartment of a three-family house (six girls in the girls' room, four boys in the boys' room, and a bathroom in between). My father and mother slept in the living room on a convertible couch. When people talk to me about the cramped size of New York apartments, I can only smile.

Growing up in a large family is like growing up in your own town. Everyone, whether he or she likes it or not, takes on a role. My mother, Florence, should have been running the war in Iraq. To this day, I would call her the most organized person I have ever met. She ran our household like a boot camp. Although we had one of the two biggest families in town, we also had the neatest house, and it was the house that everyone in town hung out in.

Anyone who has a business that employs more than one person knows how important systems are to making things work. My mother's organizational genius meant that she had a place for everything. If my mother had to do one thing more than once, she would create a system so that it would happen automatically. There was, for example, a sock drawer for the girls—all white, all one size—and a sock drawer for the boys, right underneath—all navy blue, all one size. It was years before I realized that not all kids have that cloth bump on the back of their ankle! The system was there so that we didn't have to waste time. This approach gave me a huge advantage in running my own business later on.

Ed's Way

The other key person in my life was my father. Ed was totally different from Florence—a role model for insubordination and fun. Mom commanded Dad to be home for dinner at six o'clock every evening. He was always prompt, but now and then he would say, "Guess what, kids?" and we would say, "You got fired again, Dad?"

Ed, you see, had an issue with authority. He was a skilled printing press foreman, but inevitably he would have an argument with the boss or the boss's son and be sent packing. Just as inevitably, he would find a new position within the week—thank God he was so employable. If the industry changed, he got back on his feet and found yet another job. And every evening, after the dinner and bath-time routine was done, my father headed back out to work a second job, as a truck washer for UPS, a night foreman at a factory, or a night watchman. He was a wonderful model for us as a hardworking man, but he also, clearly, should have been in business for himself. Not surprisingly, all ten of us kids went into business for ourselves. I doubt that would have happened if we hadn't grown up thinking that it was a bad thing to work for someone else.

The Importance of Fun

My father also gave us his sense of fun. In the window of time between shifts and jobs, Dad's other job, as dictated by my mom, was to play with us. My father's idea of fun was a little extreme at times, even weird. For example, one snowy day he hauled his two-story wooden ladder to the end of our side yard. On each rung, he put his ten kids. Then, with a quick shove, Dad jumped on the back of the ladder and sent it flying down the yard, hurtling toward the snow bank that rose up against the retaining wall and separated us from the street. People might say that's not very good parenting, but you have no idea how high you'd fly on that last rung when the ladder shot over the retaining wall, sailed over the sidewalk, and landed smack down in the middle of the street! We lay there, laughing until our sides hurt, and then scrambled up to do it again. Until my mother came storming down the front steps in her house slippers to put an end to such craziness, we knew we had the happiest family in Edgewater.

Later, when I ran my own business, I would rely on my dad's sense of fun to occasionally put my little team of salespeople (which grew into a bigger and bigger team) into risky and (now that I look back on it) frankly litigious situations. But I knew from my father's example that people would talk about these incidents for years. The shortcut to creating cohesiveness, after all, is to make people laugh together. In real estate, team spirit is especially complicated. Although we're all on the same team, we are also in competition with one another. So as a manager you are dealing with a weird balance. Most real estate brokerages in New York have found room for only one superstar. This is understandable, because like a queen bee, a real estate sales star is very territorial by nature. From the beginning I had two, three, and even four or more superstars on my team of brokers, more than any other company in town. How did I pull this off? By putting people into situations where there would be no choice but to have fun and learn to love one another. I didn't have expensive budgets for perks or high salaries to create loyalty. I used downright ridiculous fun to build my business.

One of the most important lessons I ever got from my mother was the ability to underline the positives. She decided, practically from the moment we were born, what our gift was, and reinforced it over and over. As for me, she declared that my gift was my wonderful imagination. Whether it was true or not, I believed it. She constantly placed me in the role of entertaining the other kids, putting on Broadway shows in the basement or running chalk games on the sidewalk. I'm sure that this was also an easy form of baby-sitting on her part, but I thought it was an honor.

My mother also chose to ignore the negatives. I distinctly remember the day when I was in third grade and was told to go back to the second-grade classroom after school. I knew something was wrong. I knew that everyone in third grade was reading books that I couldn't read. When I walked into the second-grade classroom and saw the students who were in there, such as Rudy Valentino, I knew the jig was up. "Rudy from the boat," as we called him, was an Italian kid who couldn't speak English. Kids measure themselves. Until that moment I had always known something was wrong, but I thought I was hiding it. Sitting next to Rudy and the others, I realized I was stupid.

From that day on, I became the quiet child at school. What an unbelievable waste of time and spirit. But thank God I went home to a mother who focused on the positives. One of our routines at dinner was that we had to go around the table and say what had been good about our day. It was our lesson in how to converse. When it was my turn on that day, I could hardly talk. So after dinner, my mother kept me at the table and told me that she had gotten a call from the school, and the sister had told her I was having trouble reading. My mother didn't focus on the problem; she focused on the positives. She said, "You know, Barbara, you don't even have to worry about that. You have a wonderful imagination. You'll fill in the blanks." In other words, she chose to ignore it. Nowadays, parents would put their kids into special education or give them extra reading, but my parents didn't have the time or the resources, so my mother went heavy on the positives. As much as I felt like a loser or failure at school, I could come home and be "the child with the wonderful imagination" for her. In other words, I had a choice. I could be the Barbara at school, or the Barbara at home. Thankfully, I kept choosing to be my mother's Barbara.

Always Offer the Bigger Piece

I met my future business partner while waitressing at the Fort Lee Diner, just north of our hometown of Edgewater. I was competing for tips against a blonde bombshell named Gloria who was a dead ringer for Dolly Parton. I mean, she had a set of breasts that were like shelves, a beehive hairdo, and a teeny waist. "Dolly" had one counter and I had the other, but it was Dolly that put the Fort Lee Diner on the map. Men waited in line on the double steps outside to sit at Dolly's counter, even when my counter was wide open. I'd been working there for a few weeks when I whined to my mom about how unfair it was to tag-team with Gloria. This, of course, did not go over well. My mother said, "You know, Barbara, if you don't have big breasts, why don't you go put ribbons on your pigtails." In this way, my mother, who knew nothing about business, gave me my first marketing lesson: you need a gimmick. So for a while, flapping little ribbons in my pigtails was my marketing strategy.

With renewed confidence, I met Ramone Simone, from the Basque Country of Spain.[1] He walked through the restaurant like a cat on the prowl, with jet-black hair and dark skin. He took a seat at my counter, and that's how I found my future business partner.

My parents hated Ramone on sight. He became my boyfriend anyway. I found out later that he wasn't Ramone Simone from the Basque Country; he was Ray Simon from 125th Street. (I guess he knew a little bit about marketing, too.) Ray loaned me the $1,000 I needed to start my business. Without him, I never would have gotten the money. Together, we started a real estate company. We weren't quite equal partners, though. Because Ray was taking all the risk, as he put it, he got 51 percent and I got 49 percent.

Our company was a business of one at first, just me in a tiny little office in Manhattan. I moved in with Ray, and we were raising his three girls together. I hadn't even known he had children until I moved in with him. Then, almost seven years to the day when I first met him, Ray came home one night for dinner and told me some big news. I was dumping pasta in the strainer, and he said, "Barbara, you and I have something very important to discuss." I thought it was going to be the kind of conversation you usually have at night. But Ray said, "I'm going to marry your secretary."

I think I stopped breathing. I thought it was a joke, actually. I couldn't believe it. I said, "Tina? You're going to marry Tina?" He told me that it was true and that I could take my time moving out. That was a relief, because I needed every one of those eighteen seconds to pack my bags and leave.

That was an ending. And how did I deal with it? For the first time in my life I was hit by depression. I couldn't get up, couldn't function. In one fell swoop, the confidence I'd been building by raising a nice family, doing a great job, and having a boyfriend in what I thought was a great relationship—vanished. At work, I had fourteen salespeople under me. Business wasn't thriving, but I was making a living. Suddenly, I was a nobody in my own mind. It took four or five days of crying before my good friend Cathy threw me off the couch and sent me back to the business.

I worked for two more years with what I called the "Ray and Tina" show. I couldn't fire Tina, though I wanted to, because Ray was the controlling partner. I went through the motions of thinking life was OK. Little by little, I got my confidence back, and I finally realized that I could run this business on my own. I walked into Ray's business one day and told him I was going to end the partnership.

Ray was shocked. To get him to agree to my terms, I once again mimicked my mother. As children, if we had Duncan Hines cake, the pieces were cut into a grid in the pan. This left some pieces bigger than others. Mom always made us bigger kids offer the bigger piece. She told us, "If you offer the bigger piece, yours will taste better." We thought that was ridiculous. How could a smaller piece taste better? But when I decided to end the business, I did it the way my mother made us share cake: I took the smaller piece.

I told Ray that we were going to start by dividing our salespeople into two groups, and I let him pick first and me second. Next I let Ray decide whether he wanted to keep the old phone number or get a new one, stay in the old office space or go to a new one. Ray picked the best salesperson, took the existing phone number, and decided to stay in the current office. In many people's eyes, this meant I got the short end of the stick; but I actually got a much more long-term and meaningful thing: a feeling of pride that I had operated above and beyond the call of duty in the fairness department. I wasn't this vindictive woman who had been trying to get back. I had given Ray the bigger piece. So in thirty minutes we divided up the company, settled everything, wrote the checks, went to the bank together, closed our joint checking account, opened new checking accounts, and parted ways. I only wish I had divided my first marriage that efficiently.

Ray and I were not quite done yet. When I was going out the door, he gave me a great gift. He said, "Barbara, you know you'll never succeed without me." You can imagine how that made me feel. I knew I would rather die than have him see me not succeed. So in the next chapter of my business career, whenever I thought I had exhausted every last channel and there was nothing left for me to try, I would think of Ray. Even when I was ready to throw in the towel with dignity because everyone else was failing too, I would remember Ray's words, and somehow one more idea would pop into my head, and I would try that too. I couldn't stand the thought that he might see me fail. It might have been bad motivation, it might have been coming from the wrong place, but it worked for me. I continued to build the business over the years with that motivation at my back.

Falling with Style

What I've learned about myself over the years may surprise you. More than anything else, the thing I am great at is failure. For whatever reason, all the big jumps forward in my life have come as a result of being put down, pushed down, or pulling myself down. The falling back position has always provided me with the momentum or spring to push right back up. Whenever I've had a crisis, that's when I've done my best. Whether it was interest rates skyrocketing to 18 percent in 1981 or the stock market crash in 1987 that plunged real estate prices and sent our business down by 70 percent—no matter what, even when most of our competitors were going out of business, we figured out how to keep going.

For me, every breakthrough has taken place because of failure. When I announced to my salespeople that I was going to put all my apartments on videotape so people wouldn't have to go around the city to figure out what they wanted to see, everyone thought I was a genius. But I spent my entire $71,000 profit for the year on making copies and publishing tapes that no one was interested in. I was old enough and smart enough by then to know that another opportunity would emerge from that debacle. So in 1990, when real estate was in a recession once again, I looked around and saw my rotten old videotapes and had a new idea. My husband had just gotten back from "playing war games in real time" on something called the Internet. I asked what he meant by that, and an idea was born. I had a big sales meeting coming up, so I thought, I'll announce that this homes-on-video idea was a prelude to taking our listings into cyberspace.

We became the first real estate broker in America to put our properties on the Internet. Did I think it would work? Of course not. Was I saving face? Of course. But within the first week of putting those images onto the Web, most of the properties were sold. Our new clients were not from New York; they were from Europe. By the time the local markets improved and our competitors had the money to get started, we had already tested fifty different angles and reorganized our approach a hundred times. Our Web address was well known, and we had staked out a dominant presence in a market no one had seen coming.

It wasn't that I was so smart—it was simply that I was failing well. For those of you who have children, you have probably seen a movie called *Toy Story*, which explains what I am talking about. In the movie, Buzz Lightyear, one of the toys, is a macho astronaut flying with the aid of a toy rocket. The other toys look on in awe and say, "It's incredible. He's flying! He's flying!" And Buzz shouts, "It's not flying! It's falling . . . with style!"

In my business, in which a handful of superstars make $2 to $3 million a year and a great number of others don't, I've found only one difference between the top 10 percent and the rest. It's not about success—it's about failing well. The top salespeople take more hits because they're out there more. They don't get knocked down by the rejection, however; they jump back up. I've been studying failure for some time, and to me that's the critical difference. People who fail well, who bounce back quicker than others, are the ones who excel in my field. As my mother would insist, there's no room for whining or feeling sorry for yourself. And that message, for me, was the real gift of a lifetime.

As the author of *Rhythm of Compassion: Caring for Self, Connecting to Society* and *Empowerment: The Art of Creating Your Life as You Want It*, Gail Straub has been a teacher and activist for more than two decades, leading countless people through training that helps them integrate their spiritual development with social and ecological responsibility. She is considered a leading authority on empowerment, having worked with thousands of people throughout the world through the company that she cofounded, Empowerment Training Programs. She also codirects the Empowerment Institute, a school for transformative leadership. And she is the creative force behind *Grace: A Spiritual Growth Training Program*, a special program for leaders who want to integrate spiritual development with social responsibility.

As leaders, what is our calling? What are our gifts, and how can they best be deployed? In this chapter, Gail helps us answer these questions so that we can lead with courage and strength while replenishing and nourishing the self. Along the way, she helps us identify the space where the expression of ourselves as leaders in work meets our human need for purpose and passion.

PHOTO CREDIT: Gail Straub by Leif Zurmuhlen

5

WORK AS LOVE MADE VISIBLE

Finding Your Passion

Gail Straub

At the heart of what is meaningful in life, we think of many things: our families, our communities, our most important relationships, and even the social challenges that inspire us to take action in causes much larger than ourselves. It's rare that we think of work, yet so much of our modern life is devoted to a job. We're immersed in that work for much of each day, surrounded by others who are participating with us in a common endeavor, engaged in efforts that often require our full capacity and then some. If we are driven to seek larger meaning in life, it is obvious that we would do well to seek that in our work. In other words, I am suggesting that we view work not as a job, a paycheck, a struggle, or a confrontation, nor as something that we do to support our efforts in more precious areas, but as a source of meaning in itself. This search for meaningful work is the call to discover your passion.

In writing this chapter, I thought a great deal about passion and calling in life. I thought about the many people I have worked with who followed their passion, and I also thought a lot about how I found a unique engagement with my own life and its meaning. No one showed me how to follow my passion, but somehow that is the path I have always traveled. In that sense, I have been blessed. I was the first high school–age woman to be sent to the poorest part of South America as an American Field Service student. I attended the Sorbonne University in Paris during the students' 1968 revolution and took active part in those wild days of political unrest. I went on to serve in the Peace Corps in West Africa. I became passionately involved in the women's movement during the 1970s. In the 1980s, I became a global peace activist engaged with citizen diplomacy in various hot spots throughout the world. In the last decades, I've worked to create environmental sustainability, a field in which my husband David Gershon is a leading force. In 1981, David and I founded our business, Empowerment Training Programs, to help others find their passion. Over the last twenty years, working with thousands of people in many parts of the world, I have learned a number of things about passionate work.

I wish I could say that the search for passionate work is easy or straightforward. But the truth is that there are always reasons why we feel the need to put off that search, and always roadblocks we can't see beyond. We need only compare the eras we've lived through in the last five years to realize how critical, yet how elusive, the search for passion and calling can be. During the economic high times of the late 1990s, many of us fell under the spell of the trickster of busy-ness. We offered up our lives for the promise of a payoff that would lead to freedom, only to find that the rewards we sought were often illusory. That busy-ness created a malaise and emptiness that brought many people to a search for something more fulfilling.

The nature of that emptiness shifted with September 11. Fear and anxiety turned many of us inward in a reexamination of larger life priorities. At that moment, there was a kind of spiritual vitality present for many people, a deeper inquiry going on, an understanding that time is short and life is precious. But the economic downturn that followed made many people conservative about their dreams and less inclined to take risks. As a result, discovering and pursuing your passion has become a challenge once again, for different reasons than before.

Not everyone who needs help to discover her passion needs it because of a crisis in her work. Yes, there are those who need to leave their jobs because they are dying spiritually or emotionally. But some blessed people are extremely happy and fulfilled in their work and are looking for ways to sustain that. In between those two extremes there is, perhaps, a more silent majority who are treading water, neither satisfied nor moved to desperate measures. The reasons for the call to passion, like the journeys themselves, are myriad.

I've come to believe that the authentic search for passion requires a profoundly honest self-inquiry and the courage to face our deepest fears and unknowns. In this chapter, I will share with you what I've found that may help you face your challenges in the quest for passion. Through engaging with this process, you will, I hope, be able to answer some fundamental questions: What is my calling? What is my unique engagement with life? Where do I belong? What are my gifts, and how can I fully contribute them to the world?

I want you to ask yourself, in the deepest sense: Who am I? It is my hope that the answers fill you with surprise while allowing you to recognize your passion.

The Quest

In his classic book, *The Prophet*, Kahlil Gibran said this about the quest for passionate work:

> When you work you fulfill a part of earth's furthest dream assigned to you when that dream was born, and in keeping yourself with labour you are in truth loving life. And to love life through labour is to be intimate with life's inmost secret.
>
> And what is it to work with love? It is to weave the cloth with threads drawn from your heart, even as if your beloved were to wear that cloth. It is to build a house with affection, even as if your beloved were to dwell in that house. It is to sow seeds with tenderness and reap the harvest with joy, even as if your beloved were to eat the fruit. It is to charge all things you fashion with a breath of your own spirit, and to know that all the blessed dead are standing about you and watching.
>
> Work is love made visible. And if you cannot work with love but only with distaste, it is better that you should leave your work and sit at the gate of the temple and take alms of those who work with joy.

For if you bake bread with indifference, you bake a bitter bread that feeds but half man's hunger. And if you grudge the crushing of the grapes, your grudge distils a poison in the wine. And if you sing though as angels, and love not the singing, you muffle man's ear to the voices of the day and the voices of the night.[1]

The search for passionate work reflects all the classic phases of mythic journey:

- Call
- Awakening
- Journey
- Descent into darkness
- Epiphany
- Ascent

The good news is that this rigorous quest brings real joy and authentic meaning to our lives. How do we engage in work that is love made visible? There are two aspects to the quest for passion. First, there is the quest to find our passionate work. Second, there are the practices that sustain that passion—some of which we will explore in the next few pages.

In the journey to passion, we all start from a particular place. I have found that people fall into five broad categories in their search for passion. Each raises a different question for people searching for more meaning in their work. Perhaps one of these situations will resonate with you.

I Need to Leave My Current Work, or I'll Never Find My Passion

"Where is my passion? How do I find it?"

Leslie was a vice president at an international corporation. Early in her career she obtained a very desirable global assignment. Because she excelled at that position, she began to climb the ladder quite rapidly and rose high in the ranks. She enjoyed her "golden girl" status, loved her work, and found her career path very satisfying for fifteen years. Then things began to unravel for her.

When she reflected on where things had gone wrong, she realized that over the course of her career she had driven herself so hard and fast, and given so much of herself for so long, that she felt incomplete as a person. Although she thrived in that dynamic work environment during her twenties and thirties, by her mid-forties she realized that she had absolutely no interior life. She had simply ignored it for too long.

Leslie never blamed the job. She did not try to rewrite history or dishonor the enjoyment she'd had for fifteen years. But she realized that it was time for a change. She needed to find passionate work again.

To do so, she needed to try some things that were difficult for her. First, she had to get quiet in order to hear what life was telling her. Next, she had to make a brave move and step off the fast track. For someone who had risen as high as Leslie, that took serious courage. She understood that she had to jump into the void of the unknown in order to face all her most intimidating fears. "I'll be nothing if I leave my position," she worried. "I'll become depressed. I'll lose my community of colleagues and friends." She was wise enough to get some counseling to see her though that in-between period.

Eventually, after about six months of thinking and searching, Leslie discovered something new and very different. She decided to go back to school to become a therapist.

I found Leslie personally inspiring. She loved the work she had been doing at the corporation, then she realized that her passion was no longer there and knew she needed something else. She didn't gripe and moan or blame the job. Instead, she had the courage to take decisive action. Unlike so many successful people, she did not stagnate in the trap of her own accomplishments but stepped out of that trap and found a new home.

Leslie had found tremendous happiness and vitality in her work for many years. But when it began to unravel, she could feel herself becoming depressed. She knew how important it was to confront those fears directly rather than poison something that had given her so much joy. She was also smart enough to know that she shouldn't go it alone. Because of that courage and care, she was able to reengage with life through work in a different and rejuvenated way.

I Had Passion in My Work, But I've Lost It and Need to Rekindle It

"How do I reengage with my passion in a sustainable way?"

If you are just getting by in your job, you neither like nor dislike your present work. Although there's nothing offensive about the job, it doesn't excite you or engage your passion. Perhaps you've fallen into a rut and don't face any challenges. Perhaps you are bored or burned out.

Ella was a gifted clinical psychologist. She'd been working one-on-one with patients for ten years before it became very boring to her. There was no fire left. When she began examining what would reignite her passion, she felt that she needed to do more group work, so she volunteered at a shelter for battered women. This experience lit her fire. She made a tremendous contribution to the shelter and realized something even more important—she needed to work with a more diverse population. The highly educated, upper-middle-class patients with whom she'd been working were very comfortable to her. By moving out of that comfort zone and giving to a wider world, she found the love of her calling again.

I have seen a great many people reignite their passion by connecting that passion to the larger world. Doctors, lawyers, business executives—at a certain point, they may develop a need to push themselves beyond the confines of their everyday responsibilities in order to encounter people and life issues they would not normally be touched by. I know doctors who've gone off to work in refugee camps or business executives who mentor young leaders, high school students, or inner-city children. Although their service sometimes takes people in entirely new directions, more often than not it connects their passion to their work in a slightly new or innovative way. This pattern exhibits something true about passion: it needs to incorporate "giving," almost as though giving is the kindling that keeps the fire going. Sometimes, by making certain subtle but strategic shifts in your thinking, you can fall back in love with your work or create a new iteration of that work that reengages your passion.

I Am in Transition Between Jobs

"What is my passion? Am I actively seeking it?"

When you are in transition, you are between jobs and wide open to what's next. You may be searching for a new career in a field in which you have no experience, or you may want to continue your current field of work but hope for a job that is more fulfilling. Perhaps you need time to just "be" before you get back to work. Perhaps you are actively searching for your next job.

The wonderful thing about being in transition is that you are in an excellent position to start with a clean slate. This is an opportunity to clarify your vision and make sure that your next work experience is all you want it to be.

Candice was a stockbroker. She had loved that work intensely for a long time, then felt so burned out that she needed to quit immediately. To her credit, she did not try to hang on to something that was unhealthy—she let it go. Candice's problem was that she did not have a clue in the world about what she wanted to do next. She wanted "another life" but did not know what that meant. Through the process of getting quiet and befriending her fears and barriers, she began to hear the call of her earliest passion. After college, she had been a volunteer teacher at a high school. She thought back on what had been so exciting for her at that time in life, and remembered all the good and bad aspects. It gave her a picture of what she might want to do next. As the vision gained clarity and took shape, she decided that she wanted to work with young adults in college who were struggling with what shape their own lives should take. This new passion, radically different from what had occupied her through her career as a stockbroker, was connected directly to her earliest work. By rediscovering that passion and updating it to fit her experiences and current interests, she made a major shift into what could honestly be described as "another life."

I Am in a Stepping-Stone Phase in My Career and Am Headed Toward My Passion

"Am I still actively learning from this stepping stone, or am I where I am because of inertia?"

When you are in a stepping-stone phase, you are doing work that you know is not your final destination. That work is providing you with training and experience in a field you will either stay in or adapt to a similar field. You are learning a lot of practical skills, and your work is fulfilling. You still face a learning curve. You sometimes question, however, whether the step is still relevant. You wonder if you are still making progress toward your destination.

Sometimes you need to sharpen your vision of where your path is ultimately leading you so as to make sure you are getting the most out of your present situation. Paula was another therapist who had become tired of that work and knew she wanted to do something different. She decided that she wanted to join the corporate world, so she became a management consultant. She knew that management consulting was a stepping-stone to the business world and that it would provide her with valuable training and experience.

Even though her management consulting work did not take full advantage of her capabilities, Paula found it satisfying for a time because of the learning involved. After a while, however, the work became boring to her, and she decided to figure out where her passion was taking her within the business world.

She realized that the level at which she was working was not satisfying. Paula wanted to help executives at senior levels, so she decided to become an executive coach. Her management consulting role put her in position to develop those capabilities and gain the right experience. She was also very smart about using the support network around her. She talked to her boss openly about her larger goals. When the time came for her to move on, he was the first one to point out that she was ready and became an advocate for her move within the company.

Becoming an executive coach was, in many ways, a reconnection to her original passion as a therapist. But she needed to take a slightly roundabout route to get to that position. In other words, in order to sustain her passion in therapy, she needed to be truthful about her feelings for her work and place herself on the next growing edge of challenge.

I've Found My Passion; My Work Is Love Made Visible

"How do I sustain my own passion and create an environment that empowers others to find and sustain their passion?"

Sarah is the executive director of a regional AIDS program—one of the model agencies. Her story is compelling because of its lessons for leadership. The passion that Sarah, her staff, the social workers, and volunteers at the agency had for people dying of AIDS was immense. As is often the case in such situations, however, the danger of despair and burnout was very high. It's as though the fire of passion can burn so intensely that we become consumed by it. In Sarah's case, she was so immersed in her work that her marriage began to suffer, and she felt that her inner life was in need of protection.

Sarah thought long and hard about the practices needed to sustain her passion. She could have rationalized the daily sacrifice of time and energy that was hurting her family and marriage, but she knew she needed to safeguard that wellspring of support if she was to be fulfilled as a person and a leader. She had a passion separate from work—for being in nature—so she followed that by hiking and skiing with her family in order to spend more time with them. She also developed a strong spiritual practice that became critical in feeding her resilience.

Because Sarah was a visionary leader, she knew she had to sustain the passion of the people around her as well, including her staff, the people dying of AIDS, the social workers, and the volunteers, a group that collectively numbered in the hundreds. She empowered them to such a degree that even in the midst of extraordinary suffering there was a sense of meaning and joy. Sarah found that the passion of others was sustaining her own passion as well. It was as if passion had to flow out of her to be sustained.

Leadership can be a draining and lonely affair if passion is not sustained. As Sarah's story reflects, it is critical to preserve the inner life of the leader. And it is just as important to develop support systems around the leader to feed the passion of all involved. When you have full passion for the work you do, you experience that work as love made visible. When that passion is sustaining, you have created a work situation that is deeply fulfilling to your mind, heart, spirit, and body. The work remains challenging to you, both for personal and professional growth. There is no difference between work and play. Your work is your earthly playground, and you are very blessed.

Finding Your Passion

The process of finding your passion is a gestalt with many interconnected qualities. For most leaders I've worked with, that process encompasses seven stages, as follows:

Get Quiet Enough to Hear Your Passion Calling You

Many of us are so busy, so overstimulated and crowded within, that there's no space for our passion to grow, and no quiet from which to hear its call. And yet our deepest creativity is born in silence. As my dear friend Gunilla Norris says in her beautiful book *Inviting Silence*,

> *Within each of us there is a silence*
> *a silence as vast as the universe.*

We are afraid of it . . . and we long for it.
When we experience that silence, we remember
Who we are: creatures of the stars, created
from the birth of galaxies, created
from the cooling of this planet, created
from dust and gas, created
from the elements, created
from time and space . . . created
from silence.
Silence is the source of all that exists,
The unfathomable stillness where vibration began
the first oscillation, the first word,
from which life emerged. Silence is our deepest nature,
our home, our common ground, our peace.
Silence reveals. Silence heals.
Silence is where God dwells.
We yearn to be there. We yearn to share it.[2]

The seeds of your passion are born in this silence. To discover it, you need to cultivate quiet in your life. You can do this through meditation, prayer, or formal retreat. You can do it through quiet walks in nature or even by turning off the radio on your commute. You can create silence with your family before meals, or within your own mind just before you fall asleep.

Have Courage to Heed the Call

Once you hear the call of your passion, it will be obvious that tremendous courage is required to heed that call. To follow your passion requires that you face fears, losses, challenges, and failures. The cultivation of your courage comes as you face some difficult questions: What am I willing to give up in order to pursue my passion? What am I losing by not pursuing my passion? Am I dead inside and just going through the motions at work? Am I burned out? Have I given away my soul to my job? Am I courageous enough to risk the security of the known and pursue my passion, finding my gifts and giving them fully to the world?

The beloved Indian poet Kabir called us to courage in this way:

> *Friend, hope for the Guest while you are alive.*
> *Jump into experience while you are alive!*
> *Think . . . and think . . . while you are alive.*
> *What you call "salvation" belongs to the time before death.*
> *If you don't break your ropes while you're alive,*
> *do you think*
> *ghosts will do it after?*[3]

Face and Befriend Your Fears

This courage then guides us to the third stage of passion where we are asked to face and befriend our fears. Most of us want to run from our fears. Paradoxically, it is by going toward our fears that we move toward our passion. We are not asked to overcome or resolve our fears completely. Rather, we are asked to befriend them. Fear is a necessary ingredient to passion. Indeed, it is part of what keeps the fire hot.

Often the fears that keep us from claiming our passion are deeply hidden and unconscious. These fears include the following:

- Fear of disobeying an idealized father figure
- Fear of disobeying a patriarchal organization or culture
- Fear of betraying our mother who didn't follow her passion
- Fear of displeasing or threatening our lover or spouse
- Fear of the inner critic who tells you that you are worthless and can't follow your passion, that you don't have what it takes, that you're not enough
- Fear of confronting the litany of excuses that blocks your real passion: fear of failure, disappointment, not enough money, not enough time, not enough staff, not enough . . .

These fears are inevitable as we claim our passion. We need to go toward them in order to uncover them, talk about them, and transform them with mentors, counselors, or trusted colleagues. We need to use them as part of the fuel that fires our passion.

Face and Befriend the Unknown

Like all mythic quests, the journey to passion also requires us to face and befriend the unknown. To find our passion we often have to leave the familiar before we know exactly where we are going.

Most poetry, music, and art that moves us deeply is in some way about going to the edge and leaping empty-handed into the vast unknown. In the deep waters of the unfamiliar, creativity and passion live and thrive. The unknown may be scary to us, but it's a fertile and friendly environment to the two sisters, creativity and passion. In her poem "At the Shore," Mary Oliver speaks to us about befriending the unknown so that we may know passion (see page 92). As you read it, imagine risking what is familiar and safe in your work so that you might find what is passionate.

Revisit Your Earliest Passion

It is challenging to face your fears and unknowns, but there are some lovely aspects of the journey as well. Revisiting what Emily Dickinson calls your "original joy" will almost always give you clues to your life's passion. The blueprint for passion is set early for most of us. That blueprint shows up where we felt our greatest sense of belonging as children—in the natural world, with books, music, dressing up, building things, organizing tree house clubs, or finding new and dangerous adventures. My sister, for example, was forever in the creek behind our house. Only in mud and plants, with frogs and snakes for company, was she completely at home. Today she has found her passion as a wetlands ecologist—not such a far cry from her play in our childhood creek. Another friend enjoyed her greatest moments of belonging while listening to her grandmother tell

At the Shore

This morning
wind that light-limbed dancer was all
over the sky while
ocean slapped up against
the shore's black-beaked rocks
row after row of waves
humped and fringed and exactly
different from each other and
above them one white gull
whirled slant and fast then
dipped its wings turned
in a soft and descending decision its
leafy feet touched
pale water just beyond
breakage of waves it settled
shook itself open
its spoony beak cranked
like a pump. Listen!
Here is the white and silky trumpet of nothing.
Here is the beautiful Nothing, body of happy,
meaningless fire, wildfire, shaking the heart.[4]

---

stories. It was the deep listening that totally engaged her. Today she is a talented therapist, healing people through her gift of listening deeply to their stories.

Remember What Is Essential in Life

What were you passionate about early in your story? What was your original joy? At the deepest level our passion is in close relationship with what is essential in life. Ironically, finding and living your passion have a close relationship to the questions you will ask at the end of your life: Did I love well? How have I touched the people at work, at home, and in my community? Have I given my best? Who, what, and how you love is inextricably bound to your passion.

This is what Gibran was talking about in the earlier passage when he said, "To love life through labour is to be intimate with life's inmost secret. It is to charge all things you fashion with a breath of your own spirit, and to know that all the blessed dead are standing about you and watching."

In working as a hospice volunteer, I've had the privilege of helping people review their lives before they die. Again and again, what was essential to most people centered around doing what they really loved, giving their best to life, and loving well. Recently I coached a minister who was working with firemen and rescue workers on the front lines at Ground Zero in New York City. He was struggling to understand the relationship between the indomitable passion he saw in the rescue workers and the unfathomable death all around them. In our dialogue it became clear that the death around them had brought out their very best. It had made them realize how short and precious life is, how important it is to give our best and not to hold back. Perhaps this is what September 11 asked of all of us.

Start a Passion Journal

Finally I want to switch from the sublime to the pragmatic and mention the final stage—starting a passion journal. This is a great support in the process of discovering your passion. In the spirit of Julia Cameron's wonderful book *The Artist's Way,* a passion journal is a simple diary in which each day you record one thing that generates passion.[5] This can be something specifically related to your work, such as having lunch with a mentor or colleague who inspires you; or it can be something more general that ignites your creativity, such as arranging a vase of flowers, listening to music you love, taking out the hidden-away box of watercolors, or walking in a beautiful place. A daily journal entry exercises your passion muscles and gives you the flexibility to move out beyond familiar boundaries into the unknown.

Sustaining Your Passion

Working with these seven stages of the journey can help us discover our passion. But how do we sustain it? Passion is an ongoing, living process that needs reigniting on a regular basis. Not surprisingly, most of the elements that sustain passion are precisely the same ongoing practices that sustain quality of life in general. In particular, there are five practices I can describe that will help you sustain passion, regardless of your environment. Discuss these practices at length in my book *The Rhythm of Compassion*.

Engage in a Spiritual Practice

Ultimately, to sustain passion we need some kind of spiritual practice that helps us cultivate a strong center. Prayer, meditation, yoga, solitude, time in nature—regardless of the form your spiritual practice takes, it is essential to sustaining your passion. Without a spiritual practice we're like a tiny boat without oars or rudder on the great turbulent sea of life. In fact, your spiritual practice is the most powerful tool you have for staying healthy—mentally, emotionally, and spiritually—amid the enormous stress and complexity of passionate work. When you find your passionate calling, complexity and challenges increase, and more is demanded of you on all levels. You need a place to stop to refuel and to replenish your energy and confidence. It is your spiritual practice that will sustain the courage and energy required for passionate work.

In the last several years, I've had the good fortune to do much of my teaching in a beautiful Benedictine monastery on the Hudson River in New York. I've grown very close to the monks at this monastery, and they have taught me an enormous amount about passion and spiritual practice. This is a vibrant working monastery where the brothers host thousands of visitors a year and lead hundreds of dynamic programs on spiritual development. These brothers are as busy as anyone who works and leads, yet they pray five times a day to cultivate a strong spiritual center. Having this center allows them to be present though each moment of the day. In a multitude of ways, I have witnessed their deep attention to each person, each challenge, and each stress. They have taught me that many present moments add up to an entire passionate life.

Practice Self-Responsibility, Showing Up, and Being Real

The next practice is easy to describe but hard to do. So often we lose our passion in work because we're hiding. What are we hiding? Well, to name a few things, we are hiding our gifts, our ideas, our enthusiasm, our boredom, our anger, our power, our originality, our disagreement, our failure, our success, or our exhaustion. The energy it takes to hide our real self steals vital energy from doing passionate creative work.

The degree of passion you sustain in your work is equivalent to how real you are. What does it mean to be real at work? It means that who you are at work is who you really are. In other words, there is no split between work and the rest of your life. There is a large component of personal responsibility inherent in this idea. A person who is who she is at work must take responsibility for the good, the bad, and the ugly without blaming others. A passionate person does not hide from herself or from the world. A passionate person shows up, beautiful mess and all, and generously gives her gifts to the world.

Rumi taught us this about showing up:

> The breeze at dawn has secrets to tell you.
> Don't go back to sleep.
> You must ask for what you really want.
> Don't go back to sleep.
> People are going back and forth across the doorsill
> where the two worlds touch.
> The door is round and open.
> Don't go back to sleep.[6]

Stay on the Next Growing Edge of Challenge

To sustain passion in our work we need to be honest with ourselves about when we are stale. Such stagnation can build subtly when we've found work that we're passionate about. Because we love the work, we coast too long without stretching ourselves with vital new challenges.

In my own case, for instance, I am absolutely passionate about my work as a teacher and a trainer, but I have to stay alert for the dangers of becoming too comfortable. Some years ago, I noticed that I was becoming bored with my work. I was still helping transform people's lives, but I wasn't transforming myself anymore. I realized that I needed to work much more deeply and for longer periods of time with the same students if I was to reengage with that sense of personal transformation. To that end, I created a yearlong spiritual growth training program that took people into the most fundamental questions about themselves and the nature of the human condition. I was, to put it mildly, challenged by this endeavor and found that my passion was reignited. After some years of doing this work I was so inspired by my students that I wanted to write a book about what I was learning. My inner critic said, "Don't even try!" But I knew that writing was the next challenge I needed in order to keep growing and learning. As hard as it was, and still is, writing is now a rich part of what brings passion to my work.

Protect Your Inner Life

Like everything in life, passion has a shadow. The shadow of passion is called workaholism and burnout. Without the balance of an inner life, your passionate work is an empty shell. Sooner or later you will find yourself automatically going through the motions of an outer life that will lead to burnout. As someone who has experienced the shadow of my own passion—I am susceptible to both workaholism and burnout—I can tell you, in no uncertain terms, that passion cannot survive without an inner life.

In her wonderful book A *Woman's Education*, Jill Ker Conway— the first woman president of Smith College and a leading educational visionary—says this about protecting the inner life: "I wasn't quite forty when I arrived at Smith and ran instantly into one of the major challenges of adulthood. That challenge is to protect and sustain the inner self while entering passionately into the complexity of one's work. I was stressed. Not so much by all the public commitments but by the lack of solitude. I thought the Benedictine rule of work, prayer, and meditation saner than any other rule for life I knew, and I began to lose my zest for life if I couldn't find some approximation of it."[7]

Then Jill goes on to describe how she and her husband found a way to protect their inner lives: "Our life in Conway took place on snatched fragments of weekends, holidays, and summers. It revolved around creating a garden, hiking to enjoy the striking beauty of the natural landscape, poetry, which we read aloud to one another almost every evening we were alone, and music."[8]

I use the metaphor of the breath to represent our need for both the in-breath of self-care and the out-breath of giving our gifts to the world. To thrive on all levels, we need to find our balance of breathing in (caring for self) and breathing out (offering our best to life). We know our passion has turned into workaholism when we find we don't have a life outside work anymore.

There's only one thing to do at that point. We need to take that radically courageous first step of reclaiming our inner life. We need to start gardening again, or playing the piano. We need to take a silent retreat, go back to our dance class or our morning yoga. I've found that even a small dose of in-breath—a long hike, a beautiful dinner with friends, an evening of reading or music, an afternoon of silence—goes a long way to protecting the inner life. Our inner life doesn't require a lot; it simply requires that we honor it.

Create Ongoing Support Systems

Last, and definitely not least, I want to mention the crucial need for creating support systems to sustain passion in our work. The very essence of passion is the support with which you surround yourself. To meet the risks, challenges, and demands of doing passionate work, we first need the support of our family. Our partners and children need to be on our team all through the journey. This includes the phase in which we jump empty-handed into the unknown, as well as the times when we have wild successes or dismal failures and are confused, elated, or overwhelmed. Our family needs to know why it is important for us to follow and fulfill our calling in life. We also need to support them in their doing the same. Passion, after all, is contagious.

Our family support provides us with an even deeper level of self-knowledge than we may be aware of. After all, the roots of our passion are in our own lineage. We may have a father who inspires superb negotiation skills, a mother who is the consummate team builder, a grandmother who was a genius at multitasking long before the word was invented, or a grandfather whose courage remains a vibrant and living inspiration. This lineage gives us profound insight into our passion. In our toughest moments we can go to back to our roots to find the strength we need.

We also need support systems among our colleagues and mentors. Such people are invaluable resources when it comes to talking things through, testing ideas, collaborating, obtaining honest feedback, and staying on the cutting edge in our chosen fields. I have been in a woman's support group for over twenty years, and I am absolutely clear that these colleagues and dear friends have been an intrinsic part of sustaining my own passion. One of the most crucial things that your family and your collegial support system can offer is to let you know if you've fallen into the shadows of passionate work. They are there to remind you to protect your inner life.

Signing Up for Life

Some people come to their passion naturally and easily; such people are blessed. For others, there's a crisis—a divorce or an illness—through which they recognize that change has occurred. It sounds glib, but at such moments one really does realize that life is short. The question that follows (What do I really want to do with my life?) can provide a powerful redirection. The majority of women, however, are in the poignant and difficult category. They're going along well enough, but there's no spark. The voice in their heads is soft but insistent: *This is not what I signed up to do for the next twenty years of my life!* What such people do in response to that voice makes all the difference in the world.

It takes a very brave person to leave her job or reshape it, especially when that carries her beyond a zone of comfort and security. It takes courage to push the envelope of what provides subsistence for our lives in order to go for something that is truly nourishing. Especially in this conservative era, few people are inclined to take such risks. I see many corporate women, in particular, who are sitting on their passion these days yet who want to reclaim their lives.

As leaders we are conditioned to think about what needs to change in the world and to take action. We know how necessary it is to take a stand in that external sense; but it is just as important that we take a stand with regard to our interior lives. Without that stand, we burn out, falter, or lose spirit, and our lives are less integrated and rewarding. When we touch our innermost vision of how we want to express ourselves on this planet, we release our life energy. This energy fills us with creativity and provides us with an innate ability to bring energy forth in others. In these trying times, there can be no greater thing we do for those around us.

Be still. Listen to your calling. Be brave. Find support. Take the leap. Bring others with you. The rewards will return to you many times over.

Stacy Blake-Beard, Ph.D., is a profound voice in the field of mentorship. She is an associate professor of management at the Simmons School of Management, where she teaches organizational behavior. She is also affiliated faculty in the Center for Gender in Organizations at Simmons. Before joining Simmons, she was on the faculty at the Harvard University Graduate School of Education and worked in sales and marketing at Procter & Gamble as well as the human resources department at Xerox. She currently sits on the advisory board of a number of important organizations, including MentorNet, Peace Games, Jobs for the Future, and the Harvard Project on Tenure. She has also been the recipient of numerous grants and fellowships, most recently from the Ford Foundation.

In this chapter, Stacy clarifies the link between mentoring and leadership. Blending a review of the latest research with her own experience as a consultant, a scholar, and an individual who has been touched by mentors, she makes a compelling and personal case for the critical impact of mentoring in shaping our next generation of leaders.

PHOTO CREDIT: Stacy Blake-Beard by John Gillooly

6

THE INEXTRICABLE LINK BETWEEN MENTORING AND LEADERSHIP

Stacy Blake-Beard

We wear the mask that grins and lies,
It hides our cheeks and shades our eyes,
This debt we pay to human guile;
With torn and bleeding hearts we smile,
And mouth with myriad subtleties.
Why should the world be overwise
In counting all our tears and sighs?
Nay, let them only see us, while
We wear the mask.
We smile, but, O great Christ, our cries
To thee from tortured souls arise.
We sing, but oh, the clay is vile
Beneath our feet, and long the mile;
But let the world dream otherwise,
We wear the mask.

—Paul Lawrence Dunbar[1]

The haunting imagery raised by Dunbar's poem is very familiar to me. As long as I can remember, whenever I have read this poem, I've been filled with a melancholy awareness, a recognition that the spectral beings in Dunbar's poem could be any number of my colleagues in twenty-first-century organizations. In fact, Dunbar could be talking about me. Dunbar's poem resonates with my own experience as an African American woman who has lived my whole professional life in traditionally white institutions— as an "outsider within."[2]

The mask alluded to in Dunbar's poem is not mine alone; many women face challenges that compel them to wear a mask, to survive by appearing to be something they are not. Esteemed legal scholar Lani Guinier describes her experience with a male law professor during her graduate studies. At the start of each class, her professor offered a greeting to his male and female students alike: "Good morning, gentlemen." Guinier shares the implicit message with which this professor inculcated his class: there was an expectation that each student was on the journey to becoming a professional and that this journey entailed becoming a "gentleman"—detached, problem-solving, unemotional advocates. She describes how alienating and isolating her experiences were in law school; for her, the forum of legal education had not been a safe place. In her research on the experiences of female law students (with colleagues Michelle Fine and Jane Balin), Guinier "chronicles the disappointments of women as they entered previously male-dominated institutions and, to a surprising extent, remain isolated, marginalized and dissatisfied."[3] Although their study was set in a legal context, their findings are representative of the experiences of women in many other professions, including medicine, sports, education, and management. In spite of our many advances, women still encounter organizations where wearing the mask is a viable strategy for survival.

I started studying mentoring relationships in 1989 because for me, on a very personal level, mentoring relationships have always been about having a safe haven in the landscape that Guinier described in the research or recollection described earlier, a space to lower the mask to which Dunbar so eloquently refers. Guinier suggests that how leaders take up this challenge to women is crucial to building organizations that are inclusive and supportive of women. She also highlights the importance of mentoring as a tool by which women are given access to opportunities and exposure to traditional and alternative models of success.

Mentoring as a Tool for the Development and Advancement of Women

Mentoring is a critical tool in the career development of women.[4] Access to mentoring is one of the most significant enablers of women executives' career advancement, according to research by Catalyst.[5] Likewise, Catalyst studies have noted that the most significant barrier to women executives' advancement is lack of access to mentoring. These conclusions are borne out when we examine two organizations that have adopted formal mentoring as one aspect of their endeavor to recruit, retain, and advance women.

Procter & Gamble (P&G) is an example of one organization that focused on mentoring as a way to better understand and support the careers of female employees. In P&G's Mentor Up program, senior male executives were partnered with more junior women in the organization, an example of reverse mentoring.[6] The impetus for the Mentor Up program was the results from a "regretted loss" survey of employees who had recently left P&G; female employees indicated that they wanted to hear explicitly about their value and their contributions and to be given opportunities for open discussions about their career path and development. Formal mentoring was offered as a way to address concerns raised by female employees. These pairings were also done to give senior executives a glimpse into the challenges and experiences of women in the company. One of the reasons the program has received so much attention is that it challenged the paradigm of mentoring that suggests that an older, wiser male is the ultimate fountain of wisdom. Early results from this experimental program suggest that male senior executives gained important learning from their mentoring relationships with their junior colleagues. Senior male leaders in the Mentor Up program have tapped into advice and perspectives on various cross-gender job situations. Participants say that beyond fresh thinking related to cross-gender communication, they have received insights and suggestions that have strengthened their relationships with men as well as women in P&G. And "regretted losses" of female employees were down 25 percent and are now on par with losses for male managers; there have been some organizational benefits as well.

P&G is not the only company that faces challenges in retaining women managers. In 1991, Deloitte & Touche held a similarly dismal record for the retention and advancement of female partners. They confronted startling statistics that indicated that of fifty candidates being nominated for partnership in that year, only four were women. When Deloitte & Touche partnered with Catalyst to determine why women were leaving, they found three crucial problem areas related to the advancement and retention of women: a male-dominated environment, fewer opportunities for career advancement, and challenging work-life balance issues.[7] Deloitte & Touche faced two challenges: (1) although the company was recruiting women aggressively, it was not advancing them to partnership status, and (2) in an industry characterized by fierce competition for talent, women were leaving in droves. One partner shared that the Catalyst report sent a clear message: "You know what, guys? You grew up here and you think this is a great place. But there is a whole class of people who don't agree with you. . . . And if you think you're going to grow this business 25 percent to 30 percent a year with 25 percent to 30 percent of the people leaving, you've got another thing coming."[8]

In 1993, Deloitte & Touche announced an Initiative for the Retention and Advancement of Women. The task force charged with implementing this initiative undertook a number of actions to address the three issues identified as barriers for women at Deloitte & Touche. A key component of their recommendations and implementation strategy was acknowledgment that women did not have access to crucial developmental opportunities or the critical guidance of mentors and sponsors. For Deloitte & Touche, creating an environment that was more hospitable to women included an explicit focus on mentoring.[9] This focus has been associated with some positive benefits. Since the initiative began, the number of key leadership positions held by women grew from 14 to 118. In addition, the number of women partners and directors jumped to 368 in 2000 from 97 in 1993; at the time that these figures were reported, Deloitte & Touche had a greater percentage of women in these positions than any of its large competitors.[10] Not only were women advancing in greater numbers, they were also leaving in fewer numbers. By 1995, the turnover rate for female senior managers dropped to 15 percent from 26 percent in 1992. In March 1995, Deloitte & Touche received a Catalyst award as one of the best organizations in the country in the area of gender equality in the workplace. With considerable effort, including attention to mentoring opportunities for women, the culture has changed significantly at Deloitte & Touche.

Beyond the Business Case for Mentoring Women

As the cases from both P&G and Deloitte & Touche illustrate, there is a business case for mentoring. Recent examples and organizational programs confirm the importance and increasing use of mentoring as a strategic initiative.[11] Drawing on the extant research, we know that mentoring has been linked to easier socialization, less turnover, more productivity, and increased loyalty and commitment.[12] A study of the benefits of mentoring programs reported that organizations use these formal initiatives for a number of reasons, including retention of employees, enhancement of career development, the development of new leaders, and support of high potential employees.[13]

But we need to go beyond the business case to fully understand the rich potential and implications of mentoring as a source of organizational strength and renewal. The very essence of mentoring is that the process signals, "I care." Mentoring communicates a clear message: I think enough of your potential and capabilities that I am willing to invest time, training, and access to critical opportunities in your growth and development. We often think that "I" refers only to mentors who invest in mentoring; in fact, organizations that support and nurture mentoring efforts are also sending this message, which is potent in and of itself. The importance of organizational care was illustrated for me as I worked with a large financial services company that was rolling out a formal mentoring initiative to four hundred employees. On the first day of training, one woman sat listening in the front row, skepticism written all over her face. At the lunch break, she approached me. Considering the looks of doubt she had been transmitting throughout the morning, I watched her approach with some concern. She shared with me that she was surprised and pleased that the company was investing in mentoring. In fact, she had been about to begin the process of seeking other employment. But with the start of her participation in this mentoring initiative, she expressed an interest in staying with the company; she wanted to see if their mentoring initiative would make a difference in her chances for development and advancement. Although this woman is only one person, her story speaks to a larger issue. Sometimes we are so busy looking for the business case—the hard-numbers justification—that we miss the power of what mentoring relationships can mean to people.

Leaders needing to justify an investment in mentoring can marshal at least two arguments supported by research: that mentoring has been linked to important organizational outcomes and that it sends a message that the organization values its most precious resource, the women and men who do the work and fulfill the mission of the organization every day.

Best Practices for Leveraging Mentoring Relationships

There are a number of steps that leaders in organizations can take to ensure that women are receiving access to mentoring relationships as they move through their careers. A first step that I often offer to organizations is for them to ask themselves why they are interested in using mentoring, as opposed to some other initiative, to leverage opportunities for women. Mentoring is such a popular topic that sometimes organizations latch on to it as a default or because their peer organizations are using mentoring. Neither of these is a good reason to institute formal mentoring in an organization.

A more thoughtful approach allows leaders to consider the following questions:

- Why do we believe that mentoring is the right tool to use for our situation?
- What aspects of our culture will be supportive of a formal mentoring initiative?
- Are there aspects of the culture that might make it difficult to build a formal mentoring initiative?
- Who will be the champion for this effort—how have important and powerful organizational leaders connected to this initiative?
- Does the organization have the infrastructure to support a formal mentoring initiative?

Some leaders still have the misconception that mentoring is a quick, cheap fix to their people problems. In fact, a well-formulated and strategically placed mentoring initiative is neither quick nor cheap. If an organization is not willing to dedicate resources (financial and human) to its mentoring initiative, it may be better served by finding an initiative that it can fully support.

In addition to considering the questions listed here, organizations planning on using formal mentoring as a tool to aid women should give careful thought to how mentoring partners are matched, trained, and supported throughout the duration. Helping mentoring partners set realistic expectations at the outset of the relationship will give them a foundation on which to build an effective formal mentoring partnership. Leaders in organizations should take care to build in opportunities to learn from their experiences of formal mentoring. Check-ins with the mentoring partners as well as a formal evaluation at the conclusion of the program are both essential. The information gleaned in these procedures will allow program administrators to shape the program based on their learning.

There are two last caveats that leaders should consider when championing mentoring for women as a catalyst for change. Change of any magnitude requires time to take hold in organizational cultures. Leaders should be prepared to give the mentoring initiative the necessary time for results to be measured and for benefits to be gained. A second caveat is that focusing a mentoring program solely on women in your organization, to the exclusion of their male colleagues, may produce backlash. If your mentoring initiative cannot be or is not open to everyone, leaders should be prepared to offer other opportunities for developmental growth and support to those employees who are not included in the mentoring initiative.

An Ongoing Journey

I have been fortunate. At every step in my professional career, I have had the benefit of a mentor—actually, multiple mentors. A senior black male colleague walked by my side as I struggled with the decision of where to start my academic career after leaving the University of Michigan with my doctoral degree. He offered sage words of advice that provided just the right insight for me to make the best decision for me. I wanted to adapt the strength that he had, through his scholarship, to shatter the monochromatic landscape of mentoring research. A senior white female colleague held a mirror up for me to examine my tactics and strategies for integrating family and work. As I was figuring out how to fit myself into the skin of a "professor and mentoring scholar," I appreciated that this mentor never forgot or regretted that she is a mother and that her family holds a crucial and precious place at the forefront of her life. I marveled at how she was (and continues to be) able to publish rigorous and important research at prolific rates, in part through the amazing partnerships that she has built with her protégés. And I have learned from these two mentoring relationships. I know what I want to give to those who are coming behind me. Most of all, I enter each mentoring relationship with the thrill, the sheer possibility that I am going to be transformed by my partner. As a leader, I know that mentoring is an integral part of my stewardship of the organization.

Leaders are charged with creating a space that encourages their colleagues, that allows people to step out into uncertainty and be bold, and to make mistakes. This space is difficult to quantify. In my practice as a leader, and as I have studied and watched others lead, I have seen that mentoring relationships offer a phenomenal opportunity to support and be supported, to offer shelter and take risks. Mentoring is a gift that leaders today can give to themselves and their organizations.

For women, being part of an organization that values mentoring may be particularly important. Audre Lorde's question, "Am I to be cursed forever with becoming somebody else on the way to myself?"[14] is one with which I see women grappling in organizations of all types. Mentoring provides a place that welcomes women to come as they are. At its best, mentoring is a process that beckons to women and encourages them to lower their masks.

Influence is both a by-product of power and a pathway to it. As an executive coach and organizational development consultant, Kira Hower has examined many of the aspects of this influence-power connection. Kira was central to the development of the Women in Leadership practice area while working at Linkage, Inc., helping create and facilitate the *Influencing for Impact* and *Risk Taking and Decision Making* workshops, as well as other leading skill-building workshops geared specifically to women leaders. Kira is currently a senior partner with the Shambaugh Leadership Group. All told, she has had extensive experience working with hundreds of women leaders in businesses all over the country grappling with profound workplace and leadership challenges.

One of those challenges involves the inability to be heard—a problem that women leaders perceive as a consistent and systemic feature of organizational life that can impair their effectiveness on both an individual and organizational level. In this chapter, Kira discusses how we can identify and leverage our own influence styles to address that problem—and improve our workplace interactions and results.

7

INFLUENCING FOR IMPACT

Kira Hower

> When I dare to be powerful, to use my strength in
> the service of my vision, then it becomes less and
> less important whether I am afraid.
>
> *–Audre Lorde*[1]

Everyone feels frustrated at times by an inability to be heard by others. Yet many women confront this every day at work. I have spent the past four years working in the area of gender and leadership in corporate America, seeking to better understand the challenges and potential solutions for women working to gain influence and use their voices—both at work and at home. To illuminate some of the elements that contribute to women's challenges with influencing in corporate environments, I would like to address some critical questions: What is influence? How does gender communication affect women's ability to influence? What do effective influencers really do? Finally, what strategies might you or your colleagues use to strengthen your voice of influence?

Influence and Power in the Workplace

Influence happens constantly and sometimes invisibly. As a force, it is both tangible and intangible—something you experience when you see a well-defined business strategy turn into real profits or when you feel the confidence of a role model or mentor who helps shape your career and life. Linguistically speaking, influence is both a noun and a verb, something we have and something we do. The

American Heritage Dictionary defines *influence* as "A power indirectly or intangibly affecting a person or a course of events"; "power to sway or affect based on prestige, wealth, ability, or position"; "a person or thing exercising such power"; "an effect or change produced by such power"; "an occult ethereal liquid flowing from the stars to affect the fate of men." As a verb, *to influence* means "to have power over; affect"; "to cause a change in the character, thought, or action of."[2]

Although you may enjoy the image of a magic influence potion, chances are that your definition is a bit more practical. More typically, when people talk about influence as a noun, or something we possess, it tends to be used synonymously with power. This connotation, however, may be changing. More and more women in positions of authority are expressing their discomfort with the "power over others" paradigm. In 2003, *Fortune* magazine interviewed the one hundred most powerful women in the United States, many of whom claimed they did not conceptualize power in a traditional, hierarchical, or macho way.[3] Consider a few of their comments from the article:

> Power is in your face and aggressive. I'm not like that.
> > —Jenny Ming, president of Old Navy

> Power has a negative connotation.
> > —Meg Whitman, CEO of eBay

> I'm afraid of it.
> > —Gail Berman, president of Fox Entertainment

As the article states, many women "view power differently from the way that men do: They see it in terms of influence, not rank."[4] It's no surprise that many women leaders avoid power in a hierarchical sense but seek influence, the ability to effect change. It is also no surprise that there are so many women who opt out of corporations in which power is entrenched. In fact, thousands of women start their own businesses every day, at twice the rate of men.[5] For a variety of reasons—an inability to influence inevitably being one of them—women are leaving Fortune 500 corporations in numbers large enough that the leaders of these organizations should be paying close attention to the phenomenon.

When I began to research issues of women in leadership in the corporate arena, I was struck by how much communication, and specifically gendered communication, or the way that men and women communicate differently, played a role in the themes that emerged. The voices from the road (that is, my clients) went like this:

"My colleague plays the devil's advocate with me so much that I've just shut down when he comes around. It's not worth the fight."

"I get interrupted consistently in meetings."

"I'll propose an idea and it will be ignored and then picked up by a man a few minutes later and then touted as a brilliant idea!"

"I can't get my boss to listen to my new ideas."

"I try to think of my employees as family."

"I build trust with my employees before I ask for their commitment."

"I listen to concerns and try to build my case based on each team member's position."

"I ask a lot of questions and listen actively."

Each of these statements reflects an issue with influence and also power. If we were to use the term *power* not as synonymous with influence but as an element of it, the relationship between power and influence becomes clearer.

One important step in developing your influencing skills is to identify where your own power resides. Acknowledging and analyzing the bases of power that we possess do not always come easily to women. We have been socialized to downplay our strengths and not talk about our accomplishments—let alone our power. Yet much of our power, both personal and professional, comes from successfully navigating life's challenges and adventures.

When I think of personal power, I think back to when I was twenty-one. I bought a one-way ticket and moved to Italy with the goal of learning Italian. I was not a big risk taker or a thrill seeker. I was just passionate about the language and culture. I spoke very little Italian and knew hardly anyone, but my passion overrode my fears and self-doubt. Ultimately, I lived in Florence for nearly a year and learned enough Italian to get a job in a private language academy. It was a life-changing experience that helped build my self-confidence in a way I never would have experienced had I stayed in the United States. Even today, I feel powerful when I think back on that experience because I had to believe in myself and my ability to communicate with others. I often share this story with people who are considering living abroad to encourage them to take the risk. I see this as one way that I influence with my own personal power.

It is one thing to feel powerful based on entirely personal accomplishments; but many people, men and women alike, feel powerless in the workplace. The refrains from professionals range from "I can't get my boss on board with this new idea, and I know it will be a huge success" to "They [senior management] have told us to 'make this change happen' but haven't given us the resources or the necessary information to even understand why." As I said, these examples are not exclusively of women's experiences; therefore, both men and women can benefit from identifying where their power resides.

Power can come from many sources—knowledge and expertise, financial resources, position or title, and certainly the relationships you have. Following are five bases of power found in organizations of all sizes:[6]

> *Resource power* is based on having control or access to needed resources or rewards. The resources could be funding, materials, critical information, or assistance. The challenge with this base of power is that it is ephemeral. Our resources can be taken away from us very easily at the next budget cut.

Positional power is based on title and status in the organization. Positional power will certainly gain you compliance, but not necessarily commitment.

Coercive power is based on using threats and manipulation and assumes and uses positional power. Coercive tactics may get you what *you* want but will probably inspire resistance, hostility, and distrust in others.

Expert power is based on your experience, knowledge, and subject matter expertise. This is one base of power that poses a challenge to many women in business. Too often women downplay their expertise so as not to seem self-aggrandizing. In fact, some research indicates that women more commonly attribute their success to luck than do men; this is one aspect of the Imposter Syndrome.[7] This "giving away" of your expertise can have a subtle but far-reaching impact on the people you are trying to influence.

Relational power is based on who you know and the quality of those relationships—both internal and external to the organization. This base of power is predicated on trust and the length of history with the relationship.

Of these forms of power, the key to most leaders' success is relational power. It is what establishes, maintains, and builds *trust*—which, as we'll discuss in more detail later, is the most critical and often undervalued element in business (and our personal lives, for that matter). The quality and depth of your relationships gain you more influence with others than the resources or position that you hold. And if you can't build trust with people, you cannot have much influence over them.

Influence and Language

How we communicate our ideas, our expertise, or our needs is probably the greatest determinant of whether or not we are able to influence others. Yet over 90 percent of our communication takes place at a nonverbal level. A frequently cited study by Dr. Mehrabian at UCLA shows that 55 percent of what we recall about an interaction or presentation is actually based on what we perceive visually (such as body language, style, and so on); 38 percent is tone; and only 7 percent is based on the actual words spoken.[8]

When we look at language through a different lens, that of gender, we gain another means of understanding influence. How does gender communication affect a woman's ability to influence in corporate environments? Much research exists on the subject of gender communication, popularized especially by Deborah Tannen, professor of sociolinguistics at Georgetown University. Nevertheless, little of the knowledge about gender communication has infiltrated corporate cultures. Clichéd generalizations occasionally surface in the groups I have worked with, but few managers have a sophisticated grasp of the issues. Undoubtedly, business schools could benefit from building gender communication and gender dynamics into their curricula for future leaders. One institution in Boston that is doing just that is Simmons School of Management, providing the only all-female MBA program in the United States. The Center for Gender in Organizations at Simmons is a wonderful resource for research on gender and business for those interested in understanding at a deeper level many of the issues of power and leadership for women.

According to most gender communication theories, as well as those of relational psychologists such as Carol Gilligan, men and women experience the world differently. Tannen proposes that men and women actually "see" the world through different lenses, affecting how they experience and interact with others. From her perspective, women view the world through a "connection" lens and men through a "status" lens.[9] Similarly, in Gilligan's and Jean Baker Miller's research, women gravitate toward a more relational orientation (connection) and men toward a more independent and hierarchical one (status).[10]

How does this play out in an actual conversation? For example, for two men talking about past experiences, the "status" lens could sound something like this:

Tom: Where did you used to work?

John: At the World Bank in D.C.

Tom: What position did you hold?

John: I worked in human resources in the Organizational Effectiveness Division.

Tom: Hmmm. How long were you there?

John: Two years at the D.C. office and then a year abroad.

Tom: Did you work for Tim O'Brien?

In a similar conversation between two women, the "connection" lens could sound like this:

Tammy: Where did you used to work?

Joan: At the World Bank in D.C.

Tammy: Really? I used to know Nina Miller there. Do you know her? And what did you do there?

Joan: No, actually I didn't. I worked in human resources in the Organizational Effectiveness Division. I'm not sure where she worked.

Tammy: I don't remember exactly. HR? I've always been interested in that field. How has your experience been with it?

These are subtle differences, and it would be overly simplistic to suggest that men don't look for connection and women don't seek status. Yet these nuances can cause serious disconnects between men and women. Seeing the world through a connection lens works to a woman's advantage, especially when trying to build influence, because fostering relationships and establishing trust and credibility require a personal connection. Nevertheless, there are also "conversational rituals," as Tannen calls them, that can inhibit a woman's ability to influence in the workplace. The rituals that I see as the most damaging to our ability to influence, and the most common, cause us to be silenced by others or to silence ourselves. The most recognizable of these rituals are playing devil's advocate and interrupting others.

Devil's Advocate

Most of us have experienced what it feels like when someone plays devil's advocate. Despite whatever intellectual understanding of gender communication theory we may have, such tactics can still press our emotional buttons in the real world. As a personal example, I worked in the product development group creating and delivering leadership workshops in a midsize consulting firm. My responsibility was to generate innovative learning experiences based on current and emerging research in the field of leadership and communications. Most days I loved my job and my team, except when we would have design sessions with an outside contractor whom I will call Rob. He was a perfectly nice person, and certainly very intelligent and verbal, but when we got to brainstorming ideas, he would shoot down every suggestion that hit the table. It didn't take long for me to shut down. I began to dread his visits and those meetings, and I also began to personalize these interactions. I felt attacked by him and decided that he was arrogant and pompous. I even considered finding a new job.

It wasn't until I began my research on gender communication that I realized I was experiencing a conversational ritual that Rob was using, one in which I was not well versed: playing devil's advocate. When I discovered that this was a very common source of gender conflict in organizations, I shared Tannen's video *Talking 9 to 5* with Rob. He was stunned, and said, "I never realized that you could have taken it personally. I was brought up to believe that my whole purpose in life was to help people see the holes in their arguments. I never saw any harm in it." Then it was time for me to be stunned. "Brought up to help people what . . . ?!?" I thought with shock. Obviously, the role of devil's advocate is a critical one in organizations in helping ensure that decisions aren't made blindly. But great ideas, great people, and team harmony can be lost as a result.

Rob and I learned a great deal about each other in that one conversation. Yet it took my caring enough about the relationship (and my career) to bring the issue to his attention. It was not an easy conversation, because I had come close to deciding that he might as well have been the Devil himself. It took every ounce of self-esteem, an open mind (that was pretty closed at that point), and some vulnerability and honesty on my part to tell him that his actions were affecting me and my behavior. The experience also forced me to look at my own actions. I chose to silence myself when he began his questioning. That was my first mistake. In silencing myself I lost the ability to influence.

Think of a person on your team or in your organization who plays devil's advocate with you or others. What impact is that person having? What reactions does the behavior bring to the surface? What results come out of those interactions? I would suggest that the quest for better products often leads instead to frustrated employees. Consider, instead, thinking about this ritual as an opportunity to discuss openly how you and your team interact in meetings. What's working? What's not working? I'll bet that you will find a range of reactions to this conversational ritual. But if even one person is silencing himself or herself because of these power issues, isn't it worth having the conversation?

Another option for teams that are stuck in the conversational inferno with the Devil is to play a different "game": angel's advocate. Deborah Myerson proposes this in her book *Tempered Radicals*.[11] When a person offers up an idea, share first what you like about the idea, what intrigues you, and what you think has potential. See what reaction and energy you get from that mode of thinking. It is easier to go back and look at potential loopholes once you've discussed what works.

Interruptions

Interruptions are another frustrating conversational ritual. In terms of gender communication, research indicates that men interrupt twice as much as women,[12] a significant tally when played out in meetings or the boardroom. Our workdays comprise a series of inter-actions in which we share ideas and information, make decisions, and strategize for the future. These interactions are opportunities to have your voice heard, to gain recognition, and to build credibility and influence. In some corporations, especially the highly entrepreneur-ial and competitive ones, fighting for airtime becomes a part of the culture. Both male and female managers need to be aware of how the conversational ritual of interruption plays out on their teams and what the effect may be on some people (male or female) who are self-silencing. For leaders, examining group norms around interruptions is an effective place to start making changes by providing the more silent members of your team some much-needed airtime.

When it comes to interpersonal communication, most of us have been significantly influenced by our families and cultures. You can learn a lot about your team if you simply ask, "How were inter-ruptions addressed in your family? In your culture? What was ac-ceptable or not?" I was not surprised to learn that my own boss, who interrupted a lot and loved to play devil's advocate with Rob, grew up with eleven siblings. Fighting for airtime became a natural defense mechanism and a communication strategy that proved use-ful in his career.

Other Rituals of Influence

Another aspect of gender communication that affects our ability to influence is the level of directness we use. Women and men often use varying levels of indirect and direct communication. This de-pends, usually, on their cultural or geographical background and their comfort level with the people with whom they are interacting. Research suggests, however, that women tend to be more indirect when they want someone to do something for them, and men may be more indirect if they are in a lower status position.[13]

The biggest benefit to using an indirect style is that it helps build rapport. We influence because we have engaged others through a relationship, in the moment, as opposed to being demanding. One of the most significant drawbacks to using an indirect style is that your request may be viewed as optional, which means you could be denied or misinterpreted.

The following scenario illustrates. First, the indirect approach:

> *Kate:* Tom is really swamped this week. What do you think about helping him out?
> *Gustavo:* OK.
> *Kate:* Great. I know he'd really appreciate it.

Now for the direct approach:

> *Peter:* Tom is really swamped this week. I want you to help him until he gets his project done. Block out all day tomorrow.
> *Gustavo:* OK.
> *Peter:* Great. Thanks.

In the first dialogue, Kate assumes that Gustavo will help Tom as needed—and as requested. Yet there is a good chance that Gustavo doesn't see it that way. In the example of the direct approach, there is no wiggle room or possibility of misinterpreting the request, yet the approach may seem forceful. The direct style is certainly an advantage in terms of efficiency when decisions are time limited and others' input is not as critical.

The easiest way to check for level of directness is to start proofreading your emails and voice mails. Is the message concrete? Is there potential for misunderstanding? Imagine that you are the receiver of the message. How might someone interpret your request differently from what you intended? Where can you edit to ensure crystal-clear communication? Keep in mind that when either gender uses a conversational approach that is not perceived to "fit" with their gender role, recipients "feel" a mismatch or incongruence. For example, a woman who is extremely direct and assertive can be viewed as "bossy," and a man who is indirect and not aggressive can be seen as a "wimp." Women try not to be too direct because they fear they will be seen as aggressive—something that is viewed as exceptionally negative in females.[14] Women often cite this as one of the most common double binds, also known as a Catch-22. Rosabeth Moss Kanter refers to them as "self-defeating traps."[15] According to feminist scholar Kathleen Hall Jamieson, "a double bind is a rhetorical construct that posits two and only two alternatives, one or both penalizing the person being offered them."[16] Double binds can strongly affect our ability to influence.

Along with indirect and direct language, women often use other common conversational rituals that can diminish their influence or credibility. These are small but potentially damaging if overused.

Disclaimers are conversational rituals commonly used at the beginning of sentences, preceding the speaker's own thoughts. These sentences are used to downplay status and accomplishments while simultaneously attempting to soften the blow of criticism and minimize the potential for conflict. Examples include "I'm not sure about this; however . . ."; "I don't know if this will work, but . . ."; "Maybe it's me, but . . ."

Fillers are short utterances and words that we unconsciously add to sentences but that have no real meaning. Everyone uses them, yet women have been cited for using fillers more often than men. Fillers can include the following: "Um," "You know," "Well," "Like," and "Uh."

Hedges are words that diminish the strength of a sentence and make the speaker sound unsure: "kind of," "sort of," "something like," and "maybe."

Question tags are short questions at the end of sentences that are used to confirm understanding or connect with another person's thoughts or feelings. Question tags help create balance by linguistically involving the other person in the conversation. An overuse of question tags can lead to a misperception that the speaker lacks confidence, knowledge, and individual opinions. Examples include "That report was really well written, wasn't it?" "I believe it's the best way to do it. OK?" "Our presentation seemed to hit the mark, didn't it?"

Neither the traditional male conversational rituals nor the traditional female conversational rituals are better. Each approach has its advantages and disadvantages—especially in corporate environments. What is important is to learn each other's rituals and be aware that when we use a style with someone who doesn't share that style, we put ourselves at risk of creating misunderstandings. We also need to maintain our focus on strategic choice. Your potential for influencing someone increases when you know, and can match, the approaches to which that person is most receptive. With all of these conversational rituals, two keys to improving your communication and influence effectiveness are to show flexibility in your own use and to be flexible and respectful in your perceptions and interpretations of others' approaches.

Actions of Influencers

What do effective influencers do? Some say that influencing is less about what you do and more about who you are—or at least who you are believed to be. Annette Simmons, author of *The Story Factor*, calls this a "believability index" or test with which we evaluate a person in terms of how much we believe them.[17] This brings us squarely to the element of trust. Although being an influencer has a great deal to do with who you are, I believe that what you do—your actions and behaviors—will affect how successful you are at influencing others.

Good Influencers Build Trust

Bob, an entrepreneur and engineer by trade, is introduced to an extremely intelligent scholar who is fundraising for women's rights. Bob has never donated to women's causes before but decides to invest both time and money to promote this scholar and her foundation. When asked why he chose this cause over many others, he stated, "Because I trusted her." Building trust is the most critical step toward building influence.

Think of someone with whom you need to build trust. It could be a person who is new to your team whom you don't know very well or someone with whom you have strained relations. For most people, the latter is the most challenging (and most important) person with whom to build trust, because we have a tendency to turn our backs on people once trust has been broken. Yet in organizations it is critical to build and rebuild trust—we cannot get our work done without it. If you think about it, you have no reason to trust your colleagues—initially they are complete strangers. Over time, our colleagues prove themselves to us and we to them. Meeting deadlines, surpassing expectations, upholding commitments, and communicating honestly and openly all help build trust. What step could you make toward building trust tomorrow? Or better yet, today?

Good Influencers Are Authentic

Being authentic begins with a deep understanding of yourself. To influence with the highest level of integrity and impact, don't check your true self at the door of your office building. Bring it with you to work. Let people know who you are. The more open and authentic you are with them, the more they will want to be themselves with you. For those of you who are reading and rolling your eyes saying, "Yeah, yeah, I could never be myself at work," I challenge you to ask yourself why. What is missing from your organization's culture or team, or from the job itself, that keeps you from being able to share who you are with your colleagues? What is the price you are paying—emotional, physical, or psychological—by not being authentic? Why are you holding yourself back? And what is the worst thing that could happen if you showed them just a little bit of yourself?

Good Influencers Have Integrity

Leaders know they have power because it comes with their position of responsibility and authority. There are some who thrive on the power and abuse it, as we have seen time and again in corporate corruption scandals of late. There are other leaders who recognize that with power comes a responsibility to use it with integrity. There are many leaders who use fear and threats to get results. But at what cost? Think back to the times when you felt that someone above you was using coercive power to get you to do something. How did you feel about that person? The work itself? Yourself? It probably got you moving into action but not without resistance, resentment, and possibly even outright hostility. Using coercive power will gain you compliance—at best, but never the level of commitment you really need from employees.

Good Influencers Show
Both Confidence and Compassion

Melissa, a first-time manager responsible for a team of twenty-five, shared with me that she was concerned that her employees would view her as "too nice." This fear was coming from a strong, assertive, and incredibly intelligent woman who is certainly very nice but by no means a pushover. I reminded her of how she is with her friends and family—she supports them but challenges them when she feels it is necessary. Her natural tendencies should come forth at work. Employees respect a manager who can be both confident and empathic. Leaders from the old command-and-control world of management may view empathy, understanding, and compassion as showing vulnerability, also known as "poor management skills." In reality, the more human and balanced you are in being confident and compassionate, the more successful you will be—because employees want to be treated as human beings, not as human "doers." Certainly this does not mean that you need to roll over every time an employee makes a request or takes advantage of your kindness, but it does mean being aware of the balance in your everyday interactions.

Good Influencers Speak Up for What They Believe

You cannot influence change if you don't speak up. It's as simple as that. How would Sherron Watkins have changed the way we view corporate corruption if she had not come forth and shared the truth about what was happening behind closed doors at Enron? Change happens through thoughts and ideas—and ideas become reality through language. Certainly, when you have to be the one to blow the whistle, the stakes are enormous, and there are consequences. Yet when turning a blind eye becomes a greater risk to one's personal well-being than speaking up, then the solution becomes a lot clearer. Further, the notion of speaking up does not have to be hugely risky. Debra Myerson refers to the concept of "small wins," lending to the idea that even small changes in how and what we communicate can make a difference.[18]

Good Influencers Listen to Others

The adage "Seek first to understand and then be understood," although overused, is still valid. Active listening skills are among the most critical to leaders today. Engaging those skills is a challenge because we are inundated with information and pressure. Melissa, the new manager, told me that she now gets over 350 emails a day in her new role. How is she expected to manage people (which means listening to a lot of people every day) and do her own individual work when she is barraged with this amount of correspondence? The easiest way to think about it is that an email can wait a few minutes longer than the employee standing in your doorstep who needs to speak with you. Telling her "I have five minutes; is that enough for this conversation?" is better than saying "I only have five minutes." Give her the option to reschedule to a time when you will be able to give her your full attention. John

Kotter, from the Harvard Business School, shared that in studying successful managers and leaders, one in particular stood out because he carried a notepad around with him everywhere and took notes of conversations he had in passing. His note taking showed he was actively listening, showed respect for the other person's ideas or issues, and helped him be able to organize his task list throughout the day.[19]

Good Influencers Allow Themselves to Be Influenced by Others

Think back to your worst boss. How much did he or she listen to and implement your ideas? Now think back to your best boss and ask yourself the same question. Chances are that there is a wide difference between the two. Research on married couples by Dr. John Gottman at the University of Washington shows that the single biggest thing a husband can do to end a marriage is consistently reject his wife's attempts to influence.[20] I believe the same holds true between a boss and employee. We all need to know that our opinions and ideas are valid and worth listening to. Many managers mistakenly believe that their role is to come up with and implement new ideas, yet there are endless opportunities for seeking other people's opinions and ideas. Think back to an idea that an employee recently proposed. What aspect of that can you implement and give your employee credit for? When you do it, watch for his or her reaction and increase in motivation. *That* is influence in action.

Good Influencers Know Their Facts

In business, no knowledge means no influence. It's as simple as that. Pat, a CFO in an investment firm, presents financial reports on a weekly basis. Her numbers were consistently a bit askew. She always explained that it was a simple accounting error or that one invoice hadn't been inputted yet. She shrugged it off, and nobody ever called her on it, due to a conflict-averse corporate culture. But when it came time for her annual review, she wanted a promotion (and substantial raise), and the CEO refused to grant it to her. One of his reasons was that her numbers were not accurate. Can you blame him? In this competitive climate, we can't afford to be inaccurate and sloppy with our facts. If you think back to your greatest influencers, how well did they know their facts? Probably very well. If you want to influence a person or a situation, do as much digging as you can bear—and then do some more. People respect that you know what you are talking about, and facts and data will help build your case when it's time to influence change.

Strategies to Build Influence

Now that we've seen what successful influencers actually do, let's look at some strategies women can use to increase their visibility and influence in an organization.

Identify Your Power

Your ability to influence a situation is dependent on your understanding of the source of your power in a particular circumstance. If relational power is the source of your ability to influence a person or outcome, your awareness of gender communications theory will also be very helpful.

Identify Your Skills

Also key is having a solid idea of the expertise and skills you bring to the table. Many women (and some men) have trouble articulating their strengths because they have been socialized to downplay their accomplishments and even to "forget" their expertise. Women can start by compiling a list of the qualities and skills that make them unique, and bearing these in mind especially during periods of difficulty or stress and self-doubt.

Build Self-Confidence

Building your self-confidence starts by valuing the knowledge and expertise that you have. Identify the unique qualities and skills you have that you most value and that are valued organizationally. Then determine which of those qualities and skills need to be made more public.

Repeat Your Personal PR Message

It is imperative that you communicate your contributions and strengths to others. This can be especially challenging for women who have been taught not to talk about their achievements. Yet this strategy is critical for women who want to achieve and maintain positions of leadership, especially in male-dominated organizations.

Find High-Profile Projects

It is not enough to be competent and able to talk about how competent you are. If you want to be given more responsibility, you need to seek it out. Build your network, internally and externally, in order to uncover those sought-after projects. And then ask, when necessary, to be assigned to a key role. As Harriet Rubin suggests in her book *The Princessa: Machiavelli for Women*, "Ask for everything."[21] (I like to put the emphasis on *everything*—not on the asking part!)

Get a Mentor; Be a Mentor

Leaders often cite having a mentor as critical to their success. Women are natural mentors. (In fact, Mentor was the name taken by the Greek goddess Athena while disguised as a man!) Women can benefit greatly from finding mentors both within and outside their organizations. Furthermore, being a mentor and sharing your wisdom and expertise with others are beneficial for you and the organization.[22]

What Can Men Do?

There are also strategies that men can take to give women opportunities to influence more.

Protect Your Investments and Strategic Assets

As research shows, companies with the highest number of women in senior management positions are more profitable than their competitors with much lower numbers of women represented in top management—by approximately 35 percent.[23] Why leave money on the table and continue to pay the high costs of turnover when you don't have to? Male managers can provide leadership development opportunities for their female employees, which will help put more women in the running for positions with greater responsibility and influence.

Stay Open-Minded and Curious

Listening to diverse viewpoints can be draining, challenging, and sometimes threatening, because doing so forces us to reflect on who we are—especially as we relate to other people. Because men tend to have more difficulty listening than women do, one simple but effective goal to aim for is the 70-20-10 rule: seek to listen 70 percent of the time, inquire 20 percent, and summarize 10 percent.

Check Your Assumptions About Women's Aspirations, Experience, and Skills

Research suggests that stereotypes about gender may be the main reason why women do not get promoted into leadership positions.[24] As hard as it is to do, check yourself the next time you think, "She doesn't want to travel overseas," or "She probably isn't up to the task," or "She has what it takes, but she isn't a strategic thinker." Get the facts to back up those assumptions—by checking with her about her preferences and interests and by talking with a range of reliable colleagues about her skills and experience.

Back to the Basics: Be Real and Be Present

Influence does not merely require authenticity: it demands it. Finding your authentic voice takes courage, vulnerability, and personal power. Influencing with integrity and impact requires you to understand what your ethical boundaries are and how to use your voice in ways that people respect and respond to, in order to build trusting, genuine relationships.

We all want to know how to be heard more, to be taken seriously, to be known for the unique people we are. Yet there is no silver bullet for how to influence others or to be seen as influential. Influence happens over time. It happens when there is a significant amount of trust present. It happens when you least expect it—because all you were doing was being yourself. It happens when you don't even know it. We never can really know how far-reaching our influence is. All we can be sure of is that if you don't use your voice, you will not be heard, and therefore you cannot influence.

Helen E. Fisher, Ph.D., has written extensively on gender differences in the brain and behavior; the evolution of human sexuality; and the future of men, women, business, sex, and family life in the twenty-first century. The *New York Times Book Review* selected her book, *The First Sex: The Natural Talents of Women and How They Are Changing the World*, as a Notable Book of 1999. She currently serves as research professor at the Center for Human Evolutionary Studies in the Department of Anthropology at Rutgers University. Helen has also served as an anthropological commentator, consultant and lecturer for businesses and the media, including NBC's *Today Show*, the BBC, the Canadian Broadcasting Corporation, *Reader's Digest*, Time-Life Books, the Smithsonian Institution, Bank of America, Salomon Smith Barney, and *Fortune*.

In this chapter, Helen explores how women's "web thinking," intuition, mental flexibility, long-term planning, creativity, imagination and verbal and social skills—as well as their different views of power—create undeniable win-win strategies in business.

PHOTO CREDIT: Helen E. Fisher by Richard J. Berenson

8

THE NATURAL LEADERSHIP TALENTS OF WOMEN

Helen E. Fisher

"If ever the world sees a time when women shall come together purely and simply for the benefit and good of mankind, it will be a power such as the world has never known." Nineteenth-century poet Matthew Arnold believed that women can change the world. He was prophetic. At this critical time in history, many are seeking alternatives to the traditional command-and-control models of leadership. This chapter describes some of the biological underpinnings of women's natural leadership talents. Myriad diverse factors contribute to leadership performance in both women and men, including an individual's personality traits, thinking and feeling styles, values, motivations, childhood experiences, and cultural milieu. Nevertheless, a great deal of scientific evidence has now demonstrated that in some respects the sexes are, *on average,* not alike.

No wonder. For millions of years, men and women did different jobs, tasks that required different skills. As natural selection weeded out less able workers, time carved differences in the male and female brain. No two human beings are alike. Countless cultural forces influence how men and women think and act. And each one of us is an elaborate mix of both male and female traits. Yet, *on average,* each sex has its own range of abilities; each is a living archive of its distinctive past.

In my research, I have identified some talents that women express more regularly than men,[1] aptitudes that stem, in part, from women's brain architecture and hormones, skills that leadership theorists now espouse as essential to leadership effectiveness. These talents are not exclusive to women, of course, yet women display them more regularly than men.

Web Thinking: Women's Contextual View

One remarkable difference is the way that men and women tend to think. Psychologists report that when women cogitate, they gather details somewhat differently than men. Women integrate more details faster and arrange these bits of data into more complex patterns. As they make decisions, women tend to weigh more variables, consider more options, and see a wider array of possible solutions to a problem. Women tend to generalize, to synthesize, to take a broader, more holistic, more contextual perspective of any issue. They tend to think in webs of factors, not straight lines. So I coined a term for this broad, contextual, feminine way of reasoning: *web thinking*.

Men are more likely to focus their attention on one thing at a time. They tend to compartmentalize relevant material, discard what they regard as extraneous data, and analyze information in a more linear, causal path. I call this male pattern of cogitation *step thinking*.

We are beginning to know how these capacities for web thinking and step thinking are created. The female brain has more nerve cables connecting the two brain hemispheres; the male brain is more compartmentalized so sections operate more independently. Moreover, testosterone tends to focus one's attention. Women's lower levels of this hormone may contribute to their broader, more contextual view. Scientists even know the locations of some of the brain regions for these thinking processes. And some of the genes that construct these regions vary between the sexes. One gene, for example, is active in 50 percent of women and silenced in all men.

Women's proclivity for web thinking probably evolved millions of years ago when ancestral females needed to do many things at once to rear their young, whereas men's step thinking probably emerged as ancestral hunters focused on the pursuit of game. Both web thinking and step thinking are still valuable, but in the contemporary business community, buzzwords include "depth of vision," "breadth of vision," and "systems thinking." In this highly complex marketplace, a contextual view is a distinct asset. Women are built to employ this perspective. In fact, in one study of Fortune 500 companies, senior executives were asked to describe women's most outstanding business contribution. Their consensus: women's more varied, less conventional point of view.

Women's web thinking provides them with other natural leadership qualities. According to social scientists and business analysts, women are better able to tolerate ambiguity—a trait that most likely stems from their ability to hold several things simultaneously in mind. And if I had to sum up the modern business environment in one word, I would call it ambiguous. Women are well endowed for this indefinite business climate.

Women's web thinking also enables them to exercise more intuition—and intuition plays a productive, if often unrecognized, role in managerial decision making. This mental capacity has been explained by psychologist Herbert Simon. He maintains that as people learn how to analyze the stock market, run a business, or follow a political issue, they begin to recognize the patterns involved and mentally organize these data into blocks of knowledge—a process Simon calls chunking. With time, more and more related patterns are chunked, and clusters of knowledge are stored in long-term memory. Then when a single detail of a complex situation appears, the experienced person can instantly recognize the larger design and predict outcomes that another must deduce with plodding sequential thought. Sherlock Holmes remarked of this, "From long habit, the train of thought ran so swiftly through my mind that I arrived at the conclusion without being consciously aware of the intermediate steps." Women, on average, excel at this form of thought.

Also related to web thinking is long-term planning—the ability to assess multiple, complex scenarios and plot a long-term course. Two scholars have studied gender differences in long-term planning and found a significant variation.[2] Some business analysts believe that women are apt to think long term more regularly as well, whereas men are more likely to focus on the here and now. Women definitely use long-term strategies more regularly in their financial affairs. In fact, in a study of 6,000 investors, three-quarters of the women had no short-term investment goals; moreover, the trading records of 35,000 clients of a large brokerage firm showed that men traded 45 percent more often than women.

There is, most likely, a biological component to women's long-term approach. When scientists inject men with testosterone, their thinking becomes more focused on the present. So it is possible that women's hormonal make-up contributes to their tendency to plan long term. Women may have evolved the propensity to think long term to plan for their children's distant future. Today, however, this faculty predisposes women to see business issues from a longer perspective—an essential element of leadership.

Mental Flexibility

Women's brain architecture for web thinking has endowed them with another natural talent—mental flexibility. Mental flexibility is an essential trait of leadership in our dynamic global economy.

In a recent study of nine hundred managers at top U.S. corporations, researchers reported that "women's effectiveness as managers, leaders and teammates outstrips the abilities of their male counterparts in 28 out of 31 managerial skill areas."[3] Among these skills was "generating new ideas." I suspect that the ability to generate new ideas is the product of women's mental flexibility, as well as yet another aspect of women's web thinking: imagination. What is imagination but the capacity to reach into the depths of one's stored knowledge, assemble chunks of data in new ways, examine these myriad combinations, and "suppose" how various arrangements might play out? All are aspects of web thinking—women's forte. John F. Kennedy once said, "We need men who can dream of things that never were." We need the female mind as well.

Verbal Articulation: Words Are Women's Tools

Women have other skills that enable them to lead. An exceptional female talent is the ability to find the right word rapidly—basic articulation. As Mark Twain said, "The difference between the right word and the almost right word is the difference between lightening and the lightning bug."

Women's verbal skills begin to emerge in early childhood. Infant girls babble more than infant boys. They speak sooner, with longer utterances and more complex grammatical constructions. By age twelve, girls excel at grammar and spelling and at understanding and remembering what they read. Moreover, American women share this verbal fluency with women in Japan, Nepal, England, and every other country where these skills have been tested—most likely because women's verbal aptitudes are associated with gender differences in the brain, as well as the female hormone, estrogen. In fact, a woman's facility with words increases during the middle of the monthly menstrual cycle when estrogen levels peak.

Women are born to talk—a feminine acuity that probably evolved to enable ancestral women to comfort, cajole, and educate their little ones, chastise, even ostracize group members who failed to meet their responsibilities, reward those who did and maintain harmony in the community. Words were women's tools. Words still sway minds and hearts. And as contemporary women leaders have opportunities to express their "voices" in the workplace, their power will increase.

Executive Social Skills

Women have what scientists call "executive social skills." From millennia of rearing prelinguistic babies, women have evolved a keener ability to pick up the nuances of posture and gesture, read complex emotions in faces, and hear slight changes in tone of voice. Women, on average, have a better sense of taste, touch, smell, and hearing. They see better in the dark, have better peripheral vision, and remember more objects in the room or landscape. As novelist Sarah Orne Jewett remarked, "Tact is, after all, a kind of mind reading." With these skills, women are built to read minds. In fact, several of these "people skills" are associated with the female hormone, estrogen. So it's not surprising that women already hold over 60 percent of jobs in the booming service sector of the world economy— another way they lead.

Networking, Collaboration, and Empathy

Along with women's executive social skills are their remarkable facilities for networking, collaboration, empathy, inclusion, and sharing power. Men tend to cast themselves within hierarchies and view power as rank and status; women, on the other hand, form cliques and tend to regard power as an egalitarian network of supportive connections. These traits have also been linked with hormones. When birds and mammals are injected with the predominantly male hormone, testosterone, they begin to fight for rank; infusions of estrogen tend to produce nurturing and connecting behaviors instead. These feminine dispositions to work in egalitarian teams, network, and support others were unquestionably vital to ancestral women who needed to support one another and their children. Today these traits are still more impressive contributions to the contemporary business environment.

The Coming Collaborative Society

Web thinking, mental flexibility, the ability to embrace ambiguity, intuition, imagination, a penchant for long-term planning, verbal acuity, executive social skills, the capacity to collaborate, and empathy are all essential leadership traits in the new global economy. But this is not to suggest that women will run the world. Many men display these traits to a considerable degree. Moreover, men have a host of other skills that make them natural leaders as well. Men are, *on average*, superior at all sorts of spacial and engineering skills, gifts associated with testosterone. Using these capabilities, men have long been building our "high-tech" society, vastly improving human health and welfare.

Men and women are like two feet—they need each other to get ahead. Nevertheless, the world is changing in ways that can profit from women's skills *as well as those of men*. Today, the business services and health care industries, the media, the law, not-for-profit organizations, and service professions are all burgeoning. All can benefit from women's natural talents.

Indeed, the business world has begun to feel the impact of women's leadership skills. As educated women become influential in offices of all kinds around the world, they are spreading their taste for cooperation, flexibility, and egalitarian team playing, as well as providing a broader perspective and new ideas. On television, women have supplied more sensitive depictions of women, more ethnic and age diversity, more visual and performance arts, more programming for children, and a broader, more contextual perspective on many issues. Women's faculty for language and appetite for complexity are also enriching what we read in newspapers, magazines, and books.

With their "people skills" and imagination, women have begun to provide all sorts of professional services that bring comfort and novelty to our work and leisure hours. Women bring compassion, patience, team playing, and a broader perspective to hands-on healing. They offer creativity in the classroom. And because women tend to have different views on child abuse, sexual harassment, abortion, and criminality in general, women in the law are enlarging our view of justice.

With their influential role in not-for-profit organizations, women are improving the welfare of women, children, minorities, the elderly, and the disabled and disadvantaged, as well as the environment. They are gradually making a difference in government. And with their votes, women are more prominently placing the issues of education, health, child care, poverty, and the environment on the national and international agenda.

Women are also changing family life. Marriage is undergoing a reformation. The traditional patriarchal family headed by the male is metamorphosing into new family forms. Most important, more couples are forming what sociologists call "companionate marriages" or "peer marriages," marriages between economic and social equals.

Peer marriages are not new. Throughout deep history, women commuted to work to gather fruits and vegetables, contributing 60 to 80 percent of the evening meal. In hunting-gathering societies, the double-income family was the rule. Men and women were economic, social, and sexual equals. When our forebears settled down to farm, women lost much of their economic and social power. But today we are returning to our original ancestral lifestyle. The twenty-first century may be the first in the modern era to see the sexes live as their forebears lived a million years ago: as equals. We are inching toward a collaborative society, a global culture in which the merits of both men and women are becoming understood, valued, and employed.

Albert Einstein once said, "The significant problems we face today cannot be solved by the same level of thinking that created them." Women bring a different way of thinking; a cooperative spirit; a gift for "reading" people; patience; empathy; networking abilities; negotiating skills; a drive to nurture children, kin, business connections, and the local and world community; an interest in ethnic diversity and education; a keen imagination; a win-win attitude; mental flexibility; an ability to embrace ambiguity; and the predisposition to examine complex social, environmental, and political issues with a broad, contextual, long-term view. As the female mind becomes unleashed on our modern world, societies will benefit—even in lands where it is currently shackled.

Gail Evans has made it her life's work to help women leaders understand what they need to know about the nature of hierarchy and power to flourish professionally. Much of that bottom-line insight and advice has found its way into a series of acclaimed books, including the *New York Times* bestsellers *Play Like a Man, Win Like a Woman* and *She Wins, You Win*. A former White House aide, Gail was also CNN's first female executive vice president. While at CNN, she was responsible for creating some of the network's most successful shows, including *TalkBack Live*.

In this chapter, Gail describes how women leaders can get ahead in the workplace by learning the unwritten rules of business that men "wrote" and play by—and, further, by creating one's own rules to change the nature of the game. In so doing, she is an inspiring voice—and a compelling advocate for the principle that all of us must look out for one another.

PHOTO CREDIT: Gail Evans by CNN

9

ARE WE LOOKING AFTER EACH OTHER?

Women Leaders Winning the Game

Gail Evans

Golf is a game that many women associate with men who are in power. Metaphorically, it's about relationships. But a lot of women find the nature of the game to be somewhat mysterious. A good example came up when I made a speech at the National Association of Women School Superintendents. One of the women listening to what I had to say about leadership shared her belief that she could be more successful by learning how to play golf. I asked whether it was working for her. She said that she wasn't sure yet. She'd only had three-and-a-half years of lessons and still wasn't perfect, so she hadn't played with anyone.

For many women, business is like golf. We work on our individual skills to compete in a game that is really about relationships. Striving for perfection does not get us any closer to success. In fact, it takes us out of the real game altogether. So how do we succeed in business? We need to figure out the rules and understand the strategy. The rules of business, as we all know, were written by the guys. They weren't written to leave us out intentionally; in truth, few women were playing the game back then. Instead, the rules were established according to the laws of how little boys play. Just as little boys play very differently than little girls, so big boys and girls play differently, too. It really is that simple.

Let me give you a few examples to illustrate my point. I go to my grandchildren's birthday parties. Even though my granddaughter's party takes place in a gym, it's all about magic wands and pink and purple tiaras. At my grandson's party, on the other hand, the presents are all about team games and strategy. I don't think we have to take away the tiaras and magic wands from our daughters, but we do have to make sure that we're teaching them strategy and how to play on a team. One woman told me that she has a son who is eight and a daughter who is five. When her son was first learning how to play games, his interests were very clear: all he wanted to do was win, win, win. Because she didn't like that very much, she tried to teach him how to be a good winner. Now that her daughter is playing games, she realizes that she's doing something different: she's teaching her how to be a good loser. The truth is, it's very difficult for us not to infuse such stereotypes into gender. We need to watch ourselves all the time.

Our words reflect those constructs very clearly. Some women say that they don't like to negotiate raises. In their view, negotiation always comes down to the feeling of "deserve," which brings up associations of "better or worse than." In my experience, *deserve* is not a very empowering word. If you want a raise, you want a raise. Walking into your boss's office and saying you deserve a raise is a good way to put your boss in a bad mood. He'll quickly think of all kinds of reasons why you don't.

Another word that women commonly use is *hope*. I think it's a wonderful word when associated with our spiritual concerns but a terrible word for use in our business life. Try to eliminate "hope" from your vocabulary. See for yourself how many times a day you "hope" something will happen, as if that magically calls something into being. Substitute another word, like "will," instead. You'll be fascinated to discover that when you get rid of hope, you are forced into action. And if you take action, you are one step closer to achieving your goal. In the end, a simple change in vocabulary leaves you more empowered.

Women in business also know that it's difficult to be heard. Although there are a lot of concrete reasons why this is a real problem, I suggest that we also contribute willingly to that problem. At a presentation, women fill the room from the center to the back, men from the center to the front. We associate being at the front with being in charge. Generally, the only women who sit at the front of the room are the organizers, the people who know they belong there.

When the meeting is convened, don't we sit at chairs that put us safely out of the center of attention? Don't we act as though the smartest thing to do is to keep a low profile and not speak up? I used to fume when my best ideas were taken by someone not as smart as I am who chose to speak up. When I got tired of that happening, I learned to prepare for meetings with a female colleague by practicing our one-liners together. It sounds silly or trite, but being able to say something empowering that just rolled off our tongues made it easier for us to be heard. This is not a minor problem. Every woman knows what it's like when she says something in a meeting and the men in the room mutter "interesting" and move on to more discussion. Then, ten or twenty minutes later one of the men repeats the point and gets the credit. When the meeting is over, he walks out talking to the boss about your idea, and you walk out of the room with one of the other women talking about how he stole your idea. I would like to suggest that he did not steal your idea—you gave it away. It was terrible what he did. But he's now closer to that promotion, and you're the aggrieved victim, yet again.

When we do get that promotion, do we understand the nuances of how power is perceived by others? At upper levels, when two or three people are promoted at the same time, there are usually one or two good offices available and another that is clearly less prestigious. Do you push for the room with the best view? I'm not suggesting that you get into a fight about it, but the larger windows matter. It's part of the perception of power. To establish yourself in that regard you need to look out for yourself from the beginning.

Women have a tendency to accept responsibility without authority. We're great at problem solving. At the middle management ranks, we're quick to accept that role and the habit follows us into the executive levels. But when there's a problem to be solved, you need the authority to solve it. Otherwise you are the one who will be burned if it doesn't work out right.

Many of the "problems" that I've mentioned thus far can be changed at the individual level. But there is another, more serious problem I want to bring up that belongs to women collectively. I call this problem the "elephant in the room": Are we taking care of each other? Are we playing on the same team? Writing about these ideas and speaking to women all over the country, I have become convinced that we aren't all playing on the same team. In fact, we view the workplace through the lens of gender scarcity. We are pitted against each other, rather than supportive of each other. We don't understand the connection between our success and our failure. The world does not forget that a leader is a woman when she is promoted or demoted. For every woman who succeeds, the rest of us succeed with them. For every woman who fails, the rest of us fail as well.

One of the things that men understand that I think women would do well to learn is how to play on a team. Watching school sports, I have observed over time that on boys' teams, the best player believes that the team is only as good as its weakest player. On good teams, for example, you will often see the star player working with the one who strikes out all the time. Women are more prone to get rid of the weakest player.

It's very interesting to think about that in the context of life and business. For instance, I have been told by younger women that they feel older women give them a hard time. Those older women made tough sacrifices. Some of them chose not to have children because they couldn't afford to take the time from a career. In turn, their attitude seems to be that it is necessary to toughen up the younger generation. From the perspective of that younger generation, this message is very confusing. They've been told all their lives that they can be the best and have it all—then suddenly they are told that there are some dreams they must let go. My question to women in that regard is simple: Are we taking care of each other? Are we making it fashionable to be good to each other?

One way we take care of each other is by mentoring. I know of too many women who are first in their field. We need to show the younger generation the way so that it is not as hard for them as it has been for us. Another critical skill is networking. We network brilliantly about our personal lives. We feel no hesitation to approach someone and ask her anything if it has to do with her personal life. But when it comes to networking for business advantage, we have a whole different set of ethical rules or boundaries, which leads to hesitation. Women don't hire relatives; men don't hesitate. Women feel that it's inappropriate to talk to or do business with another soccer mom because there's a split between their personal and business lives. Men would not give it a second thought. And is that boundary as real as we think? Why is there always someone from the office in the bridal party? Isn't that one of the most intimate and personal moments in your life? We're not good at this thing called networking. It doesn't suit our sensibilities. But it's critical for success when the game is all about relationships.

In addition to mentoring and networking, we have another responsibility as women leaders. Are we considering each other when it comes to hiring? Affirmative action has taken women and minorities very far. But we have further to go, and no diversity plan can take us all the way. When a woman leader does not make the extra effort to find another woman to be a candidate on the short list, then she is not keeping up her end. This applies not just in your business life but in your personal life as well. How many of us hire a photographer for the anniversary party who is a woman? How many of us, when we are getting work done on the house, look for contractors who are women? It can be difficult, and the numbers may be scarce, but we have to stop waiting for the system to fix itself. We need to think of each other. We don't need to favor each other; all we need to do is make sure that another woman gets the chance to compete.

Ultimately, are we talking to each other? Getting back to the issue of negotiating a raise, statistics tell us that women make about seventy-six cents on the dollar compared to men. In my experience, a great many women are simply unaware of what a job will pay. Without that information, how can we expect to negotiate the best price? It's not our boss's job to say that we have undersold ourselves. That understanding only becomes possible if we talk to each other.

I knew a fun group of women, from different divisions of a major corporation, who had all made it to a certain level. At one point, they decided that they needed their own retreat. The men had their getaways. They went to sporting events or on hunting or fishing trips. The women decided to go to a spa. Of course, they ended up paying for that themselves. So the next year, one of them joined the corporate retreat committee and had spas included. This brought everyone closer together, and they developed into a tight group.

Of course, the women talked about personal things on those trips, but they also talked about business. Each one of them, they discovered, knew more than anyone else in the company about the area they were in. When they started sharing that information, they went from being isolated experts to big-picture people. They understood how the implications of what they wanted to do in their own groups would impact the company as a whole. When they walked into meetings they were all a lot smarter as a result.

We are all connected, and we all make different choices. But some of those choices support our success and others don't. Hoarding information. Holding other women to higher standards. Resisting being seen with women socially because we don't want to be thought of as separate from the main group. These kinds of choices hurt us. We need to help each other succeed, not help each other fail. If we want to change society and want the corporation to be more family-friendly and want the executive team to understand the work-life balance issues that women face, then we need to be supportive of each other. It's not going to happen until we see our successes as connected.

We've done a lot as individuals to change ourselves and become smarter about playing the game, but the game itself is not won by individual advances. I think it's our game to change, and we need to start playing on the same team. We've seen a lot of "firsts" for women in the last fifty years, but the next level of accomplishment will not come about because of individual achievement. People often ask, "When will we finally see a woman President of the United States?" The answer is simple: when the women of the United States decide they want one.

Susan Brady and Gabriella Salvatore are codirectors in the Corporate Education practice at Vantage Partners, a relationship management training and consulting firm based in Boston, Massachusetts. As codirectors, Susan oversees business development, sales, and client management, while Gabriella leads product development, delivery, and operations. They have formed a partnership—at work as they blend their unique areas of expertise and experience and at home where they have come to support each other and their respective families in the process of integrating working and mothering. Like many young women who are leaders at work, they are continually forced to grapple with the choice of furthering their careers or starting and growing their families. Some of the questions that were catalyzed for them, and for which they went searching for answers, were: Do these options have to represent an either-or-breaking point? Or are there new models for creating wholeness in our lives?

In this chapter, Susan and Gabriella outline the process they implemented to analyze these and other personal questions facing young mothers who are also driven leaders. They identify a set of common concerns, experiences, and motivations—as well as an insightful range of success strategies for any woman leader seeking to lead an integrated life.

PHOTO CREDIT: Susan Brady and Gabriella Salvatore by Allison Evans

10

WITH CHILDREN

Leading an Integrated Life

Susan Brady and Gabriella Salvatore

Like so many others, we were recently faced with the paradox of our desire to lead at work and our deep devotion to and love of our children. We decided to try to resolve this paradox by talking and learning from other working mothers. But our initial expressions about the complexities of managing professional self and mothering self were met with a mere, "It's tricky balancing it all, isn't it?"

Not only did the notion of "balance" seem empty, but the very thought of trying to equalize our work lives and our home and mothering lives seemed unrealistic. We don't lead two lives; we lead one. We don't have two selves; we have one. We can't (as of yet) figure out how to check our professional desires at the door nor our personal desires at the office such that we can experience this thing called "balance." In fact, compartmentalizing our lives into discrete parts only leads us to feelings of guilt or inadequacy. It seems a rare moment when we are doing any one thing well.

So we wondered, "Is this all there is? Is the notion of 'seeking a balanced life' the only language we have for working mothers?" We have come to believe that the discussion deserves a new paradigm. The term *continual integration*, as opposed to *balance*, allows for a more complex conversation. Life is moving so quickly; the demands on our time have only increased since having children, and the notion of a *state of balance* is what seemed so challenging—as if when we arrive at this desired state, we'll be OK, less stressed, even happier.

Why should we continue to perpetuate the notion of balance as the elusive yet ultimate goal? It does not serve us in the way that the concept of continual integration can when faced with trying to do it all. Working mothers are ultimately successful by allowing for and expecting constant checks and balances, frequent check-ins on how it's all going, and a ton of self-forgiveness for not getting it "right" all the time.

Beyond the Balancing Act

Once we were able to move into a new paradigm for thinking and talking about the blend of motherhood and work, we then were able to articulate our deeper problem: despite the fact that we knew many working mothers, we felt alone in our quest to manage it all. We felt confused about why it was as hard as it was, and we had little insight into what was actually driving us not to give up on our work.

In particular, and mainly for those moments that are still really hard (like leaving behind our children on a Monday morning, or having to miss a really important meeting with a client because our kids have a fever and there's no child care back up), we wanted something to go back to that reminded us *why* we were trying to do both—work and mothering. We wanted to know what things we could do (per the advice of other working mothers) to make the journey of integration a bit less painful and a bit more fulfilling. We also wanted to share our findings with other working mothers who were attempting to weave together their mothering and working selves.

We hope that our findings will help women who are expecting a child or thinking about having children and who plan to stay in the working world. We want them to know what may lie ahead. Feeling torn, feeling at times unmotivated to go to work, questioning if the path chosen is indeed the right one—all are normal thoughts and feelings as women integrate work back into their lives after the baby comes.

Working Mothers Speak:
The Whys, the Rewards, and the Challenges

I had the opportunity to close a business deal once, and I was the
only woman at the table. It was a table full of men, and they all said
that they never see their kids. One man said, "I see my kids two
hours a week." If women were running businesses we wouldn't have
that kind of life. It's just not acceptable.

> —Thirty-something mother of an infant,
> executive at an insurance company

Wondering how others integrate, we decided to expand our conversation to include a number of working mothers. We found many who
wanted to talk about why women desire, need, and pursue both
motherhood and work. The challenges, successes, and lessons learned
quickly came to the forefront of the dialogue.

We started on this path of inquiry by inviting four women to
our first focus group. Our purpose was to test our assumptions that
many working mothers are like us—dissatisfied with the idea of
committing fully to either work or home, intent on finding a dual
path that lets them have the proverbial "all."

In this first focus group, we asked the women whom among
famous working mothers interested them. Would they be interested
in hearing how Katie Couric, Madeleine Albright, Annie Lenox,
Madonna, or others manage their working mother integration?
Resoundingly, the working mothers we spoke with told us that they
wanted to know how "everyday working moms" are feeling about
the integration and how they manage to make it all happen.

In addition to the clarity regarding the women from whom we
should be looking to learn, our hypothesis coming out of that focus
group was that working and mothering give a woman a feeling of
efficacy and agency. Seeking to focus on the general themes of motivation, challenge, and success that surfaced in the focus group, we
created a questionnaire to continue testing our assumptions.

We administered that questionnaire to twenty respondents. The women we talked to are much like us: ambitious, driven professionals and committed mothers, opting to work, choosing to mother, and intent on interweaving the two. For the most part, we spoke with college-educated thirty- to forty-year-olds who are in a committed relationship and earn upwards of $50,000 per year.

At the outset, we would like to acknowledge that, when it comes to the subject of working and mothering, there are many women who have chosen the path of staying home full time. In addition, we understand that many families are unable to afford child care, thus requiring one parent to be home full time, and many single mothers are forced to do it all. And then there are others, the ones we spoke to most often—those who have the desire to both work and mother (regardless of income) because they don't feel "complete" if they do only one or the other.

It has been confirming to find that the challenges and rewards we have experienced are not personal to us but run rampant, and resonate throughout a network of working mothers. What follows is their truth, which begins to point to the ups and downs, motivations and setbacks that make continual integration a necessary lens through which to view working and mothering.

Why Both Work and Mother?

We asked the working mothers, "Why do you do both?" Why is neither motherhood alone nor work alone enough? Here's what we learned:

Why Work?

• *Intellectual stimulation*. The dual life makes sense and feels worth it when the work being done away from children is exciting. Examples include completing a creative project at work, engaging in a great conversation, and accomplishing something that really has impact. These are the moments when working mothers report that their "brains are in gear," and this leaves them feeling good about themselves, feeling whole.

- *Complete self-expression, being a "whole" person.* Many of the women we talked to said that they need to be both mother and worker to feel whole, to fully express the width and breadth of who they are—their interests, their intellect, their ability to make a difference in the world. The story of a retired CPA, mother of two, resonated with many: "My career was rewarding to me in ways that motherhood alone could not be. I was a happier person as a working mother and therefore a better mother."

- *A full range of rewards.* One set of rewards here, of course, comes in the form of the money earned in the workplace that provides additional or supplemental family income. On a daily and pragmatic basis, the fruits of working moms' labor show up through their children—the clothes that they wear, the rooms that they keep clean, the character that they exhibit with their friends, their teachers, and fellow family members, and so on.

A quality assurance professional in a pharmaceutical company, mother of an eight-month-old, talks about the pleasure her role as the sole provider in her home gives her. "I feel rewarded when I look into my son's eyes and know that I am providing him with as much as I can and ensuring a successful future for our family." Among the women we interviewed, similar realizations instilled pride in themselves and for the work done at home and at the office.

- *Recognition, a sense of achievement.* Working mothers value the sense of achievement that comes from a job well done. It matters that people notice the contributions they make. Working moms we talked to seem to be hungry for that public recognition of their professionalism. For whatever cost there is to integrating mothering and working, this is a definite benefit.

A business owner and author, mother of two in her thirties, described it this way: "Partly I am motivated to work for the measurable success and feedback. It's pretty rare for my son to say, 'I learned so much today. Thank you.' It's so much more gradual and implicit. At work I get the tangible success: revenue numbers; a happy client."

- *Influence, the ability to effect change and contribute to the larger society.* A chiropractor, just back to work in her own practice, seemed to capture the essence of what this is about: "I have a gift and I've changed people's lives. I felt like I was hiding it, it was dormant [when I wasn't working]. To be able to express that and help people is one of the biggest joys in life."

How Do You Define Success?

> I am a working mother. That's my identity. That's who I am now.
> —Thirty-something corporate executive

We asked working mothers, "When do you feel rewarded by doing both?" What keeps you going? What we learned from them was that they felt most rewarded when it all "works." The good news: there are identifiable occasions when they feel that the struggle of juggling work and motherhood is very much worth it. There's something about the double win and the quest for it that keeps working mothers going and feeling "fed." Some of the working mothers we spoke with reported living for moments like these:

> "When I have success at work and come home to a house not in total chaos."
>
> "When I have a day with a lot of energy and I'm able to do great work at work and come home and spend quality time with the baby."
>
> "When she is happy and greets me with a big hug—it's these days I feel like I have it all."

When mothers feel connected with their children and when they see the direct positive impact that their work has on their children's lives, there is a sense of great reward.

> "Being able to move to a home that the children would love; bring them to places I didn't see until I was an adult; give them a wonderful school to go to."

"A good fun day with my kids makes it all worth it."

"When I am at work and I know no matter what our son has one mom at home and the other at work and both moms are constantly working to ensure our happiness."

The feeling of success on the job is the parallel strand to feeling connected with their children and to knowing that their work is making a good life for them. Here are some of the moments that working moms say bring the greatest satisfaction:

"When I receive reward and recognition from my boss and peers."

"When an accomplishment at work really has impact."

"When I engage in a great conversation with a colleague and can participate in the creation of something new and better."

"When clients thank me for the work I do."

An anesthesiologist, mother of two, shared with us the times when she feels most rewarded: "My kids' teachers and friends' parents ask me for professional advice and my husband tells me he is proud of me." She adds that in this way, her being both a mom and a doctor teaches important values to her children. "My kids talk to friends and other adults and talk about mommy working and know that a woman can do anything. It is rewarding that my kids think that it is normal for their mother and all women to contribute to the world outside of the home."

What Are the Challenges?

I don't think you can have it all, at least not at the same time. That's okay because you're making sacrifices on each side. You're just trying to make the best sacrifices for you.

—Business owner, consultant, author, mother of two

Of course "doing it all" carries a price, as most mothers can attest. We asked working mothers, "What do you find most challenging about being a working mother?" Not surprisingly, many of the challenges they expressed were similar. Here are the top five:

Lack of Time to Get It All Done.   Resoundingly, women told us that their biggest challenge is not having enough time. We all seem to be perpetually flummoxed by the need to get it all done.

> "I am a Type A personality. I always feel like I have to do it all everywhere, and you can't. It's just not possible. For me part of being a working mother is coming to terms with a new definition of perfection."
>
> "When I don't plan ahead, or something unforeseen happens, my stress level goes way up. I simply don't have the time I need to get everything done."

Feeling Guilty.   Being at the office, be it on the third floor of your home or in another town, means that you miss out on the day-to-day. For some working mothers, the nanny or partner or day-care provider spends more time with their children than they do. They worry about not being around enough and how that might impact the growth of their children, as well as the crucial mother-child bond.

> "I am afraid she won't know how much I love her."
>
> "This has been the hardest part in going back to work full time, pacing up and down my days worrying about the impact of my absence on my son and our relationship. Will we still be bonded? Will he be hurt?"

The women we heard from also expressed guilt in feeling they are not doing either job—home or work—well: "I feel like a Jack of all trades, master of none. Spreading myself thinner than I'd like in both camps, and the truth is I can only do so much in a day."

Another source of guilt comes from wanting to work in the first place. If you admit such a desire, do you also have to admit that you are, in fact, not completely fulfilled by motherhood alone? Rightly or wrongly, some women reach such a conclusion—and find it to be problematic for it feels like a disparaging statement about motherhood as opposed to an empowering statement about who they are as mother and leader.

Physical Self-Care.   Many working moms we spoke with said that taking care of their physical well-being is, in the words of one, "next to impossible." Despite the very real and pragmatic challenges involved though, physical self-care remains a critical area for working moms. And the payoff is, of course, enormous.

> "I've turned the New York City Ballet Workout tape on at 6 A.M. after my son's 5 A.M. rising. He usually scrambles under my feet, pulls on my pajama bottoms, grunts for my attention. I usually give up. I only have until 8 A.M. and then I have to go to work, so I tell myself I shouldn't waste a precious second not being totally focused on him. So I let it go, and therefore let myself go."

> "It never ceases to amaze me how restored my perspective is after I work out. I feel rejuvenated, able to manage."

Emotional and Spiritual Self-Care.   Perhaps even harder to manage than physical self-care, but something we believe to be just as important, is scheduling nonwork, nonmothering personal time. Without a doubt, in the balance of things, this gets shortest shrift. Other areas receive attention first because they appear more urgent. It seems like the demands of life create a hierarchy, and although the ordering may vary for different women, it often falls out like this:

Kids first: sleep, feed, cuddle

Work next: projects, voice mail and email, accountability, success

Then relationship: time to talk, time together, sex

After that, home stuff: laundry and taking out the trash

Finally, self . . .

Although it might be last on the list (rightly or wrongly), personal time is just as important. This is the time that allows you to self-center, reflect, and just "be." Such time can be sacrificed only at your peril.

Managing the Integration

All the feedback from our focus group and the data we collected via survey led us to conclude that integration *must* be a continual process. To think that we'll find a perfect, permanent, and dependable mix of things we can do (and not do) isn't realistic. We need to look *continually* at our lives and ask questions: What's working, and what's not working? How can this be easier—less stressful, more manageable, more gratifying? How can we make ourselves more whole? We asked working mothers for suggestions and advice on how we can answer these questions—and learn from one another.

The responses that we received here do not yield any magic formula for how best to manage the often complex and conflicting demands of work life and mothering life. None of the women that we asked professed to have such a formula. Nor did they claim to have all the answers. To the contrary, each expressed feelings of frustration and even confusion as to those moments when the integration gets hard and doesn't work so well.

The working mothers that we spoke with, however, also described those moments when integration of family and work has gelled. From this data, we were able to identify a set of concrete recommendations to make working and mothering less stressful and more satisfying for working mothers. Some of these recommendations require simple, practical action. Others, on the other hand, hinge more on mindset and attitude. Taken together, they offer invaluable guidance on how to achieve success—and even joy—

both at home with children and partners and at work as leaders and contributors. For all of us who are in the thick of integrating our lives, there is indeed hope!

Be Gentle with Yourself!

Worry, judgment, and guilt—these are all real feelings that seem to accompany the choices we make. Most of us have thought at some point, "I am not being a good mother. I am not spending enough time with my child. I haven't made the right choice." So in addition to trying to figure out a way to get it all done, we may beat ourselves up along the way.

Every working mother we heard from tended to think that if she demanded less of herself and ignored the judgments of others, integration would be easier. The suggestions that follow pertain to something over which we all have control: how we chose to think about ourselves and who we chose to listen to along the way. Although we realize that ignoring the naysayer and overcoming self-doubt are difficult, the following advice from working mothers could serve as a wise prescription:

Worry Less About Perfection

- Believe that "good enough" really does exist.
- Be realistic about what you can and can't do.
- Give yourself room to make mistakes.
- Accept that your best is your best and that it is OK.
- Resolve the guilt early about not being 100 percent in either place.

Trust Yourself

- Listen to your own voice: don't waste energy on feeling guilty because others manage their lives differently.
- Ignore the fanatics who try to convince you of what's right and what's wrong when it comes to breastfeeding, staying

home full time, working full time, public school, private school—there will always be an argument for the choice you didn't make, and that's OK!

- Don't let the opinion of others derail you; you don't need anyone's permission or approval.

Remember That You Have Choices

- Question the "trap" you feel yourself in. Even if you feel like you can't choose a different life, *you can.*
- Learn to let go.
- Enjoy the process.
- Don't worry too much about the stuff you need to get done around the house. Your kids will only be young once.

Negotiate Work That Fits Your Life

Although working mothers are still taking on the lion's share of the burden when it comes to finding flexible work arrangements (as opposed to having employers who just offer up options), there is a growing number of employers that are more open to nontraditional working arrangements. Our research is telling: of the twenty mothers surveyed, twelve work Monday through Friday, which means that 40 percent have some kind of alternative arrangement. Many have negotiated a schedule with their employer that meets the needs of the organization but also is responsive to the needs of their home and family life. Here are specific suggestions from the working mothers we heard from.

Negotiate a Role and a Schedule That Accommodate Home and Work

- Be clear about what you do and don't want in a nontraditional work arrangement.

- Before talking with your employer about changing your schedule, think about your employer's interests—and present your understanding of their interests along with your own.

- Be creative with your employer when generating different schedule options. Ask for his or her creative thinking too.

- Be sure that your employer knows that you are committed to the organization.

- Find an employer who has an understanding of you as a working mother.

- Know that you will not be able to work the hours you worked before having the baby and that that is OK.

- Set expectations at work and at home for when you will (and will not) be available.

Be Prepared and Efficient

- Never leave the office without planning to work from home the next day—you never know when you will have to.

- If you commute, use your travel time to work so that you can focus on being a mom when you get home.

Ask for Help or Hire Help When Possible

Many of the working mothers we spoke with found that asking for help (and, when affordable, hiring help) enabled them not only to get it all done but also to enjoy life along the way. The crux of this advice is to identify areas where you think you will need help—shopping, cleaning, a night out—and ask for support from partners, friends, and family. One working mother suggests, "Outsource everything you can afford!" Although we recognize that some of the fun in the journey of integration is the sense of accomplishment that comes with getting it all done, we need to get real! We were not meant to do it all on our own—and don't have to.

Get Support from Your Partner!

A relationship today is not just about staying connected—it's about sharing the load. The load of laundry, the load of details, the load of scheduling, and the load of work at home that comes along with having a family. Many working mothers we spoke with advise negotiating early and often with partners about who does what. Clarifying roles and responsibilities—regardless of the demands of each partner's professional life—is essential. Setting expectations with one another will pay off!

Find the Best Available Care for Your Child

We heard it time and again: if there is only one thing you can do as a mother committed to integration, it is to find the most reliable and convenient day-care arrangement you can. Settling on child care because of price, location, timing, or anything else is simply not worth it; high-quality, trusted care for your children is invaluable.

Plan Ahead

We found that planning played a big role in the success of integration. When you take the time to carefully plan schedules, appointments, child care, work engagements, and everything else that demands the attention of a working mother, everyone is saved a lot of stress and anxiety. Specific planning advice from working mothers includes the following:

- Prepare meals in advance.
- Sit down with your partner and look at the calendar at the beginning of each week. If there are days you know you need to work late or know you need to be available for the kids, be sure to think through how to make it happen in advance. Don't wait until the last minute!

- Try to organize the best you can—create a system that works for you and lets you find your keys in the morning and the email you printed out in preparation for your morning meeting.

Make Time for Yourself to Rejuvenate

This is one of the most difficult challenges for working moms. Many advised women to "schedule alone time, whether it's a class at a gym, walk in the woods, movie, or coffee with a friend. Make some time each week just for you."

Be Present Wherever You Are

We found that working mothers tend to contribute to their own stress by being mentally at home when they work or mentally at work when they are home with the kids. Many of the women we spoke with suggested being wherever you are in the moment. This way, our employers get us when we work, and our families get us when we're home. One mom described it as "sequentially mono-tasking." Having to take a work call at home or rush out of the office to pick up a sick child from school or day care is par for the course. But if you can, enhance your sense of well-being by fully engaging in what you do when you do it. You'll feel less guilty.

Use Your Mommy Network!

Creating a support system of women who "get it" is essential for making continual integration successful. Find a friend in the same situation and swap stories about how to make the working mother schedule successful. Talk to other moms—working and nonwork-ing—about how they handle the challenging times with children. Reach out to one another and keep the dialogue going—not to complain or to advise but to be on the journey together instead of alone.

Integrated Leadership: Creating Understanding, Choice, and Community

We learned many things from the working mothers with whom we spoke. As we reflected on these conversations and our own experience as leaders and mothers, we came to the conclusion that continual integration is an alternative to what is too often (and unfairly) seen as a binary choice between work and family. Indeed, it is not enough to offer women the right to their career at the expense of their children and families. Nor is it enough to offer women the gift of their families for the price of their ambition and drive for achievement.

If we are to acknowledge the tension in our hearts as we manage life between work and home, we need a vision that moves us beyond the notion of "balance." We cannot in fact strive for balance because there is no such perfectly equalized state to which we can arrive. The concept of continual integration assumes that there are challenges; it assumes that the rewards make those challenges worthwhile; and it assumes you can't get it wrong because there is no one right way. There is only constant evaluation and innovation in the face of the current needs of your family and job.

Continual integration is about giving women a window to understand better why they might have chosen what they chose—and the challenges, rewards, and further choices they have as they seek a fulfilling life. With such understanding, we can embark on a journey of integration that breathes new life into the concept of "having it all."

Ellen Wingard, one of the co-editors of this volume, is considered an early innovator in the field of executive coaching. Ellen has coached CEOs, executive teams, and emerging leaders to achieve desired business results while enhancing their resilience and renewal. She has honed her craft in Fortune 500 companies, leading academic medical centers, universities, nonprofit organizations, and other organizations in industries such as biotech, telecommunications, and financial services. Ellen is on the faculty of the Institute for Women's Leadership in Redwood City, California, and the Duke Corporate Education Program in Chapel Hill, North Carolina. She is also a member of the Women's Leadership Board of the John F. Kennedy School of Government at Harvard University. A former senior consultant for Linkage, Inc., Ellen was an early developer of the Linkage coaching program and has been on the Advisory Board of Linkage's Women in Leadership Summit since its inception.

In this chapter, Ellen brings to light the importance of practicing reflective leadership as an essential capability in reimagining power. Ellen invites leaders to cultivate a "still point," a present-centered sense of *being* from which to lead. Through three reflective practices, we learn how leaders can enhance resilience and lead effectively while mending the fragmentation prevalent in workplaces and society.

PHOTO CREDIT: Ellen Wingard by Lynn McCann

11

Cultivating the Still Point

The Power of Reflective Leadership

Ellen Wingard

For the past twenty-five years, I have been asking women leaders to be quiet.

This is not an invitation to suppress our voices as women in the world. Rather, the quiet here is one of deep resolve that arises when we pause, breathe, and allow the noise levels of constant distractions and contradictory pulls to give way to a direct internal knowing. This quiet allows us to locate a sense of present-centered awareness from which we can observe and shift our habitual thinking to awaken new perspectives. Here, we cultivate the "still point" where the tributaries of intellect, emotions, instincts, light, and shadow converge to reflect our core being. From this core, we are able to discern our own best counsel and give voice to wise solutions in the midst of seemingly insolvable daily complexity. The paradox of this quiet is that by pausing to reflect, we become more effective in the rigors of our day-to-day actions.

This description of leading from the "still point" may sound self-indulgent or naïve. It may read like yet one more set of externally imposed ideals that cannot possibly be met. In any given day while making the rounds with clients in corporate offices, I am struck by how difficult it is to live idealized versions of the latest leadership theory.

In pace-setting environments that reward the "extreme sports" of multi-tasking and overcommitment, cynicism prevails and over-doing compensates for the inner lack of meaning. However, it is my premise that twenty-five years of clinical applications, recent neuro-science discoveries, and the perennial wisdom of contemplative practices gathered throughout the centuries speak to a dimension of leadership performance that goes beyond *doing*.[1] My own experience with hundreds of talented leaders who make a difference in the same corporate corridors mentioned above has shown me consistent evidence that these practices in fact redefine performance as a unifying fusion of action and reflection, while also producing exceptional results. This premise is not new nor is it original. Leadership theories abound with the notion of self-reflection as a fundamental requirement for effective leadership, and thousands of professionals enlist coaches, consultants, and clinicians to gain perspective. However, the practices for achieving this fusion are often left as the "add on" to a more substantive strategy discussion or compressed agenda of the "real work."

The following chapter offers three reflective practices that have been shown to legitimize reflection as an essential element of leadership: (1) present-centered awareness that helps us locate a "still point" of *being*, (2) 360-degree feedback from colleagues and peers to polish the lens of our self-perceptions, and (3) collective reflection to build community and connection. All three practices will be illustrated through the stories of insightful women leaders, each at a unique life stage, whose challenges—how to advance while overcoming external perceptions of one's "style," how to sustain work/life integration, and how to reawaken purpose for meaningful work—all represent themes of many of the women with whom I work.

Many people ask me about gender issues related to reflective leadership. Clearly we cannot ignore the social and cultural contexts that continue to affect equity issues and caregiver responsibilities for women. In fact, it is often dispiriting for women who read the current leadership theories when they do not find many examples that reflect their realities. Further, it is my experience that longing for more purposeful work in a life-sustaining environment that fosters health and family time is a human (not gender-specific) longing. Thus, the practices described here are equally relevant for women *and* men seeking to become more effective leaders.

I am not suggesting that by incorporating these practices into one's daily life, one necessarily achieves a higher moral ground or ceases to cast a shadow in one's organization or home. To the contrary, the leaders presented here embody a vital element of enlightenment: to be awake to one's essential nature *and* mindful of the light and shadow one casts.

Early Lessons in Reflective Practices and Leadership

My understanding of the first practice—the development of present-centered awareness—begins with an early learning experience.

It is the summer of 1980, and I am in an evening class with a young cell biologist from MIT who is teaching an introductory class on "mindfulness." I sit cross-legged, assured that I know a lot about meditation, having taught movement therapy to kids and adults in my early career through the 1970s. Our instructor explains that mindfulness is a concentration tool to cultivate a nonjudgmental level of awareness. He guides us through the simple instructions of paying attention to the rise and fall of one's breath while observing thoughts, feelings, and sensations without judgment.

A bell is rung minutes later, and the instructor inquires about our experience. I wax eloquent about the blissful relaxation and near sleep state I have achieved. The instructor, Jon Kabat-Zinn, looks at me and says, "Clearly, you have much to learn about meditation. Mindfulness is a focused intentional awareness and a way of being, not just a technique to arrive at a pleasant destination. Mindfulness is not about dozing—it is about being awake."

For me, the early awakening of that first mindfulness class would have a life-altering impact. I would become a student of mindfulness, and devote years to the application of this practice in the workplace. It was during the AT&T divestiture in the early 1980s where I would first learn its meaning for leadership.

Around that time, the number of people experiencing heart attacks increased dramatically in corporate settings around the Boston area.[2] An innovative cardiac rehabilitation program was designed by a local hospital, and I was hired to be part of a medical team providing a regimen of exercise and lifestyle counseling for executives recovering from heart attacks. During their thirty-six weeks with us, I taught mindfulness several times a week to a group of these high achievers. We began, for thirty minutes a day, focusing awareness on the breath, noting thoughts, experiencing sensations and emotions, anchoring attention in the present moment, not trying to "relax" or change, just observing non-judgmentally. Other self-regulation methods—such as visualization and body awareness techniques—were offered. And a mindfulness tape was provided for at home use.

It is a late summer day well into the program, and a group of us sit together in the mindfulness practice. Gail is a senior manager for a telecommunications firm and the only woman in her organization. Mel is a government administrator almost ready for retirement. Roger is a young entrepreneur, and Evelyn is scientist from a local MIT think tank.

"Is this meditation a cult or a religion?" asks Evelyn.

I respond, "No, but all contemplative traditions East and West have a version of it, depending on your spiritual or secular beliefs. Mindfulness is an ancient tool with roots in Buddhism but it is widely used now in medical clinics around the country. The Buddhists recognized that the only 'constant' in life is change and impermanence. The tool helps us alleviate suffering and stress by allowing us to live more fully in the present." Everyone nods. Impermanence is a concept this group can grasp following a near-death experience.

"Will I lose my edge and become passive?" worries Gail.

"Actually," I explain, "this practice is used with Olympic athletes to 'sharpen their edge,' to increase the capacity for mental rehearsal and concentration. Businesspeople use these skills every day to brainstorm creative thinking and new innovations by getting out of their habitual mind-sets and gaining different perspectives."

"*This sitting still business is making me nervous. I really don't have time for this.*" Everyone laughs while Roger squirms in his seat and taps his foot.

"*Sitting still isn't for everyone,*" I allow. "*If you just can't or won't sit still, focus on establishing a rhythmic breath when you exercise or play sports. The key is to pay attention to how much of our time we are distracted, not listening, and checked out, and to the impact on our moment-to-moment experience of missing out on life. About the time issue: time urgency raises our anxiety and stress hormones. Mindfulness gives us more of a sense of time expansion, more of an ability to concentrate on 'now.'*"

Gail chimes in. "*This all sounds good for you folks, but when I stop and observe my thoughts, I've got a whole committee in there going in different directions! And I don't really like my present reality, so why do I want to focus on it sitting here breathing? My boss has told me that I have to come back full time whether I am ready or not. My staff can't function without me. My kids are saying I am killing myself with overwork. I get chest pains yelling at them. It's a little ridiculous to think I can just flow through it all.*"

Mel steps in, "*No, it's not about avoiding what is. What I have learned here is that anger isn't bad. Sounds like you have a lot to be angry about, and it can be energizing. It's when it gets stored as resentment. Notice what the stress is doing to your body, catch yourself in the act, right here, right now. We are all so used to being in charge, being high achievers, having a short fuse. We need to come to grips with getting stopped in our tracks, notice the cost of this stress, and face it. Remember what Woody Allen says, 'Death is nature's way of telling you to slow down.'*"

We laugh together, and the group turns to problem solving and offers suggestions on how to set aside time for their health without abandoning their important responsibilities to work and family.

Several months later, they are all completing the program. Gail begins: "*I have recognized how indispensable I think I am, and the fact is my staff and my kids actually have done pretty well on their own. I used to think I was the firefighter rushing in to save the day. Apparently I am* the arsonist." Everyone chuckles, and Gail continues on a more serious note. "I've also lost about fifteen pounds through the exercise and by catching my habit of eating under stress. I demanded a half hour of alone time every day at home and am carving that out now. I am less resentful of everyone, more able to connect."

Others nod and express regret for their self-absorption and their failure to recognize the needs and concerns of those around them. They speak about lost passion for their work and the emptiness of going through the motions for personal gain and enhanced status. Many break down and weep with grief and anger over the preoccupying conflicts that had consumed their time and strained their most intimate connections.

In the follow-up to the program after returning to work, Gail, Mel, and others gave a picture of how the mindfulness, exercise, and group support had contributed to shifting the way they approached leadership and business. They described going back to work with a renewed vigor to listen more and control less. Each began to express their energy and passion for the work at hand and communicate how their employees contributed to the larger context. Some instituted their own stress reduction programs and created more open forums for dialogue. As they recovered their health, they also began to express more qualities of heart—the courage to express more vulnerability, the conviction to take more risks, and the capacity to release blame and resentment. These were not sentimental platitudes but remedies for what had been absent in their lives and workplaces.

Later research would confirm what we knew intuitively at the time. In the words of Pascal, "the heart has reasons that reason knows not of." The collective spirit of the group created what scientists would eventually call *limbic resonance*—a deep emotional heart-brain connection.[3] This heart-brain connection is now understood to be a primary factor in leadership effectiveness and the healing benefits of empathy and altruism.

This resonance had created a climate of encouragement in which each leader had taken a rigorous personal inventory, and each had learned about tools to sustain moment-to-moment awareness. Together, they had shared their fears of imminent death and the challenges—the triumphs, losses, achievements, and uncertainties of leading and living more consciously.

Most important, each member had been strengthened at their core by the experience of healing and reflecting together in community. No longer able to rely on role or status, each had, in a very real sense, been forced to reflect deeply on who they had become and how they might want to shift focus or attitude. Although they always acknowledged the staff for the experience, they unanimously attributed their transformation to their community of peers.

I continue to hear from some participants and the great team of professionals who worked together. Mel is now in his early eighties and thriving with his devoted wife Lenore and their family. We joke that I am still learning mindfulness as I "mindfully rush" from city to city for my work. Mel claims he still practices his tape. He always ends his greetings with "Just remember, we only have moments to live!"

Reflective Practices & Leadership Today

Today, mindfulness is a mainstream phenomenon due to the work of Jon Kabat-Zinn, the same young cell biologist who, as mentioned above, first helped introduce me to the essence of the practice back in the summer of 1980. Kabat-Zinn and his colleague Saki Santorelli went on to establish a world-renowned mindfulness-based stress reduction clinic. Leveraging more than 25 years of clinical research, that clinic has validated the practice of mindfulness-based stress reduction (MBSR) to alleviate pain, reduce anxiety, improve sleep, address immune-related disease, face life-threatening diagnoses, and reduce workplace stress.[4] Since 1979, more than 16,000 participants have completed the program offered by the clinic. Today, approximately 200 healthcare systems offer MBSR programs.

Mindfulness research is also the foundation for much of the emotional intelligence work introduced by Daniel Goleman, Richard Boyatzis, Annie McKee, and others.[5] Their groundbreaking synthesis of neuroscience and mindfulness has elevated self-awareness from a soft skill to a leadership necessity. Other pioneering researchers, such as Joan Borysenko and Evelyn Rosch, have been instrumental to our understanding of mindfulness and health as well.[6]

The theory and practice of mindfulness continues to advance today. For instance, the positive benefits of mindfulness in the workplace were recently researched and validated by Kabat-Zinn and Richard Davidson at the University of Wisconsin. R&D scientists from a biotech firm participated in an eight-week program led by Kabat-Zinn. Blood work and brain imaging revealed that the program yielded significant results: reduced stress hormones, enhanced immune function, and prefrontal brain activity associated with positive emotions.[7] Workers reported higher-order thinking in problem solving and positive shifts in handling workplace stress and negative emotions such as hostility and resentment. They also identified an increased capacity to express empathy, compassion, and gratitude.

On a personal level, the significance of the mindfulness research is brought home to me each day while witnessing the daunting challenges experienced by leaders who seek to stay awake and make a difference in the midst of our post-9/11 geopolitical reality, a deeply polarized society, corporate malfeasances, and economic instability. In spite of how much more we know about the positive effects of mindfulness, yoga, and other still point practices, our physiological vigilance to threats around us has only increased.

The *New York Times* recently reported that workplace stress continues to cost the nation $300 billion in healthcare annually.[8] Depression and anxiety disorders persist, and our attempts to "cope" result in addictive behaviors. Quoted in the *Times* article, Dr. Arlie Hochschild describes the phenomenon of our "splintered selves," distracted and unable to give attention to where it is needed—to ourselves and each other.[9]

An Opportunity for Leaders: Listening to the Wake Up Call

As Lin Coughlin, my co-editor and colleague, stated in the Introduction to this book, a growing number of enlightened leaders are looking for ways to create humane workplaces of collaboration and inclusion. However, the best of intentions to pause and reflect are usually the first thoughts to evaporate in any given workday. Most leaders cannot imagine *just* sitting still given their schedule and job demands. The very thought often creates anxiety. Perhaps most significantly, to pause requires us to face difficult truths in our personal lives or work situation that then often require action rather than avoidance. But at some point we find that we can no longer avoid these truths. Whether by crisis or choice, we come to recognize that our own daily leadership behaviors are sabotaging our best intentions and that we owe it to ourselves and the organizations we serve to become more self-aware.

Reflective leadership requires that we interrupt habits of overcommitment, time urgency, and lack of fulfillment and examine our own self-imposed barriers to change. On close examination, we discover that even our greatest strengths as leaders can work against us.

The Center for Creative Leadership conducted classic research describing how leaders derail by overdoing their strengths.[10] An example of a strength becoming a liability is a high achievement orientation that results in burnout and workaholism. John O'Neill, Connie Zweig, and many others have also explored the "paradox of success" and the "shadow of achievement."[11] In addition to CCL research, theories of the Enneagram, a sophisticated system of psychological types, correlate with my own observations that effective leadership styles can have unintended impact. Taken to extremes:[12]

1. Impeccable standards and integrity result in a critical perfectionism.
2. Service orientation as a giver results in overcommitment, burnout, and resentment.

3. Zest for achievement results in constantly auditioning and polishing an image.

4. The search for significance and meaning results in mood shifts that create toxic emotional states.

5. An intellectual quest for knowledge results in data overload and subsequent social withdrawal.

6. Troubleshooting and scenario planning result in worst-case thinking and doubt.

7. Imaginative, creative thinking results in distraction and avoidance.

8. Direct, authoritative approach results in over-controlling.

9. Peace seeking and harmony result in conflict avoidance and passivity.

As you review this list, you may find that more than one consequence has significance for you, creating inner contradictions and conflicting priorities when expressed in daily life. Still point practices can provide a way of observing and integrating these diverse selves within a larger sense of *being*.

Tara Bennett-Goleman notes this when she describes the value of mindfulness in observing our multitudinous selves and in knowing that we are more than our contradictory thoughts, emotions, moods, and impulses: "Instead of seeing personality as a fixed set of tendencies, modern psychology is coming around to a view that who we are shifts, sometimes radically, from moment to moment and from context to context—though the coexistence of these differing realities does not release us from the responsibility for what we do."[13]

Daily Practices for Leaders: Collecting Ourselves

We can remember core leadership strengths and shift away from self-sabotaging behaviors by cultivating the still point practices. Let me recommend the following:

1. *Begin to explore resources for starting a still point practice.* There are hundreds of excellent resources in the marketplace now. See the partial list provided at the end of this chapter. I suggest a qualified mindfulness instructor, a structured CD program, or an extended retreat. A particular effective practice combines yoga, Pilates, or other body-based discipline with the present-centered awareness.

2. *Create a space in your home office that has visual symbols or images that remind you to shift from overdoing or "being."* Enlist the support of loved ones and work colleagues to protect your commitment to taking time. Thirty minutes a day of "being time" can make a significant impact.

3. *Once you have begun a formal mindfulness practice, bring in present-centered awareness to moments throughout your workday.* Even five minutes of modulated breathing per day will begin to have a carry over effect to reduce strain and increase concentration and energy. It is important not to wait to "feel like" attending to this concentration practice, but rather to engage in the practice and then observe the shift in awareness that can occur. In fact, every transition in the day offers an opportunity to be more present: early morning, during the commute, while preparing for a challenging conversation or meeting presentation, while exercising, while eating, at one's desk, during a break, before bedtime, even when you are frantic, upset, or stressed. Essentially, any moment is an opportunity to ask, "Where is my attention right now?"

4. *Pay attention to potential triggers due to overdone strengths.* In the course of any given work day, enormous frustrations, missed deadlines, or perceived violations of trust combined with our own over-functioning can offer multiple opportunities to be more awake to our habits.[14] Over time (usually within days of beginning a guided practice), you will begin to observe your inner narrative and the corresponding physiological impact of your moods, thoughts, and emotions.

These practices can be enormously useful to quickly recover your clarity in the heart of a contentious workplace situation. As you cultivate more of ability to experience, observe, and release the grip these triggers have on you, you will also be more likely to create an environment of mutual respect and an orientation toward resolution rather than blame. Over time, you can express and release a range of emotions while increasing your capacity for empathy, candor, and transparency.

5. *Apply still points as a tool of self-compassion rather than as a blunt instrument of self-judgment*. Many people resist a reflective practice because they think that it will amplify the noisy inner critic or other voices of self-judgment. In fact, harsh self-blame is often the loudest "inner narrative" of high achievers. The intent here, however, is to acknowledge rather than silence the inner "hecklers." You may find that when you approach the inner narrative with curiosity, you will be able to observe how habitual, automatic, and often inaccurate these internal assessments can be. Cultivating compassion for perceived failures and inadequacies can begin to dissolve the corrosive nature of self-blame.

Other barriers, too, such as procrastination and perfectionism, are intensified by non-acceptance and tend to shift naturally when you decide to observe them without judgment. By creating an atmosphere of acceptance, we are more likely to get the cooperation of even the most recalcitrant aspects of our being.

6. *Create positive interruptions to practice*. For many of us who are caught in a pattern of time constraints leading to self-neglect, it can take an interruptive situation to point us toward the need for daily still point practice. As the cardiac patients often said, it is not necessary to wait for a near-death experience, a religious awakening, or a work crisis to begin living more fully in the present. You can choose instead to wake yourself up and book a retreat or spa vacation where you can get expert guidance and see immediate results.

7. *Consider other daily practices even if you can't sit still*. If you simply cannot sit still and decide the sitting practice is not for you, be assured that there are hundreds of powerful practices to heighten your senses, expand your perceptual field, nourish your being, and reset your physiology. Imagine yourself engaged fully in activities where you are both focused and spacious, such as gardening, paint-

ing, poetry, singing, sports, music, journal writing, massage therapy, martial arts, prayer, crafts, savoring beauty in nature, visualization.

For conscientious leaders who also devote non-work time as caregivers, it is important to create a rationale of how your "time out" will result in generous dividends to others by your enhanced capacity to handle triggers, recover more quickly, and experience fulfillment and joy of being present with those you love.

You may ask, "How will cultivating the still point actually make a difference in day to day leadership?" I have observed that those who attend to these practices demonstrate the following reflective leadership at work:

- *Excel in "pattern recognition" and adapt to rapidly changing external conditions* moment to moment while sustaining a clear sense of purpose, linking each person's contribution to the business imperatives

- *Create rigorous performance expectations* while welcoming humor, imagination, and social connection as part of the fabric of high performance

- *Set a tone of openness by listening and asking questions* to test hypotheses, challenge sacred assumptions, and learn through candid dialogue without fear of retribution

- *Be present to team members* and engaged fully in the requirements of the moment while providing alternative time availability if they can't give their attention

- *Foster the diverse strengths and talents of each team member* and provide one-on-one time for regular developmental conversations

- *Handle performance breakdowns quickly with clear expectations* that preserve dignity and inspire commitment rather than compliance

- *Create a flexible environment to support the health and boundary setting of team members* as they live whole lives while continuing to achieve results

- *Encourage risk-taking to address conflict and violations of trust* through transparent conversations that identify impact, reduce blame, and focus on clear requests for positive resolution
- *Examine personal biases* regularly and find trusted peers to handle setbacks, highlight the rewards, address the challenges, and reduce the isolation that can accompany a leadership role

Reflective Leadership in Action: Three Stories

To see how these still point practices might be integrated into "real life," we'll look at the experiences of three leaders who became awake to their power through rigorous self-reflection and a willingness to confront their own self-limiting behaviors. In each case, a practice of mindfulness served as the foundation of their awakening and was then enhanced by 360-degree feedback and a positive, reflective community in which these leaders shared their values and principles in order to galvanize a sense of purpose and connection.

Alyssa: Becoming an Inspirational Leader

> One does not become enlightened by imagining figures of light, but by making the darkness conscious.
>
> —Carl Jung, *Alchemical Studies*, Vol. 15

"I am ambitious, and apparently that's a problem." Alyssa, a charismatic high performer, had requested coaching following a promotion as a managing director in a financial services firm. A quick-witted, vivacious extravert who spoke with concise language and penetrating directness, Alyssa wanted to "accelerate" her learning curve following a recent promotion. Yet the conversation quickly turned to her dissatisfaction with her current situation. She described success after success and a pervasive feeling of emptiness. "For all purposes, I should be happy here, but I have gotten feedback that I am too upwardly mobile. I am just trying to learn the ropes here quickly. I have attempted to drive some initiatives but am frustrated that the organization isn't thinking or talking at a larger enterprise level—and on top of it to be 'labeled' for my competence! The criticism has stung me. I have a lot to offer and want to give it. What's the point of doing this if I can't make a difference?"

Alyssa described beating the odds to become as accomplished and financially secure as she was—a Harvard MBA, several years in the financial services world, and cover stories on several leading financial services magazines. Alyssa and her husband had put their careers first and were now questioning the contribution they were making in the world. To paraphrase Joseph Campbell, Alyssa was asking whether the ladder of success was perched against the right wall.

Becoming Aware. We established two goals. First, she wanted to find more equanimity and fulfillment in her day-to-day life as she sorted out the "big questions." Second, she wanted to address others' perception of her driving ambition.

Alyssa immediately applied her high level of discipline to the mindfulness practice. She also started to use a computerized biofeedback program called Heartmath, which has been found to be extremely effective in restoring people's "coherence" and calm throughout the workday.[15]

Alyssa began to observe her multiple internal narratives and notice the triggers that would cause a defensive posture, sharp tone, and impatient body language. She also explored several leadership inventories. She learned about the virtues of her achievement orientation and the shadow of constant striving based on a deep vulnerability that she revealed related to the hardships of her upbringing. Alyssa began to observe her shifts in mood and recognize them as a protective response to perceived threats to her image: "I can see how intolerant I am of incompetence. I don't want to look bad. My success has defined my worth. Failure is very threatening to me. I am now aware of how often I have triggers throughout the day. The mindfulness is helping me know I do have an essential nature that is more than my image or the approval of others. I realize that the way through is to have more compassion and empathy for myself and others."

Polishing the Lens of Perception: The Use of 360-Degree Feedback. At one time in her career, Alyssa had elected to go through a 360-degree feedback process that she described as "dev-astating" because the collector focused so heavily on her perceived deficiencies, rather than balancing with her strengths. We talked about the benefits and hazards of collective feedback. Often the process can be misused to send a message that should have been delivered by a manager. In Alyssa's case, she believed the collector of the feedback lacked sensitivity to the subtleties and nuances of sharing data. We did agree, however, that gaining these collective perspectives can illuminate the systemic and cultural context of the leader's behavior and her propensity to see "through a glass darkly."

As rigorous as any meditation teacher who speaks to the human propensity for self-deception, the workplace is an environment where our blind spots are like open secrets to the people with whom we work. We are often the last to know.

Alyssa decided to brace herself for another round of feedback to understand how she could address and turn around negative perceptions. Feedback was collected from stakeholders all around the organization as well as from her manager and direct reports. Positive assessments rolled in on Alyssa's brilliant conceptual and strategic skills, her verbal quickness, and her ability to execute.

On the personal development side, she gained an understanding that she had not read the organizational culture's informal "rules" about how to enter into a new organization and build social networks outside her group. Her self-promoting behavior was interpreted as self-aggrandizing, as if she were always auditioning for her role. Alyssa's rapid, no-nonsense communication style was experienced as intimidating and disrespectful of others.

Building a Community Through Presence. Meanwhile, Alyssa began to pay much more attention to others, listening more actively and encouraging solutions rather than assuming that she knew best. She came to focus on her "leadership presence" in terms of her tone and approachability, as described by Halpern and Lubar.[16] In addition, Alyssa developed awareness of the mood she projected during public presentations. Following suggestions from corporate communications coach Peter Bubriski, she became more comfortable connecting with the audience and communicating her genuine warmth rather than rushing through a scripted "performance."[17]

As Alyssa later reported on her experience:

> The truth is I was oblivious to the signals I was sending to people. I thought I was being helpful in giving my great advice across the organization early on. I wanted approval. When the discomfort shows up and I seem insincere it usually means I am experiencing some threat, some insecurity. It is a signal I have lost touch with my genuineness, my authenticity. At the same time, I do have to have difficult conversations every day and address tough issues. I find I am able to get to the heart of an issue faster and be direct without bulldozing my way.
>
> The power of the still point practice was first that it just reduced the noise level and helped me get a visceral sense of being more centered to manage my reactions. I have learned that not everyone holds my beliefs for how things should be and that they have their own very diverse strengths and shadows that get triggered. My job as a leader is to understand these differences and focus on their success rather than on how they make me look.

Alyssa was able to tap into a deep and genuine commitment to her team and the great innovations occurring that would affect the whole company. At an off-site retreat, Alyssa spoke with transparency and vulnerability in acknowledging what she had been missing and what she was working on to be present as a leader. People in the room were visibly moved. She invited others to call her on her behavior and to speak up if there was a disconnect between her words and actions. Most important, her focus turned to the team and she highlighted the contribution each person made and invoked the compelling future they would achieve together.

Nine months later, a post-360 feedback check-in resulted in continual "raves" for Alyssa's responsiveness and availability. Her manager said, "We all knew Alyssa was brilliant; now we know she is real." A team member said, "In the past we would have followed Alyssa because she just is so bright and we all respect her—and we would have been scared if we didn't. Now we follow her because she genuinely connects with us and inspires us. We want to deliver for her and we love coming to work. It's a real community here."

Today, Alyssa, who is still an achiever seeking results, says she has gained insight into the "big questions":

> The first step in this time of reflection was to get an understanding of who I am and who I want to be. Yet I have learned that focusing on numbers and innovation, which I can do, doesn't mean much if I am not inspiring people and building the organization—it's a positive-sum balance. I am thrilled by the accomplishments of my team this year and just received very positive feedback from the president on the impact we made.
>
> There is a lot of pain in organizations right now. Most people I know are asking if the effort is worth the cost. I want to be an inspiring leader where people feel they belong to something bigger than just a business. I am now working with a group to bring more social responsibility issues into business and use our talents beyond the bottom line. I still witness the "striver" in me who now strives to be better at being mindful! However, I catch myself. When I first started these practices, I think I was searching for a better mask; instead I discovered much more about myself. I am making a lot of connections now and starting to feel as though I can and do belong.

Juliana: Healing the Divide at Work and Home

> If you carefully observe the flow of your breathing, you will discover that in the midst of constant change there are still points. These are revealed at the very climax of the inhalation before the exhalation begins, and at the bottom of the exhalation as the inhalation begins. . . . With practice, you can learn to be more fully present with change by building frequent pauses into your busy day.
>
> —Michelle Levy, *Living in Balance*, 1998

Juliana was in tears as she talked to me. "I want to be more present for my kids, but my 'present' just isn't working. At this point I don't believe I am a good mom *or* a decent leader." Juliana was a newly promoted analyst with a reserved and stoic demeanor. On this particular day, she had been up all night with her two-year-old and was preparing to present a strategic plan from her global IT group of fifteen reports to the president of the manufacturing firm. Juliana continued, "I know I need to do more to cope, like asking for support, working out, and taking time, but the situation is beyond that." Juliana had requested coaching to support work-life integration and to address her tendency toward perfectionism in sustaining the high quality standards in her technical work.

Although the organization she worked for promoted flexibility, Juliana believed there to be an unwritten rule that strong performers don't ask for flexible work arrangements. She believed she would be risking future promotion if the request were to be denied.

For Juliana, quieting the conflicting and contradictory internal noise through brief mindfulness sessions allowed her to recognize that she could use the mindfulness to "cope" in an intolerable situation, or she could use it to take action. She courageously faced her inner narrative of being irresponsible and her fears in addressing authority figures. At the same time, Juliana was also able to identify her love of mentoring her team and the sense of mastery in her IT work. She came to terms with the fact that all the data she had collected on self-care practices were irrelevant unless she acted on them.

Juliana committed to return to her long-distance running, which she described as her best still point practice for savoring alone time, being absorbed in nature, and feeling the freedom of speed.

Juliana realized she needed to interrupt the pattern of being overwhelmed and arrived at the decision to take a month's leave of absence to sort out her priorities. She rehearsed the conversation she planned to have with the president and the HR office, stressing her conviction about the long-term benefits to herself and to the company. She called after the meeting, astonished by their response: "Not only were they receptive, but they assured me that I can create a workable situation with flextime when I get back."

Months later, Juliana reported on what the experience was for her:

I finally caught up with myself and was able to put systems in place that have created much more of a sense of order for all of us. Knowing my tendency to withdraw and get lost in overload if I don't plan, I feel much more centered. I did follow through on my running plan, and it gives me a lot of energy and perspective to problem-solve. My partner and I spend more spacious time just being together. I have been able to observe rather than react to all the ups and downs with my kids, and that makes a big difference.

The surprise was that right after I got back to work I was offered another promotion. I was able to negotiate up front on my "conditions of satisfaction." I put my requests on the table explicitly. The best part of my job has been creating a flexible work culture in my expanded organization. We have made going home at a reasonable hour a sign of good leadership and advancement. The feedback I have gotten from my team has been terrific. I would tell other women in my position not to shortchange possibilities by suppressing your needs. So many women are leaving the workplace, smart organizations are noticing. Ask and you may be surprised. If your situation is untenable and you are doing everything you can but are stuck in a rigid environment with a boss who doesn't get it, strongly consider finding an environment that does.

Erica: Reawakening Purpose

Nothing contributes so much to tranquilize the mind as a steady purpose—a point on which the soul may fix its intellectual eye.
—Mary Wollstonecraft Shelley

"I have devoted so many years to direct care of my patients, now I am administrating in a toxic system." Erica was a seasoned leader and single physician who had been recently promoted from clinical researcher to department head at an academic medical center. She was published and widely acknowledged in her field of oncology.

Due to the grueling administrative hours and excessive demands of running the office, she was going home exhausted every night.

> I recently went through a 360-degree process and was told that I have a constantly critical tone and display a lot of negative body language in meetings. I admit I get fired up every day by some stupid comment. I believe it is my responsibility to challenge practices that have questionable integrity. But as a bit of a whistleblower, I am very isolated. Lots of the younger women medical students are reaching out to me, but to tell you the truth I am too jaded to give them advice. I am totally dedicated to my patients, but because of the administrative work I see them less and less.

Erica embarked on an inquiry to examine her deeply held belief that it was "too late" to make any significant changes in her life. She identified a chronic resentment toward the systemic conflicts of academia. She began to observe her defensive reactions and resulting tension headaches when her expertise was questioned. We spoke about the stress associated with women not supporting women in the workplace. As a researcher, she had followed the work of Shelley Taylor at UCLA, who described the health benefits of women's social networks. In what she called the "tend and befriend" study, Taylor determined that under stress women secrete oxytocin, a hormone known to chemically induce caring, tending behaviors essential to the well-being of the group. Dr. Taylor discovered that the withholding of nurturing behaviors in woman-to-woman conflict posed the highest threat and produced the most significant stress reactions in other women.[18]

Erica acknowledged that this lack of support had generated her sense of isolation and betrayal. She admitted that her whole life had become an "out of body experience" of little pleasure, rigid neck, and painful shoulders. When asked where she was experiencing passion or sense of purpose in her life, she revealed that she had been an artist prior to attending medical school and had deep regrets about "letting her creativity go."

Erica scheduled an overdue health exam and began receiving muscular therapy treatments for her stress-related symptoms. She signed up for art classes. She described a restoration of her still point and an ability to see more beauty around her by taking time to be in nature. She began to use her art with oncology patients and became quite energized. However, in spite of Erica's attempts to mend some of the deep conflict in the office, she had burned several bridges and "lost social capital." The question was, what was she here to do that mattered most? A year later, this was Erica's answer:

> I spent several months with this question. I thought about staying and "fighting the system" and then I realized I had become the system. The hostility took a real toll on me and I had lost my sense of purpose. I looked for over a year and was hired by a nonprofit foundation as executive director of oncology research. I work with an incredible team of totally dedicated providers. We do global work, and I have begun traveling to several other cultures, which puts a lot into perspective. I am also painting and working out regularly. Interestingly, I now get very positive feedback from my staff and have tremendous energy for our work and the team environment we have created. I now have people to partner with who have the same convictions. Belonging to this group has changed the way I approach issues. We debate, we get passionate about what to do, but it isn't personal and I haven't alienated anyone. It can sound like a cliché, but finding what you are here to do, what it is that makes your heart come alive, does make it all worthwhile.

All the leaders highlighted in these examples (Alyssa, Juliana, and Erica) faced real systemic challenges yet were able to turn around unsustainable situations. Each did a rigorous personal inventory and discovered a still point practice that helped them access their best inner counsel. Rather than expend energy on self-blame for not being perfect, they found energy in the practice of simply allowing co-existence for their contradictory selves. They recognized that mindfulness or any other still point practice is not a panacea but a way of being in the midst of complexity. Each developed the ability to stay present and benefited enormously, if not always comfortably, by the process of receiving feedback from colleagues and peers. And each depended upon a community to support her leadership initiatives.

Community as the Collective Still Point for Leaders

We need a new vision, a new definition of power and leadership. We must move toward a model of creative cooperation. The world needs women to come together and imagine, define, and lead us toward a sane and sustainable culture.

—Dr. Johnnetta Cole, spoken at the Women in Power Conference, Omega Institute, September 11, 2004

It is imperative that we as women today find the collective still points that return us to wholeness through community and connection. Rather than being a narcissistic pursuit, shared reflection with other women allows for candid transparency and truth telling. As Susan Ray, director of the Women in Leadership board of the John F. Kennedy School of Government at Harvard University says, "My sense of purpose comes alive the moment I sit in a room with a hundred extraordinary women who are working to change the world."[19]

Much has been written about women not supporting other women across racial lines, age, culture, and status. These barriers cannot be dissolved without making time to reflect on our differences and to create, as social commentator and actress Anna Deavere Smith says, "an irresistible fusion" across gender, age, race, and ethnicity.[20] This fusion is also critically needed in a world where we see few examples of reflective leadership.

The goal of creating communities for women is not about exclusion but rather about replenishment—about creating an environment in which our deepest longings, regardless of our diverse belief systems, find resonance with others. Whether in a peer group, leadership conference, meditation class, church, synagogue, mosque, or community center, coming together for reflection creates that irresistible fusion by allowing women to see one another beyond stereotypes and to find those inevitable places of commonality and connection. From the strengthening fabric of community, women can engage more fully in partnership with men with a renewed clarity of purpose, emboldened hearts, and a willingness to lead others to a greater level of creative cooperation.

The ramifications of reflective practices go beyond self-renewal and enhanced organizational leadership. Our need for mending the fragmentation we experience every day continually increases, as do examples of the dire consequences of non-reflective leadership.

As we consider the consequences of incompetent, unethical, and outright brutal abuses of power, it becomes clear that enlightened power is more than a soft notion that will make our lives less stressful. It is an imperative. Such reflective practices have been with us for centuries in various wisdom traditions. It is our task as current leaders to be fully awake and to utilize these practices for our sustainability and survival—on both personal and global levels. As Lao-tzu described thousands of years ago in the Chinese text, the *Tao te Ching*:

> *Empty yourself of everything*
> *Let the mind rest at peace*
> *The ten thousand things rise and fall*
> *While the self watches their return*
> *Knowing constancy the mind is open*
> *With an open mind, you will be open-hearted*
> *Being openhearted, you will act royally.*

Recommended Resources

Goleman, D. (2003). *Destructive emotions: How can we overcome them? A scientific dialogue with his holiness the Dalai Lama.* New York: Bantam Books.

Halpern, B. L., & Lubar, K. (2003). *Leadership presence: Dramatic techniques to reach out, motivate and inspire.* New York: Gotham Books.

Kabat-Zinn, J. (2005). *Coming to our senses: Healing ourselves and the world through mindfulness.* New York: Hyperion.

Kellerman, B. (2004). *Bad leadership: What it is, how it happens, why it matters.* Boston: Harvard Business School Press.

Paul, M. (2003). *It's hard to make a difference when you can't find your keys: The seven step path to becoming truly organized.* New York: Viking Compass.

Ruderman, M., & Ohlott, P. (2002). *Standing at the crossroads: Next steps for high achieving women.* San Francisco: Jossey-Bass.

Senge, P., Jaworski, J., Scharmer, C. O., & Flowers, B. S. (2004). *Presence: Human purpose and the field of the future.* Cambridge, MA: Society of Organizational Learning.

Sounds True Catalog, http://www.soundstrue.com. (Extensive resources on mindfulness CDs.)

Websites

Excellent sources of mindfulness instruction
www.mindfulnesstapes.com
www.soundtrue.com

Poetry and inspirational guidance
www.davidwhyte.com

www.oriahmountaindreamer.com
www.cherylrichardson.com

Noted Enneagram theorists and resources
www.enneagraminstitute.com
www.authenticenneagram.com

Part Two

PATHS OF POWER

If we are to achieve a richer culture, rich in
contrasting values, we must recognize the whole
gamut of human potentialities and so weave a less
arbitrary social fabric, one in which each diverse
gift will find a fitting place.

—*Margaret Mead*

In Part One we explored and established a way of *being*, a way where
we can internally generate power to address the complex demands
in leading others. In Part Two, we look at how we can express this
leadership power and fulfill that leadership calling in creating high
performing, inclusive organizations and work communities.

In the following pages, our contributors present new paths for
expressing one's power in the workplace—through bold expression,
risk-taking, innovation, conflict resolution, new models for thinking
about structure and network, and the creation of work environments
large enough in spirit to accept our diverse selves as leaders across
boundaries and cultural divides. We hear from women whose leadership has brought trust, inclusiveness, vision, values, business results,

and creativity to the center of their organizations. Their stories inspire us to see the environments in which we are immersed as living systems, capable of evolution and change. Equipped with such awareness, we can begin to feel the heartbeat and see the nerve endings of organizational life where work answers a calling beyond financial security. As a result, we gain a greater insight into how we might influence and direct the flow of power and energy in our own places of work.

As our contributors reveal, the onus of finding or creating such vibrant organizations is on us. The challenge is as simple and daunting as Gandhi's adage to be the change you seek. Scaling outward from the self, to our organizations and the world, we influence and shape the swirl of life around us—and have a far-reaching impact in the process.

 An expert on professional development, Herminia Ibarra is INSEAD chaired professor in organizational behavior and area coordinator for the Organizational Behavior Group. Prior to joining INSEAD, she served on the Harvard Business School faculty for thirteen years. Her work has been profiled in a wide range of media reaching the general public, including *The New York Times, The Wall Street Journal, The Financial Times, Fast Company,* and the *Economist.*

A native of Cuba, Herminia brings a multicultural perspective to her research and teaching. She also lectures and consults internationally on human resources, leadership, career development, and organizational change. Her new book, *Working Identity: Unconventional Strategies for Reinventing Your Career* (Harvard Business School Press, 2003), shows what conditions enable people to reinvent themselves.

In this chapter, Herminia describes powerful tools and strategies we can use for reexamining our lives and embarking on new paths to power.

PHOTO CREDIT: Herminia Ibarra by INSEAD

12

OUR MANY POSSIBLE SELVES

What Do We Want?

Herminia Ibarra

Something's missing.

I need a change, but I don't know what.

I hope I'm not doing this five years from now.

Going to work is no fun anymore, but I don't know what I want to do instead.

Thoughts like these are increasingly on the minds of the growing number of midcareer women who are at a crossroads, stuck in jobs they've lost their passion for, unable to strike a balance among their varied roles and interests, yet at a loss for a better alternative. "Am I doing what is right for me, and should I change direction?" is a question we all ask ourselves at midcareer. But for an overwhelming number of midcareer professional and business women today, this kind of questioning attains an even greater urgency.

Having achieved great successes in traditional careers and often inflexible organizations, many women find that the desire to give rein to unexpressed facets of ourselves only becomes pressing at midcareer. To make matters worse, whereas most of us can state with utter clarity what no longer works, much fewer have a clear idea of—or a reliable method for finding—a better alternative. Consider the following examples:

As a thirty-nine-year-old general manager at a large New York publishing house, Brenda Rayport attended a convention of economists to promote one of her books.

> We had hired a caricaturist to draw cartoons of the professors whose textbooks we sold, and he offered to do a caricature of me. His technique was to ask people about their hobbies and interests. He would draw the figures with their little emblems around them. I thought, what will he depict in his drawing of me? A textbook? I didn't have anything else in my life at that point. My marriage was no good. I didn't have any hobbies. I said to myself, "I'm passionate about my work, but is this what I want arrayed in the caricature of myself that I'll hang in my office? I don't think so." It really bothered me. It became clear that I was doing something very wrong in my life. The problem was that I didn't have a forward trajectory. I couldn't see where I wanted to go next. I really wanted a time-out at that point.

It took Susan Fontaine several years of planning (and gathering up the courage) to leave an unfulfilling job as partner and head of the strategy practice at a top consulting firm. She knew she wanted to travel less and to spend more time with her children. But a busy schedule had left her no time to figure out a future direction, and she felt ambivalent about making a "mommy's choice." "I was thinking about leaving, but because I had been working so hard and I had two small children, I didn't really know what I *could* do, not to mention what I wanted next. I was clear, though, that I didn't want to just go on to another big consultancy and do the same thing in a new company." Susan spent a few weeks wondering "What next?" before a close client, the CEO of a Financial Times 1000 firm, offered her the top strategy job, the "perfect" position, according to what Susan calls "the relentless logic of a post-MBA résumé." Confident that she had explained her new priorities and flattered by the extent to which they wanted her and only her, she took the position. No sooner had she started, however, that she realized the new job was no different from her old position in all the aspects she was seeking to change.

A professor of Spanish literature, June Prescott returned to her academic department after a one-year sabbatical and realized that the deep-seated discontent with academic politics and wages that had troubled her for years had become unbearable. "Once I became a mother and wife my interests and values changed. My intellectual life at the university had no importance compared with my wish to create an environment that would permit me a full dedication to my family—a real chance at making more money, giving my children good schools, being with them, and being with them out in the world in a way that would be consonant with my work life." Her idea: translate her aptitude as an amateur investor into a new career in finance. But her age and literary background would make her a tough sell to Wall Street. She spent nearly two years in sustained investigation, by which time the paucity of actual job prospects had damped the euphoria of new possibilities.

Brenda, Susan, and June had much more in common than their hard work and successful careers. Like so many of the men and women I studied,[1] they found themselves at an impasse at midcareer—dissatisfied with the old yet unable to imagine or bring to life a new, more fulfilling and economically feasible alternative. In this chapter I describe the unconventional strategies that they and dozens of other managers and professionals I studied used to explore possible futures.

Although these strategies are by no means gender specific—both men and women used them quite successfully—the women in my study shared characteristic challenges and dilemmas that extended far beyond the familiar issues of work-life balance. As they strove to define who they wanted to become and what they wanted to do next, they discovered how they really felt about money and status. They faced their own preconceived notions about "good jobs" versus "women's work." They confronted traditional wisdom about the obvious trade-offs: fame versus satisfaction, money versus fun, impact versus flexibility. Their experiences hold valuable lessons for all professional women striving to create choices beyond the binary (and rigid) thinking that pits the high-powered corporate life against the "mommy track."

Working Identity

What is identity? Most traditional definitions—the ones that are the foundation for most career advice—are based on the notion of an "inner core" or a "true self." By early adulthood, these theories suggest, people have formed a relatively stable personality structure, defined by their aptitudes, preferences, and values. Excavating this true self—often forgotten in a dead-end pursuit of fame, fortune, or social approval—should be the starting point of any career reorientation. For a person armed with the appropriate self-knowledge, obtained via introspection and psychological testing, her search for the right "match" is easier, and she is more likely to avoid the mistakes of the past.

The work of Stanford cognitive psychologist Hazel Markus and other behavioral scientists, however, offers a different definition of identity, one that is more consistent with what I discovered: we are not one but many selves, and they are defined as powerfully by our hopes and fears for the future and by our present circumstances as by our past history.[2]

Possible selves—the images and fantasies we all have of about who we hope to become, think we should become, or even fear becoming in the future—are at the heart of the career change process. Although the conventional wisdom says that fear—fueled by the growing realization that you are, in fact, becoming the person that you never wanted to become—is the only driver for change, in reality fear can create paralysis. We change only when we have tangible and enticing alternatives, ones we can feel, touch, and taste. That is why *reworking our identity* is necessarily a process of experimenting, testing, and learning about our possible selves.

How do we work and rework our identities? By doing new things and meeting new people. By telling and retelling our stories. And, of course, by taking the time that trial-and-error discovery requires. In the discussion that follows I continue the stories of Brenda, Susan, and June. As we will see, it is not in a moment of blinding insight but rather by taking small action steps that each found her way to a new career. Although not necessarily taken in the same order, together these three steps or practices describe the path that most people I studied took in re-creating their working identity.

Step One: Craft Experiments to Test Possible Selves

By far the biggest mistake people make when trying to change careers is delaying the first step until they have settled on a destination. Alternatively, like Susan, for lack of better destination they settle on a position they hope will change everything, while in fact changing nothing at all.

Few people really leap into the unknown. Instead, most of us create possible selves on the side at first, by getting involved, as Susan did, in extracurricular ventures, freelance work, and weekend projects. *Crafting experiments* refers to the practice of creating these small probes and side projects. Their great advantage is that they allow us to try out new professional roles on a limited but tangible scale without compromising our current job or leaping too quickly into the wrong position. In almost every instance of successful change that I observed, the leap was not a leap, because the person had already been deeply engaged in the new career for quite some time.

Realizing she made the wrong choice, Susan gathered her courage again and quit. But she doubted herself:

I asked myself, "Why did I accept the job when it wasn't right?" I also wondered, "If this isn't right, what is right?" I didn't want to go back to the handful of people I had been talking to about jobs. I wanted some space. But, I felt quite a bit of financial pressure. I knew I would have to work again pretty fast, but I also knew that feeling that I had to move instantly on to the next job, not spending too long deciding, had doomed me. I had the wits to see I needed some time out to have a think.

Resolved to explore a range of different possibilities, she took some freelancing assignments in her old line of work and did pro bono work for charities, as her "lifeline" to get her through this difficult period. Through that work, she began to develop contacts that led to paid charity consulting. These concrete experiences, more than any amount of self-reflection, helped her get reoriented.

Gradually Susan found herself immersed in an industry in which she had never expected to work for a living. And she found herself enjoying a style of work—freelancing—that she began only out of necessity.

> After about two years my "gift work" became my main line of work. The first realization came after a few months of freelancing, when I realized I would not look for another permanent job. I was doing well financially and enjoying the freelance lifestyle. I would not have risked a freelance career had I not taken the wrong job in the first place. But once I started doing it, I found it actually suited me very well. Two years later, when it was clear that I was making a good living, that I was able to get quite interesting work, and that my network was serving me well, I had to decide what really wanted I want to do.

By this time it was clear her heart was in the nonprofit sector.

There are many ways to set up experiments that work. As we'll see, Brenda also did freelance work as an editor as an intermediary step between her old career as a manager and her new career as a literary agent. Other people use temporary assignments, outside contracts, advisory work, and "moonlighting" to get experience or build skills in a new industry. Taking courses or picking up training and credentials in a new area is still another way of experimenting, as June did when she audited MBA classes at her university. June, in fact, did not limit her search to positions in finance; she experimented with a broad palette of possible selves: she looked at management consulting, knowing it was not for her; she considered whether or not to apply for other literature jobs; she took on a one-year volunteer project coaching high school instructors to teach literature; she revisited the idea of moving into university administration; and she investigated a range of finance possibilities.

Step Two: Shift Your Connections Toward the Future

Consider how many times we have heard someone reproach her company by saying something like, "There is no one here I want to be like." At midcareer our desire for change is rarely about only the actual work we do; it is equally if not more importantly about changing our working relationships so they are more satisfying and more inspiring. *Shifting connections* refers to the practice of finding people who can help us see and grow into our new selves. For most successful career changers whom I observed, a guiding figure or new professional community helps light the way and cushions the eventual leap.

June had grown to dislike many of the people with whom she worked. There was not a single one among them whom she wanted to be like. Still it was hard to make the break. "My academic department was family, a dysfunctional one," June says, "but one I was an intimate part of, one I joined at age seventeen when I went to college." For her, leaving academia meant not just giving up a long-term career objective but leaving the mentor and family with whom she had grown up professionally. And by leaving she was necessarily disappointing those who had been her role models and peers.

To make a break with the past we must venture into unknown networks—and not just for job leads. Making a career change requires more than a little help from mentors, guides, sounding boards, and role models. New guides and communities offer inclusion, provide a safe base for trying out new possibilities, and replace the community that is being lost. From the start, June tried to meet as many people as possible in the world of finance. Those possibilities amplified when she started auditing MBA courses at her university. "I thought it was going to feel like a divorce, a huge loss," she recounts, "but it didn't. I loved my business courses and the project groups. It's a lot easier when you feel emotionally involved in something else."

At the same time as she did the "usual networking" via the MBA career office and traditional college alumni listings, June pursued another idea: finding a person she admired and convincing him to take her on as an apprentice. One candidate was James Cramer, a financial pundit who wrote a column for the *Wall Street Journal*. June admired his wit and writing style as much as his insights into the markets. By email, she told him how much she enjoyed his writing and asked for a meeting. Cramer agreed. He advised her to keep a journal to track her impressions and experiences. A relationship began in which he challenged and guided her.

Finding people with humanities backgrounds as well as finding women who seemed to be successful while still having time for a personal life were, for June, critical tests of her options in the finance world. She made friends, for example, with her teaching assistant: "He considers that my working as a literature professor while taking business classes makes me as weird as he." At one investment bank, she was impressed with the physicist in fixed-income research, who graduated from her university. At another bank, she met a managing director with an MA in philosophy and theology. She drew inspiration from the financial columnist, who like her, had a flair for writing. She especially enjoyed an economics course taught by a professor from Spain, a country where she had spent much time and in whose culture her academic discipline was rooted. Each time June met someone from the new world she was seeking to enter, she ran them through the "Do I want to be like him?" and "Can I be like her?" tests. A "yes" led her to pursue the relationship—and the corresponding possible self—further.

Making a major career change is not simply about picking up new technical skills and repackaging one's image and résumé. It is also about finding people we want to emulate and places where we want to belong. From beginning to end, June's story is punctuated by interactions with people she met who made a difference, from the day traders and stock-market speculators who inspired her at the start to the kindred spirits who gave her encouragement and advice along the way. Her desire to move into a career in finance and out of academia grew—in appeal and in feasibility—not as an abstract idea but as a tangible reality embodied in the people she did (and did not) want to be like.

Step Three: Tell and Retell Your Story

In the middle of the confusion about which way to go, many of us hope for one event that will clarify everything, that will transform our yearning for change into a coherent trajectory. For Brenda, the cartoon episode was the "click" that got her moving. But it is possible to create our own triggers for change: infusing events—the momentous and the mundane—with special meaning and weaving them into a story about who we are becoming.

In fact, Brenda experienced a multitude of triggers. A major change in her firm's internal management (one she did not like), a new "commuter" relationship, and a looming fortieth birthday were all nudging her to reexamine her fifteen-year career in publishing.

> I met my future husband, Aaron, who lived in Chicago. As a general manager, I had completely given up any personal life. The business was global; I was on the road two weeks out of four the whole year round. Suddenly I was getting married again.
>
> I moved to Chicago determined to be a whole person again, which meant having to develop those parts of me that were quite underdeveloped. I was going to make damn sure that the next time someone had to draw a picture of me, there would be plenty of things to put around it. The big decision wasn't moving to Chicago. It was deciding not to go back to my firm in a comparable position. I could have done that, and they encouraged me to, but I really didn't want to. Then, I was headhunted by everybody, for jobs close to what I had done before. But I didn't want that. The problem was, I didn't have a forward trajectory, I couldn't see where I was going.

Not knowing what next, Brenda took a time-out. A year-and-a-half sabbatical allowed her much more than rest and recovery from her punishing schedule as a manager. Taking time, doing volunteer work, and exploring diverse alternatives allowed her to come to terms with her desire for work that was both fun and lucrative. "I thought I wanted to work in education. I volunteered in the public schools. I had to learn to listen more to myself, to reflect on what I wanted to do and what I enjoyed doing. I include being successful and making money in 'enjoy doing,' but I had to figure out how to put the pleasure back into a money-making job."

Taking a time-out also allowed Brenda the time to explore a line of work that, while appealing, she had dismissed as "women's work."

> An ongoing dialogue with my husband helped me see that education wasn't it. He urged me to look at what I did back in my twenties, what I fell in love with when I left school. I had loved being an editor. I remember having enormous discussions with him, often pretty anguished ones. I felt editing was women's work. I thought it was a submissive, or subordinate, kind of helping work. I really fought that. But that dialogue allowed me to start working as a freelance editor, which was really only a step. I thought it would lead to something else, but I didn't know what. Slowly, it began to dawn on me that being a literary agent might be the absolute best option.

Trigger events don't just jolt us out of our habitual routines; they are critical components of good stories and, therefore, the necessary elements of plot for our emerging stories. Arranging our life events into a coherent story is one of the subtlest yet most demanding challenges of a career transition. Without a story that explains why we must change, the people to whom we are pitching our reinvention remain dubious, and we too feel unsettled and uncertain of our own identity. June's attempts at explaining herself—why she wanted to make such a seemingly "crazy" career change from literature to Wall Street, why a potential employer should take a chance on her, why she was attracted to a company she had never heard of a day before—were at first provisional, sometimes clumsy ways of redefining herself. But each time she wrote a cover letter, went through an interview, or updated friends and family on her progress, she better defined what was exciting to her, and in each public declaration of her intent to change careers she committed herself further.

Good stories develop in the telling and retelling, by our putting them into the public sphere even before they are fully formed. It took Brenda close to three years after the cartoon episode to figure out a new direction. In the interim, the cartoon episode became a guiding image she used each time she came to a fork in a road, to remind herself of the feared possible self to which she was still at risk of reverting, and its counterpart, the still vague but much desired Brenda with a multifaceted, rich life.

Dropping the Rocks

Like that of many who switch careers, Susan's transition brought her back to her starting point: working full time for a top consultancy. Yet her professional life—the way she does her work, the way she relates to coworkers and employers, and the way she balances her personal and professional life—changed because of what she learned along the way. Making a career move is a chance to make fundamental changes in one's life. Many people, like Susan, have long-held dreams about their careers, but for one reason or another—including financial, family, or social pressures—have put them off. In some cases, like Susan's, the issue is less the substance of the work than the *lack of flexibility* of the institutional structure in which the work gets done. In other cases, a person may have dreamed of becoming a writer, musician, or entrepreneur, but the practicalities of life constrained her. Still others experience the deeper problem as an issue of authenticity, finding themselves caught in a work situation that asks them to suppress too much of who they are in order to fit in. Whatever the cause, a time comes when long-ignored values, priorities, and passions reassert themselves—or the inconsistencies in our lives grow too blatant to ignore.

Elizabeth McKenna, who wrote about the life and career changes of women struggling to balance work and personal life, tells a parable about a woman swimming across a lake with a rock in her hand.[3] As the woman neared the center of the lake, she started to sink from the weight of the stone. People watching from the shore urged her to drop the rock, but she kept swimming, sinking more and more with each stroke. To the gathering crowd the solution was obvious. Their "drop the rock" chorus grew louder and louder with her increasing difficulty staying afloat. But all their yelling did little good. As she sank, they heard her say, "I can't. It's mine."

McKenna uses this story of a drowning woman to illustrate how stubbornly we can hold ourselves back. Susan, in fact, had many "rocks." One was her definition of a good job and, therefore, a good career move, what she called the "relentless logic of one's post-MBA CV." That rock was made heavier by her ambivalent feelings about sacrificing her ambition in order to be a better parent. Another rock was her fear of not having enough money, an understandable but untested fear. Although she knew what deep change she sought—better balance, greater meaning—when a job came up that allowed her to hold on to the rocks, she convinced herself that it was a good move.

The inconsistencies between what Susan said she wanted and the choices she kept making created fault lines in her evolving life. Taking the wrong job led to the first "crack" in a tight system of interlocking assumptions and priorities that, consciously or not, had always informed her career decisions. But without having had time to explore options, to experiment, to assimilate discrepant experiences, she simply doubted her judgment. She still could not see her own responsibility for the out-of-whack work-life balance; hence she was unable to make full use of the new information about herself to take stock of past events or identify future steps.

Many people in transition stumble onto the fact that they derive much of their sense of identity from their title and employer and that such an overidentification with any institution can lead to stunted growth in other arenas. Far into our careers we can remain the victim of other people's values and expectations. Susan worried that peers would think she was downshifting from an ambitious consulting career to the mommy track. When she accepted the wrong job, she got lots of validation: everyone wanted her business card and asked her to have lunch. She moved, not according to her own logic, but according to the logic of a "traditional" MBA career.

Becoming our own person, breaking free from our "ought selves"—the identity molded by important people in our lives—is at heart of the transition process. June's parents were proud of her Ivy League position, and her mentor felt he had groomed her for academic fame and glory. As she began to identify with the values, norms, attitudes, and expectations of people working in the business world and began building relationships with people outside academia, her colleagues attributed her diminished engagement to marriage and motherhood. She was no longer as available for lunches and extracurricular activities. Now that she had "a personal agenda," as her mentor had put it, she was obviously less committed to the scholarly life.

June, in fact, faced a typical dilemma: how to reconcile her ambition and her family responsibility. Her desire to better provide for her children informed her desire for career change, yet she recognized that bringing up motherhood in her job interviews amounted to shooting herself in the foot. She came to understand that the most attractive places from a career standpoint would leave her little time for her family. When her stockbroker, who worked for a rapidly growing U.S. brokerage house, encouraged her to apply there, she was not interested. Her strategy was to go for the "top names," figuring that starting at one of the most prominent companies would offer the best learning opportunity. A year into the search and exploration process, she took a different view. What at first had seemed so far from the world of Wall Street, so much less glamorous than private banking, revealed a different set of advantages: independence, flexibility, good training, good public schools for the girls, the prospect of buying a house with land around it, and a less stressful environment in which to earn her stripes.

In career transitions, the basic assumptions that typically prove most resistant to change include our benchmarks for success and our preconceived notions about what are viable or appealing work arrangements. Brenda's first reaction to a trigger—the menace of a cartoon picture—was to overcompensate for the void she felt by putting her career at the bottom of her list of priorities. She did volunteer work and considered a career in education. She struggled to reconcile her natural talents with her disdain for "women's work." But stepping back led her to a more creative solution, in which she combined the best of all worlds.

Even when we start a career transition with these deeper questions in mind, it can take time to discover what we truly want to change. Trying to tackle the big changes at the beginning can be counterproductive. Our customary mind-set about who we are and what others expect undermines us in myriad subtle ways. Just as starting the change process by trying to identify one's "true self" can cause paralysis rather than progress, starting by trying to change basic assumptions inevitably leads to an exercise in abstraction and, all too often, avoidance of real change. We are simply not equipped to make these deeper changes until we come to understand what they really mean, not as concepts but as realities that define our daily lives.

A Life of Possibilities

Major career transitions take three to five years. The years preceding the actual change necessarily involve difficulty, turmoil, confusion, and uncertainty. One of the hardest tasks of reinvention is staying the course when you feel as though you are coming undone. Unfortunately, there is no alternative but foreclosure—retreating from change either by staying put in the old or taking the wrong next job as Susan did at first. It takes a while to move from old to new.

The careers of most of the women in my study are still evolving. After two years with the brokerage firm that opened the door to her financial career, June was recruited by a top Wall Street firm. In her new position she now has the means to practice her teaching vocation: she has reinvented her job as financial consultant to include financial planning seminars, educational experiences for her clients, and television commentary on market reactions. Even more important to her is the "holistic" character of her new life: "everywhere I go with the children, their schools, their field trips, can and sometimes does lead to more business. All is joined together. There is no pull between the life of the mind and the life of the heart."

Today, Susan is working with the largest U.K. consulting firm that specializes in charities. She envisions continuing her career in the nonprofit sector but recognizes that she is likely to move back and forth from independent contracting to traditional employment and from consulting to line work, and has this to say: "All I hope is that I never again make the mistake of jumping before giving myself the chance to explore what I really want to do."

After two years in partnership with a more established agent, Brenda has founded her own literary agency and moved backed to the city where she grew up. Her conclusion:

> Being an agent gives me a complete career and a complete life. There's no trade-off. Sure, I get busy and, of course, on any given task, I have to decide what comes first, my job or my life. My life is more enjoyable all around. It's not just about work versus personal life. It's about "What's my voice? Can I be creative? Am I just a corporate drone? Do I just exist as a thank-you in people's prefaces? Am I a writer?" If someone were to draw that cartoon of me now, what would I tell the artist about myself? Lots: arts boards, philanthropy, a dog, a great marriage, a Jewish faith, Pilates, dance class . . .

Most of us know what we are trying to escape: the lockstep of a narrowly defined career, inauthentic or unstimulating work, numbing corporate politics, a lack of time for life outside work. But finding an alternative that truly fits, like findings one's mission in life, is not a problem that can be solved overnight. It takes time. Whether we feel closer to June Prescott, who struggled to leave the literary life she had so loved as a younger woman, or to Susan Fontaine, who lost her way following the logic of a "good MBA career," there is no substitute for constant exploration. We don't find ourselves in a blinding flash of insight, nor do we change overnight. We learn by doing, and each new experience is part answer and part question. Whatever the first step, the process gradually changes the nature of what we know and what we seek to learn. Transformation happens less by grand design or careful strategy than by the ongoing experiments that enhance our capacity to become the myriad possibilities that define us.

Sharon P. Whiteley has embraced the entrepreneurial path, launching and leading new businesses and helping business related non-profit organizations flourish. In her latest venture, she serves as CEO of ThirdAge, Inc, a content, research, and marketing company focused on aging baby boomers. She was previously founder and CEO of Peacock Papers, an innovative manufacturer of consumer products focused on celebrating aging. She is also on the board of directors of the Committee of 200, an international organization of preeminent women business leaders, and the recent author of *The Old Girls Network: Insider Advice for Women Building Businesses in a Man's World*.

In this chapter, Sharon identifies the key entrepreneurial challenges that women leaders face, as well as the unique opportunities and advantages that women bring to the table when leading new ventures. And she explains why, as consummate networkers inclined to connect hearts to minds (instead of brains), entrepreneurial women are uniquely poised to build sustainable organizations.

PHOTO CREDIT: Sharon P. Whiteley by Charles Vendetti

13

WOMEN BUILDING BUSINESSES

Courage to Find Your Way

Sharon P. Whiteley

I am an entrepreneur. I was born that way. I've built five companies so far and have coached a number of other businesswomen to do the same. Along the way, I've experienced the roller-coaster ride of conception, capitalization, start-up, launch, and growth—in good times and in bad. I know how entrepreneurs tap capital markets successfully, and I've led investment groups in making those decisions on the other side of the table. Most important, I've learned over the last few years a great deal more about what it takes for people to commit to a vision, persist through killer obstacles, and create a profitable and sustainable venture.

This is no easy task for any leader, and it is often particularly challenging for women. Not only is the ability to tap capital markets seriously biased toward men, but the dreams of women are less frequently expressed through the medium of business. Few of us were coached or encouraged to consider the possibilities that business brings. We don't naturally think about how creating and selling products and services can fulfill us. Most women dream about what kind of person they can become or what kind of positive influence they can have in the world. Before anything else, it's important for us to recognize that business is a powerful means for expressing our dreams and our urges for collaborating, nurturing, doing good—and, yes, our urges for achievement too.

Although entrepreneurship is gender neutral in my book, women have capabilities for launching successful businesses hardwired into their DNA. They bring certain natural instincts to leadership, which can be instrumental to the success of emerging or struggling businesses. In this chapter I will talk a little about my own most recent experiences founding and leading a new company, as an example of some of the challenges that exist for women in today's business environment. I'll describe the vision and passion that drive a real-life venture, and show how the formative values of the company can foster the resilience necessary to survive the inevitable growing pains and unexpected hurdles. I will also talk about the strengths that women, in particular, bring to the arena. My desire is to encourage more women to express their dreams through the ventures they are launching, collaborating on, or joining.

Passion: Are Women's Dreams Less Worthy of Investment?

The starting point behind every business idea is passion. For entrepreneurs, passion is the urge or compulsion to express our creativity by bringing something new into the world—something that we may have daydreamed about for many years, something that excites and energizes us to the core. Often, successful businesses spring from a lifelong interest, a particular strength or a hobby from which we now want to earn a livelihood—or make our fortune. One needs to distinguish between a vision of what's possible, however, and a mere fleeting fantasy.

The business I'm currently leading is called ThirdAge, Inc. It is an online lifestage company focused exclusively on serving the needs and interests of aging first-wave baby boomers—midlife adults generally in their forties through sixties—and those who want to reach them. It was founded in 1996 as ThirdAge Media, a company that gained rapid success and celebrity as a promising Internet darling. In 2000, following the collapse of the high-tech bubble, the company was purchased by an Internet company in the ancestry business, MyFamily.com. Nine months later, in 2001, several investors and I bought the company through our investment group, 8 Wings Ventures LLC, and renamed it ThirdAge, Inc.

Although ThirdAge technically isn't a start-up, it clearly would not constitute an organization in a mature phase of growth. The business community would likely classify it as a restart; I prefer the term *fresh start*. As was the case with many Internet companies, ThirdAge experienced an early phase of heady growth, then fell into dire straits because of the downturn in the economy and a flawed business model. It was resuscitated by our group of angel investors who believed that under an expanded business plan, there was a long-range opportunity. Where it goes from here depends very much on our vision, skill, perseverance, and good fortune in steering it toward sustainable profitability.

Even though I did not found the company or develop the original idea, ThirdAge fit my own passion like a glove. For starters, I felt the possibilities for the business almost viscerally. The market was magnificent; the company's brand was trusted; and with expanded, more diverse revenue streams, it represented an opportunity waiting to happen. I felt that through an expansion of targeted products and services and a synergistic set of distribution channels, the company could take off. It was, after all, focused on the needs and lifestage issues of the fastest-growing, wealthiest segment of the population. It was not just a hollow and abandoned dot-com. If we enrolled the right team, employed the right strategy, and executed well, we could become profitable, benefit many during a critical stage in their lives, and help positively redefine what it means to age in today's world.

The market for ThirdAgers is an increasingly compelling demographic that represents tremendous opportunity. By 2005, close to 108 million people in America will be over the age of forty-five—that's about 40 percent of the population.[1] And this dynamic group will control the majority of buying power in the country. ThirdAgers over the age of forty-five account for 70 percent of U.S. net worth[2] and have an estimated annual spending power of over 2 trillion dollars. To me that was going to make the tipping point look like a seesaw.

ThirdAge Media (the name of the old company) was a trusted brand in the business sector it served. The company understood its audience well—their preferences, priorities, and needs, and, as important, what was in their hearts and minds. It didn't see ThirdAgers as just a generic demographic slice of the pie. Rather, the company understood them at a much deeper level in terms of their values and their aspirations. So, whereas the original business model was no longer intact, what did survive the bust were two vital assets: a great reputation and a loyal following.

Passion for the business remained, as well. I felt a deep personal connection to this market. I am a ThirdAger myself, and earlier in my career I'd founded and built a company, Peacock Papers, that manufactured consumer products focused on positive and celebratory messages around aging milestones. Through that experience and my own life I knew that ThirdAgers were an untapped, misunderstood, and extremely potent group.

Incredibly diverse on one level, ThirdAgers are similar on others. Most are likely to have experienced one of those many midlife changes, transitions, or milestones that can shake a person to her core. For instance, they might have recently lost a parent; they might have been or be going through a divorce; they might have just changed careers. Their kids may have just left home—or they may worry about the success of those who already have. Not everyone reacts the same way to such disruptions, however. Some ignore the issue, others sink and don't rebound, and still others develop a new perspective and make profound and positive changes in their lives.

Regardless, today's ThirdAgers (or aging baby boomers, if you prefer) tend to have a different take on life. We don't view ourselves as seniors or as "grey-hairs." These are terms that simply don't resonate with us. In fact, today there's really no vocabulary that appropriately describes our wants and needs accurately. Speaking broadly, we feel free and empowered. We are interested in possibility and renewal. We may have discovered something about ourselves that we didn't know was there. We have an appreciation for exploring and learning new things and for giving back. We are interested in positive yet realistic messages about the aging process. We celebrate living and appreciate life. I would be remiss if I didn't add that we want to look as good as we feel. Quite simply we are redefining what it means to age.

As you can probably tell, I'm passionate about this market. I am also clear about my vision for the company and the values that need to be our guideposts. When it comes to turning dreams into action-able business ideas, nothing could be more important.

Vision

> The soul never thinks without a picture
>
> —Aristotle[3]

Vision is a clear articulation of your passion. It's a motivating force for enrolling and bringing others along with you. And it is a crucial step in building your business. Having described your vision, the next stages involve determining whether it can be translated into a profitable and sustainable venture.

In order to do this, you need to ask yourself some hard questions about your business concept. Is it a real business opportunity? Will you be able to compete successfully in the marketplace? What does your product or service look like? Who wants it? How do you deliver it? What value does it provide for your targeted customers? What do your competitors offer, and how well do they provide that product or service? Why would anyone want to join your company, and what would make them excited about the work? Does your idea stand the test of time, or is it vulnerable to an imminent shift in the market or other trends? If you cannot nail each question with a bulletproof response, go back to the drawing board. If, on the other hand, you decide that you do have a real business proposition and you can competitively and profitably sustain yourself, then the next query is, How do you go about securing the capital to fund your plan?

As a woman, you should know some hard facts. On average, 95 percent of all investor financing goes to men.[4] Despite this, women's businesses generate more than half the private sector output of our gross domestic product, and women-owned businesses employ more people than the Fortune 500 companies combined.[5]

So, if women-owned businesses are so successful, why is there such gender bias in the capitalization of those businesses? Women who start businesses have the same motivation as men: self-actualization, personal achievement, autonomy, and wealth. But the truth is, a double standard exists. We are still laboring under inequality—externally and internally imposed—and our culture and societal upbringing leave us at a disadvantage. For most women, there is not a long list of role models or mentors we can follow or seek as guides in raising capital and launching a business. Schools can provide us with knowledge, but the process is still very much an "old boy's network." The vast majority of deals are funded by referral through established networks. Less than 10 percent of venture capital partners are women, and only an estimated 5 percent of angel investors are women.[6]

Typical (read male) investors tend to have preset ideas of what is and isn't a profitable business. The types of businesses that women start are often seen as cottage industries, small and lifestyle-focused, that enable one to work part time or stay at home. When coming to the table to negotiate with investors, women bring a different approach and perspective. Generally speaking, we have different presentation styles from men and a lower level of comfort when it comes to talking about our own capabilities, expertise, and accomplishments. We tend to undersell ourselves rather than express our ideas in more assertive (rather than grandiose) terms.

Securing funding is also a highly critical process. Women tend to internalize criticism rather than use it to improve, making us more susceptible to the doubts and strain of the process. Although these are certainly generalizations, they do tend to ring true for most.

At the same time, women have some unique advantages. The myth of the entrepreneur is that "he" is a rugged individualist. The reality is that successful entrepreneurs are consummate networkers.

They know that relationship building is the essential link to capital, employees, strategic alliance partners, and all who contribute to their future success. Women are also not afraid to ask people for advice, introductions, expertise, and understanding. We are particularly adept at building relationships before we need them.

Not All Money Is the Same Color Green

Gaining access to funding channels also requires that you gain entry into a connected community. It requires knowing what your options are—from maxing out your credit cards (which I don't recommend) to gaining face time with angels or that coveted meeting with the elite world of venture capitalists. You should also know that 55 percent of all new businesses are started with an average of $5,000 from the entrepreneur's own pocket.[7] Understanding who and what type of person or institution is likely to fund your business is strategically key to your success. You must also be careful about what funding sources you turn to. Not all money is the same color green. Some investors will amplify your energy and the alignment of your values. Others, if they don't fundamentally believe in the same things that you believe in, may withdraw their support for your venture when the going gets rough or the opportunity to cash out presents itself.

Ultimately, the extent of your ability to obtain funding is tied to your credibility and experience as a leader, the type of industry you are in, the size of the market opportunity, and the rate of growth of the enterprise—its uniqueness and profitability. Nobody can predict the future, but you can predetermine the kind and size of business that fits your needs, your lifestyle, and your aspirations—and plan accordingly.

The final questions to ask yourself about your passion and the opportunities associated with your business venture are more self-critical. Put very simply, ask yourself, Will my efforts be worth it? What is my projected return on my investment? Will it be worth it to me personally, professionally, and monetarily, as well as to my investors?

Another way of asking these questions is to identify your real needs and your absolute, definitive, personal limits. These are key concerns because during challenging times—and, rest assured, they will be there—your passion will be the only fuel in your tank. Will your passion sustain you and be sustained by your efforts? Generally, I think there are two types of people who engage in launching and building a business. There are those who, metaphorically speaking, "will die" if they can't express themselves through the medium of business creation. For them it is their destiny. And then there are those who somewhat dispassionately have competently developed the skills to start and successfully build a company. If I were betting my money on an idea proposed to me by two such individuals, I would go with the first type, all other factors being equal. There's simply no substitute for passion and its twin, tenacity, when it comes to developing and sustaining a business through all reasonable obstacles and even those occasional unreasonable ones.

Leadership: How Do You Sustain Passion?

I was somewhat naive when our investment group first came on board as the new owners of ThirdAge. In hindsight, I'm sure that we were seen as wolves in sheep's clothing by the employees, but in reality this wasn't the case. My intentions for the company were sincere, but I needed to make that clear to everyone involved through my actions, not just my words.

Ten days into our tenure, the world and we were hit by September 11. The energy and strategy brought to the first critical months were violently and shockingly disrupted. Given this and every other challenge that we faced, we could only hunker down and try to stay alive. We weren't certain that there would be a future for the business at all.

As every entrepreneur knows, there are no guarantees, but your success depends on your commitment to your idea. I knew we needed to be tenacious and to persevere. This required more than just dogged determination. We needed to be resilient—and to tap into the optimism that is endemic to entrepreneurs. That optimism is how we find the confidence to drum up the money in the first place—and keep drumming it from stage to stage even when the well is dry. It's how we can hear criticism, ask questions, and even process negative news. And it's how we navigate through stormy seas on nothing more than a patched-up life raft.

Being optimistic doesn't mean that we beat our heads repeatedly against the same wall until we knock ourselves silly. Nor does it mean that when we hit rock bottom, we deny the problem or our feelings of fear, frustration, and anxiety. We need to somehow carve out time even to cry, scream, pull the sheets over our head, and withdraw into a fetal position for a day. Then we need to get up and face the issues. If we hit the wall, we need to find a way to go over it, around it, beneath it, or through it. In the early going at ThirdAge, it happened to us more often than I care to remember.

The truth is, I know that we would not exist as a company today if there hadn't been a constant inflow of positive energy that kept our vision in sight. I believe that energy follows thought, energy follows word, and energy follows voice. Along with a sense of purpose and meaning, these so-called softer sides of leadership are critical elements without which no leader or company can be successful.

Values Create Culture

From the beginning at ThirdAge, all who remained on board believed in the same overarching mission—to develop a great company authentically serving the aging midlife boomer population. The transition from the old leadership to the new also required us to be aligned in our values and to create a new culture together. One of the first things we did was work together establishing specific values we all believed would define what made ThirdAge and our purpose uniquely ours. We created a ritual to make the values explicit and seal our intention. The only thing that gives your values life, however, is to live them.

The work that goes into that value creation helps forge the culture of your enterprise—in essence, what becomes the soul of your company. Your culture is the manifestation of the values you live by. It's the foundation on which you build your business. It informs the critical decisions you make and the actions you take, as well as those you choose to pass over. No matter what values you espouse, your behavior, not your words, will define your culture. Competitors can copy your products, services, and pricing, but they can't "me-too" a high-performance, passionate, and fulfilling culture.

This change to a newly articulated set of values and a new culture was not easy for some people at ThirdAge. There were split allegiances between the former founder, whom I encouraged to stay involved early on, and the new leadership team that needed to be resolved. Lesson number one: a company, no matter how inclusive, cannot have more than one leader.

At the same time, I wanted—and needed—to respect and acknowledge what had come before us. Employees appreciated this consideration and acknowledgment of their prior efforts and accomplishments. This extra care contributed to the trust and commitment critical to survival. Lesson number two: respect the past and use what is positive from it to build your future.

The day-to-day challenges that occur in survival mode are softened by that sense of trust and safety. People needed to believe in me as their leader. They needed to trust my intentions in every action that I took even if they disagreed with the decision or the reasoning behind the action.

To create that sense of safety, you have to be a good listener, to grant people respect, and, when appropriate, to show compassion. Let them know they are appreciated for being truthful and authentic. This leads to lesson number three: truth hearing is as important as truth telling.

At the same time, being in survival mode requires vigilance in maintaining a positive environment. Negative energy is toxic in any environment, but for a company fighting for its life, it's a sure way to go belly-up. Negative energy, like all energy, is cellular. It expands.

It erodes creativity, precious spirit, passion, and ultimately your ability to perform. Lesson number four: do not tolerate negativity.

What Women Bring to the Table

Just as men have their unique strengths that they tend to bring to the business setting, I believe women have particular attributes that are useful to leaders. Many of these innate skills simply have not been consciously honed for business. The good news is that they can be easily translated and rapidly applied to the challenges that businesses face.

These attributes are not limited to women. Like all traits and abilities, they cross gender lines. But women tend to possess them more frequently and more markedly, representing both a cultural dynamic and a biological condition. The following are some of these core innate attributes.

Multitaskers

Numerous studies have examined the physiological difference in women's brains that makes them highly skilled at keeping a number of balls in the air at the same time.[8] A leader needs to touch on many issues, ideas, and problems simultaneously if he or she is going to thrive in today's business climate. The intensity and demands of leadership, along with the need to hold sometimes contradictory directions in mind at once, make for a great mental stretching that linear thinkers find nearly impossible.

Natural Resource Optimizers

A company often starts with a person and a vision and very little else. There's no product, no accounting system, no infrastructure, and no staff. Without the ability to optimize the resources available, few leaders will survive the early days. Women are natural resource optimizers, able to access energy and ideas that may be left untapped by a traditional business perspective.

Highly Empathic

Women have an ability to forge connections and to put themselves in someone else's shoes. We are also great nurturers. With all the difficulties, downsizing, changes, and stresses that businesses face, women are naturally skilled at being able to understand what someone is feeling, and we are more inclined to care about how much that matters. We are also able to show the flexibility necessary to manage people in different stages of their lives and with different styles of working.

Intuitive

Women don't have a monopoly on intuition; however, we are credited with being more in touch and socially more comfortable relying on this "inner wisdom." In today's business environment, when many decisions need to be made quickly and data are inconclusive at best, intuition is a powerful tool.

Natural Collaborators and Partnership Builders

Women are community builders. This ability is ancient and it's tribal—it's in our DNA. We are also inclusive by nature, inclined to seek multiple points of view and able to see value in a range of perspectives. This openness to diverse thinking gives us an advantage in today's business environment. We know how to align people's hearts and minds around an overarching vision and enroll in a collaborative fashion.

People—Not a Person—Build Companies

People build companies. Vision drives people, and values guide them. You can't build or lead an organization without really believing in something. We all know that. And you can't do it alone. If the people in your organization share your passion and feel inside that there's a reason for them to be there, then the best of their care and creativity will be released. As leaders we need to consciously foster flexible environments where people can grow, flourish, and be fulfilled. At the end of the day, people need to feel that they've gotten more from their work than their weekly paychecks, and they must know that they've contributed to something that matters to them—that has purpose. I call this connecting our hearts to our minds.

Women are particularly aware of what it takes to connect hearts to minds. We are certainly more aware when that connection is not being made. We question work, strategy, and vision when it does not make sense to us. We also are more concerned with nurturing and aligning people in a way that makes them more integrated in their work.

ThirdAge has managed at times to survive on not much more than "spirit fumes" because of a fierce determination, passion, and genuine intention we brought to our efforts. There is authenticity in our purpose that fuels us, and as a result we are smarter, more resilient, and more resourceful than we would be otherwise.

For the last few decades, many have written about the challenges of the glass ceiling for women, saying that their inability to smash through was the reason they chose to get off the climb. I don't think that's true. I believe that their choice relates to the availability and appeal of other opportunities. Whether those opportunities are in the corporate arena or the entrepreneurial field, greener pastures are always sprouting. It is incumbent upon leaders to till the ground in which people can nurture their own passions, unleash their brilliance, feel appreciated, and be acknowledged for their unique contributions. Leadership is as simple—and as difficult—as that.

 Two smart women, one great idea, zero regrets. That's how the new math works for Cynthia Cunningham and Shelley Murray, the authors of this chapter. Several years ago, Cynthia and Shelley found themselves working sixty-hour weeks to achieve success as BankBoston branch managers. They both wanted more time with their children, and the long hours on the job were creating a major barrier to motherhood. So they decided to change their lives. The solution was self-evident: share one job together. But it was also risky. They knew they would be subject to new (and potentially unfair) levels of scrutiny. They knew they would likely have to fend off subtle and not so subtle criticism, if not outright challenges. And they knew that sustaining their arrangement would require marathon-level resilience and perseverance. Given all of this, could they really have it all?

In this chapter, Cynthia and Shelley describe how they packaged themselves as one candidate, lobbied for a single vice president position, and excelled in that role once they attained it, operating at the highest levels of performance despite being constantly under a microscope. Their lessons are valuable for anyone contemplating an alternative career path for any reason.

PHOTO CREDIT: Cynthia Cunningham and Shelley Murray by Steve Robb

14

TAKING RISK

Lessons from an
Unconventional Career Arrangement

Cynthia Cunningham and Shelley Murray

We are two women who shared one job. For six years, working twenty hours a week each, we held a single full-time position as vice presidents in the Global Rate Markets Group at Fleet Boston Financial (formerly BankBoston). This was not a temporary solution to provide us with more flexible working hours during a particular stage of life; this was the right lifestyle choice for us, which we plan to continue for many years to come.

Imagine how radical our work arrangement seemed in the very conventional world of a major financial institution. We are very different individuals who shared one set of responsibilities, one set of performance objectives, and one performance review. Not only was our circumstance unusual, but so were our working hours. Most people who have flexible work arrangements cram longer hours into a shortened number of days, but we drew our limits differently. We each worked two full days and one half day a week, overlapping on Tuesdays. So neither one of us was physically present at our desks for the standard forty hours per week. On a busy trading floor, where the pace rarely slows down, the act of going home early carries with it special burdens. It was never easy to rise from our desks, nod good-bye to coworkers who barely looked up from their own work, and leave for our personal lives—but it was always worth it.

While such an arrangement is certainly not right for everyone, we made that choice because the opportunity for a more well-rounded and integrated life was too important for us to pass up. Just the same, the path we took was filled with difficult challenges. *There is no such thing as having it all.* It takes as much sacrifice, hard work, and stress to maintain work-life balance as it does to succumb to a lack of balance. The opposition from peers, the resistance from managers, and the worry of friends and family were difficult to overcome, as were the threats to our ambition, status, and income. Just the same, because so many women have asked us for advice about how to make an alternative career path work, we know there is a great desire among others to redefine the game. To that end we would like to be candid and detailed about the challenges and opportunities.

But before you begin to consider how to make a flexible arrangement work for yourself, we ask you to consider why you feel moved to take the risk in the first place. We strongly believe that the particular reasons for choosing an unconventional career path shouldn't matter to your employer or your peers. The reasons should matter only to you. Spending more time with your children is as legitimate as looking after your health, writing a novel, or working for a social cause. Whatever aspect of your life is calling out for more attention or devotion, an alternative career path might be the right way for you to answer that call. In the pages that follow, we want to tell you about our journey and experience, and outline some of the keys we found for making the best of the choice we made.

Selling a Radical Proposal

Six years ago, we were both successful BankBoston branch managers working sixty-hour workweeks. We knew each other by reputation as high performers. We also met at monthly branch manager meetings as peers. We recognized a similar drive, work ethic, and ambition in each other, as well as a similar strain. Our long and intense work hours were helping to further our careers, but those careers were also creating a major barrier to motherhood. We both wanted to continue to excel in our jobs, and we also wanted more time with our children. It seemed an impossible balance.

That's when Cindy approached Shelley with a novel idea. Why not package and promote ourselves as one candidate (with a combined thirty-five years of experience in the banking industry) to share a single job? We could spend half as much time at work, and much more time with our families. Despite the part about cutting our income in half, the idea sounded great. Yet it still took time for Cindy to convince Shelley to take the chance. Friends and peers asked, "Are you sure you want to do this?" Even putting the proposal forward to the bank seemed risky to our careers.

We knew that our arrangement had to make business sense to the bank. In retrospect, this was the most critical element to making our idea succeed. How were we going to help the bank exceed its goals while we worked in a different capacity? When we had sketched out our proposal and combined our résumés, we found that we had an appealing package, so we sent letters to all of the key senior executives notifying them of our interest. Many of them were intrigued and agreed to meet with us. One of those senior executives was a woman Cindy had gotten to know at a recent diversity retreat. She listened to our pitch. Although she didn't have a position available in her group, she sent an email to five of her peers, amplifying our message.

That letter helped get us in the door at the Global Rate Markets Group. Our experience as branch managers, combined with our sales, marketing, and analytical skills, made us an ideal candidate for the job. We received an offer that in fact doubled our combined salaries. We became responsible for the sales and marketing of commercial foreign exchange products through a delivery network of the bank's retail branches. In addition, we educated employees and clients on small business foreign exchange products and services.

In our proposal, we each agreed to work twenty hours a week, splitting the salary. Fortunately, and to BankBoston's credit, twenty hours a week did make us eligible for full benefits. One of us would be in the office from early in the morning until three in the afternoon on Mondays, Tuesdays, Wednesdays, and Fridays. We would leave by noon on Thursdays but remain responsible for voice mail remotely through the end of the day. Our responsibilities and objectives would be decided on as if we were one full-time employee. In other words, even if one of us had more aptitude for a particular aspect of the job, we would maintain seamlessness between us in how we fulfilled the responsibilities of our role. Likewise, our performance would be evaluated as if we were one employee.

Although it may sound logical and clear to have developed our parameters in such a way, it took a great deal of thought and some careful negotiation. For those considering their own proposal, it's best when a company has a flexible work arrangement policy in writing. When developing your arrangement, you need to map out all expectations clearly. The specifics should be in writing to reduce the number of surprises for both employer and employee. Such a document needs to cover the hours that will be worked and the flexibility that will be required from both sides. For example, what will you do if you have an important meeting on your day off but have personal constraints that prevent you from being there? Will you need to check voice mail and email every day? What will your manager expect? Although you cannot plan for every situation, clear boundaries are important.

Communication between employer and employee—and, to be sure, between the job-sharing employees themselves—is crucial. The situation works best when the manager demonstrates open support in the presence of team members and colleagues, and when the employee is as flexible as possible in meeting the business need. There is a fine line, however, between flexibility and personal compromise. If the employee allows that line to be crossed too frequently or in a precedent-setting way—either from personal volition or because of the pressure from managers or peers—then the progress that has been made may prove unsustainable.

Our first week in our new job-share arrangement provided us with an immediate trial by fire that set the tone for the challenges to come. Not only were we job sharing for the first time, but we had also joined a different side of the bank and were learning an entirely new business with a new set of teammates. Suddenly, our managing director called Shelley into his office. It was already midday, but he told Shelley that he had an important task that he needed her to complete before the end of the day. Shelley agreed to take on this mystery assignment with an enthusiastic smile. Her smile soon fell, however, when she learned what he actually wanted. It turned out that one of the senior executives was leaving the division for another position that very day. Our managing director needed a creative gift for that person. He needed it by four o'clock. And he needed it *engraved*.

Shelley was supposed to leave at three o'clock to pick up her son from school. She made other arrangements for his ride. Still, the challenge remained: how could she find a suitable gift and get it engraved in only four hours? The day was freezing cold. She hailed a cab, went to Shreve, Crump & Low on the other side of town, and spent a great deal of the bank's money on a beautiful picture frame. She asked if the store could do the engraving within a few hours, but they thought she was kidding. She left the store, found another cab, and headed toward the jewelry district in downtown Boston. The sixth jeweler she talked to agreed to do the job. When it was completed, she caught another cab back to the office and presented the gift to our managing director just in time.

He was thrilled with the present and the engraving job. The day had been saved, but Shelley was left wondering why she had been chosen for this task. Was it because she was one of a handful of women employed on the trading floor? Or was it because the managing director thought she had good taste? Or was he testing her to see how she reacted in a stressful situation? She suspected it was a combination of all three. Certainly, the ability to think quickly under stressful circumstances was a critical skill we were going to need.

Later, the managing director admitted that he had indeed wanted to see how we would respond to such an unusual request. Despite that challenge to our new status, or perhaps because of it, he became one of our biggest supporters from that day on. We found many times in the next few years that having his backing was critical to winning over our colleagues and navigating unimagined dangers. Although our managing director retired, he continued to support and mentor us.

Meeting and Exceeding the Daily Challenges

If we hadn't fully realized it already, we certainly received an early lesson in the need to overachieve and prove ourselves above and beyond the call. That sort of roller-coaster crisis management characterized our working life. Because we were constantly being watched and tested, overtly or otherwise, we needed to perform at high levels 100 percent of the time. We learned that you must always be on top of your game. And make no mistake: despite how seriously you may view the stakes, it *is* a game.

How does that game play out? One of the pitfalls of our arrangement was how severely our schedules limited networking with coworkers. This set into motion all kinds of ramifications and complications. On the job, we were working full speed as much as possible. Most days, people get up from their desks to exchange small talk, ideas, and even crucial information only after the trading day winds down. By that time, we had been gone for several hours. Nor did we have time for evening events either, something that also had a negative impact on our relationships with team members. One of our previous managers drove this point home when he told us, confidentially, that we were seen as an "enigma" by others in the group because they didn't really know us on a personal basis. Although an outsider might have felt that our manager had a reasonable point, his observation struck us as extremely unfair. To our minds, there were many people on our large trading floor who did not know each other well or at all. Yet because of our special status we were held to a different standard by peers and managers alike.

Some of the inevitable jealousy from coworkers was quite understandable. Our limits on working late hours were clearly defined, but most people, especially those with fewer personal commitments, are vulnerable when it comes to such boundaries. In our view, this is unfair to those who are asked to shoulder more of the load, yet it made us natural targets for the frustration that results. Although most of our colleagues said they supported our career choice, in reality some of those same coworkers tried to undermine our success. The fact is, you have to watch your back. Teammates may want you to fail, and you are not always going to be there to defend yourself. One of our colleagues, for instance, made a point of publicly asking what time we were leaving for the day even though our hours were posted on our desk for all to see. This was not an occasional or unintended moment of forgetfulness. . . . *He asked us this question every day for five years.*

In some ways, we can't even blame this colleague for his lack of understanding. Unfortunately, seat time or "face time" is still considered an indication of productivity. Even organizations that say they measure performance by objective standards of productivity still, unconsciously perhaps, judge effort by how early you arrive and how late you leave. Therefore, we were always battling the misconceptions of coworkers and the management team. We were not seen by everyone as completely committed or as fully engaged in the game. Even during friendly interactions, this bias revealed itself. When we ran into male colleagues, for example, they invariably asked about our personal life and family rather than a business concern or office issue.

The impact of this perception on our career growth was hard to overcome. Management did not necessarily believe that we really wanted to climb the corporate ladder—or that we were able to. We were made aware of how real this problem was come annual review time. Despite the fact that we continued to meet and exceed goals that are the same as those of our colleagues and that we consistently received high performance ratings, in at least one instance we received a lower evaluation and bonus than a colleague whom we outperformed. The difference? This colleague was in the office all the time.

In reality, however, we were mentally engaged with work 100 percent of the time, even when we were not at the office. We found it necessary to develop split personalities to manage our balancing act. Life between work and personal time was in constant transition, and we were always changing hats. In the midst of chaos at home, there were times when we needed to devote full attention to the job. We found, for instance, that it was necessary to provide each other with lengthy messages regularly during the day, describing in great detail what occurred on the job. Usually this kind of communication could be managed smoothly and required only an hour or so over the course of an off-day. But one experience of Shelley's was typical of what an afternoon could be like.

Shelley was in the kitchen cooking dinner. Her dog was running around frantically because it was time to eat. Her son was upstairs doing homework. She called for him to come down for dinner as it was time to eat and then leave for soccer practice. He called out that he would be down in a minute. She decided to make good use of that minute, so she told her dog to be patient a bit longer, and called in to check voicemail. Even though she'd checked her messages an hour before, anything could have happened in the interim. As she concentrated on an important message, her son came barreling down the stairs with his soccer gear, and her dog saw a squirrel in the backyard. This time, the dog ran straight through the screen. Once again, her work world and her personal world had collided with a bang.

As many challenges as there were in the office, there were just as many outside it. All professionals struggle with reducing their take-home work, but with our limited office hours this problem became magnified. We needed to know how and where to draw the line. Ironically, we both tend to overcommit outside the office. Because we have more time to be in our communities, it is nice to be able to devote ourselves to important issues. We are on school boards and local committees and are frequently asked to do more. Things get hectic, naturally, but it is a "good" hectic for a change. It is a pleasure to be able to say yes once in a while rather than no all the time.

Not everyone can work in this way. We were lucky that we had each other. Many people in flexible work arrangements have no one with whom to share their frustrations. We could vent to the one other person in the world who truly understood. If we had an issue with a colleague or a concern with a manager, we could put our heads together and come up with a strategic answer as to how we should handle this latest challenge. Thinking it through, we could decide to give up some tactical ground, push back hard, or change course altogether. Without that political and emotional support between us, neither of us is sure how we would have survived so long. The stress, frustration, and anxiety can eat you up.

The Bank of America–FleetBoston merger reminded us of how real and present this constant dark cloud of stress and anxiety could feel. When the merger was announced, our division executive gathered all of us who worked on the trading floor into a conference room to discuss as many details as were known and answer any questions she could. Out of sixty people in the audience, perhaps five of us were women. Looking around the room, we were struck by how surprised and anxious the men seemed. All we could think was, *they look like we feel every day.* Suddenly, the dark cloud was over their heads. As much as we could feel sympathy for the fear and uncertainty they were experiencing, we were also reminded of how the two of us lived with this feeling most of the time.

Staying the Course and Reaping the Benefits

We felt many threats to our job-sharing arrangement throughout our six-year journey. Two years ago, for example, we were suddenly asked to submit a proposal for our current job, as if we were coming into it for the very first time. It seemed likely that the expectation was that we would feel pressured by this request and would come back with a proposal that would involve us spending more time in the office. We held firm, however, and managed to preserve our limits. It wasn't easy, but it was always worth it. A bad manager can use an arrangement such as ours as a weapon to force you into a more difficult position. A good manager will evaluate your performance objectively and applaud you for your contributions to the team's success.

We have focused on the challenges and pitfalls in this chapter because those difficulties were an important part of our experience. Nevertheless, we do not want to leave you with the impression that this path has been a mistake. Given everything that was at stake, we have since realized that the far greater risk would have been not to take the chance at all. We talk to others about our experience because, when all is said and done, it is a very positive story that we want to share widely.

From the employer's side of the equation, there were many benefits. First of all, there was a cost savings to the company because it retained two talented employees. Second, the need for us to be focused 100 percent of the time made us more efficient; the company thereby achieved an increase in productivity, and, most important, we generated millions of dollars in revenue for the corporation. Third, our balanced lifestyle resulted in our being well adjusted and content, reducing the burnout that plagued so many of our colleagues. Finally, our success as job-sharing pioneers was good for the bank's image, inside and outside the company.

From our perspective, too, this was a positive experience. Fundamentally, we obtained exactly what we wanted. We spent more time with our children—time we simply didn't have before. We chose to set our priorities, and by being able to make those choices, we felt empowered and in control of our lives. We also developed new personal skills by necessity. For example, we became better communicators. To make our arrangement work so well, we had to be completely honest and trusting with each other. We noticed that this openness helped us in other relationships as well. Professionally, our individual strengths not only combined to create "a single," more complete, more well-rounded employee but also afforded us the opportunity to learn from each other. The net result: each of us became a better, more skilled, and more effective professional.

As balanced people, we gained the ability to give back to our communities through our involvement in the schools and various social issues. On top of all that, we felt better in terms of our overall physical and emotional well-being. For most people, there is a large gap between what is important to them and what they do with their time. With our arrangement, we didn't have that gap. It's a powerful way to be in the world.

There are difficult trade-offs, tests, and challenges, but in the end, our balancing act is one worth mastering. We can imagine no other way to live, and do not see ourselves giving up this lifestyle choice, even when our children no longer need us at home. At that time, we will be able to take on other priorities, callings, and desires to balance and enrich our lives in new ways. Part of that formula is work and the satisfaction gained from performing at top levels in a challenging and stimulating environment. But the space outside of work is just as important.

How important to you is that time outside of work? How would you benefit by developing a different relationship with your employment? Imagine what you would do with your life if you worked only twenty hours a week. If changing your lifestyle is important to you, we are certain that you can manage an alternative career path in this day and age. Doing so is only going to get easier, as more of us prove that success in our personal lives does not preclude success in our working lives. As a wise person once said, no one on their deathbed wishes they had spent more time at the office. We think that work should balance and serve your life, not the other way around. We hope our story helps you see the possibilities in your own life.

 Karen Stephenson, Ph.D., is a unique visionary and a pioneer in the rapidly emerging field of social network analysis. She has forged an innovative approach that integrates the natural sciences (quantum physics and chemistry) with the social sciences (anthropology). This approach has transformed the concept of network analysis—and won Karen international recognition as a foremost corporate anthropologist. Karen is the president of NetForm and a professor of management currently teaching at Harvard's Graduate School of Design. She previously held a position on the faculty of the UCLA Graduate School of Management as well as visiting anthropologist and scholar positions at Bolt, Beranek and Newman; MIT's Sloan School of Management; and IBM's Advanced Business Institute. Karen is also the author of the forthcoming book *The Quantum Theory of Trust*.

In this chapter, Karen helps us understand what happens behind the scenes of an organization's hierarchy. She confirms what many women leaders have long known: that networks are the central nervous system of an organization, and its signals cannot be ignored.

PHOTO CREDIT: Karen Stephenson by Bob Seidemann

15

TRAFFICKING IN TRUST

The Art and Science of
Human Knowledge Networks

Karen Stephenson

First they ignore you, then they laugh at you, then
they fight you, then you win.

—Ghandi

She had been mentored by the very best. It was all because the CEO
had had an epiphany. He had looked around his company and seen
that he was wheeling and dealing mostly with men—where were the
women in the equation? Why weren't they involved? And then he
realized that he was the sole party responsible for both the absence
and silence of women. In a quiet promise to himself, he decided to
change the context and shift the equation. And he did—she was
now CEO. But the appointment alone was not enough to garner the
impact he sought. Oh sure, he saw the press rally 'round her—both
praising and picking. But that's not the kind of recognition he was
expecting for his new successor. Instead, what he saw was that the
male managers within the enterprise didn't trust the new female
CEO—perhaps because they had difficulty trusting *any* woman.
Quite frankly, he had not spent much time in nurturing those relationships to get past that ol' familiar "gender issue." He also saw that
women managers did not trust the new woman CEO either! Did she
sell out? What did she do that they had not done or would not do?
Surely her promotion was not the result of mere meritocracy!!

If time is appropriately spent in building collegial relationships in the leadership network, gender issues can become irrelevant. But when leaders don't do their homework and fail to establish their networks, then other factors, like gender take center stage. In the final analysis, merit matters, but only when networks are nurtured.

Why Is the Web of Relationships So Important?

I have spent my entire professional career in hot pursuit of this single question. I've come to realize that the only way to inspire change, stir activity, or get anything done at all is to explore the hidden world of social networks—"grey markets" of rights, riddles, and rituals.

Such social networks exist within your organization. And if you are a woman leader, these are forces that you should not and cannot ignore. Indeed, because women leaders have so long been on the outside looking in, they in particular need to understand the various sources of power that exist within an organization. It's not just about simple and straightforward hierarchy anymore. It's also about social networks. Recognizing, understanding, and leveraging these social networks, then, are critical for women leaders who want or need to secure power within their organizations.

In this chapter, we'll review significant moments, milestones, and insights relating to the power of social networks. And we'll discuss the importance of the art and science of network analysis.

First, let me provide a quick overview about the research that forms the foundation of this art and science. As a corporate anthropologist, I enter an organization through any number of access points. About 30 percent of my access comes through human resources, 30 percent through the chief financial officer or chief operating officer, and 30 percent through the chief executive officer directly. I survey the population using a simple paper form, an online form, or, in some cases, interviews. No matter what the medium, the method is the same. With whom do you work directly? To whom do you turn for advice? To whom do you look for new ideas and new information? With whom do you collaborate and socialize? After I aggregate the answers to these questions across the entire organization, a series of cultural knowledge maps is produced.

I am talking here about how the relationships between people in an organization create the real pathways of knowledge, for the actual power of an organization exists in the structure of a human network, not in the architecture of command and control superimposed on it. My research is about making invisible workplace relationships visible by computer modeling the web of social exchange in both two- and three-dimensional forms. And the data always reveal some significant answers to a host of significant questions: Who is talking to whom (before and after the formal agenda-driven meeting)? Where do ideas get bottlenecked, and how do they get widely dispersed? Who has the authority, and who has the ability to make things happen? Why are the top salespeople effective, and what does that have to do with their proximity to customer service? Which candidate for CEO has a finger on the pulse of the organization, and which candidate has merely grabbed the current CEO's ear? Who among the senior partners is informally mentoring a younger generation of potential successors, and what does that have to do with their smoking habits? Why is the merger, which looked so promising on paper, failing to gel? Why did the latest middle-management layoffs, less severe than in previous rounds, leave the organization so much more decimated? Why did one factory plant become so efficient as compared to two identical ones?

By x-raying the social network of an organization, we in effect provide another and new way of seeing. Until very recently, we perceived organizations as a structural hierarchy that was both blind and deaf to another life force fomenting within. Tacit knowledge—the critical information that makes organizations functional—is in fact transferred not through established channels within the formal hierarchy but instead through informal relationships. And the medium of exchange is not just the *authority* of transactions but, significantly, the *trust* within relationships.

Without an understanding of this other world and its operating principles, women leaders will find genuine power to be potentially within their grasp yet nevertheless, frustratingly, at arm's length. And they will be marginally effective, at best, at managing and influencing their own culture. The missteps and misreads that result during reorganizations, layoffs, strategic initiatives, and promotion decisions are just a few signs of a larger cultural illiteracy that can bedevil all leaders (male and female) who fail to understand the social networks at work.

Such corporate failings usually indicate an incomplete portfolio of knowledge. An overreliance on explicit, procedural knowledge that can be readily taught or passed on in notes, instructions, or textbooks is the culprit. Tacit knowledge, in contrast, is developed through embodied experience; stored away in impressions, intuition, and instinct; and subsequently shared with trusted colleagues. The best leaders understand that this knowledge is a critical component of success. How one interacts with customers, navigates a bureaucracy, generates innovations, blows off steam without stressing the system, or increases the efficiency of a warehouse storage facility is not information that is always readily accessible. Such knowledge cannot be stored in databases or captured in instructional manuals so that it can be tapped when needed. Instead, it invisibly resides in each person's knowledge bank and is exchanged, distributed, or blocked depending on who that person encounters, trusts, or fears.

To understand how information flows through a network of relationships, I have focused on three archetypes of information sharers that exist in every social system—people I call Hubs, Gatekeepers, and Pulsetakers. Together they constitute a culture's DNA. Knowledge is encoded in these positions because they are located at the nucleus of trust. Knowledge is then replicated throughout the social system via trust-based relationships, which hold these key positions in place (see Figure 15.1).

Figure 15.1. The DNA of Social Capital

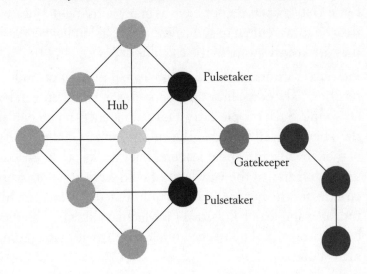

- *Hubs* are people who are socially connected to the nth degree. They have the highest number of "direct ties" to others and hold numerous face-to-face conversations, like the center of a star in a classic hub-and-spoke system. They are also effective multitaskers who can juggle many activities, concepts, and relationships. You have to be careful what you say to Hubs. Although they are not malicious, they are so connected that any message may be quickly spread and potentially damaging. A Hub can thus accidentally cause harm, much in the same way a child unwittingly causes embarrassment by speaking the unadorned truth.

- *Gatekeepers* serve as important links or bridges within an organization, functioning as human way stations on critical pathways between parts of an organization or between Hubs. When information must funnel through one person on the way to another, a Gatekeeper is the conduit. If this person likes you, he or she can act as a valuable broker. Conversely, if the Gatekeeper does not support you, he or she can slow down your progress by withholding critical information. Because Gatekeepers do not have as many activities to juggle, they have more time to survey the political landscape. And they are keenly aware of the calculus of power.

- *Pulsetakers* are connected through a great number of "indirect ties." They are almost the opposites of Hubs, unseen but all-seeing. Such people carry a lot of influence, much of it subtle. They are well versed in the culture, and a good proportion of them evolve into great leaders. They are key to knowledge succession and, at the very least, should serve as mentors and coaches for the newly hired and uninitiated. My favorite historical example of a Pulsetaker is Machiavelli, who observed court intrigue and influenced it masterfully without a prominent station.

These are the types of people at the nexus of knowledge within a network. And they transmit information amid a web of relationships using the powerful, cementing force of trust.

The Force Field of Trust

For a long time I did not realize that by studying networks I was actually staring at trust. Knowledge is biased and does not travel neutrally like currency in an electronic communication network (ECN), or electric currents in utility lines. Instead, knowledge ebbs and flows down hallways, in meetings, and in private conversations inside and outside the office. The key to the way that knowledge travels lies in the relationships that can bypass the standard organization chart. The quality, kind, and extent of those relationships are much more influential than most leaders recognize. Relationships are the true medium of knowledge exchange, and trust is the glue that holds them altogether.

What does all this mean for the individual woman leader? Among other things, it dictates that her effectiveness and power depend not on her position or title but, instead, on her connections to others in a variety of intertwined networks. As a woman leader, you have to pay attention to those many and varied connections. And you have to make sure that those relationships are infused with trust. Only then can you fully access the many important strands of knowledge existing in your organization's social networks.

Consider the idea that members of an organization are wired to others to produce a ganglia of interconnected nerve endings (Figure 15.2). Studying the figure, you begin to realize that the network is a collective intelligence that is greater than the sum of its parts. Conversely, this also means that the insight of any one person about his or her own network (the egocentric network) is, by definition, fundamentally flawed. Why? Because it is engulfed by the whole of the organizational network. If a woman leader can fly over the network or through it, she can also understand how to produce a tipping point—and how to best influence the organization more effectively through its key network nodes. Indeed, new knowledge or strategy will be accepted by the organization only if adopted by the networks.

Figure 15.2. Models of a Human Network Nervous System (Left) and of Biological Nerve Complexes (Right)

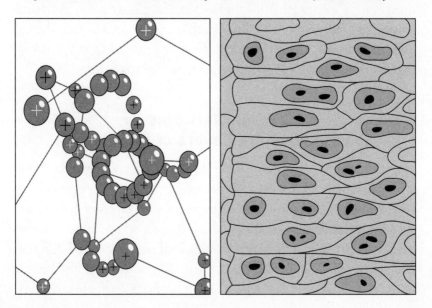

Despite the perceived authority of the formal hierarchy, an organization's real value is at the mercy of its social networks.

Let's take three examples that evidence the impact of relationships, trust, and social networks in everyday work life: mentoring, contract law, and office politics.

Mentoring is one of the oldest forms of knowledge transfer and, in many ways, still the most efficient. Mentoring programs that thrive do so because they rely on the building of a real relationship between mentor and mentee. Mentoring programs that fail do so because they force the relationship on the participants without the understanding that trust is the foundation for the real connection. It is the quality, not quantity, of reciprocal exchange that is proportional to a high level of trust.

Contracts that adjudicate between organizations fill a void where trust has not yet formed by controlling for the costs of transactions across organizational divisions. At the same time, when trust is present, contracts ensure that there is clean separation between transaction costs and trust so that the relationship may continue unfettered.

In terms of office politics, how many successful executive underlings have found that it is critical to gain the trust of the CEO's administrative assistant? Without tacit knowledge of the CEO's time constraints, meeting availability, priorities, and moods (which the top executive assistant can choose to share or withhold), it is unlikely that one will succeed in effectively communicating with the CEO.

Seven Networks
(and Seven Core Layers of Knowledge)

You can achieve complete cultural literacy by understanding that all organizational knowledge is not created equally. Specifically, in any organizational culture, there are seven core layers of knowledge, each with its own informal network of people who exchange information. Individual people move among all networks. And different people may play different roles in each—for example, a Hub in one network may be a Pulsetaker in another. So it is *who* in *what* network that shapes organizational knowledge. The following sections describe the seven social networks that I regularly use to discern the stratigraphic layers of knowledge.

The Work Network

With whom do you exchange information as part of your daily work routine? The everyday contacts of routine operations represent the habitual "resting pulse" of the organization. This network contains functional and dysfunctional processes. It is a *baseline* of knowledge containing valuable nuance as well as noise.

The Social Network

With whom do you *check in* to find out what is going on? This network is a strong indicator of trust. Healthy organizations have social networks strong enough to withstand stress and uncertainty but not overly demanding of people's personal or productive time. When social networks are sparse, it can mean two things: either the organization has just been formed and trust is nascent, or the organization has suffered a setback and trust is betrayed.

The Innovation Network

With whom do you collaborate to kick around new ideas? In this network, people talk openly about ideas, perceptions, and experiments without political concerns. People in this network do not hold sacred cows in esteem and may clash with keepers of corporate customs. There is a healthy amount of trust and irreverence in this network.

The Expert Knowledge Network

To whom do you turn for expertise or advice? Organizations have core networks possessed by key members who take solace in the legacy of the enterprise. They are the keepers of past traditions and procedures that they helped establish. As such, they are often uncomfortable or threatened by innovation. The people in this network form tight-knit core groups or cliques of closely held trust.

The Career Guidance or Strategic Network

To whom do you go for advice about the future? If people tend to rely on others in the same company for mentoring and career guidance, that in itself indicates a high level of trust. This network often directly influences corporate strategy, decisions about careers, and strategic moves.

The Learning Network

With whom do you work to improve existing processes or methods? Key people in this network may end up as bridges between Hubs in the expert knowledge and innovation networks, translating between the old guard and the new. Because most people are afraid of genuine change, this network tends to lie dormant until the change awakens a renewed sense of trust. It takes a tough kind of love to entrust people to poke holes in your established habits, rules, and practices.

The Decision-Making Network

To whom do you go in order to get decisions made expeditiously? Key people in this network know how to "work" the system, use old processes for new purposes, and in general get things done. This network is usually sparse because, under normal conditions, decisions are made through established processes and procedures. When this network is dense, it is indicative that existing procedures are in all likelihood broken, irrelevant, or never existed. In these instances, decisions become like market transactions and occur instantaneously.

An individual woman leader's understanding of the social networks within her organization usually determines her access to critical organizational knowledge—and thus the extent of her power, influence, and impact within the enterprise. Not surprisingly, a woman leader's understanding of social networks usually shapes her satisfaction with her leadership position and the organization in general.

Mapping Trust:
Decoding the DNA of the Organization

More broadly, understanding networks and the roles people play in them is the key to decoding the DNA of the organization. Network analysis can be used as a diagnostic tool in many ways. Insights rendered can be critical for the success of mergers, acquisitions, talent management, corporate restructuring, innovation, improving efficiency, succession planning, and deploying a communication strategy, to name just a few areas. Network analyses have been used by architects and interior designers to determine optimal workspace planning, CLOs who want to tap real knowledge and innovation potential, and the U.S. government in unraveling the networked world of al Qaeda. Here are several real-world cases taken from the NetForm database exemplifying a smattering of the applications.

The aerospace giant **TRW** learned that a procurement staffer three layers below the divisional hierarchy was an informal "personnel department." She was assessing the competencies of colleagues and matching them to the right jobs or directing them to appropriate training. Our work helped identify this shadow leader. The organization recognized and rewarded her. She was coached in the ways of the hierarchy so that in six months her promotion would result in a smooth and successful transition.

A medieval—er, rather a midlevel—university administrator at **UCLA** was, as a control mechanism, letting work collect on his desk, thus keeping it out of the hands of others. He'd taken up with a clique of grousers who reinforced his negative aura. The surprising solution? A promotion. It's hard, after all, to fire someone in academia—but promoting him disconnected him from his negative support group and removed him as a bottleneck.

The **Los Angeles Philharmonic Orchestra,** dependent on donor goodwill, upset some sponsors by failing to print their names in the programs. Information was dropping between the cracks. No one was able to understand how this could happen. The real reason? The development staff consisted of young new hires, whereas the marketing staff was made up of fifteen-year veterans. The net result: the two groups talked past each other when it came to thinking up new ways to do things. Hubs, Gatekeepers, and Pulsetakers were assembled in a task team to ensure that nothing more fell through the cracks (see Figure 15.3).

Hewlett-Packard was reorganizing and reinventing itself in the late 1990s. The company's founders, now deceased, had made famous their management approach (the HP Way). I employed network analysis and confirmed the long-held cultural belief that the HP Way consisted of management by walking around (MBWA)—in essence, nurturing the networks. I uncovered that the root cause of organizational pathologies was not the HP networks but a vacuum of authority, for example, hierarchy missing in action. The HP response was an organizational swap whereby powerful networks begrudgingly gave ground to a new imposed hierarchy.

The royal tombs in ancient Egypt were home to the bones of the dead. So it was with a sense of irony that I was staring up at a six-story modern pyramid of **Steelcase,** a manufacturing firm, home to research and development. The company's tacit policy was "creativity on demand" producing over the years a state of cultural exhaustion. A return to former levels of creativity was achieved by diagnosing undiscovered but thriving areas of innovation. The solution consisted of integrating the measurement of the networks as part of individual and collective performance, reinforced with a redesign of the workspace.

Figure 15.3. The Innovation Network at the Los Angeles Philharmonic

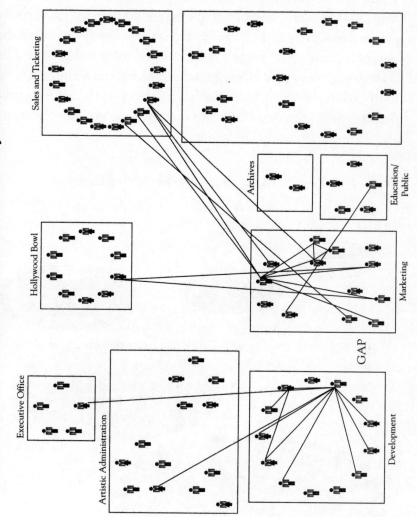

Social networks also proved to be key for the naval operations for Warfare Requirements and Programs at the **Pentagon.** Figure 15.4 is the image of an organizational analysis conducted of the U.S. government, three hierarchical layers down from the president. Within each organizational segment you can see smaller subgroups denoted by densely connected circles. The perimeter of the circles is made up of microscopic dots denoting real people. The crisscrossing lines that fill each circle represent the reciprocal communications between individuals. It is obvious that the relative density within the circles eclipses the connections between them,

Figure 15.4. Work Network, Pentagon

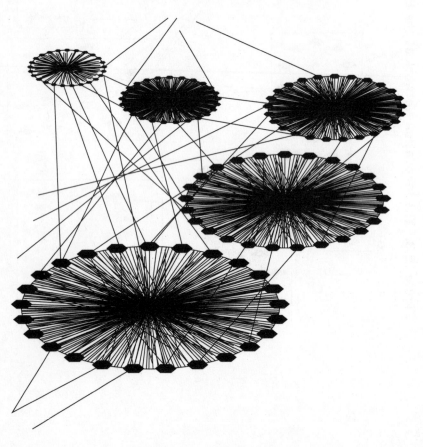

indicating that people spend their limited resources arbitraging information within segmentary or "siloed" divisions. The unhappy result: competing for scarce information produced a perilous mix of politics and human error compromising overall effectiveness. New technology was put in place to eliminate human error, freeing individuals to do the one thing that technology cannot—innovate.

A network analysis of a largely female-run **Head Start** agency revealed an unusual pattern, one in which men were communicating exclusively through a subset of the women. There seemed to be no rhyme or reason for this particular pattern, as it cut across division, function, and tribe. On reviewing the anomaly with the company's president (who was not a member of the clique), she too was stumped. On hearing the names read to her, she proclaimed, "I've got it—they're all smokers!" One further note: none of the men had previously smoked. They nevertheless risked potential long-term health hazards for short-term access to information.

In a merger of two container plants, **International Paper** had to wrestle with decisions around what would be outsourced and what would remain with the new entity. Management quickly came to certain decisions about retaining key players. Our network analysis indicated, however, that the key players were only a part of a greater knowledge network. Management's initial decisions about retention of talent were based on individuals, not on the collective intellectual capital of the network. When they considered the broader implications of outsourcing in light of organizational knowledge, they came to a different set of decisions.

Women made up less than one percent of the directors at **JP Morgan** in the early 1990s. By 2001, the firm's population of directors was fifty percent men and fifty percent women. A network analysis showed that the statistically balanced population at the director level shared a healthy dialogue between male and female counterparts. Closer examination, however, revealed a hidden pathology. Men talked to each other at the director level eighty percent more than women talked to each other. Why? Female directors were still treating men as their mentors, modeling their behavior on their female predecessors, who in fact did rely on male mentors. But now, in a day of gender equity, this survival behavior was disabling rather than enabling. By still communicating through a male conduit, women were spending more time in circuitous female-to-male communications rather than communicating directly with each other, woman to woman. Building trust and true cooperation (and not competition) among the female cohorts was the next step in achieving effective operations by overcoming the legacy of gender bias.

Moments of Seeing

"Deep tissue" network analysis described in these case studies provides information most people sense but can't see. Executives are satisfied with these revelations because they can at last see what's really going on and are able to influence their organizations in a more profound and knowledgeable way. Rank-and-file employees are relieved because there is a rationale for recognizing their role in collecting, facilitating, and distributing tacit knowledge. This results in both management's and employees' having greater confidence in each other.

I have personally conducted many network analyses. And I have done so as an anthropologist. My goal here has been to decipher what real working knowledge is. People in organizations are intimately familiar with their own context, while the anthropologist is not. To a real extent people are right about what they are describing to me—it is their reality. But they know too much and see too little. That's where an anthropologist's interpretive eye serves as a corrective lens. What do I mean?

Every time I step across the threshold of an organization, I remember the research done on children's art. Most children draw what they know, not what they see. Similarly, when the untrained eye of a leader draws a picture of the organization, he or she does it on the basis of what he or she knows. The resulting image is usually a flattened organization chart, distorted in perspective; long on opinion and short on reality. To draw what you see, you must forget what you know. You must erase any preconceived notion of what the object is and draw only what is there. If all of us can do this, then we truly see.

The sad fact is that what people usually see inside their organizations is what they know—an explicit structure—in exactly the same way that we walk into any building and see its physical architecture. What they do not see is the shape of an invisible culture that fills the organization, in much the same way that people can't see the shape of the space that fills a building. Although there is safety, security, and certainty in the explicit hierarchical structure of organized work, there is precious little representation of another, equally valid, and very real worldview of its hidden culture. By connecting the dots revealed by network analysis, an anthropologist can bring into focus an emergent, shadow world beneath the formal one.

The Accidental Anthropologist: A Nonconformist's Triumph over Bureaucracy

I am fortunate to be an anthropologist, if only by accident. The story of my journey to that discipline (and to my passion for social networks) is a tale of two identities, one with relevance for any woman leader. For that tale is illustrative of the value in nonconformity—and the stifling danger of playing by and with the rules of the bureaucracy.

I vividly remember an early, crystallizing moment in that journey. I had graduated from college and was working as a research chemist in Salt Lake City. One evening, after ruminating over molecular structures all day in my office, I glanced down from the mezzanine onto the laboratory floor below. Chemists, physicists, and technicians were milling about the lab benches enmeshed in their work, colliding and dispersing in a swirl of motion that reminded me of the way molecules or subatomic particles interact. I froze. Instantly, a picture formed in my mind, and I saw a pattern of connections formed from familiar exchanges that had been invisible to me before. Over the next few months, I continued to observe such patterns in action.

I saw these patterns largely because of the parallel lives I had been living in both the arts and sciences. While pursing my undergraduate studies in chemistry and physics at Austin College in Texas, I also privately maintained my lifelong studies in the visual arts. Although I was unwilling to substitute art for chemistry, I was willing to make art my second major. And, eventually, I was drawn to the field of iconography of art—and indirectly to the discipline of anthropology by using art and artifacts to reconstruct the ancient trading patterns of the Mayans and Egyptians.

Track back to that moment on the mezzanine. When I saw the pattern of human interactions taking place in real life and coupled them with the archeological work I had done in reconstructing ancient human interactions, I decided that the idea was robust enough to follow up on in a disciplined way. After all, it was all about recognizing patterns. So I transferred all of my postgraduate studies in quantum chemistry and mathematics—much to the chagrin of Professor Henry Eyring in the chemistry department—to the department of anthropology. I subsequently received a master's degree for developing a new mathematical model for analyzing human networks.

Five years later, I moved to Boston with my husband and son, landing at Harvard. I did not find it easy to carve an innovative path while fulfilling requirements for my Ph.D. Perhaps because I had been in the corporate world, I had little patience for the antiquated rituals of academia. Yet I pressed on, regardless of the obstacles. The folks at Harvard initially urged me to become an archaeologist. I demurred—I was tired of piecing together the incomplete puzzles of dead people's cultures. I wanted to understand living cultures in which all the pieces are alive and moving. Meeting me halfway, my professors suggested that I model myself after Margaret Mead and live among tribal elders, such as the Mayans. But if I were going to study strange, exotic behavior, I wanted to go where the real action was—to strike at the solar plexus of the modern corporation, an unexamined heart of darkness. Although not the usual anthropological fare, it was compelling to me.

Persuading professors, corporations, and potential funders of my idea proved daunting—and ultimately unsuccessful. But I didn't give up and decided that I could pay my own way through by consulting. Toss in a few scholarships, I figured, and I just might make it. The lesson here: have the integrity to hold true to your ideas and it will immunize you against institutional attempts to transform you into a Stepford student. Who wants to be a professor's clone (aka protégé), when you can be an independent product of your own thinking?

After pounding on many corporate doors and having as many slammed in my face, Bolt, Beranek and Newman (BBN), the technology company founded by MIT professors (they are the ones responsible for the @ sign in email), decided to enlist me. My professor's skepticism about my unique approach evaporated upon their recognition that the Harvard Business School (HBS) was jealous of my opportunity to study BBN, an opportunity long denied to them. It's always heartwarming when one vice trumps another. Later, I discovered that BBN founder Richard Bolt was a personal friend of Margaret Mead. Coincidence?

During my dissertation writing, I was a careful listener, responding discreetly and respectfully. As attempts among BBNers to surreptitiously play me for information failed, they began to trust me. In method, I functioned exactly like a cultural anthropologist studying a hunter-gatherer tribe. I took copious notes, attended meetings, watched how and in what order people spoke. As part of my thesis, I developed formulae for ranking the significance of individuals as knowledge conduits, and began calculating how networks emerged and changed over time.

With Ph.D. in hand, I went west to the business school at UCLA to continue my research. And it was there that I finally and fully ran into the obstacle of bureaucracy. As the only anthropologist in the business school and the newest junior member to join the faculty of this public institution, I was a bit taken aback at the sheer number of private, closed-door meetings during which faculty members obsessed over unwritten rules, behaviors, and dress. Social scores were kept over every slight. Differing ideas about scientific research were taken personally. I was explicitly instructed to steer clear from the Margaret Mead model of reaching out to the public and to instead adopt a competitive strategy of narrowing my field of potential discussants. My goal according to the academic bureaucrats was to create an intellectual fortress built up through years of obfuscation with the tools of an arcane academic language. Following such an approach, if I played my cards right, I could eventually work my way up the ladder to an apotheosis, at which point there would be only one other person in the world with whom I could have a conversation about my research. This was allegedly the height of intellectual achievement.

I have never and will never conform to such a stifling bureaucracy. And I didn't then, either. For instance, when I pointed out the relativity of hierarchical rules, one UCLA economics professor (a rumored confidant of the deified Alan Greenspan), proclaimed, "What hierarchy? I see no hierarchy here at UCLA." My deadpan response: "Well, if you look 'straight out' from the top of a hierarchy, you can't see the organization below." I'm not sure if my comment ever fully registered.

After a decade at UCLA, my resignation in 2000 marked my coming of age in academia. I gleefully accepted Harvard's invitation to come back east and teach at the Graduate School of Design. I had, in a sense, returned to art. And, in so doing, I encountered far less bureaucracy. Perhaps this was due to the fact that Harvard doesn't care about becoming "the UCLA of the East" and is instead focused, for better or worse, on being "the Harvard of Harvard." Or perhaps this had nothing to do with a particular institution at all. Perhaps it was because I had finally learned how to triumph over bureaucracy—by completely ignoring it.

Lessons Learned

Here's one important truth that I have learned from my personal journey: streamlined org charts, precise reporting relationships, and established bureaucratic procedures create a traffic grid, a visual composition of formal structures for how things should work. The fact that things actually work much differently, and sometimes at complete odds with the formal apparatus, leads us to the discovery of a second world, buried beneath the first.

It was a bitter pill to swallow when the test case for my theories came from the World Trade Center towers, not the ivory tower. The field of research and practice I had spawned in the 1990s was growing—competition surged. But then the cacophony of entrepreneurialism was stilled with the collapse of the World Trade Center towers on September 11, 2001. Never was the case for the power of networks made more obvious than on that day in that single event, but not in the way most people think. Al Qaeda is a network, but any network's success depends on its host. And what better host than a U.S. government that did not or would not talk or walk across organizational walls and halls? It was the same bureaucratic phenomenon I had earlier witnessed within the American university system—a problem that is plainly not unique to that system.

The lesson here for women leaders in today's organization? We ignore trust-based networks at our peril. When we do, key employees are not retained over time. Mentorship breaks down. Institutional memory seeps away. Manipulative blowhards who have the boss's ear get promoted over more talented but less visible rivals. Lacking the psychological safety net of trust, many employees run away from risk rather than run toward it.

Please don't consider this an indictment of hierarchy, however. Hierarchy is an important aspect of an organization's structural integrity. It is, in fact, half of the knowledge equation. But hierarchy's power cannot be confused with that of the equally real and relevant social networks that account for so much organizational knowledge. In the final analysis, hierarchy and networks should be yoked together to ensure balance and accountability.

By respecting the social networks in her organization, keeping the trust of its powerful Pulsetakers, forming alliances with the Gatekeepers, and strategically positioning herself with the Hubs, today's woman leader can optimize power, innovation, and efficiency. At the same time, she needs to remember that only the hierarchy can turn all of this cellular anarchy into order. The woman leader should respect and leverage the hierarchy accordingly.

I have been branded the "Queen of Between" for my contribution to the network theory and its application. Guilty as charged. In truth, I'm really a closet hierarchist because I recognize that hierarchies will always have their place in organizational structure. Hierarchies can neutralize networks but networks can unhinge hierarchy. In the end, it is a dilemma—and an uneasy balance of power.

Bruce Patton, Michele Gravelle, and Scott Peppet, collaborators at Vantage Partners LLC, coach leaders around the world to handle negotiations and difficult conversations more productively. One of the founders of the Harvard Negotiation Project, Bruce is a coauthor of the best-sellers *Getting to YES* and *Difficult Conversations*. He has conducted interventions within numerous leading organizations as well as on the world stage (for example, training all parties before the constitutional talks that led to the end of apartheid in South Africa and working at the behest of both governments to resolve the U.S.-Iran hostage crisis in 1980). Michele Gravelle is an independent consultant who was formerly the executive director of Vantage Partners's corporate education business. Her work focuses on teaching individuals and organizations how to manage their most important relationships more effectively. Scott Peppet is a professor at the University of Colorado School of Law and a recognized leader in the field of negotiation and alternative dispute resolution ethics.

This chapter provides us with tools to communicate in respectful, productive ways in the face of conflicts in the workplace that endanger performance, productivity, morale, and trust. It explains how today's leaders, equipped with these tools, can change the nature of power and partnership.

PHOTO CREDITS: Bruce Patton by Stephen Jennings; Michele Gravelle by Linda Holt; Scott Peppet by Casey A. Cass, University of Colorado, Publications & Creative Services

16

ENLIGHTENED POWER THROUGH DIFFICULT CONVERSATIONS

Bruce Patton, Michele Gravelle, and Scott Peppet

Every leader faces vexing dilemmas in using her power to further group goals. Traditional leaders, for example, are tempted to articulate a comprehensive vision and pull whatever levers are at their disposal to ensure that followers enact that vision. Indeed, for many this is the definition of leadership—a willingness to stick one's neck out, say one's piece, and take the consequences if decisions go awry.

Such a leader may look decisive, efficient, confident, honest, transparent, and forthright, and others may indeed follow, whether because they agree with the leader's views or because it doesn't seem worthwhile to disagree. In either case, subordinates may value knowing where the captain is steering the ship.

But this top-down approach to leadership may also look power-hungry, domineering, overconfident, arrogant, or brash, and it often fails to achieve the intended goals. It may alienate colleagues and staff and cause them to shut down, withdraw, or second-guess in private. Followers who do not participate in or agree with the vision are less likely to enact it enthusiastically (lack of "buy-in") or effectively (lack of understanding). Moreover, a vision informed only by one person's experience is likely to be less robust (less able to foresee and cope with contingencies) than one reflecting multiple diverse perspectives and experience.

Women leaders, because of lingering cultural stereotypes, are especially vulnerable to some of the negative perceptions associated with an assertive, top-down style, and many, perhaps because of more "relational" socialization, are more sensitive to the costs of this style. As a result, many women leaders seek to exercise their power in a more "enlightened" and inclusive way.

Unfortunately, a leader who seeks to overcome the limitations of a top-down approach by being inclusive faces the reality that the more people who are involved in decision making, the slower the process becomes. Indeed, the more inclusive a decision-making process, the more likely that divergent views will emerge that are not easily reconciled. If broad participation results in de facto joint decision making, no consensus may be possible, and a "majority rules" decision may also do little to engender buy-in. In a world of competition moving at Internet speed, delay or deadlock can be deadly.

Moreover, in the urge to be inclusive, the leader may be tempted to mute her own perspective and restrain her judgment so that others are less withholding or "political" in their own input. But a leader often brings unique and broader insight that, even if not perfect, may still be among the most valuable inputs into a discussion. Censoring or delaying that input may put the organization at a competitive disadvantage. In addition, people may second-guess the leader and spend inordinate amounts of time "reading the tea leaves" to ascertain the leader's true feelings and intentions. Cliques may form of those in or out of the proverbial loop, if the leader shares an honest view with certain trusted colleagues while obscuring the message for others. People may even lose confidence in the leader's ability and wonder at her unwillingness to state her views clearly.

More generally, leaders, like other managers, often find themselves torn about how direct to be in offering feedback, especially negative feedback. Being forthcoming ensures that the recipient gets the message clearly, but it may also be demotivating and hurtful, with negative consequences for the ongoing relationship and even for relationships with others who witness or hear about the conversation and wonder who will be next. Yet being less direct, perhaps by "easing in" through leading questions, can be frustrating for both parties and is usually no more effective in improving performance and motivation. Over time, avoiding direct conversation may itself erode trust and put strain on a relationship.

A Fruitless Discussion

To make these ideas concrete, let's look at Barbara's story, which is an amalgam of several real situations. Barbara is a midlevel manager at a financial services firm, with six direct reports. Barbara finds it easy to be encouraging, supportive, and compassionate with her colleagues and reports. When it comes to delivering bad news, however, she becomes tongue-tied, loses her confidence, and stumbles through conversations. She fears that others will get upset, go over her head, dislike her, or think poorly of her if she confronts them directly with negative feedback.

Now Barbara needs to let Sally, one of her reports, know that Sally's recent work was unacceptable. Barbara's tendency is to sugarcoat difficult facts and beat around the bush. This makes her feel better about the relationship—she doesn't worry as much that she has offended a subordinate, even though she knows that her message gets a little muddled this way.

Her conversation with Sally is no exception. Barbara begins by alluding to her dissatisfaction with something in Sally's work, but remains very general and vague about what exactly the trouble is. They then talk about several tangential matters, as well as some personal issues. Finally, Barbara comes back to the issue at hand, saying the following:

> *Barbara:* So, Sally, what I really want to know is how you think you handled the Jackson account last quarter. I mean, did you feel that it met your targets?
>
> *Sally:* Well, I thought it went OK. I mean, obviously we didn't get the returns we expected, but overall I was happier at the end of the quarter than I expected to be.
>
> *Barbara:* That's good . . . that's good. I know it was a difficult quarter for everyone. Is that what you think led to the

below-target figures, or was there something particular to this account that we should work on?

Sally: I think the problem, honestly, is that the sales team gave us poor information at the start of the quarter, and we didn't know the client's real needs until too late in the game. I would have been more aggressive, but I just didn't have the information I needed.

Barbara: Well, OK. It sounds as if you expect things to improve now. I certainly would like to see you succeed with this account, so I'll be counting on you to get those numbers in by quarter-end this time!

Barbara is using various strategies to try to deliver her message without being too direct or aggressive. She doesn't want to come across as too bossy or negative, and she says that her purpose is to "keep Sally's morale and energy up." She therefore avoids coming right out and telling Sally that her performance was unacceptable. Nor does she tell Sally what Barbara really believes—that Sally has been distracted by her planning with several friends to create a start-up company on the side. Instead, Barbara hedges her statements and asks questions to try to lead Sally to what she sees as the right conclusion—that Sally dropped the ball.

Unfortunately, it doesn't work out that way. Sally leaves this conversation feeling unsure about Barbara's message and intentions. It is clear to Sally that Barbara was trying to say something about Sally's performance, but she doesn't know exactly what. More important, Sally has no clear idea about what to do differently going forward—other than to produce better results. If Sally was unaware of what she might do differently, she remains so after this conversation.

Some may think at this point that the answer is simply for Barbara to be more direct: "Sally, your performance this past quarter has not been up to standard. I know the economy is difficult, but that just means you needed to work harder, and you didn't. . . . I don't want to hear excuses about how others are to blame. I want you to look at what *you* should have done differently. To be frank, I think you spent too much time planning your start-up and not enough time doing your job. In fact, I think you were so distracted that you didn't even realize you were dropping the ball."

This would be clearer, but it is not without its own costs. Sally may not feel understood or fairly treated. Barbara's concern that Sally will become demotivated may be well-founded. Sally may conclude that Barbara has already made up her mind and isn't interested in hearing "the truth" (which to Sally is more complicated), leaving Sally angry and alienated even as she says something to get Barbara off her back: "I didn't realize you saw it that way. I'll definitely try to do better next quarter." Sally, who doesn't see "more time" as an answer, doesn't learn what she *could* do differently, and Barbara doesn't learn if there *is* a problem with marketing.

Intriguingly, neither Barbara nor Sally is likely to see the problematic results of this conversation (whichever way it went) as *her* responsibility. If asked, Sally would say something like "Barbara wasn't being very clear. I know she wants me to do better, but she just isn't very good at giving helpful advice. And she really doesn't understand what I'm up against." Perhaps more important for our purposes here, Barbara would similarly deflect. If asked why the conversation unfolded as it did, she might say something like, "Sally is so impossible. I really don't think she wants to learn or improve. She gets so defensive; she's always coming up with excuses. Frankly, I've about had it with her. All I can say is that she better improve her results."

In our work with leaders of all types, we have learned that most individuals have difficulty speaking effectively about sensitive issues, and even more difficulty taking responsibility for that fact. Managers and executives come up with all sorts of useful strategies to dodge being direct, and to dodge looking at their dodging! One organization we work with, for example, recently changed its year-end performance appraisal system. Managers began giving 2s instead of 1s to some of their direct reports, after acknowledging to each other that not everyone in every work group deserved the highest possible mark on every evaluation. When employees pushed back, however, the managers shrank from honest feedback. They didn't want to take responsibility for their assessments face-to-face, so they blamed the upper-level executive team by saying that the executives had restricted the number of 1s that the managers could award. It was easier to blame the system than engage in the difficult conversations about performance that needed to happen.

The Costs of Mismanaging These Dilemmas

Unfortunately, leaders who can't have productive conversations about difficult subjects can't effectively exercise "enlightened" power or manage the dilemmas of inclusive leadership. Like Barbara, they incur at least three sets of costs:

First, their role as leader suffers. Barbara knows that she didn't give Sally direct feedback, and she knows that others know as well. People have already been talking at the water cooler about whether Barbara will step up and do anything about Sally's performance. If nothing changes, the team will feel frustrated, upset, and disappointed in Barbara. They may lose faith in her ability to take a stand and to manage their work. They may ask themselves whether she is effective in representing them when she negotiates with others in their company, or with clients, on their behalf. They may doubt the feedback she has given them personally, or begin to believe that they too can shirk their responsibilities. On the other hand, if Barbara tells Sally what she is really thinking, the water cooler conversation may be about how Barbara is a hardass who never listens and doesn't want to hear bad news. Either way, her effectiveness as a leader is undermined.

Second, their relationships suffer. Whether or not Barbara has been clear with Sally during their conversation, she expects Sally's behavior to improve. If it doesn't—if Sally continues to get poor results and continues to seem distracted, Barbara is likely to become increasingly frustrated. Sally, meanwhile, may also become frustrated if Barbara keeps returning to these performance issues without being direct or without seeming to take seriously her view of the situation. Sally may wonder whether Barbara has just come to dislike her. Or she may come up with a story about Barbara's intentions—for example, that Barbara feels threatened by Sally's entrepreneurial ability or resents that Sally has enough family money to pursue a start-up. All of this is likely to put strain on their relationship, eroding trust and respect and making it difficult for them to work together effectively.

Third, they may suffer as individuals. Barbara is miserable. She knows that she seems unable to effect change on her team. She is aware of the damage to her reputation when she soft-pedals things, but she also doesn't want to be one of "those" women who pushes people around and develops a reputation for being cold, hard, and ruthless. She knows, in short, that she hasn't made Sally angry, but that she also hasn't garnered Sally's—or anyone else's—respect. She begins to doubt whether she can be a good leader.

Why Does This Happen?

Assuming that Barbara is a reasonably skilled, intelligent, competent manager, why does this happen? Why doesn't Barbara see the results of her flawed communication style—and change her behavior to get *better* results?

Unfortunately, it's not that easy. First, Barbara doesn't know what to do instead. She sees her choice as being between maintaining the relationship but losing the message (being indirect or ambiguous, not confronting Sally) or being direct but losing the relationship (telling Sally off). She is aware that neither is satisfactory, but sees no better alternative. She is stuck.

Of course, there is an alternative, known as balancing advocacy with inquiry and acknowledgment,[1] but it doesn't come naturally, and there are surprisingly few skilled practitioners available as role models. It is a skillset that has to be learned through hard work, practice, and reflection, so it is not surprising that Barbara and other leaders are not proficient, especially under stress.

Balancing advocacy with inquiry and acknowledgment means three things. First, your point of view should be expressed during the conversation. However, it should not be expressed as the truth or the final word, but rather as a hypothesis that you are actively testing. "What am I missing?" "Who sees it *differently?*" Second, it means that you should work as hard to elicit, understand, and demonstrate your understanding of different views as you do to express yours. Assume that others' views make sense given what they are seeing, and ask questions until you understand why. Then demonstrate (and test) your understanding by paraphrasing it back and asking whether you have fairly and accurately captured their thinking and feelings.

Third, for difficult conversations to be productive, the *quality* of your advocacy, inquiry, and acknowledgment needs to be sufficiently high. Quality in this context reflects an understanding of a tool called the Ladder of Inference, which shows why people can (and so frequently do) see things differently without either person being entirely right—or wrong (see Figure 16.1).[2]

The Ladder of Inference posits first that each of us has access to somewhat different information. Second, we can focus only on a

Figure 16.1. Explore Each Other's Reasoning with the Ladder of Inference

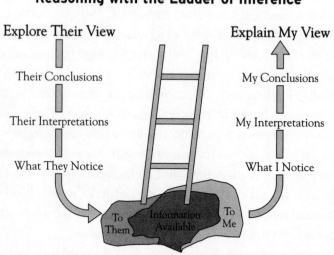

manageable subset of the information we do have, and different people will tend to focus on somewhat different things. For example, some of us will focus more on feelings, whereas others will focus more on logic and meaning, and still others on status and power. Third, from this subset of selected information, we each construct a cause-and-effect story about what is going on. Constructing a story, however, requires us to make inferences (guesses) about information that we don't have, especially other people's intentions. We base these inferences on observations of others' actions and our personal views of how people and the world work, reflecting our own experience. Unfortunately, a vast body of research suggests that as a rule we vastly overestimate the validity of our inferences.[3] Finally, we reach judgments and conclusions about people and events in line with our stories.

High-quality inquiry and advocacy involves sharing not just one another's conclusions but also the information, assumptions, inferences, and reasoning that underlie and explain those conclusions. If the other person's story makes sense as far as it goes, but seems to leave out key factors, note those issues and why you think they are important, then ask how the other thinks about them (rather than assuming that she hasn't). Likewise, when you are finished telling *your* story, help people test it by asking what is *missing* or *un*persuasive, rather than whether your view makes sense.

In this way, the goal of the dialogue becomes first to understand the internal coherence of different views and then to identify the key differences in information, interpretations, and assumptions that give rise to the divergence. From there, the parties can move to problem solving based on a more sophisticated understanding of the situation, or they can jointly construct tests of key differing assumptions to find out which are justified in this particular situation.

With the Ladder of Inference in mind, it is easy to understand why people so often genuinely see situations differently: they are working from different information, they emphasize different aspects of that information, and they are making systematically different assumptions about information that neither in fact has access to. Indeed, it is a wonder that people ever agree! The reality is that most situations are in fact ambiguous and more complicated than we realize, and any story or interpretation depends heavily on untested assumptions—usually much more heavily than people realize or acknowledge in their thinking.

This is the second source of Barbara's dilemma. Barbara doesn't realize the ways in which *she* has created an impasse. First, she doesn't question the completeness of her view of the situation. She assumes that her story is the "truth" about what is happening, so she isn't looking to test that view or find out whether Sally sees things differently with good reason. As long as Barbara continues to think about the situation this way, she will remain stuck. Like a moth trapped behind glass, she keeps trying to escape in ways that don't help—and may even make her situation worse. As the impasse with Sally goes on, Barbara becomes increasingly frustrated and increasingly blames Sally for their shared problems. Soon, she contemplates letting Sally go and fervently wishes that Sally would either shape up or leave of her own accord.

Second, Barbara is blind to the ways her own behavior mirrors those aspects of Sally's behavior that she criticizes. She blames Sally for being defensive, but ignores her own defensiveness. She faults Sally for making up excuses to explain poor performance, while making up excuses for why she doesn't talk more productively with Sally. She condemns Sally for not admitting that her outside activities are affecting her work, while keeping her judgments about that issue equally private and untestable.

Barbara and Sally are stuck because they, like many managers, leaders, and employees today, are trying to get somewhere with blinders on. Barbara is so focused on what's obvious to her—Sally's behavior—that she ignores the one thing she can actually influence: her own behavior. Barbara has no magic wand to transform Sally into the perfect employee. All Barbara can do (other than fire Sally) is try to change what *is* changeable: how *she* is acting in these exchanges with Sally. And that requires changing how she is thinking.

The Way Out: Shift Our Own Thinking

As Albert Einstein once said, you can't solve a problem using the same thinking that created it. To break free of the dilemmas of inclusive leadership and to exercise enlightened power by crafting actions that both lead and include others' perspectives, we must shift both the way we act *and the way we think*.

This is easier said than done. First, we must become aware of and learn to recognize how we are thinking now and how it affects our conversations. Second, we must learn to make five key shifts in the way we think about difficult situations, so that we can make corresponding productive shifts in our behavior. (We describe these shifts in detail later in the chapter.) Then we need to practice, because making these shifts is not something that we can do once and be done with it. Being human, we are never going to get rid of the problematic first thoughts and reactions that lead toward impasse and insoluble dilemmas. Our goal is simply to insert a new *second* reaction, a step of reflection and internal negotiation with ourselves, before we seek to respond to others and to lead.

Become Aware of Your Internal Voice

Sit still for a moment. What do you notice? Even if you're in a quiet room—no television, no telephone ringing, no colleagues talking to you—a quiet moment can actually be pretty loud. In fact, the more still you become, the more you realize that there's someone talking to you—you!

We all have an internal voice, a steady stream of conversation with ourselves inside our minds. That internal voice may be asking a question right now, such as "How long until dinner?" or "I wonder if I'll have the time to finish this chapter?" It may be daydreaming, worrying, or fantasizing. Or it may be coming up with a counterargument, such as "I do *not* have an internal voice!" Regardless, it is probably active—talking away even as you read these words.

Perhaps paradoxically, our advice is not to try to turn down the volume on this internal voice, but to turn it up. A leader trying to manage a potentially difficult conversation productively needs to become more aware of her internal voice. What is the internal voice saying while she's in that conversation? Is it helpful? Distracting? How is it either helping or hurting her ability to balance high-quality advocacy with high-quality inquiry and acknowledgment?

Most of the time, if we stop to examine our internal voice *during a moment of stress, conflict, or embarrassment,* such as Barbara's conversation with Sally, we discover a discomforting reality. Usually, the internal voice is not very nice, and it's not very helpful. Generally, it is full of judgments ("He's wrong"), blame ("This was her fault"), negative attributions ("She doesn't believe that; she's just trying to protect her turf"), strong feelings (hurt, fear, anger, frustration), and defensiveness about our own ego and identity ("I'm *not* a bad manager"). We call such thoughts "toxic," because they are poisonous to share or even to keep inside. We try to bottle them up in our internal voice precisely because we know that sharing them straight out would be provocative and unhelpful. But keeping such thoughts to ourselves is also difficult. We feel mistreated or cowardly. ("Why can't I stand up for myself?") And like toxic waste, such thinking tends to leak out in our tone of voice or turn of phrase, even if we don't pour it out. ("Yes, you *would* think that, wouldn't you?")

Before we can shift such thoughts into more productive channels, we must first become aware of them. We need to be able to recognize when our thinking is starting to resemble a toxic waste dump. Let's return to our example of Barbara and Sally.

Imagine that we could hear what was going on inside Barbara's head during the conversation with Sally that we described earlier. We might experience something like what's shown in the left column of Figure 16.2, which details Barbara's unexpressed thoughts and feelings during the conversation.[4]

Not surprisingly, Barbara's internal voice is pretty toxic. It is full of judgments, attributions, and accusations that she isn't sharing. She believes that Sally is fully to blame for the low numbers and

Figure 16.2. A Difficult Conversation

What Barbara Was Thinking and Feeling But Not Saying	*What Barbara and Sally Said*
I've got to say something about this, but I can't be too tough. Of course she didn't meet her targets— she was slacking off.	*Barbara:* So, Sally, what I really want to know is how you think you handled the Jackson account last quarter. I mean, did you feel that it met your targets?
You were happier than expected?! How can you say that! You are so blind.	*Sally:* Well, I thought it went OK. I mean, obviously we didn't get the returns we expected, but overall I was happier at the end of the quarter than I expected to be.
Now what do I say? She's got me on the spot—if she thinks it was so great, I'll really look like an ogre if I tell her off. Let her save face and show me she understands there was a problem.	*Barbara:* That's good . . . that's good. I know it was a difficult quarter for everyone. Is that what you think led to the below-target figures, or was there something particular to this account that we should work on?
There she goes again, blaming others and not taking any responsibility. She's so frustrating (and I'm so frustrated).	*Sally:* I think the problem, honestly, is that the sales team gave us poor information at the start of the quarter, and we didn't know the client's real needs until too late in the game. I would have been more aggressive, but I just didn't have the information I needed.
I can't help her. She's so blind. She just needs to get her numbers up—there's nothing I can do.	*Barbara:* Well, OK. It sounds as if you expect things to improve now. I certainly would like to see you succeed with this account, so I'll be counting on you to get those numbers in by quarter-end this time!

also fully to blame for the way this conversation unfolds. She has theories in her head about why Sally is so frustrating (she's slacking off, she's blind to her own failings, she takes no responsibility) and why she is responsible for the outcome of this conversation (to the extent that Barbara is ineffective, it is because Sally has Barbara "on the spot" and there's nothing Barbara can do).

Barbara does not say much of this to Sally, *nor should she*. Barbara's thinking here isn't very helpful. If she were to dump it into the conversation, it would make things worse, not better. Instead, Barbara needs to listen to and reflect on her internal voice, and realize how it is compromising her ability to act effectively in this conversation. When Barbara is thinking these toxic things during the conversation, it becomes difficult for her to say much of anything. When she is thinking Sally was "slacking off," she knows she can't say that. Instead she asks a leading question. ("I mean, did you feel that it met your targets?") This confuses the conversation. Sally is left wondering what Barbara really thinks and wondering how to answer the question. You can't be an effective leader if your thoughts are not discussable, either because you recognize their toxicity and choose not to share them, or because you do share them and others hear that you have already made up your mind.

Five Key Shifts in Thinking

Barbara's thinking is problematic in five specific ways. Each one points to a shift in thinking that will allow Barbara both to share her view *and* promote a dialogue in which her view is informed and enriched by the views of others.

From Debating "Who's Right?" to Understanding Different Perspectives

The first and most fundamental key shift in thinking is from "My view is right; so theirs must be wrong" to "My view seems to make sense, but they seem to disagree. I wonder what I know or see that they don't, or what they know or see that I don't?" You shift from *certainty* to *curiosity*. It can help to remind yourself of a time when you were sure you were right and then learned one small additional piece of information that changed everything. How do you know this might not be another time like that? You can't for sure. And the more confident you are in your view, the less risk there should be in framing your view as a hypothesis and offering it up for testing.

From Blaming to Exploring Joint Contribution

No one likes to be blamed, especially unfairly. Blame says that you not only caused something to happen but were wrong to do so. And the implication is generally that if *you* were to blame, *I'm* off the hook. This sets up a needlessly adversarial and simplistic conversation. It may well be that each person is to blame in the other's story. Or perhaps neither is to blame; sometimes unfortunate things just happen. But more important is that in most real business situations, blame is not as important as contribution, and contribution is almost always joint.

Blame looks backward to affix moral judgment and punishment, and it tends to be either-or. Contribution asks what it will take to avoid the problem in the future. In practice, you have to choose which is more important, because once you focus on blame, everyone runs for cover. Yet when you focus on avoiding repetition, you immediately see that many parties can contribute to that. (Perhaps Employee X did embezzle funds, but where were the checks and balances to prevent that? Who had doubts and kept quiet? Who encouraged that reticence by reacting negatively to a prior effort to speak up?) Contributions may not be equal and they may not be blameworthy; they are by definition simply things that might make a difference. Own up to yours, and also point out those of others.

From Making Attributions (Equating Impact with Intent) to Exploring Others' Intentions and Your Impact

Barbara's frustration leads her to conclude that Sally, consciously or unconsciously, doesn't want to own up to her responsibility for the poor results. Barbara attributes intent based on the impact of Sally's actions. But actions often have unintended consequences, and when they are *our* actions that have a bad impact, we are quick to point out that that wasn't our intention and that we were distracted, or couldn't have known, or whatever. Even when an impact is foreseeable, we can't know what is in other people's heads, no matter how obvious it may seem. (When a parent misses their child's soccer game, the child may think she is unloved; she doesn't realize the greater hurt the parent feared if she lost her job.) Nor, by the way, can we assume that our good intentions will necessarily have positive impacts.

Thus we must turn attributions about others' intentions or our impact into hypotheses to be tested. "When you did this, the impact on me was . . . Was that your intention?" "When I did that, I was trying to . . . What was the impact?" We simply cannot automatically equate intentions and impact.

From Avoiding Feelings to Understanding Them

Before, during, and after their conversation, both Barbara and Sally have feelings that remain unexpressed and unresolved and for which each blames the other. Despite the fact that many believe feelings don't "belong" in the workplace, they are there, they are human, and they aren't going away.

In many situations, the feelings (of disrespect, lack of appreciation, unfair treatment, and such) are actually more important to the participants than the substantive outcome of the interaction, and their resolution or lack thereof may be the most important determinant of the quality of the working relationship going forward. Blaming the other for these feelings, however, virtually ensures that they will either not be expressed (with a chance to be resolved) or will be expressed in a blaming frame that is far more likely to escalate feelings than resolve them. Meanwhile, the presence of strong feelings, which tends to be communicated and infectious even when the feelings remain unexpressed, causes chemical changes in the brain that decrease our ability to think logically. Just when we need our rational faculties most, our brain is on drugs!

Rather than bury your feelings during a difficult conversation, ask yourself what you are feeling and why, and ask yourself what feelings may be driving others. If feelings seem to be at the heart of the matter or standing in the way of moving on, consider discussing them directly. If expressing your own feelings, share the feelings, not attributions about the other. ("When you did that, I felt . . ." not "You are selfish and ungrateful!") If you want to address others' feelings, acknowledge them—without agreeing or disagreeing with the underlying story. "Wow! If you thought I was trying to undercut you, that must have felt like a terrible betrayal of our friendship." In acknowledging, a question is always implied to confirm or disconfirm your understanding.

From Defending an Impossible Identity to Growing a Strong One

The essential reason Barbara is stuck in dealing with Sally is that she doesn't want to see herself as "one of 'those' women who pushes people around and develops a reputation for being cold, hard, and ruthless." This is an implicit statement about how Barbara defines herself, an aspect of her identity that matters to her. She would rather be ineffective than violate this self-image.

Perceived threats to our identity are routinely at the heart of difficult conversations and the leadership dilemmas that we experience. One of the main reasons we may resist inquiring into another person's story and helping her climb down her Ladder of Inference is that we fear to discover in her story a credible view of ourselves playing a role at odds with our self-image and self-respect.

The root of the challenge is a tendency to define ourselves unconsciously in all-or-nothing terms that are impossible to live up to and that we don't hold others to. We know that others can be good people and still occasionally do selfish or hurtful things, but we tend to see ourselves as either lovable or unlovable, competent or incompetent, caring or callous. Obviously, as long as we hold to such an unsustainable self-identity, we face the world teetering on a knifepoint—terrified, waiting for the buffeting winds of reality to strike. We are constantly in danger of losing our psychological balance. Not surprisingly, this tension fuels many of the strong feelings we experience in such situations.

The way out is to embrace a more realistically grounded and balanced identity, one that permits error and exceptions without giving up on our essential values. This is a shift that needs to occur over time and in stages as we come to understand ourselves better, but one that offers the greatest payoff for the effort.

Barbara and Sally Redux

To the extent you have made these five key shifts in your thinking, you are much more likely and able to act effectively in a conversation. You'll naturally be more curious about the other person's perspective, intentions, and feelings. You'll acknowledge your own contribution to the problem and be willing to explore it. And you'll feel less mindlessly defensive about your identity and ego.

Imagine, for example, that Barbara and Sally had a second chance to have their conversation—they got a "do over." How might Barbara implement our advice and do a better job?

If Barbara attends to her internal voice and works her way through our five shifts, she will realize that she is full of judgments about Sally's performance that may or may not be justified. She has a theory about Sally's poor results—that the low numbers resulted from Sally's being distracted and slacking off while she focused on her start-up planning. But Barbara might get curious about whether this is really true or whether it is the *whole* truth. Was Sally absent more (either physically or mentally) during the last quarter than she had been previously? Did others see Sally's start-up planning as a distracting influence on Sally's performance? How does Sally see the impact of her outside activities? Did others in the group have poor results, which would suggest that perhaps a larger economic downturn was responsible for Sally's results? Have others had difficulties getting timely or complete information from the sales team? And so on.

Barbara may also realize that her own identity is on the line during this conversation. If she avoids really talking with Sally, Barbara will become upset with herself and feel as though she has failed. On the other hand, to have a productive conversation with Sally, Barbara must be ready for Sally to feel hurt or to "push back" on Barbara's points and perspective. Barbara must feel balanced and steady, prepared to share *and test* her views and to understand *and explore* Sally's views. She must be prepared to accept that if Sally is upset by the conversation, it doesn't mean that Barbara is a bad person; Sally *may* be hurt by Barbara's feedback, but she would be hurt *worse* without it. Remember: the original scenario ended with Sally's being fired or leaving in disgust.

Figure 16.3 shows such a reworked conversation in which Barbara *thinks* quite differently throughout and thus *acts* quite differently. As you read her thoughts and what was said during the conversation, ask yourself whether you think Barbara is being a more or less effective leader than she was the first time around.

The Challenge of Inclusive Leadership

Exercising enlightened power as an inclusive leader is harder than it sounds. The path is fraught with dilemmas that few leaders are well equipped to manage—and women leaders, in particular, who aspire to be inclusive may find themselves ensnared in more than their share of difficult conversations. How do you ensure participation *and* speed? Promote participation *without* degenerating into joint decision making? Encourage an empowered workforce with diverse opinions *and* still ensure consistent execution of a chosen strategy? Hear what others *really* think while also advocating your own vision honestly and with the passion you feel and the organization may need? These and similar dilemmas confront inclusive leaders in almost every decision and interaction they face, often causing them to feel that they face potentially difficult conversations at every turn.

This chapter offers a systematic approach for managing such dilemmas and making potentially difficult conversations productive. It was drawn from and built on our experience coaching thousands

Figure 16.3. A More Productive Conversation

What Barbara Was Thinking and Feeling But Not Saying	What Barbara and Sally Said
This is an important issue for both of us. We need to figure out what happened. Let me start with Sally's view.	*Barbara:* Sally, I'm concerned about your performance last quarter. The numbers slipped, and I'd like to talk with you about why. What's your take on what happened?
That's interesting. I hadn't heard that. I wonder if others have had difficulties with the sales team?	[Sally explains her concerns about the sales team not giving her information she needs.]
Let me acknowledge what I've heard and check my understanding.	*Barbara:* So you didn't feel you got the information you needed until it was too late to push as aggressively as you might have?
Sounds like I got it right.	*Sally:* Right.
Still, this may not be the only explanation.	*Barbara:* Is there anything else that contributed to the quarter's results?
Hmm. I wonder if that's true, or if Sally would be uncomfortable saying more. Her identity as a "professional" might be threatened by acknowledging a personal challenge.	*Sally:* Not really.
Let me share my view in a straightforward way to indicate I think the subject is discussable, and ask for her reaction.	*Barbara:* Well, I'm concerned that your outside business planning activities have been taking up a lot of time, and may be distracting you some from your work. What is your sense of that?
She seems taken aback. I hope she doesn't think I disapprove of her entrepreneurship. Let me clarify.	*Sally:* Um . . . I'm not sure.
I think I should share more of the information and reasoning in my Ladder of Inference, so she knows where I'm coming from.	*Barbara:* Let me be clear: I'm not trying to interfere in your personal life or discourage your entrepreneurship. In fact, I applaud your initiative. And at the same time I wonder whether you are spending enough time with your clients, and whether you're as focused as you've traditionally been. Our executive sponsor on the Jackson account, for example, told me that they haven't seen you as much recently. She asked if you'd been sick.
I like Sally! Some people might get really defensive about this, but she is taking it seriously.	*Sally:* Really? Hmm. I hadn't considered that. I didn't think my new venture planning was impacting my work, but I'm surprised to hear that from the Jackson account.

of executives over many years at the Harvard Negotiation Project and Vantage Partners. At its core, the approach argues that success lies as much in *thinking* differently in such situations as in acting differently, because our actions reflect our thoughts. This explains why the catch phrases and behaviors that characterize the best-intended efforts of today (such as "I statements" and "active listening") are so often insufficient: although the specific suggestions are good ones, you can't pull them off if you don't really believe in them. Without genuine curiosity, for example, a leader's real thinking will leak out in tone of voice and leading questions— "Let me see if I understand the stupid way you are thinking about this"—with a predictably negative impact. Results tend to be quite different if you first negotiate yourself into a place where you genuinely wonder what could lead this arguably intelligent person to see the situation as she does.

In today's increasingly large and diverse organizations and rapidly evolving markets, successful leadership (whether by men or women) requires a skillful commitment to relationship building, collaborative problem solving, and inclusive decision making—in short, to the exercise of enlightened power. The best solutions often need the input of divergent views, and the best execution requires multiple actors working with a common vision and purpose. If leaders are equipped with the skills to manage the dilemmas and difficult conversations inherent in such collaborative inclusion, diverse and divergent views can become the fuel of success, and conflict the engine of excellence, innovation, and growth.

Barbara McMahon has studied how the best women leaders convince others to follow them in creating organizational change. As an organizational consultant, executive coach, and trainer, she has worked with a wide variety of professional organizations, including those in business, media, high-risk occupations, hospitality, mental health, and education. She has done so both through the Center for Transitional Management (the Orinda, California, company that she founded) as well as with Marshall Goldsmith and the Alliance for Strategic Leadership. Barbara's areas of expertise include leadership development, team building, change management, and building strategic partnerships. Her personal passion has also spawned an expertise in women in leadership. She has helped develop programs on a national and international level for Shell International, Intel Corporation, Social Venture Network, *Working Woman* magazine, and countless others. She is currently writing a book titled *When I Rise: A Guidebook for Women in Leadership*.

In this chapter, Barbara describes her framework for leading others through the process of change with conviction.

PHOTO CREDIT: Barbara McMahon by Jamie Westdahl

17

CROSSING OVER

Leadership That Makes Others Want to Follow

Barbara McMahon

It's an age-old story reiterated through time—the Exodus . . . Lewis and Clark—the challenge of moving people from one place to another with the promise and belief that there is something better to be found on the other side. These stories bring to mind the ultimate challenge and adventure of leadership. Imagine holding the lives of people in your hands as you lead them toward an unknown place the way that Moses held the lives of the Israelites in his hands. In some ways it's hard to relate with such a challenge, yet don't we as leaders do this every day?

Whose safety and well-being is held in your hands? It might be your company, the team you work with, or your family. As leaders today, we are required to be flexible and quick to embrace change. It's one thing to inspire yourself to change, but how do you motivate others? How do you get buy-in from others so that they move swiftly in the direction of the needed change? What does a leader do that makes others want to follow?

As a coach and consultant, I have the privilege of working with modern-day heroines, women who have been masterful in taking on the challenge of leading their teams (whether family members, partners, or entire organizations) through significant transitions. Having heard all these stories and through years of experience, I've developed a framework and methodology for leading both ourselves and others through the process of change. It begins with first constructing a foundation of meaning, which is established by clarifying the purpose for the change and then building on that foundation with what I call the three R's (roles, resources, and the art of renegotiation).

By understanding each of these elements and using them as a framework for leadership, you will enable not only yourself but your entire team to be committed to something greater than just the task at hand. When you can engage an entire team in moving toward a goal with personal conviction, you can create an environment where everyone gives their best, and excellence is the norm. You will be leading not by *influence* but by *engagement*. People will be drawn to follow you because they can see your own conviction and your commitment to the team.

Constructing a Foundation of Meaning

In the last decade, there has been a tremendous shift in the values that drive leadership. The fundamental expectations of leadership have changed. Gone are the days when a leader could just say, "Follow me!" Today people want to be involved in the leadership process, to be cocreators. In the new form of leadership, it is no longer *doctrine* that creates a following; it is *dialogue*. It's more valuable to be able to *engage* than to *influence*. Command and control has shifted to collaboration and empowerment. Remnants of the old form of leadership can still be found, but even within our most traditional "old guard" systems, leadership continues to be redefined.

Women not only have been responsible for this shift in leadership style, as a result of our own involvement in business and other nontraditional settings, but also possess natural strengths and competencies in these approaches. These business values are at the very core of our own internal values, which gives us unique abilities as leaders today. By involving our teams in the process of change and helping them explore and clarify their own values, we create the bedrock for our teams to stand on as they cross over any challenge.

Very rarely can you simply dictate action to your team. Today it is critical to create a *dialogue* about change, to *engage* the affected team and to evaluate the roles and resources for every player. Leadership is about exploring and clarifying with your team what it is that creates meaning for them. This meaning and purposefulness is what gets people involved and makes them willing to contribute to change, even when change entails being uncomfortable for a while. As a leader you must ask yourself, "What will this change do for my team? What impact will it have on them?" You can't rely only on yourself for these answers. You must go directly to your team and ask them for their perspective. How do they see themselves in this change? What might hold them back? What would make them willing to move forward?

Sometimes as leaders we are inclined to make everything appear trouble free for our team and to gloss over the negative with little acknowledgment. We believe that we're supposed to appear strong and unaffected by change so that our team will have faith in us. However, this is actually counterproductive. If you tell your people that the company is laying off twenty-five hundred workers but that it's a good and wonderful thing because together those who are left are going to build a meaner, leaner, and more efficient organization, you've done yourself a disservice. When you go to that extreme and appear to have no connection to the loss and devastation that will occur as a result of such a drastic change, you lose credibility as a leader. People begin to doubt your perspective. If, however, you approached this announcement by saying, "We've had to make some devastatingly difficult choices, and as a leader, this is one of the hardest things I've ever had to do," you can then begin to explain why you made this difficult choice and why you need the support of those who will remain. This kind of response makes it easier for people to believe that you have a clear perspective and the perseverance that can lead them through the difficult times ahead.

It is natural for people to avoid the unfamiliar. Many times people become immobile simply because they don't know what lies ahead.

It's always better to face concerns about potential problems before the feared situations come to pass. What does your team fear? What can you do to face these concerns up front with your team? What resources would be necessary to manage the anticipated negative impact if it were to occur? What can you do to secure these resources for them? When your team feels confident that the resources they need are in place, they will be much more willing to move with you.

People can draw from resources they didn't even know they had when they understand how the action or the change being considered is meaningful. When there is a strong enough connection to the purpose and meaning of their actions or behaviors, they can look within themselves for internal resources they will need to tap into in order to get the job done. How do you help your team make these connections? A great exercise for helping your team identify the meaning and purpose behind a particular action is a sentence completion exercise that I call "drilling down on the so-what factor." Complete this exercise for yourself first and then work through the exercise with your team.

Complete the following sentence:

> If I _____ (describe the change),
> then I _____ (describe the benefit).

The purpose of this exercise is to zero in on what you get from this change. *If* you take this next step, *then* what will happen for you? How will it change you? What impact will it have on your life and your own development? Answer this question once and then answer it again with another benefit. Keep moving through this exercise for at least five iterations. This will help you get from the surface benefit down to the core value that drives any type of action.

Next, repeat the process as it relates to the potential benefit of others.

If I/we _____ (describe the impending change),
then you/the team/the organization _____
(describe the positive benefit).

Once you are clear about the benefits, it is important to communicate these benefits to those who will be affected by the change. Guide them through a similar exercise for themselves. By working together to examine the meaning and purpose of the change, you will reduce resistance while increasing commitment, collaboration, and the potential for sustaining the change through time.

Constructing a Framework for Sustainable Change

Once you and your team are clear on the reason for the change and have the commitment to see it through, you can begin to make it happen together. The three R's I mentioned earlier—roles, resources, and the art of renegotiation—are a simple construct for managing this process and moving forward with purpose both within yourself and with your team. Explore each of the three R's in turn.

What is my role in this change?

What is the role of my team?

What resources do we need to carry out this change?

What do we need to renegotiate to make us confident that we can access and utilize the necessary resources?

As leaders we must constantly reevaluate our roles and our beliefs as they relate to those roles. When we are faced with a change (a new project, position, environment, or significant life change), we have to gain clarity within ourselves about the new role and any beliefs we have related to that role. What is the role that you play? What does this role require of you? What old role might you have to perform differently in order to manifest the change? By conducting your own self-assessment, you will be able to determine what resources you will need to be successful in this role.

You might be going along very smoothly in your life when suddenly a new position is offered to you. Maybe the new position is offering more money and more opportunity, but will also require more time and more travel, placing more distance between you and your family. These are the critical moments when you have to examine your roles and resources and determine any renegotiating that will be required in the relationships you hold with others.

One of my clients, a department head managing 30 people, was offered a promotion to head of a division responsible for 130 people. She was very excited about the new position, but was having trouble letting go of the old one. Her current department felt she was abandoning them, and she felt incredibly guilty about leaving. As a leader in her department, she had always been very involved with her team. In fact, whenever they got stuck, she facilitated all their design and development work.

Because she was tormented with this decision, I coached her as she did some self-evaluation, looking at her role in the current department and the resources she had there. She began to think about her role and what she believed about that role. It wasn't long before she realized that she had developed a belief that her team couldn't survive without her, that as a leader, she needed to be there with her team to guide them through their creative process. She immediately realized that this belief was a problem for her. It was not going to serve her well in the new position. (It would be impossible to work this closely with a division of 130 people.) She also realized that this belief had held back her current department. It had kept them from developing to their full potential. They hadn't learned how to tap into themselves at a deeper level and become better problem solvers.

Once she faced this belief, she had a new understanding of what was holding her back. She began to renegotiate her role with her team in a way that allowed both her and her team to move forward.

She communicated with them about the new role and what it meant for her. She also helped them see what the change would mean for them and how they, too, would have new opportunities. As a result, her team was willing to collaborate with her about how they could build capacity and source the team in a new way that would enable her to move forward into the new position. This simultaneously empowered the department to move themselves forward by developing new resources that improved their own success.

There are many roles we can assume that will make us better leaders. The first of these is the role of observer. When we step back and recognize each of the individuals in our organization and what makes him or her unique, we find more effective resources. Everyone looks at the big markers of whether a team is performing, but if you really want to tap into the best of what your team has to offer, you have to notice the smaller things: the uniqueness of each individual and what enables that person to be his or her best. You have to be willing to try different things to create a situation that meets that uniqueness and motivates the person to act. Different people are motivated by different things. Perhaps a person requires more regularity in her schedule, more flextime, more challenge, or more creative space. As an observer, you can begin to notice the resources your team needs to move forward most effectively. You can also observe what kinds of things hold them back. What are the issues they care about? What is at risk for them in making the required change?

What other roles do you play? Student, teacher, communicator, coach, cheerleader, collaborator? What do you believe about yourself? What do you want your people to believe about who they are and what they can do? What is the perspective you want them to hold about you as a leader? What resources does your team need, and what beliefs do they hold that might obstruct them from accessing these resources? What does your team believe about your role as a leader that might keep them from coming to you as a resource?

To be successful in gaining the buy-in of your team, you will need to get them involved in the process. You must consciously and explicitly go through a process of renegotiation with others, explaining the change to them and how it will affect the resources you have to offer or the resources you will need from them. By asking them what they need and how you can help support them in acquiring these resources, you will garner more of their support.

Every change we make requires resources both internal and external. Often, however, our capacity to draw on these resources is limited by our personal belief systems. These beliefs are the framework for what we perceive is appropriate or inappropriate behavior and what we believe about ourselves in relationship to others. Foundational beliefs are based on our earliest life experiences and are continually reinforced and reevaluated as we go through time. In these early experiences, we learn from the systems around us how we are supposed to be in the world—what is acceptable and not acceptable, how to be a woman, how to deal with conflict, how to deal with authority. These beliefs are accumulated from the lessons we learn about how to survive and thrive in life. Sometimes these beliefs can be barriers, and they need to be renegotiated both within ourselves and with our team.

Linda Schaffer-Vanara was one of the first female commanding officers in the U.S. Navy. Being an effective leader in this old-guard system required her to be very skilled at helping her squadron renegotiate their roles and resources. When she first assumed her position, she took on the role of observer to gain an understanding of her team in relation to her as a leader and to the system at large. She asked these questions: How do they define their roles? What is their relationship to their peers, their leader, and the system at large? What resources do they need? What needs to be renegotiated to minimize the gap between the roles they have and the resources they need in order to excel in those roles? Most important, Linda didn't make any assumptions in answering these questions. She went directly to her squadron and engaged them individually so that she could understand what motivated them and what resources they needed in order to feel successful in their roles.

She also knew that it was important for her to redefine the role relationship between herself as a leader and every member of her squadron. She did this by interacting with each of them individually and by redefining some key beliefs they each held about what could appropriately be communicated between a leader and a member of the team. For example, as part of what had been a strongly command-and-control environment, loyalty had been defined as doing what your commanding officer demanded without question. Linda opened new lines of communication with her squadron by letting them know that for her the greatest disloyalty was for her squadron to do exactly what she asked of them when they knew it was the wrong thing to do. She made it clear to them that she valued their perspective and that their voices would be heard. She knew that a willingness to negotiate with her squadron was critical to their ability to maximize performance and succeed in any mission. This kind of interaction with her squadron created a huge shift in the dynamic relationship of every member of the team by opening new lines of communication and bringing further value to each individual as part of that team.

What beliefs does your team hold about their own roles and about the relationship they have with authority? Are these beliefs minimizing their contribution or maximizing their full potential? How can you as the leader help your team renegotiate these beliefs and tap into new resources?

By articulating and negotiating your role and the positive and negative impacts of the plan with your team, you can increase the potential for buy-in and garner a greater commitment to the shared resources that will be needed to bring the plan to fruition. The individual is no longer challenged to manifest his or her plan in isolation. The team shares a common vision with benefits for all.

Today leadership is not about being the strongest and the best. These are not the characteristics that instill respect in today's business environment. Leadership today is about being able to empower others to believe in what they are doing and providing the resources they need to deliver their greatest level of skill. Today's leadership is about dynamic interaction rather than divine intervention. It is about creating an environment of trust in which each individual is respected and empowered to do his or her best.

Creating a foundation of meaning and then building a frame-work for change using the three R's can empower you whether you are negotiating with a child or an entire organization. By helping our teams explore and clarify the meaning that drives them, we cre-ate the rocks that they can stand on to safely cross over the change before them. By examining our roles and resources and then rene-gotiating our relationship with others, we lay the foundation for sus-tainable change.

As women, we possess tremendous strength in this process of engagement and dynamic interaction. As mothers, as partners, and as business leaders, we innately understand the importance of en-gaging the values of others in the process of change. We value the input of others, and we believe in leading through empowering oth-ers. This gives us a significant advantage in today's global business environment and one that positions us to lead in a way that makes others want to follow.

> If I am not for myself, who will be for me?
> If I am for myself alone, what am I?
> And if not now, when?
>
> —Rabbi Hillel[1]

 Tricia Naddaff is the president of Management Research Group (MRG), an international leader in research and in developing assessment tools for consultants, psychologists, and executive coaches. As a successful business leader for twenty years, Tricia looks for opportunities to explore meaningful and sometimes controversial topics, whether she is discussing women's leadership issues with the media or working closely with top executives around the world on becoming authentic and increasing their impact.

The dictionary defines authentic as "true to one's own personality, spirit or character." In this chapter, Tricia introduces important research on the relationship of authenticity to the effectiveness of leaders and managers. Along the way, she addresses several critical issues, including how men and women leaders express their authenticity differently—and how one can amplify one's strengths in line with the authentic self.

PHOTO CREDIT: Tricia Naddaff by Warren Roos Photography, Inc.

18

LEADING AUTHENTICALLY

New Research into the Link Between the Essential Self and Leadership Effectiveness

Tricia Naddaff

Many individuals and organizations today, exhausted emotionally and depleted materially, are looking to leaders to provide renewal, energy, and direction. But to lead others—or manage ourselves—we must draw on our own reserves of energy, ideas, and inspiration. Thus we have little choice but to know who we are and to express who we are with integrity rather than try to be someone else. This has come to be called *authentic leadership*.

This concept of authenticity has two parts. The first can be most succinctly categorized as "know thyself." It is the quest to truly understand who we are—our beliefs, values, needs, emotions, character—what our rhythms are, what makes our hearts sing. By all accounts there seems no other way to look at this other than as a lifelong quest, as we are complex and ever-changing creatures. The second part can most succinctly be labeled "express thyself." It is the effort, the set of behaviors that we use to fully express who we are, to show our true selves to the people around us.

Of course, authenticity is not a new subject. Much has been written about it over the last five years in particular. It's worth noting, however, that about 90 percent of what has been written about this topic has been written by men. And although women cannot claim any more right to the subject than men, if authenticity is about understanding and more fully expressing who we are, then clearly gender plays a significant role in both the exploration and the expression of authenticity. And we as women will benefit from spending more time thinking about it and exploring it for ourselves.

Many have treated the concepts of authenticity and leadership as a mere intellectual or philosophical topic, a softer approach to leadership that might make for good reading and even good debate but not necessarily something that has any impact on increasing the effectiveness of leaders' efforts. At MRG we have worked with more than twelve hundred coaches and consultants around the world and have learned a great deal about what women and men struggle with and work on in their quests to become more effective leaders. We also have spent many years conducting research to gain a greater understanding into many aspects of leadership, and we have just recently conducted some preliminary research that provides evidence of a real link between authenticity and increased leadership effectiveness.

In our research,[1] we have found gender differences and similarities in both parts of authenticity. Of course, whenever we generalize—in this case by gender—we will misrepresent some portion of the population that doesn't fit into the more common pattern. In general we found that women are more powerfully drawn to both parts of authenticity. Women have a more insistent desire to make the time to discover who they are, what they really want, what they really feel and believe. And they have a more insistent desire to be able to fully express themselves in the environments and relationships where they live and work. You would think, therefore, that the quest for authenticity would then be an easier journey for women than it is for men, but this does not always seem to be the case.

There are two dynamics that appear to challenge women's efforts to be fully authentic. The first is that women, again in general, seem to be more concerned with others than are their male counterparts. They are more concerned about taking care of others, more concerned about making sure others are comfortable, and sometimes more concerned about the opinions of others. Therefore, if being authentic requires that a woman put herself first or discover her true self even if it is contrary to what others want of her, or results in others' thinking less of her (even temporarily) because of the full expression of herself—she is often less likely to give herself permission and time either to discover more about herself or to fully express herself. The second barrier to female authenticity is gender bias in her environment. Our society still has such strong gender-based expectations about behavior that if a woman wants to express something other than what others are expecting, the reaction can be something less than reinforcing of her authenticity.

In general, men seem to have less desire to spend a great deal of time either being introspective—less interest in exploring their emotions and beliefs, in going deeper on a quest to "know thyself"—or fully expressing themselves in their relationships and their environments. At the same time, to some degree, men seem to encounter fewer obstacles in the quest for authenticity. Men are often less distracted by the needs of others and often less concerned about the opinions of others. Further, the gender-based expectations that exist for males in our society do not penalize men for acting in ways that are based on self-interest, at least not to the degree that it penalizes women who pursue the same.

These gender differences result in interesting patterns. If we use the analogy of a road system to summarize the differences, we might say that the route of authenticity for women is a four-lane super-highway strewn with construction, roadblocks, and detours, and the route of authenticity for men is a narrow country road with clear driving all the way.

If it can be said that we have a greater affinity for being with people who are more like ourselves, then it is easy to see why we seem to cluster by gender around the exploration of authenticity. Women seem to come together in their quests to explore themselves more fully and to navigate what can seem like the white water of the environments and relationships within which they are trying to express themselves. At the same time, men seem to group together in keeping things "more simple and straightforward"—trying to enjoy a rhythm that is less complex and less introspective, with fewer demands to fully express themselves. It also explains why men and women who do not feel they fit into these gender patterns often seek the company of the other gender. Women who are less interested in the authenticity quest may feel more comfortable in male groups than in female groups, and men who have a passion for the authenticity quest will often seek out groups of women with whom to share this exploration.

Insights Gained from the Coaches of Female and Male Leaders

In our work with leaders around the world, we are seeing increasing numbers of women who are searching for ways to lead authentically. Regarding the first part of authenticity—the "know thyself" portion—the coaches with whom we work report that women executives are increasingly interested in going beyond the standard leadership coaching to discover (or rediscover) who they really are, what they want, what they feel and believe. These leaders are seeking to expand themselves and their knowledge of themselves and seeking ways to live, lead, and be true to these self-discoveries. They are seeking to know their own wants and needs at least as well as they know the wants and needs of their partners, children, parents, staff, bosses, communities, and society. Regarding the second part of authenticity—the "express thyself" portion—we see women seeking their voices, seeking to create environments where they and others are able to express themselves more authentically without being penalized or judged. They are working on aspects they call courage or inner strength or an internal compass. They are seeking to express all the self-knowledge they are gathering in their quests for authenticity in relationships and situations both personal and professional.

When working on authenticity with their coaches, these women describe the pursuit in a way that sounds as though they are picking up the threads of self-knowing they have gained over the years through conversations with friends and family, workshops they have attended, books they have read, and journals they have kept. The work these coaches are doing with these women leaders is not the beginning of something; rather it is the continuation of something many of these women have been doing for years—often in less structured and intense ways, certainly, but doing nonetheless. These women are still extremely interested in continuing to become increasingly effective leaders; it is just that the route they are choosing to take is first to become more authentic as individuals and then to use the power of authenticity to increase their effectiveness as leaders. These women face doubt along their developmental journeys, but it appears that at some fundamental level, they believe strongly that their most true self will yield their best approach to leadership. This implies, of course, that these women do not believe in whatever latest "one size fits all" version of leadership style is being most heralded in their organization or industry, or in the newest best-selling leadership book. It also implies that these women believe that whatever approach to leadership comes from their most authentic place will be most effective for them. And many will ultimately even make the choice to leave their employer to go to another employer or to embark on their own business if, once they feel they have begun to clarify their own authentic approach to leadership, they discover that it is not valued or supported within their current organization.

These same coaches report that the work they are doing with male leaders is often quite different than the work they are doing with their female counterparts. Often the work with men is focused on a more traditional definition of helping the male leader be more effective in his professional role. This may involve working with the male leaders to become more effective communicators or more strategic or focusing more on the development of a myriad of other attributes that make up the leadership role. Many of the men being coached are less interested than their female counterparts in exploring either aspect of authenticity. When the male leader does journey into these territories, it is often as a result of a critical external event—a job loss or trouble at work, a separation or divorce, an impending retirement or an illness. These external events seem to trigger a greater need to begin a more earnest journey into authenticity. In these situations, the coaches often report that, unlike the female leaders, male leaders are often just beginning the journey. There are fewer threads to pick up from earlier discussions, explorations, courses, or readings. Men report that their conversations with other men are more often centered around politics, sports, current events, investments, and work as opposed to the conversations about themselves personally that many women report having regularly. As a result, the coaches find that the men they work with tend to struggle with the ability to discover who they are. Further, because for many this exploration starts at middle age, there is the added fear that once they begin to discover things about themselves, they risk discovering that they have spent much of their lives living and working in ways that are quite removed from their authentic selves. Men can further feel intimidated by the idea of authenticity at the "express thyself" phase. Many men believe that embarking on a path to be authentic potentially puts them at risk for looking weak, and as a male colleague of mine recently put it, "Being perceived as weak is the kiss of death in the traditional organizational landscape."

The experiences that these coaches continue to have working with male and female leaders provide a rich backdrop to help us interpret our findings from several studies.

Defining Gender Differences

In our initial gender study, we looked at self, boss, peer, and direct report feedback on twenty-two leadership behavior dimensions, as well as boss, peer, and direct report data on twenty leadership effectiveness measures. The three questions we were most interested in answering in this study were as follows:

1. What are the key similarities and differences between women and men and their approaches to leadership?

2. What are the observers' (boss, peer, and direct report) perceptions of similarities and differences between men and women in the leadership role?

3. What are the links between perceptions of leadership behavior and perceptions of leadership effectiveness, and do they differ by gender?

This was our first study of gender-based differences among leaders. At the time, our primary reason for conducting it was *not* to add to the discussion about gender differences and similarities in leadership and management. If anything, we thought that because so many studies had already been conducted on that topic, we wouldn't have anything particularly interesting to add. Our primary reason for conducting the study was mostly technical—we wanted more information on the structure and performance of our leadership assessment instrument.

As we began to work on this research project, however, we became increasingly interested in what we might be able to offer to the gender and leadership discussions. First, as we dug into the literature and reviewed the many other studies that had been conducted, we began to realize that much of that work involved very small sample sizes. More important, few of these studies matched men and women on such important demographics as job function, leadership level, years of experience, and industry. Although the observed differences in leadership approach were often described as gender based, we all know that those other demographics are very influential and just as likely an explanation as gender. In addition, several of the studies were conducted in academic settings and the results extrapolated into business settings, making those assumptions suspect as well.

For the most part, those studies revealed what we all have come to expect: female leaders get defined in traditional ways. You probably know the list by heart. We are nurturers, caretakers, communicators, and bridge builders. Male leaders, in contrast, were most often described as focused on action and results and as less oriented toward the relationship dimensions of leadership.

Our research did turn up some points that overlapped with traditional findings; for example, our work strongly supported the idea that women leaders are more expressive than male leaders, whereas male leaders tend to be more restrained. But our research also showed themes that were quite different than those reported in other studies. Two of the most significant findings demonstrated that men spend more time than women thinking and analyzing in their leadership roles and that women spend more time than men making sure results get achieved. Naturally, we thought this was worthy of deeper analysis. When we looked at data that explored underlying motivational patterns in male and female leaders, we found that men and women tend to be quite similar in their *attraction* to thinking and analyzing, and quite similar in their *motivation* for results. So why do men and women leaders express themselves so differently in this respect?

I have had the good fortune to present this research to thousands of women (and a few men) over the last several years. Most women offer a surprisingly uniform and knowing response: "We focus on achieving results because our acceptance as leaders is dependent on our proving ourselves over and over again in the only way that is recognized and valued in our organizations—bottom-line results." These women report that they would love more time to explore ideas, reflect on meaning, assess possibilities, be more creative, and reinvent and renew, but feel that doing so risks taking time away from achieving results that would put them at risk for being seen as less effective leaders. It should be noted that most male leaders, while feeling more freedom than women in this area, would also like more time to think and explore. But as a colleague once stated, focusing intensely on the thinking, creating, and achieving aspects of leadership at once is a little like reengineering your car while driving down the highway at 180 miles an hour. It's a task that is essentially impossible for even the most skilled "engineer," regardless of gender.

We also looked at the relationship between gender and perceptions of leadership effectiveness. One of the most significant findings of this research was that female and male leaders were seen as equally effective by their bosses, whereas women leaders were seen as just slightly more effective than the men by peers and direct reports. This provided further evidence that there is more than one approach to effective leadership.

Linking Authenticity to Effectiveness

As we became immersed in the discussion about gender similarities and differences, we became more interested in answering some deeper questions about the patterns we were seeing. Is there a relationship between deeper aspects of the individuals we were studying and their perceived effectiveness as leaders? By "deeper aspects" we meant a range of things. What motivates these leaders? How have their values and beliefs affected the architecture of their lives, including how they spend their time and energy? How do they view the quality of their lives and choices in that light? We have only recently completed the first study conducted in pursuit of some of those answers. The results are very relevant for our exploration about the relationship between authenticity and leadership impact.

First, let me describe the parameters of the study. We included data from 306 North American male leaders and 364 North American female leaders. That data came from two assessment instruments. We used as a base the same leadership assessment instrument that was used in our original gender and leadership study—MRG's Leadership 360®—with the same number of leadership behaviors and measures of leadership effectiveness. On top of that, each of the individuals included in the study had also completed MRG's Personal Directions® assessment. This instrument measured three different types of personal dimensions: motivation (by analyzing what situations and experiences are most compelling to the individual);

energy expenditure (by assessing what the leaders think about, worry about, or hope for, and how they spend their time); and quality of life (by analyzing the individual's views of his or her present life).

What we wanted to learn in this study was the degree to which there may be connections between how individuals described their motivations, energy expenditure, and quality of life, and the perceptions of their bosses, peers, and direct reports as to their leadership effectiveness. Frankly, we were not very optimistic that our quest would yield much. It is hard enough to find strong relationships between self and observer ratings when looking at the same dimensions; when looking at self data on one set of dimensions and observer data on completely different dimensions, it is even less likely that meaningful relationships can be determined. Accordingly, from our perspective, the fact that we did find key connections has been powerful reinforcement for our belief that there are meaningful connections between authenticity and leadership effectiveness.

Initial Findings Linking Authenticity to Leadership Effectiveness

Women who reported that they spent more time exploring their personal spirituality (defined broadly and not limited to religion), who believed that there was a greater purpose to life, and who were exploring the idea of a greater whole were seen as being more effective as leaders than women who were less inclined to such inner journeys. Furthermore, we found a positive correlation with leadership effectiveness in women who reported higher levels of satisfaction, balance, growth, and support.

The picture for men is not entirely different. There is also a positive correlation with leadership effectiveness in men who reported higher levels of satisfaction, growth, and support. Further, men who reported spending more time exploring their emotional reactions and experiences and developing themselves emotionally, who described themselves as more aware of themselves emotionally, were also seen as more effective leaders by their observers. However, our research did not show the same positive connection between the dimension we call spiritual and leadership effectiveness in men.

How Men and Women Differ

MRG's Personal Directions assessment instrument measures four dimensions that indicate the amount of energy an individual spends exploring his or her inner self: Intellectual, Ideological, Emotional, and Spiritual. Men and women indicate that they spend the same amount of energy on the dimensions called Intellectual (exploring and expanding what you know) and Ideological (exploring and expanding what you hold to be fundamental ideals). As a rule, however, women spend more energy than men do on the dimension we call Emotional (understanding and exploring your emotions; understanding the emotional component of relationships and situations). Women also spend more energy then men do on the dimension we call Spiritual (understanding, exploring, and expanding how you understand yourself spiritually). In combination, this makes a strong case in support of the more anecdotal observations that women spend more time exploring a broader range of insights into self-understanding than their male counterparts.

We also found differences in the degree of expressiveness between male and female leaders. Our initial gender research clearly shows that women are more expressive and less restrained in their leadership roles than are their male counterparts. Again, this supports anecdotal observations that women seek to reveal themselves more openly and fully in their leadership roles than do many of their male colleagues.

How Men and Women Are Alike

As noted, the results of our preliminary research demonstrate that when men and women work and live in ways that are balanced and satisfying and that provide growth and support, there is a greater likelihood that they lead in ways that their key constituents see as more effective. We also found this same link to effectiveness in women and men who made the time to understand their emotions and to grow emotionally. If we can make the case that having some degree of balance, support, growth, emotional understanding and awareness, and satisfaction is tied to this concept of authenticity, then we believe that this study makes the case that leading authentically has a direct and meaningful impact on leadership effectiveness for both women and men.

Where to Go from Here

If we start from the premise that you need first to "know thyself" before you can seriously attempt to "express thyself," then exploring who we are is the first step. If we use the research findings as an initial guide, then as women we have the opportunity to build on the themes of spirituality, emotional awareness and expression, growth, balance, support, and satisfaction, knowing that for us there is a link between our investment in our development in these areas and increased leadership effectiveness. For most of us, this means that we are talking, in practical terms, about an individual quest. Fortunately, individual coaching is an increasingly available resource to leaders at many levels. But with or without the benefit of a coach, we can rely on our personal motivation as well as the guides we encounter (friends, mentors, wise colleagues) during the course of our too-busy lives to help facilitate our exploration and growth.

Here are some of the best questions I have learned from the coaches with whom we work for exploring authenticity in the context of the leadership role:

- What do you have a passion to express?
- When do you feel you are being most authentic in your role?
- What aspects of who you are do you most want to manifest in your leadership role?

- What about this role drains you?
- When do you feel most energized in your role?
- What do you wish you could do or express in your leadership role, but don't dare to?
- When do you feel you are wearing a costume or playing a role?
- Which leaders do you admire for their authenticity?
- What kinds of people do you most enjoy working with? Why?
- What kinds of people are most difficult for you to work with? Why?

Regardless of the process we might select to continue the exploration of authenticity, what we are fundamentally trying to learn is to distinguish when we are exhilarated, peaceful, pleased, centered, happy, energized, or engaged from when we are frantic, frustrated, confused, resentful, exhausted, stuck, or bored.

Although the pace and rhythm of the journeys to authenticity vary widely, one aspect of the timing seems to be fairly consistent: this is not something that happens over the course of a weekend retreat (although weekend retreats certainly help). In a culture that is bombarded by the promise of quick solutions—"Thin Thighs in 30 Days!"—long-term commitment can be difficult to sustain. The exploration of authenticity is a lifelong journey that manifests in ongoing, evolving ways. But when all is said and done, when we've read all the books, finished reviewing all the research, attended all the workshops and seminars, listened to all the gurus, it just makes good sense to know who we are and express who we are with integrity rather than to try to be something else.

Starting (or more likely, restarting) the process is often the hardest part. If you live in a cold climate, as I do, then there is an analogy that may ring a bell. We all know the joys of a roaring fire. But if the night is cold, and we don't know where the matches are and are too exhausted to trudge into the backyard and lug back some firewood, the effort of starting the fire may seem too much. Yet if we choose to make the effort despite our reluctance, we are rewarded by the warmth, beauty, and ancient allure of a fire. From that point on, keeping the fire burning is comparatively effortless but continually compelling. We throw on another log, poke the embers, and watch the flames grow. We've built it, on our own, yet it has a timeless power beyond our understanding. It's a creation unto itself.

 As partner and chief diversity officer for Pricewater-houseCoopers (PWC), Toni Riccardi has addressed the challenges of leading large-scale change that promotes genuine inclusivity in a 125,000-person organization across 142 countries. Toni is responsible for the firm's U.S. diversity and work-life strategies. Under her direction, PWC gained national recognition (and a host of awards) for its diversity activities. Toni is also the only woman on the firm's twelve-member U.S. management committee. Prior to joining PWC, Toni was in academia, directing alumnae and external affairs for Simmons College Graduate School of Management.

In this chapter, Toni lays out a strategy for companies seeking to profit from diversity, describes how she has developed firmwide consensus and support for diversity and work-life initiatives, and tells the enlightening story of her own rise to the senior management of one of the country's premier professional services firms.

PHOTO CREDIT: Toni Riccardi by Kristin Hynes, DiversityInc magazine

19

COMPLETING THE CIRCLE

The Business Imperative for Diversity

Toni Riccardi

I was talking about change recently with some friends at dinner. We were reflecting on how much change we have seen occur in our lifetimes, yet how hard it is to create change deliberately. Naturally, the conversation turned to a discussion of 8-track players. Remember those? Before iPods and MP3s, before the CD player, the Discman, and even the Walkman, we had the 8-track player. I said that the last 8-track player I remembered was in my mother's round bed. This offhand comment, I quickly noticed, was a conversation stopper. I needed to explain myself.

As I described my mother's round bed to my friends, their eyes widened in astonishment. It had a simulated mink cover. The headboard was a curved shell, as if someone had taken an egg and cut it in half lengthwise. At the head of the bed was an 8-track player. There was marble-mirrored glass in the interior of the eggshell. With your head on the pillow you could look up and watch the TV poised above you.

"Didn't everyone's mother have a round bed with an 8-track player?" I asked, sensing their disbelief.

"Are you sure you're not adopted, Toni?" came the reply.

Once again, I was struck by the wonderful strangeness of the world I come from and how that connects to the world I am part of now. I am the Chief Diversity Officer at PricewaterhouseCoopers, the world's largest accounting firm. I am the only woman sitting at the table when the U.S. executive management team meets. How

I got there is an interesting story. Where I come from is even more important to me. Being able to embrace that identity in my job was critical to my ability to perform and contribute my best. After all, diversity is about acknowledging and benefiting from our rich variety of backgrounds, experiences, and viewpoints, instead of suppressing them because they fail to fit a narrower view of the culture. It is about having the freedom to bring ourselves whole to the workplace. In today's global business context, diversity should and must be about completing the circle, not parsing it into discrete segments.

Naturally, this talk of circles reminds me, once again, of my mother's round bed. She was, as one can imagine, quite a character. I credit her with my own appreciation for difference. During my youth, she dyed her hair the color of her clothing for different holidays (green for St. Patrick's Day, pink for Christmas, turquoise with eggs in it for Easter back when beehives were in style). She had a wardrobe to rival her hair. It consisted of an incredible variety of outfits, from gold lamé cowboy boots with matching jacket and jeans to a dress with a light-up Christmas tree and stiletto pumps with birdcage heels, each with a bird inside. My mom had one criterion for anything she purchased, from furniture to clothing: it had to be different.

Growing up, my mom and my dad, and later just my mom, owned bars where I met and learned to be comfortable around all kinds of people. My folks also took me everywhere with them as a child, and I was exposed to different places, people, and experiences. All of that has been helpful to me throughout my career.

At each stage in my career, my appreciation for difference deepened. My undergraduate degree is in art. My first career was in academia at Northwestern, Cornell, and then Simmons Graduate School of Management, where I came to be the director of alumnae and external affairs. That led to an MBA. About a year after I got the degree, I received a call from an alum who asked, "Aren't you the person who always wanted to move to New York City?" I said yes, and at age forty accepted a job managing college relations and college recruiting in the national office of Coopers & Lybrand.

My Introduction to the
"Real World" and to Public Accounting

When I joined the firm, I intended to stay for two years because that's how long you have to stay to prove you had successfully made the leap into the "real world" from the "ivory tower." I knew that I needed to learn how the organization worked in order to navigate it and get things done. I didn't care how hierarchical it was at the time, because I didn't plan to stay for very long anyway. So I networked widely and enjoyed connecting and talking to people. It's amazing what others will tell you when you show a readiness to listen. The information and connections helped me develop the programs I was working on and accomplish things politically. I knew how to share information so that I could keep advancing the causes I was aligned with, and make change happen, little by little.

Essentially, I succeeded in the firm and was made a partner, not because I was able to fit in to the culture but because I was different from it. I had a background and personality that was not typical within the firm. The skills I brought were also different but not so different that they were rejected. People remembered me, either because I was the only woman (or one of a few) or because I had a name that is unique enough to be memorable but not so unique as to be a showstopper.

Near the end of the second year, the director of what was essentially the R&D function in human resources asked if I would join his group as a manager. I was quite surprised by this and asked, "Why me?" He said, "Because I need people who are curious." So I took the job.

Two years later he left the firm, and I took over as director. I was having a great time with the job and enjoying New York City. Then we got a new vice chairman of human resources, a woman who had stepped out of one of our business units to take the role for two years. She lived in Chicago, had two young children, and took her position on the condition that she would not move to New York City, our headquarters, but only travel there when needed.

She wanted to start a small group in Chicago and asked if I would move to join them. I thought long and hard about that decision. I had wanted to move to New York from the time I was ten, and childhood aspirations can be hard to give up. But in the end, I decided she was someone from whom I could learn a lot. She was a terrific role model for having success on your own terms. So I said yes. Two years later, she was my sponsor for partner.

Be Careful What You Ask For

In my early years as a partner, I asked three times before I got the lead role in diversity. First, when I was a new partner, our global head of human capital, a man who was British, asked me what role I wanted. I said I wanted to be head of diversity. He informed me that diversity was only a U.S. issue, to which I replied, "You have obviously never been to the ladies room in the United Kingdom, or you would know that's not true." Nevertheless, he won that round, and I spent my first year as a human resources partner on a global People-Soft project—a role that taught me some wonderful lessons about diversity outside the United States as well as about my own diversity that I never would have learned without a global assignment.

The next year, the firm decided to create a diversity position, so I raised my hand again. This time, for political and merger-related reasons, I still didn't get the job. A year after that, the firm finally created the position of chief diversity officer and asked me to take the role. The following year, our new chairman called and said he did not believe we would make significant progress on diversity unless I was appointed to the twelve-member management team that runs the U.S. firm. So I joined the team and, as they say, became one of the guys.

Interestingly, after having advanced within the organization to the point of joining the management team, I realized that I had forgotten what made me successful when I first joined the firm. If I had come in from the outside, I would have sat and talked with every leader. I would have said, "Tell me about your business. Tell me about what you do. Tell me where you want to go and how far. And let me tell you what I need from you if we are going to be successful." I didn't do any of that because I figured that I knew these people well enough already. I forgot how valuable it is to actively seek out the nuances and differences within everyone, even those who seem, on the surface, to be at one with the culture and his or her role.

Nevertheless, as the only woman on a twelve-member management team, I am often reminded of how my traits as a female make me different from my male colleagues. The clichés, at least on some level, hold true. Women work collaboratively rather than hierarchically. Women talk openly about what's wrong as an opportunity for change, where men might be more political and cautious in order to protect their position and credibility. As Barbara Annis suggests in her book *Same Words, Different Language*, women bond in conversation, men in games and tasks; women look for areas of agreement, and men look for gaps; women are validated in relationships, and men are validated by accomplishments; women share problems in the formative stages, as a way to learn and to gain buy-in, and men share problems after they have been solved; women are multitaskers who switch topics frequently in conversation, and men are linear thinkers who stick to the issue at hand.[1] That last point really set me apart, believe me. In an accounting firm with a hundred-year-old culture, linear thinking is definitely the norm.

Finding My Way

Inside myself, I felt some resistance to acknowledging those differences, and perhaps even a little rebellion. It's difficult to say how much of that resistance was gender based, how much cultural, and how much just the dynamics of a team. But no matter who you are and how fluent you may be at conversing and interacting with others, doubt can creep in when you are surrounded by people who do not look, think, or speak like you. It can be lonely at the top, as they say.

I don't shy away from saying that, because I believe that large-scale change begins from a personal stance and cascades outward.

It's very much about the "I," meaning that change starts with you and extends to everyone around you. It is not easy, and it takes time. You have to understand every element of change to make it happen, from the personal implications to the organizational implications. Although people like me, in roles like mine, can initiate programs and policies that help make a difference, real change happens one person, one "I" at a time. It happens at all levels of the organization through people who are living the change they want to see. In other words, if you don't move people with change that is meaningful to them, there can't be any sustainable large-scale change.

I believe there are some other "I's" that create or hinder the possibility for and the momentum of large-scale change:

Ignite. You need someone to jump-start the process. There has to be an individual spark to create a larger flame.

Involvement. If you don't have involvement from the senior leadership team *and* at the grassroots level, you are not going to see change gain momentum.

Inertia. If you don't reveal and change the context for the existing organization's assumptions around the way things are done, you're not going to get anyplace. People are unlikely to challenge the status quo and will revert to past assumptions as a way to deal with the future.

Integrate. Organizational systems must complement the change you are making. If you make large-scale change around diversity, for instance, you need to align the change with and include it in training, compensation, performance management systems, coaching, and business objectives.

Incentive. Individuals must understand what's in it for them. They need to feel they will benefit from the change.

In other words, there needs to be a business imperative as well as an individual incentive to make large-scale change happen. Diversity was on the firm's radar screen when I first joined in 1989, but it was approached more from a philanthropic standpoint than as a business driver. Today, businesses in general are catching on to the significance of diversity because their lack of competency in that area is costing them talent, market share, and revenue. When the new chairman invited me to be part of the management committee, it was because he believed that if we don't view diversity as a strategic necessity, we won't grow and succeed as a firm in the long term. In my business, for example, we can lose engagements if we don't have a diverse team. Many clients simply will not sign up with us without clear evidence of our cultural, geographical, and demographic diversity. Nor will we attract and retain the best people if we don't recognize and support diversity of lifestyle, background, and perspective.

What the Numbers Tell Us

Consider the demographics. Once the baby boomers are gone, we will face a shortage of professional labor. Women make up nearly 60 percent of the people on college campuses today. Women account for over 50 percent of the people involved in professional programs, such as law and medicine, with the exception being MBA programs, where the percentage of women remains in the mid-thirties.[2] Without a doubt, many of the women who become employees of our firm are going to have babies at some point during their career. If we want their careers to continue within the firm, we need to create an environment that's agile enough to allow those employees to take leave or reduce their responsibilities for a period of time and then return at full throttle later. The number of our employees who are people of color is also growing. If we want our business to be successful, we need that diversity. Accordingly, if we want those employees to advance to the top ranks of the organization, we need a culture that embraces diversity as a mosaic rather than a melting pot.

All these changes and imperatives go beyond race and gender, of course. Thinking styles and perspectives, although less visible, are also important. But race and gender are countable and can be indicative of diversity in thinking styles. For that reason, we use race and gender as primary drivers of our diversity efforts, and we measure that progress.

The Changing Marketplace

Our business model has been the same for over a hundred years. When the two founding firms started, they were staffed entirely by men, all of whom were married, all of whom expected to stay with the business for a lifetime. Now we are global and multicultural, actively seeking talent while trying to retain it as well. Our people travel extensively and work across multiple time zones. We need to accommodate an entirely new set of demands created by that globalization. We also need to respond to demands that have emerged from other sources. Recently, for example, we've experienced a major shift in operating due to the passing of the Sarbanes-Oxley Act, making us an even more highly regulated industry. This has had significant impact on how we organize and function. As an example, one provision of the act requires that we change the lead partners on all publicly traded clients (SEC), every five years. If the partner is working in a small office, that means that he or she may need to transfer fairly frequently to another office, as smaller offices have only a few SEC clients. Consider the fact that many people are part of two-career families, and you begin to see just how complex it is to deal with the realities of our 24/7, global world.

We had made important progress as a firm by 1999 when I first assumed the role of head of diversity, but we still had—and have— work to do. Without question, women and men with families find the professional services industry a difficult sector to navigate at different stages of their lives. The time demands of extensive travel and intensive client engagements make it a challenge to balance career and family.

By studying our own most adept partners, we gained a better understanding of the importance of flextime. Women who were top performers didn't want to "steal" time from their work life to spend time with their families. They needed permission and encouragement to make flex arrangements an acceptable and supported aspect of their career at the firm. Without flextime, we were eventually going to lose those women leaders. The personal guilt and negative impact people felt in asking for flextime was a tremendous barrier to retaining talent. We decided that flex had to be linked to career advancement and must be available to men as well as women to make it widely adopted and culturally acceptable.

In addition to flextime, we expanded our telecommuting program, reduced the eligibility time for parental leave from three years to three months, and created such services as emergency child care and reimbursement, a new mom's lactation program, and adoption services. These programs benefit all our employees, and our communities, in different ways. They also recognize that for the firm to succeed, we need our women leaders, and that our women leaders need us to support their efforts in order for them to succeed.

None of this makes a real difference, however, unless the fundamentals of the culture and the operating system are also changed. It's not easy to convince people that they can work an alternative schedule and still keep their careers on track. It takes personal courage for the individual to stand up and say, "My work is done today, and even though my boss is still here, I'm going to go home and spend time with my kids."

When it comes to balancing work and life, the issues are as numerous as the people themselves. We cannot address all those issues with policy but need to create a climate of trust, appropriate recognition, and positive definitions of contribution. Some people don't have kids in their lives but may have a band they play in or a church they are a member of or a triathlon they are training for. We need to empower people at every level to define what work-life integration means to them. This change happens one person at a time. The closer to home we can instill that power, the faster we will get there.

Often, in a majority culture, underrepresented groups need to validate their experiences and seek advice and council from others like themselves who have "been there," before gaining comfort with fuller interactions with the larger community. We initiated affinity groups, called Circles, to bring together like people—for example, women, racial minorities, gays and lesbians, and some parenting groups—to address important issues, such as professional development, networking and mentoring, communications and connectivity, and recruiting and retention. In just three years, we went from one Minority Circle to sixteen, increased the number of Women's Circles by ten, added two Gay or Lesbian Circles, and have a number of Parenting-Related Circles. The firm recognizes these groups as valuable contributors to retention as well as a place where participants report generating business leads.

My team at PWC has a private vision, one you will not see on our website but that we are committed to and feel strongly about. Our goal is to change the face and style of leadership at PWC *and* around the world. We were very specific about the words we chose. Yes, we are committed to seeing more diverse leaders, more women and people of color at the top of our firm. But we are equally committed to helping men find new ways to work. We want to expand the possibilities for change and create an environment in which one style does not fit all.

That vision extends beyond our firm to the world at large. If we can help people see and achieve what is possible, even if they leave us, we hope that they will pass that capability and experience on. Implicit in that idea is our recognition that people don't stay forever. They join an organization for the learning. We need to do a great deal to encourage them to stay for as long as we can. But we also need to recognize the benefits that accrue to us even when they leave. If we open their minds to another way and they go somewhere else, they can help spread that view within their new organization. They might remember us fondly and even hire us on an engagement someday. And they might rejoin us at a later date, with other valuable experience and knowledge in tow.

We give and we gain. We let go and we see people return. We allow people to come whole to the organization, and they give us more of themselves. We do a little bit better by the world, and the world reaches a hand back to us. The efforts and the energy behind caring passionately for diversity in all forms returns to us full circle. We can't always anticipate those benefits or even measure them, but we believe that they are there and will multiply many times.

In just three short years, with a commitment of senior leadership and the work of a great team, we have been able to accomplish a great deal. The number of women in our recent new partner classes has grown from the midteens to a high of more than 27 percent. We have increased our hiring of minorities at the entry level by 85 percent. The percentage of minorities at the senior manager level, the pool from which our partners come, has increased by 6 percent in the last three years. A Hispanic male has joined me on the U.S. management team, and a second woman now serves on our board. Of our women partners, 10 percent are on a flexible schedule. Our climate survey scores, conducted every six months, indicate steadily increasing satisfaction on the work life and diversity questions within the survey. We established a three-week parental leave, for men and women to use in any way they choose, in the first year of their child's life. For women, this is in addition to their maternity leave, and it can, for example, be used to return to work at a 50 percent schedule for six weeks following the end of their maternity leave. For men, this policy represents a leadership position within our industry. And in 2003 we recognized that everyone needs more than time off with pay; people need time away from their phone, fax, and email. For the first time in our over hundred-year history, we closed the firm for ten days in December and asked people to stay offline and off the phone—to truly get away—and they did.

Yet with all the progress and recognition—internally and in the media—there is still much to do. PWC and other U.S. companies need to continue to focus on the whole person, recognizing that if you want people to be productive at work, they need time to accomplish the things that are important to them outside of work. I see this becoming increasingly important as, for the first time, we have four generations in the workplace—each generation and perhaps each individual with different needs. Organizations will need to learn more about how to tailor experiences, career paths, and benefits for their people.

We need to recognize that diversity—managing and leading across differences—is not an initiative or a program; it should be a competency that anyone who manages people must learn if he or she is to be an effective leader.

Peggy Klaus is a unique expert on the art of communicating your talents and accomplishments in a way that leads to key assignments, promotions, raises, and stronger professional relationships. Much of that insight and advice is captured in her best-selling book, *BRAG! The Art of Tooting Your Own Horn Without Blowing It* (Warner Books). Her candid, colorful approach has been the subject of features and profiles in a number of national media outlets, including the *Wall Street Journal*, the *New York Times*, *Fortune*, CNN, and NBC's *Today Show*. That approach also resonates among women leaders. Indeed, for five years running, her session has been the most popular at Linkage, Inc.'s annual Women in Leadership Summit. When not speaking or writing, Peggy serves as the president of Klaus & Associates as well as part owner of Lost Canyon Winery with her husband.

This chapter has been adapted from *BRAG! The Art of Tooting Your Own Horn Without Blowing It*[1] to help young girls and women leaders master the art and practice of self-promotion.

PHOTO CREDIT: Peggy Klaus by Lisa Keating

20

GOOD GIRLS DON'T BRAG, DO THEY?

Peggy Klaus

In my work with high-achieving women around the world, I have found that, to the surprise of many, Americans don't know how to brag. Some—for instance, those people who are walking billboards and flagrant self-promoters—elbow their way in and talk constantly about how they are harder working, more deserving, and downright better than everyone else. Others simply don't brag at all.

Men in our culture often fall into the walking billboard category (sorry, guys!), whereas women tend to avoid bragging at all costs—most would rather have root canal work than talk about themselves or their accomplishments. But in today's competitive business climate, bragging has become a necessity, not a choice. Still, many talented women continue to abide by the outdated myth that "good girls don't brag" and that it's unbecoming or aggressive to promote themselves. Although their parents may have told them they could do anything they wanted, there was also a big *but*. And that *but* was don't celebrate your own glory. It was OK for boys to vie for the limelight and even one-up each other, but girls were taught to share success with others. Even then, though, it was best not to draw too much attention to themselves. The disinclination among professional women to self-promote has far-reaching consequences. It affects promotions, salary and bonus, high-visibility assignments, negotiations over work schedule, and referrals—as well as makes our blood boil from watching the guys continue to get ahead faster.

The Fear of Bragging

Throughout the years, I've worked with my female clients on changing the beliefs and behaviors that interfere with self-promotion, including ones resulting from a fear of upstaging male colleagues. I once coached a physician from Harvard who was preparing a presentation to a large conference of her peers. Although only in her thirties, she had a tremendous amount of credibility in her field and a great deal of experience speaking at conferences. Yet when she practiced her presentation at my studio, she didn't come across as an assured, confident academic and scientist. Instead, she failed to appropriately introduce herself or her credentials, lacking a sense of urgency and excitement about her new breakthrough. She also rambled, and suppressed all the delightful personality and sense of humor she had revealed in our earlier conversations. When I asked what was holding her back, she told me she didn't want to appear too "big" or too "braggy." She was concerned that her achievements would make her older, mostly male colleagues feel uncomfortable. As a result, she had prepared an unconvincing and boring recitation of her findings.

Fortunately, when I played back a video of her performance in my studio, she didn't like what she saw. She decided to take the risk of stepping into the spotlight to present a fuller, more authentic version of herself. This didn't translate into acting more traditionally male or changing her personality. Instead, she learned to present herself with conviction and conscience by using direct eye contact, a sense of humor, and a conversational speaking style. She talked about herself and her credentials with enthusiasm, convincing her audience of the importance of her research. If she believed she was the expert and worthy of recognition, so would they.

This tug-of-war between showing humility and showcasing personal accomplishment is played out daily in the work lives of women across America, even in the brashest of industries. Recently, while conducting a workshop at a major Wall Street investment bank, I asked a group of young men and women to update me on the successes they had experienced since our last meeting, when we had worked on crafting more compelling sales pitches.

From the back of the room, I overheard one guy encouraging Patty—a twenty-six-year-old, perfectly coiffed junior banker—to share her success story. Even though she had just landed an account worth $10 million, Patty seemed reluctant. Following prodding by the entire group, she finally stood up. With her eyes directed toward the floor, her shoulders shaped like an orangutan's, and in a whispery voice that barely rose above the white noise of the conference room, she said:

> Oh, well, it's really nothing. It was a team effort. There was this guy I had read about in the paper, so I wrote him and later called his assistant who said that he wanted to meet with me. I went in and told him about the services of the bank and what we could do for him. He said it sounded interesting and asked, "Where do we go from here?" And I said, "Well, let's make another appointment, and I'll bring the portfolio manager and my senior banker with me." So we showed up at his office two weeks later. I led off the meeting, but the senior person did most of the talking. Then yesterday we got a call, and he's giving us ten million dollars.

Then she sat down.

I asked the group for some feedback. The fellow who initially encouraged her was flabbergasted. "Patty, what was that? You heard about this guy, you called him up, you met with him, and he gave you ten million dollars! You told it like you had nothing to do with it. Quite frankly, you sound like a real wimp."

Patty replied, "Yeah, well you know, a lot of people helped out. I didn't want to sound like I was bragging and taking all the credit."

Seeing that Patty was missing the point, I encouraged the coworker, David, to get up and act as though the same thing had happened to him. This is how *he* told the story:

Oh man, I read about this guy in the paper. I got really excited about it and wrote him a fabulous letter. I called his assistant to set up a meeting with him. On the day of the appointment, I was nervous, but we still had a great conversation. I was really on my game that day. And he said, "What's the next step?" And I said, "I'll come back with my boss and portfolio manager. You're going to love them." When we walked in two weeks later, I introduced everyone to set the stage. Then they did their thing. Just yesterday the guy contacted me to give us his ten-million-dollar account. I'm so psyched! I nursed this baby from beginning to end.

I asked the group to describe the differences between the two versions of the story. The remarks were revealing: David really owned it. He came across as excited about what happened. He seemed authentic. He didn't come off like he was stretching the truth. You could tell he was really proud of what he had done.

Patty said, "Now that I've seen how David told the story and how people responded so positively, maybe it won't feel as uncomfortable to promote myself in this way next time." Like so many others I have coached, Patty was learning to overcome the whispers from her past, those similar to ones I heard from my father, like "You're going to break an arm patting yourself on the back too much."

Stepping into the Limelight

Too often women relinquish their victories by remaining faithful to a traditional female role. They "shrink" themselves so as not to appear too big or powerful: their voices get softer, breathier, lighter, higher in pitch, and monotone—resembling the voice of a little girl rather than that of an accomplished professional. They state declaratives with an upward inflection, making their intention sound more like an appeal for agreement or validation than a statement of opinion. They take up less space at a conference table or in a room, using gestures that are small and close to the body. They become stiff and humorless like mannequins, to avoid offending anyone. To eliminate this shrinking behavior, I encourage my women clients to

- Stand tall and imagine a string attached to the body like a puppet's, pulling the head and spine into alignment
- Get rid of the all-too-common tilted head that throws stance and directness slightly off course
- Maintain direct eye contact and avoid dropping their gaze to the floor
- Stop using self-deprecating remarks when stating credentials and stature
- Step into the light and show their real stuff—intelligence, authority, accomplishment, power, *and* personality

During nearly a decade of teaching professional women how to step into the light, I've frequently heard clients say they wished they had learned about this years ago. The mothers among them add that they want their daughters to learn self-promotion skills sooner rather than later. And even though their girls tend to excel during the school years by being conscientious, organized, and cooperative, they often lose out as young adults in the real world where assertiveness and the ability to promote oneself count a lot more. Although these women aspire to raise daughters who are more confident and self-assertive than they were while growing up, most of the young girls I meet still downplay their achievements. In part this stems from a desire to be one of the crowd and to not "stick out" by being known for doing something special or different. Yet many of these teens shared with me their secret hope of being recognized by others in some important way. And when they learn to bask comfortably in their unique personality and accomplishments (not the least of which is adjusting to the hormonal roller-coaster ride from ages thirteen to seventeen!), astounding talent and energy are unleashed. Although I had occasionally offered communication workshops for teen girls at conferences and schools, the comments from my clients kept tugging at me. What if girls were taught from the get-go how to brag (the right way, of course)? What if they learned from an early age how to communicate their achievements and to bask in the limelight? Maybe I could help more girls become like Rebecca Sealforn who, upon winning the National Spelling Bee at age thirteen, screamed and leaped around the stage in celebration of her hard-won victory. She was proud, confident, and happy to share her success with the world.

Making the Connection

Although we've "come a long way baby," even teens raised on Britney Spears are uncomfortable promoting their accomplishments at school, on the sports field, and ultimately in the workplace. After delivering one of my interactive, meet-and-greet networking workshops (called a BRAG! Party) for the organization 100 Women in Hedge Funds, once again many of the women commented on how worthwhile they found the workshop and how invaluable this type of information would have been to them as teenagers. Finally, I decided to take action and launch the cross-generational BRAG! Connections Corporate Outreach—a two-hour program pairing aspiring girls with seasoned female executives—to teach networking and self-promotion skills.

The first BRAG! Connections was held at the Manhattan offices of JP Morgan Chase, matching up around eighty junior and senior high school girls from the Young Women's Leadership School of East Harlem with members of 100 Women in Hedge Funds. The program was a huge success, and the students and teachers were buzzing about the transformations resulting from the program. The students experienced firsthand the importance of self-promotion. They discovered that when they talked about their accomplishments in a brief, conversational, and storylike manner, no one thought they were bragging. In fact, people actually wanted to find out more about them. These same girls are now using their newly developed skills when interviewing for college, asking for financial aid, or applying for jobs, internships, and volunteer positions. Fortunately for them, they have learned at an early age that working hard at their academics and outside interests is not enough. To succeed, they must also work at telling people about who they really are and what they have accomplished.

Since that first BRAG! Connections event, many more have been held around the country, with similar results. We meet not only the needs of the participants but also the goals of enlightened corporate outreach departments seeking to provide innovative programs for developing youth—their employees of tomorrow. By training teen girls to embrace and express their authentic selves—to step into the light and up to the plate—we are preparing the next generation of women leaders for taking on a full partnership role in creating the productive organizations of our future. And after working with these amazing youth, I'm counting on them! Aren't we all?

Tracey Warson is the executive vice president in charge of private client services in San Francisco and the Bay Area for Wells Fargo and Company, a diversified financial services company that was recently ranked the only Moody's Triple-A rated bank in North America. In her position, Tracey has consciously set out to create an empowering environment that brings out the very best in people.

In this interview, Tracey reveals her style of leadership, which includes treating all people the same regardless of status, maintaining consistency in her message and values, leading with authenticity and energy, and honoring personal commitments to family, health, and well-being. Tracey also explains how she has used a multi-tiered learning approach (involving "generative" learning at multiple levels) to inspire greatness, high performance, and loyalty in her team and among her clients.

PHOTO CREDIT: Tracey Warson by Russ Fischella

21

AN UNWAVERING
STAND FOR RESULTS

A Leader's Perspective

Tracey Warson

Editors

You recently moved from leading the foreign exchange department at Wells Fargo to the retail side of the bank, where you serve high net worth individuals. What was the significance of that move for you as a leader?

Warson

Private client services is part of the retail area of the bank, and retail is the engine that drives earnings for the company. I knew that if I wanted to move up in the company, I needed to eventually broaden my experience to include these core areas. Growing a niche business is fun, but influencing our core business within Wells Fargo and executing on our number one strategic priority is an exciting challenge and ultimately more meaningful.

Editors

When you were interviewed in *Working Mother* magazine, you talked about needing to act from what you want to become, not from what you are today. Now that you've begun a new role that you had aspired to, have you reflected on whether that perspective was an aspect of your success?

Warson

I think that from day one I've had a new injection of confidence. I don't know where it's coming from, but my current position is all about what I want to be. I *am* this person and this leader, and we *are* going to be successful. I operate from the idea that I *want* to become one of the top leaders at Wells. But I also know that you get there by executing and delivering great results.

Editors

So that belief is the basis of your confidence?

Warson

The basis of my confidence is the springboard of the business I came from. We delivered incredible results in foreign exchange and financial risk management. Before I left foreign exchange, my team organized a going-away event for me. They came in from all around the country. It was really inspiring. They recognized me and were very supportive, and they were also very vocal with the leaders of the group I am now in about who I am. They had already sold me quite a bit by saying, "Hey, this is who she is, and this is what she does." So I came into this side of the bank from a strong position. It's a whole different starting place.

Editors

You're known for providing recognition for your people. Why is recognition so important for a leader to provide and receive?

Warson

The group I am in right now has a very inclusive culture. It's a bit like a partnership in a law firm. All of the key managers here work together and are focused on partnering to produce great results and to give honest feedback. I think it's hard to create a sense of self-recognition without feedback. I'm fortunate in that I've always had great acknowledgment and support from senior leaders within the company. So I've tried to generate that kind of feedback and recognition for my team as well.

Editors

How do you think you are perceived within the company?

Warson

I think others perceive me as somebody who executes and who generates results. I do that by empowering the people around me. Empowerment is an overused word, but I am really trying to widen or broaden the playing field so that everybody is inspired to do his or her very best. I want people to know that they're going to be rewarded and recognized. I want them to know they have a lot of room to run things like they own it and that I'm there to support them.

Editors

Is that something you had to work at or be deliberately conscious about doing?

Warson

I think that when I was younger, when I was first managing, I wasn't as good at that. But the more you are that way, the more you can see that it works. As I've accumulated more confidence as a leader, I've realized that I could do or be more of that. I think that when a lot of people are starting out, they don't have that confidence. They think that if they make someone else look good, that person is going to leave them behind. We all have those kinds of insecurities. But if you just dismiss all that, and champion other people on your team, I think you can be a lot more powerful.

Editors

As you become cognizant of your own strengths, do you try to amplify them or work on them? Or is it just a matter of finding out what works and going with that?

Warson

I find the whole notion of *being* versus *doing* very powerful. I think you have to identify who you want to be—in life and in your work—and then make sure you have the right people around you in the right jobs. That's an old and very basic idea expressed well in Larry Bossidy and Ram Charan's book *Execution:* get the right people in the right jobs.[1]

Editors

What have you done to make that happen?

Warson

When I came into this role, the first thing I did was review the leadership team and really get to know them. I wanted to listen to them and figure out who's who. It was a very interesting experience. I don't think they felt that they'd been listened to in that way before. They were really candid with me, and we made a lot of changes. I was direct with them in turn, but in a nice way. We collaborated on the organizational changes and I think that they now all know who I am: a person who takes *an unwavering stand for everybody's success*. I'm going to succeed because that's just who I am, and they're all going to succeed with me, individually and as a team. That's the "being" part, and it's probably the hardest part about being a leader. You have to get up every morning and have that skip in your step. You need to get people excited and have that energy yourself. I watch that demonstrated by our CEO all the time. He exudes energy and charisma, and he's genuine. That's what you have to get up and be every day.

Editors

How does your approach to leadership today differ from what you've seen in more traditional settings?

Warson

Many leaders make decisions without a lot of information, because perfect information is not available. It's all about the people, and if you stop and sit down and listen to them, you find things out. I was in a great position when I came into this role because I didn't know anything. I wasn't married to old assumptions. I just came in as a clean slate. I think it was fun for my team, because they could tell me everything. People tend to be proud of what they do, and they want to share it. It's just so fundamental. You go in, listen to people, and hear what they have to say. You find out what they love about what they're doing, and what they're excited about.

Editors

Do you have an example of how you do this?

Warson

In one of my first meetings, there was a man who was so passionate about what he was doing that he was leaning forward as he
talked about it. He talked ten times longer than everybody else.
When you have people like that you've got to give them more because they want to generate more. That was an example of coming
in and watching people and identifying who you have and what
role they should be in.

I don't mean that it's all positive. You might have someone
who's all about process when you need the group to be operating at
high velocity all the time. As a leader, I've learned that you don't
fire people who work hard but don't fit; you find them another role
where they can thrive. When you make those tough decisions, you
orchestrate it so that the person doesn't feel disempowered and
angry. You find ways to get things done without being cruel. And
then there are people who don't really show up for work and don't
care or try, and you need to make those kinds of decisions too.

Editors

In what ways does this improve people's performance?

Warson

There's one person who works on my team who's hungry for support
and wants to move up in the organization. He likes and needs a lot
of recognition. One of the things that excites him is speaking to the
head of our whole division directly. So I suggested that when they
run into each other in the hall or find a spontaneous moment to
chat, he should bring his ideas forward.

The irony is that in getting out of his way, I received a tremendous benefit also. This man ended up praising me by telling our boss
how "fearless" I am, and so on. It was really unexpected. But he has

said to me several times that he's never felt so excited about coming to work and that it's a completely different place for him now. He wants to work hard and make the results happen. We've had a couple of heart-to-hearts, and he'll seek my input regarding what I think he needs to work on. One day, I asked him what time he gets to work in the morning; he wondered what I was talking about, and I said, "Well, you've got to model the way for others." And now he gets in at six in the morning, and he's always bouncing around and excited. It's fun when you can affect somebody so quickly.

Editors

You've had great success building collaborative relationships in the company—for instance, having some of your own people report to managers in another division as a way to achieve shared goals. How do you have faith that such trust and collaboration are going to take root? Is it because of the culture of the organization or the experiences you've had, or is it a vision that you couldn't let go of no matter what?

Warson

I just don't let go. And I hold to the goal in a way that is nonthreatening. I say, "Hey, we know that our company's number one strategic priority is to grow private client services, so how can you and I work together to deliver what we provide to customers and enhance their customer experience?" I show an understanding of what's important to them, and I help them see how our collaboration can value what they're up to and how it can further what's good for the company.

Editors

They trust that you will be on their side.

Warson

The wholesale banking group trusts me because I worked with them for fifteen years. On the retail side, I don't know those folks as well, yet I'm trying to operate from the same level of inclusiveness. It's not about the fact that one is senior to another; it's about how we can collectively deliver this "wow" experience to our customers. What I try to do is just foster relationships and alignment with others by being a role model. I am suggesting that all of us, as partners in business, collaborate together and do it better and bigger than anyone else is doing it, and thereby create great opportunity. People get excited about that.

Editors

We've talked about the "being and doing" of leadership in an organizational sense. Does this extend to other parts of your life?

Warson

As a mother, I think it does. I'm trying to get my two daughters to know and feel good about the fact that they can be anything and do anything. I know that they know that I take an unwavering stand on supporting their whole lives. I'm talking about life much more than their success per se. I'm always there to support them, and I know they know that. Outside of that, I don't know if I'm really great from a friendship standpoint, because I don't have any time between my job and my family.

Editors

You've spoken often about work-life integration. How do you pull that off?

Warson

It's all about commitment. What are you committed to? You need to declare that and remind yourself of it every day. When you are aware of your commitments, all your actions will align around them. I write up my goals every year. A lot of those goals are around the relationship I want to have with my kids and the time I'm going to spend with them. Some people say that as long as you have quality time, quantity doesn't matter. I don't believe that. I think you have to be present for them as much as possible. In my old job, I had to travel a lot, so I had a "two-day rule." I promised my daughters that I would never be gone from them for more than two days. So I would fly red-eyes, do twelve appointments in a day, and whatever was necessary to honor that commitment. But that's the way I would design it and live it. There were a couple of exceptions, but that's what I did. When you create these little rules for yourself, they help you keep your commitments.

Editors

Do you have those kinds of rules for work-related issues as well?

Warson

Not consciously. I don't have the same need. The parenting is different. I have to create certain structures to make sure that I don't lose sight of anything. That was always my greatest fear: that I would get so sucked in by ambition that I would neglect my children. It just doesn't happen if you're committed to them and they know that. They can feel it, just like the people who work for you can feel it.

Editors

If you were talking to someone who is coming up, someone who has your ambition and wants to make these things happen for herself too, what advice would you give?

Warson

One of the biggest things I learned, ten years ago, was not to waste energy on negative people or negative experiences. There are a lot of people who might try to make your life difficult, but you need to redirect that energy toward the positive and to generate results.

I think women especially struggle with this problem. If you can just ask yourself what are the results you need to achieve that are important to your division and the company and then focus on actually generating that, other people can never say that those results didn't happen. Most people have a thousand different excuses why they can't get something done, but generally, if you're accountable and you know what you're trying to accomplish and why, and you do it right, the rest will follow. Having a results focus is critical.

Then, I think people need to speak up about their accomplishments. They need to communicate what they're contributing. Sometimes I've had to finds ways to communicate what we've accomplished because I wasn't getting direct support. In those instances, we might have used the company newsletter or told some great customer service stories to get out the news. It wasn't *about* me. It was about the results that we were generating and how that was enhancing the collective mission of the company.

The third area that I've found critical is relationships. You need to develop relationships with others. You need to seek out mentors and build relationships with people within the company because that's how things really get done.

Editors

These issues are all germane to women, but do you see them as relevant for leaders in general?

Warson

I think they are pretty general. There was a white paper I read about the glass ceiling that wasn't gender specific but that I found fascinating. The authors were contending that a lot of people get to a certain level because organizations are meritocracies. But then, once you get to that level, you find that it's not a meritocracy anymore. If you keep running over bodies along the way, you're not going to get into the next job because you'll have irritated everybody. So you have to stop, look around, discover how these relationships work, and figure out who's who. A lot of times women trip up because they're so conditioned to outperform. But at a certain point, you need to stop and think about what relationships you need to build, not just what you can do yourself.

That's a big distinction. When I read that report, I said, "Wow, that's exactly what I'm doing wrong." Because once you get to an executive vice president level, that's wonderful, but how are you going to get to the next level? Even if I doubled our business again, they would say, "Nice job, thanks." But if you can go out and build relationships with others who are going to support you, they will know who you are when it comes time to consider who will be right for the next level up. It's not about schmoozing. It's about respecting where other people are coming from and trying to build some common ground with them so you can form a relationship. That's how I got this role. And boom—now I'm doing something different that has more influence, more visibility, and a lot more opportunity.[2]

As professor of international management at McGill University in Montreal, Canada, Nancy J. Adler has consulted and conducted extensive research on global leadership and cross-cultural management. She is the author of more than one hundred articles as well as the books *International Dimensions of Organizational Behavior, Women in Management Worldwide, Competitive Frontiers: Women Managers in a Global Economy, Women Managing Worldwide*, and *From Boston to Beijing: Managing with a Worldview*. Nancy is also an established artist whose paintings increasingly enrich her work as a global business consultant and leadership expert.

In this chapter, Nancy provides a bridge between our individual and organizational "paths to power" and the use of "power in the world." Specifically, she describes her twenty-five-year research journey into the role of significant leadership in creating a better, more equitable world. The chapter is drawn from a keynote address that she gave to the executive leadership of the United Nations at the Hofburg Palace in Vienna, Austria—mere blocks from her mother's childhood home and the scene of a personal and humanitarian tragedy with lasting historical and global ramifications.

22

LEADING BEYOND BOUNDARIES

The Courage to Enrich the World

Nancy J. Adler

> Do not forget, you are here to enrich the world. You
> impoverish yourself if you ever forget that errand.
> —*Woodrow Wilson, 28th President of the United States*

Vienna symbolizes the height of human civilization, having given
the world great architecture, art, music, philosophy, psychology, and
so much more. The Hofburg Palace stands in the center of Vienna
as elegant testament to Austrian power, past and present. As executives from the twenty-three major United Nations organizations
and their colleagues in international development and the private
sector enter the palace in early fall 2003, they cannot help but feel
awed by the grandeur of the sculptural facades elevating each building beyond the majesty of its neighbor, beyond mere practicality
and everyday ordinariness.

Vienna also symbolizes the nadir of civilization, and both the
heights and the nadir are present this morning as I walk toward the
palace along Vienna's grand boulevards and meander through her
beautifully manicured gardens. *Was this the park where my mother
played as a young girl? Is this the street where Nazi thugs kicked yet another Jew until he fell to the ground, and continued kicking while they
forced him to scrub the boulevard with a toothbrush?*

I enter the Hofburg Palace. My invitation is to deliver the keynote address on women's contributions to global leadership to the
assembled conferees, all of whom care equally passionately about

the performance of their organizations and the quality of civilization on this planet.

As I move toward the podium, I am aware of the necklace my grandmother smuggled out of Austria more than sixty years ago lying gently around my neck. Encircling my words is the strength, love, and support of multiple generations of my family, with its lineage of strong women, each of whom was a leader in her own time in history. Although my voice comes from inside me, it also comes from these strong and beautiful women. They died so I might be born; their voices cannot be denied: "Speak your truth, Nancy, for if you do not, we died in vain."

Even moments before I begin to speak, I am still unclear as to exactly what I want to say. Yet as I begin, the words flow without hesitation.

> Nobody in this room chose their profession randomly. . . . All of us chose our profession—our calling—because we know that the world is in trouble. All of us know we must do better than we have done historically. I too did not choose my profession randomly. I did not choose to focus on global leadership without reason. The reasons for my choice are embedded right here, in Vienna. As I remember my Viennese great-grandmothers, grandmother, and mother, all of whom lived in this city, I understand my choice, and I understand, at the deepest levels, why we must do much, much better.

> My mother was born in Vienna less than ten minutes from the Hofburg Palace. My mother's first thirteen years were filled with all the splendor that has given Vienna its worldwide reputation for high culture. Then 1938 arrived, and my mother's world, along with that of all her neighbors, descended from cultured heaven into unadulterated hell. If it had not been for an Austrian family from a completely different religious and cultural background than that of my mother—a family who, unlike the vast majority of Viennese, chose not to deny the new horrifying and inhumane reality—my mother would not have lived. If it had not been for a family with extraordinary courage, that risked the life of every member of their household

to hide a little girl, my mother would never have escaped, and I, needless to say, would never have been born. Good transcends evil, even as evil eclipses good.

Nobel Peace Prize laureate Elie Wiesel reminds us that it is human to have hope, that hope is not an empirical conclusion based on the evidence at hand, but rather an individual choice to assert our humanity.[1] Former U.S. president Woodrow Wilson insisted that our job, as leaders and as human beings, is to enrich the world. Our job is to confront reality with hope—not with a trite, superficial hope, but with a strong, robust hope founded on all our collective wisdom and experience. Fundamentally, leadership is about committing ourselves to things far greater than ourselves.[2] It's about returning an unacceptable reality back to the positive realm of possibility.

There is no possibility that we can return the world to a civilization we are proud of without including the voices, wisdom, talents, and experience of people from all continents and countries. We need the very best of what women and men worldwide can contribute. Yet, up until now, the world has rarely listened to most people, including ignoring the voices of most women. The message from those women, like my great-grandmothers, grandmother, and mother, who walked these streets and witnessed the apex of civilization dissolve overnight into its nadir, is that global leadership is too important to attempt alone. It is too important for us not to draw on the wisest among us, whether male or female; Buddhist, Christian, Jew, Jain, or Muslim; European or Asian, African or American. As poet David Whyte reminds us,

> [T]he journey begins right here. In the middle of the road. Right beneath your feet. This is the place. There is no other place. There is no other time.[3]

At this moment, the collage of wisdom I had created with poetry, paintings, and music appears—an esthetic reflection supporting profound and courageous leadership. The collage invites the audience of leaders to return to the deeper reasons they remain so committed to the world and its inherent possibilities, even in the face of terrorism and unimaginable inequities. As Hewlett-Packard's former CEO Carly Fiorina would describe it, the collage invites each executive into a "world of dreams expressed in art; [a world] freed from the laws of every day."[4]

Competitive Frontiers:
Women Managers and Global Economy

At this point in history, what does it mean to be a woman and a global leader? I have known for years that a global perspective was essential for twenty-first-century leadership and have conducted research on both male and female leaders for more than a quarter-century. In the late 1970s, however, as I finished my doctorate at the University of California at Los Angeles and began looking for an academic home, I found few management schools at major U.S. universities interested in taking a global perspective. In interview after interview, I was told that international management constituted too narrow a focus. "Strange," I thought. "They view domestic studies as appropriately broad, and global studies as too narrow." At one top-ranked university, I was even told that they would offer me a professorship if I promised never to teach "that stuff" (referring to international management) to their MBAs. I declined their offer and accepted a faculty position in Canada at McGill University. In Montreal's multilingual and multicultural setting, I found a management school where the overall perspective was so cosmopolitan that no seminar needed to be explicitly labeled international—for what would the other seminars be labeled? Parochial? Offering managers a choice between the international and parochial (domestic) versions of a particular curriculum—be it marketing, finance, or strategy—seemed clearly absurd to me as well as to my new McGill colleagues.

My research in the early 1980s focused on a broad range of cross-cultural management issues facing companies, including the

Collage of Wisdom

The unimaginable is now possible. The survival of the human species can no longer be taken for granted. The human species is now an endangered species.

    —Joseph Rotblat

[Artist] Marc Chagall gave this nihilist century a worthy concept—hope.

    —Alan Riding

We are all born with the potential to become human. How we choose to live [and to lead] will be the measure of our humanness. Civilization does not assure our civility. Nor does being born into the human species assure our humanity. We must each find our own path to becoming human.

    —David Krieger

When I feel what it feels like to be really human, I hear music.

    —Carman Moore

At school we are programmed to give science and technology the last word, but in the maelstrom of our civilization we long to hear the first word.

    —Ramon Munoz Soler

What we cannot comprehend by analysis, we become aware of in awe.

    —Abraham Joshua Heschel

We do, with astonishing frequency, produce moments of nobility. Our culture just doesn't choose to feature them on the nightly news.

    —Donella Meadows

Note: Reference information for these quotes is on page 507.

complexities of strategic international human resource management. Given that I, along with many other observers of the rapidly shifting geopolitical landscape, was already convinced that successful businesses could no longer remain local, the paucity of women gaining international experience concerned me. No matter how much emphasis North Americans placed on employment equity, especially for the increasing number of women managers, it seemed highly unlikely that anyone would be promoted into the senior leadership of the next generation of global companies if he or she had not had the opportunity to work abroad. The results from my research on women expatriate managers confirmed my fears: whereas more than 40 percent of domestic North American managers by that time were women, less than 3 percent of the people being sent abroad by major multinationals on expatriate assignments were women.[5] With this preponderance of men defining the universe of future corporate leaders, the situation did not bode well for either women or their companies as they entered the most competitive economic era that business had ever faced.

Why were multinational companies continuing to limit their competitiveness by restricting their choices to men? At that time, most multinational companies believed three myths and used them to explain the dearth of women managers being sent abroad. None of the three myths had ever been tested, however.

Myth 1: Women do not want to become international managers.

Myth 2: Companies refuse to send women abroad.

Myth 3: Foreigners' prejudice against women renders women ineffective, even when they are interested in going abroad and succeed in having their companies send them.

We researched each of the three myths to assess whether or not they were true. Myth 1, we discovered, was blatantly false. Whereas women from prior generations may have hesitated to take foreign assignments, by the 1980s women and men had become equally interested in seeking opportunities to work abroad.[6]

Myth 2, in contrast, proved true. The majority of multinational companies did hesitate, if not altogether refuse, to provide their women professionals with opportunities for international experience.

Myth 3 was more difficult to assess, but ultimately proved false. For years, companies had assumed that the level of resistance to expatriate managers varied according to the cultural traditions of host countries. To our surprise, however, we discovered that 97 percent of the women who were sent abroad succeeded, regardless of country— a much higher success rate than that of their male counterparts. Indeed, almost half the women (42 percent) reported that being a woman offered them more advantages to their professional success than disadvantages. Only 20 percent reported that being a woman was a net disadvantage.[7] Such evidence proved that the belief that host-country discrimination acts as a barrier against foreign women managers' success was, in most cases, a myth. Host nationals, in most cases, treat foreign women managers with the respect they need to succeed.

In the 1970s and 1980s, the women who worked as expatriate managers were pioneers. Typically, they were the first women their companies had ever sent abroad. Many had to persistently encourage their companies to send them, and often had to position themselves strategically within the company to seize international opportunities when they arose. Because there was in most cases no woman predecessor to act as a role model, these women's deliberate choice to seek positions abroad required courage, resolve, and resiliency— qualities other women, including my great-grandmothers, had displayed in other historic settings. The major barrier to women's international success was rarely the women themselves, nor a falsely assumed discrimination by local host cultures around the world. Rather, the major barrier remained the resistance put forth by the women's own companies as the decision makers continued to believe in Myths 1 and 3 and therefore chose, with few exceptions, not to offer international assignments even to their female managers with the highest potential.

Given the increasingly competitive nature of the global economy in the 1980s and 1990s, companies needed to change their assumptions and provide more opportunities for their high-potential women and men to gain expatriate experience. As Harvard Business School professor Rosabeth Moss Kanter put it: "Meritocracy—letting talent rise to the top regardless of where it is found and whether it is male or female—is essential to business success in free-market economies. Within this context, the equality of women in the work force is no longer a political luxury. It has become a competitive necessity."[8]

To dispel the erroneous myths that were hindering companies from selecting their best candidates for international assignments, our recommendations to companies included the following:

- Don't assume that foreigners will treat expatriate women the same way they treat their local women; they won't.

- Don't assume that women in general have trouble adjusting abroad. Although male expatriates of the prior era often blamed their wives for failed assignments and early return, the role of the spouse carries with it a very different set of challenges than those faced by expatriate managers.

- Don't assume that married women will not accept international assignments. If companies want women to accept assignments abroad and to succeed once there, they need to offer them flexible benefits packages and an infrastructure of support.

Today, many companies offer packages that include executive-search facilities to help the trailing spouse find a job, airline tickets to allow commuting couples to stay connected, and other benefits designed for dual-career couples and single women expatriates. The era of simply offering a nice home and membership in the international club is over. Leading companies have discovered that they have much more control over women's worldwide success—and therefore their own competitive success—than most had ever initially imagined. They have learned that exercising initiative leads to success for both the companies and the women.

Global Leaders: No Longer Men Alone

By the early 1990s, as my research shifted from focusing on expatriate managers to global leaders, I increasingly questioned the "pipeline myth"—the belief that women just needed more time in their companies' career-path pipeline before they would naturally be promoted into top positions. As I began examining the career paths of women who had actually achieved the number one leadership position in their country or company, it became clear that the women's routes to power differed significantly from those taken by most men.[9] Rather than working their way up through the corporate hierarchy, most women laterally transferred into their leadership positions.

In the political realm, for example, most women presidents and prime ministers did not progress up through the political party hierarchy. Instead, they laterally transferred into their country's number one leadership position from other careers. Tansu Çiller, for example, taught economics at Turkey's prestigious Bogazici University until shortly before she was elected Turkey's first woman prime minister. Gro Harlem Brundtland, after having begun her career as a medical doctor, was elected as Norway's first woman prime minister and subsequently reelected for two additional terms before going on to lead the World Health Organization. In the business realm, a similar pattern holds true for many of the women who become CEOs of major multinational companies. Those who succeed usually gain the number one position by laterally transferring into the CEO position in one company after having built their career in another company. Carly Fiorina is one of the most prominent current examples of this pattern. Fiorina grew her career at Lucent before being recruited to take over as CEO at Hewlett-Packard (HP), a Fortune 30 company.

Certainly, the pattern of laterally transferring into senior positions of power calls into question the belief that a glass ceiling stops women from reaching the top. It appears that many women who become CEOs find it more expeditious to go around the glass ceiling than to try to break through it. Although it is true that internal power structures in the political and corporate realms generally fail to support women as candidates for senior leadership, such lack of support does not stop the women from gaining power. Politically, for example, women often draw their support directly from the people rather than primarily from existing political party hierarchies. Former president of Ireland Mary Robinson and former prime minister of Pakistan Benazir Bhutto provide good examples. Neither gained her support from a narrow political elite, but rather each campaigned in more small communities than had any politician in her country before her. Women business leaders often exhibit similarly "democratic" approaches, drawing their power directly from the marketplace rather than primarily from the hierarchy within the company. Successful entrepreneurs, of whom an increasing proportion worldwide are women, dramatically reflect this pattern. As Mary Robinson observed in her presidential acceptance speech, "I was elected by men and women of all parties and none, by many with great moral courage who stepped out from the faded flags of Civil War and voted for a new Ireland. And above all by the women of Ireland . . . who instead of rocking the cradle, rocked the system, and who came out massively to make their mark on the ballot paper, and on a new Ireland."[10]

The nontraditional approach used by such women as Mary Robinson to obtain power and to reach the most senior positions offers an interesting model for twenty-first-century leadership that contrasts sharply with that used by most twentieth-century male leaders.

Women bring powerful public symbolism that differs markedly from that of their male counterparts when they assume senior leadership. In particular, because of their newness to such powerful positions, women are frequently viewed as symbols of hope, unity, and the possibility of change.[11] When a woman is chosen to lead her company or country, especially in circumstances in which no woman has held that office before, people begin to believe that other more substantive and significant changes are also possible.

Likewise, due largely to their newness as senior leaders, women enjoy higher visibility than most of their male contemporaries. Carly Fiorina, for example, after being selected as the first woman and first outsider to lead HP, received more press coverage in her first three months as CEO than Lew Platt, her predecessor, received in his entire eighteen years as HP's CEO. Her departure from HP in 2005, by then the eleventh largest company in the United States, ignited an avalanche of media attention.

Although the pattern is not yet clear at senior leadership levels, some studies and much anecdotal evidence suggest that women also use more democratic, inclusive, and unifying strategies than do their male counterparts.[12] In the political realm, for example, it was a woman, Agatha Uwilingiyimana, former prime minister of Rwanda, who was willing to sign the peace treaty between the warring Hutu and Tutsis in an attempt to end the war in that genocide-ravaged country. Her predecessor, a man, refused to engage in a peace process that included representatives of all factions for fear that he would be seen as disloyal by his own party and tribe. Demonstrating huge courage, Uwilingiyimana accepted the position of prime minister and signed the peace treaty at a time when no man was willing to do so. In one more tragedy in that already unimaginably tragic country, Uwilingiyimana was murdered for her leadership, not by the opposition but, sadly, by members of her own political party and tribe, who resisted her attempts to reunify the country by creating an inclusive peace.

The challenges facing today's business and political leaders require personal courage, a global perspective, and extremely broad commitments. As former Body Shop CEO Anita Roddick recognized,

"Leaders in the business world should aspire to be true planetary citizens. They have global responsibilities since their decisions affect not just the world of business, but world problems of poverty, national security and the environment. Many, sad to say, duck these responsibilities, because their vision is material rather than moral."[13]

Twenty-first-century leaders, whether women or men, derive their power from broadly based networks. They must be vision driven, globally inclusive, and multiculturally persuasive, while simultaneously exhibiting courage and humility. As global leaders they are charged with taking ideas, people, organizations, and societies on a journey. The power to shape history means that a leader's most critical task is to seek to enrich the world, rather than diminish it; to promote good and dispel evil; to propel civilization to its heights, while saving it from descending to its nadir. Economic viability and competitive success, though critically important parts of the equation, remain far from sufficient to define a leader's most significant contributions.[14]

The Art of Leadership: Giving Ourselves for Things Far Greater Than Ourselves

Do women offer a greater possibility for significant leadership than do men? Symbolically, perhaps, but there is no gender-based entitlement to virtue or efficacy. Many predicted that women would demonstrate new, more inclusive and humanistic approaches. Examples of corrupt and damaging leadership, however, can be found among women as well as among men. As we have always known, but perhaps conveniently forgotten in other eras, our task is to seek out and to grow the types of leaders our time in history requires, not to prejudge either men or women as the ready-made, guaranteed solution.

Today, to create the needed shift in our leadership approaches and vocabulary, I find myself turning away from most traditional leadership models and increasingly embracing the arts and artistic processes.[15] The move from successful to significant leadership, as former CEO and president Frances Hesselbein describes it, cannot take place within the limitations of our current dehydrated leadership vocabulary.[16] Significance is neither defined nor limited by traditional management pursuits. Achieving significance demands new concepts, new imagery, and a new language; it demands that leaders reengage with the possibility of enriching the world. World-renowned corporate architect William McDonough, recognized by *Time* magazine as the 1999 Hero of the Planet, reminds us, and our corporations, that being "less bad" does not make us good.[17] And being good—being a contribution—demands new approaches.

A leadership seminar I conducted in the late 1990s for women business executives from around the world demonstrated the power of artistic processes to open new and needed perspectives. At the beginning of the seminar, I invited each of the participants to introduce herself by describing one time in which she had been particularly powerful at work. The discussion that ensued quickly turned overwhelmingly negative. The women saw power as primarily manipulative, coercive, hierarchical, and dominantly masculine. Indeed, these business leaders seemed on the verge of rejecting the notion of power altogether until one of the most senior women challenged the others by saying, "Unless you can tell me that the world is perfect, your country is perfect, your company is perfect, your community is perfect, and your family is perfect, don't tell me that you're not interested in power." Everyone understood her message.

My goal as a professor and consultant is to help executives access and use power for worthwhile ends; it is not my role to encourage them to reject power. In the seminar, my challenge was to find a way to reunite the women executives with their power without referencing the traditional, constricted modes with which most had grown up. My challenge was to reunite them with a contrasting approach to power that could support the possibility of enriching their companies and the world, rather than the probability of diminishing either or both. Such a conception of power, of course, demands the courage to

- See reality as it actually is—to "collude against illusion" even when society and colleagues reject your perceptions[18]
- Imagine a better world—to imagine possibility even when society and colleagues consider such possibilities naive, unattainable, or foolish
- Communicate reality and possibility so powerfully that others can't help but move forward toward a better future

After my failure to engage the women executives in a productive discussion of power, I switched from words to an artistic process—in this case, to visual imagery. The following day, I offered the women a pile of art supplies and invited them to create their own image of power. Without speaking or using any words in their artwork, each executive visually explored what power meant to her. After signing and posting their art, the executives interpreted the power images of their colleagues. What emerged was the most robust, positive, and personally owned definition of power I have ever witnessed. By shifting their vocabulary from words to images—from the commonplace to the novel, from linear to holistic associations—each woman broadened her conception of power along with her relationship to its uses. The exercise allowed everyone to see again the possibility of using power to simultaneously achieve positive personal, organizational, and societal outcomes.

Following that initial experiment, other frame-breaking programs for women leaders have been successfully designed. Among the most exciting is The Judy Project, which was launched by Ben Zander, conductor of the Boston Philharmonic, who used music and artistic metaphors to open the gathered leaders to the realm of possibility. Similarly, Smith College and Dartmouth's Tuck School of Business teamed up to launch the world's first completely global program for women leaders. Did we use traditional approaches or leadership vocabulary in either program? Of course not. It was neither what we aspired to nor what would have worked.

Leader as Artist: Artist as Leader

As an artist, my own paintings have involved similar, on-going explorations. Artists, like leaders, constantly face the challenge of seeing reality as it is, even as they shift that reality into the realm of possibility and communicate it powerfully and courageously. Perhaps the era has arrived when we can no longer be leaders of the economy and society without also reclaiming our birthright as artists and citizens. Success and significance cannot be achieved within the traditional language and models of twentieth-century leadership. As I described in my artist's statement for the most recent exhibit of my paintings:

> For me, allowing a painting to be born is to stand in awe of one of life's most beautiful mysteries. Invited by the blank paper, the best of my intentions and experience enter into a dance with uncontrollable coincidence. Neither the process nor the resulting art are ever completely defined. Which way will the colors run? What surprises will the ink reveal as it, ever so gently, touches the paint? I purposely use water-based media that don't stay put where I place them on the paper. There's never any illusion that I control the process. I only enter the dance; paintings emerge out of the dance. For me, being an artist is about giving birth to the possibilities inherent in mystery. Creation—whether on a canvas of words, visual images, or action—is, in fact, about relearning to dance with God.

Vienna 2003: Music-Scapes

At the close of the United Nations conference, I walk onto the stage once again. This time, I am not preparing to speak but to paint—to visually accompany world-renowned violinist Miha Pogacik as he plays Bach.[19] As soon as the music starts, the entire audience seems to disappear, and I seemingly disappear with it, slipping into the music and the moment. The music surrounds me and becomes me. It is as though the music is choreographing me; I become a puppet following its motions. The paint gives birth to images; the music-scape is born. The audience applauds; they, Miha, and I are engulfed in the magic. "Painting is not a performing art!" "Who cares! Leadership is a performing art." I am in Vienna, where the apex and nadir of civilization have met. We are all in Vienna to engage in a new conversation about global leadership and the role that both women and men are being invited to play. No one can erase the nightmare memories of past atrocities. Each of us, however, can and will shape future history. The choice is ours, today, to enter into a new conversation. The world needs us. The world is depending on us. For without our courage and compassion, there will be no future. By creating and entering into a new conversation, the world's children will remember our contributions, and our leadership, with pride.

Part Three

A NEW POWER IN
THE WORLD

To empower women is to empower new civil
societies, to shape democracies, to change the
face of the globe.
>   —*Geraldine McAteer, global activist quoted in the*
>   *Women's Leadership Board, John F. Kennedy*
>   *School, Harvard University, May 2004*

In Part Three, our exploration of a new enlightened power in the world comes full circle.

The chapters here capture the stories of visionaries, activists, teachers, mentors, and business leaders of socially responsible organizations who address crucial questions affecting humanity in our precarious times. Through these stories, we learn how to exercise power in creating a sustainable future through service, social entrepreneurship in business, and new models of global security—and in spite of opposition, entrenched mindsets and bleak forecasts of why transformation is impossible. Through these stories, moreover, we learn how to serve our selves, our organizations, our communities, and our society all at once—and with positive impact all the way around.

These stories, then, convey the essential aspect of *enlightened power*—to be emboldened, energized, and passionate in spite of all barriers and obstacles. The legendary leaders and humanitarians at the center of theses stories show us the way. And, equally important, they help frame the obligation and privilege that we all share—that of empowering and inspiring our next generation of leaders.

Sally Helgesen is author of the groundbreaking *The Female Advantage: Women's Ways of Leadership*, widely hailed as the "classic work" on women's leadership styles, and five other books, including *The Web of Inclusion: A New Architecture for Building Great Organizations*, which was cited in the *Wall Street Journal* as one of the best books on leadership of all time. Sally is also a partner in Helgesen & Glaser, which helps clients build world-class women's programs. She has taught at the Harvard Graduate School of Education and Smith College, delivered keynotes and seminars in companies all over the world, and has consulted extensively for the United Nations.

PHOTO CREDIT: Sally Helgesen by Anthony Loew

23

THE SUSTAINABLE ADVANTAGE

Sally Helgesen

We live in a time when the signs and signals for women as leaders are increasingly contradictory—positive, and progressive on one hand, and worrying and apparently regressive on the other. I'm an optimist by nature, so I continue to believe in women's capacity to provide positive and socially critical leadership in organizations and in the larger world. I recognize, however, that the pressures women feel in today's workplace, combined with the retrenchment that has taken place in many organizations and in the political arena, present unexpected challenges to women's ability to lead. This chapter represents my ongoing effort to think more deeply about what women leaders have to offer the world, especially in regard to creating a more sustainable and inclusive model of work, economic development, and organizational success.

In its first issue of 2003, *Time* magazine broke precedent by selecting as its Person of the Year the three women who had blown the whistle in the year's three major scandals: at Enron, at World-Com, and at the FBI. Because my work as a writer, teacher, consultant, and coach focuses on defining the strengths of women and the contributions they make to organizations, I am often asked if I think it's simply a coincidence that the whistleblowers in the most notorious scandals of the last few years were women. I do not.

The reasons that women have been willing to assume this painful role are various, as anyone familiar with these events knows. One explanation is most certainly that women in large, male-dominated organizations often feel like outsiders, which means they are likely to have fresh eyes to see behaviors that are problematic. Being outside the loop, they are less likely to buy the excuse that "everybody is doing it." However, one common theme in the explanations of each of the women featured on *Time*'s cover struck a particular chord with me because it reflected something I have long noticed in my own work. Women are particularly concerned with the long-term goals and viability of their organizations. As Sherron Watkins, the Enron whistleblower, said in a forum I attended in Boston, "I came forward because I was convinced that what was going on would wreck the company in the long term, despite the short-term profits that were obviously being made." In other words, Watkins was convinced that the strategy and tactics at Enron that were dazzling the marketplace were *not sustainable* over the long term, and so would bring the organization to grief.

The other women whistleblowers expressed similar concerns, variations of which I have heard from women over the years. "These guys are riding high now, but I don't think they can keep it up," is a refrain whose variations I have heard rung by hundreds of women. Within organizations, such Cassandra-like pronouncements often earn women a reputation as naysayers who lack a bold vision, or gloom-and-doom types in thrall to pessimism. I've observed this dynamic in any number of strategy meetings. Here's a general version of how it typically goes:

> *The Big Cheese:* So that's our direction, that's our vision—aggressive acquisition! We're aiming at increasing our numbers by 30 percent this year, and to do that we'll have to move on six new targets.
>
> *Jim:* So what do we do to make that happen?
>
> *Kate:* Is that really what we want? Aren't we having enough problems integrating last year's acquisitions as it is?

The Big Cheese in this context will of course see Jim as a good team player, a potential contributor and ally, whereas Kate comes across as a "downer," focusing on the negative, too cautious to grab the opportunity and run with it.

Yet some version of Kate's response—voiced or unvoiced—was evident in the experiences of the three women who later ended up on the cover of *Time*. If their bosses had been able to listen and learn from their reservations rather than ignoring them or rejecting them as nitpicking and lacking vision, they might have been spared the reversals that culminated in catastrophe. I have likewise over the years heard hundreds of women observe that they believe that the short-term obsessions in the organizations of which they are a part are ultimately harmful. So I think it's worth pondering whether women indeed do have a greater desire to focus on the long term— and what this might have to offer in terms of leadership.

Many anthropologists and evolutionary biologists argue that a bias toward focusing on the long term is a part of the female genetic heritage, a gift of nature rather than a result of nurture. Some point to the obvious fact that women in almost every society since the dawn of humankind have been primarily responsible for the care of children, an inherently long-term project, whereas men's primary responsibility with regard to nurturing children has been to ensure their conception—almost the definition of a short-term event! Others point to the fact that women in ancestral communities had responsibility for growing, harvesting, and storing small crops, a process that took place over many months, whereas their male companions mostly hunted large animals, a process requiring short but intense expenditures of energy and skill.

I am not qualified to judge the worth of these arguments and tend to be skeptical in any case of gender prescriptions that focus on genes or biologically determined characteristics. However, my own experience over the past fifteen years, interviewing and working with women leaders around the world, has persuaded me that a desire to focus on long-term sustainability is indeed a primary characteristic of many women who have been successful at leading organizations.

Sustainability is the key word here, a word whose larger implications I would like to explore in terms of its relationship to how women lead and what women have to offer. Of course, asserting that women have a propensity to focus on the long term can be argued against by presenting contrary examples. Individual women have run companies into the ground as have men, and visionary men have built organizations for the long term. Yet I believe a case can be made that sustainability is, at least in our Western culture, often a female principle or value and that recognizing it as such can help us articulate a more powerful—and transformative—understanding of what women leaders at their best can offer.

Some years ago, I was working on a study of independent oil producers in America—a project that, needless to say, did not focus much attention on women. In the process of tracing how the oil business evolved in this country and examining its ties to the large-scale ranching that shaped the development of the American West, I learned a motto from wildcatters—independent oil producers—that both described and inspired the exploitation and development of the continent's resources: "Get while the getting's good, and move on!" Such a guiding principle, though expressed in different language, guided the progress of much of our early industrial development, which was rigorously focused on maximizing a technology or investment without much regard for its impact on the workforce, the surrounding community, or the natural world.

It was only as the result of efforts of a variety of social reformers in the early part of the twentieth century and of the modern environmental movement in the latter part that this relentlessly short-term approach to human development and progress began to be ameliorated. And it is of course notable that both these movements—in particular the first—were often led by women and were more widely supported in the political arena (once women could vote) by women. From the early reforming efforts of Jane Hull to the powerful inspirational voice of Rachel Carson, arguably the first articulator of the modern notion of "ecology," the ongoing concern with the results of resource exploitation have reflected female concerns. It is notable too that this succession of concerns has often been dismissed by "hardheaded" businessmen as effeminate, insufficiently tough, or overly refined. This is still the language and bias of those in the industrial economy who resent any efforts to constrict their short-term strategies for profit. The same objections were often voiced about the women whose concerns eventually led them to become whistleblowers within their organizations.

My point here is that women have often been carriers of long-term values and concerns and that such values have often been identified, by both supporters and opponents, as specifically feminine and nurturing, an extension of women's age-old private-sphere concern with the creation of a stable and welcoming family life. Indeed, among the early feminist industrial reformers, the stated vision was that of "making the whole world more homelike." And home is by nature an ideal of sustenance and continuity, rather than one of progress, dynamism, or bold leaps into the void.

The disproportionate involvement and influence of women in nineteenth- and twentieth-century movements that have sought to address the "get while the getting's good" approach have a parallel in developing countries today that offers additional perspectives on women and notions of sustainability. Until quite recently, development in poor nations tended to focus on funding large industrial infrastructure projects intended to catapult an impoverished region toward greater prosperity. Donors liked these programs because the data on "improvements" were easy to quantify. For example, a funder could proclaim in its annual report that the organization added 100,000 BTUs of power in the Zambesi Valley, a clear and quantifiable claim. Government ministers in poor countries promoted this approach because huge infrastructure projects provided vivid evidence of modernity—as well as many opportunities for graft.

But the actual impact of such projects on the people in nearby communities was often negligible or disastrous—villages uprooted, local subsistence crops destroyed, whole regions emptied of male labor. Nor could local populations hope to sustain enormous industrial projects that required complex skills, constant infusions of capital, and continual maintenance. As poverty persisted in the face of massive investments, support began to grow for small, innovative grassroots projects that ameliorated local problems in concrete but subtle and sustainable ways—projects that also increasingly focused on women.

This shift away from huge projects to projects that improved women's daily lives happened in part because women and their children were often the only ones left in villages decimated by war or the removal of male labor. It also happened in part because early studies, such as one commissioned by the United Nations agency for women, showed a greater return on the dollar for donors on projects aimed at women. Why? Primarily because women in developing societies tend to invest a greater proportion of resources available to them in the education of their children, rather than in acquiring status symbols such as cars and electronic equipment—or second wives! Projects that focused on women's issues thus provided multiple positive effects for whole communities. In addition, because investments aimed at women were small in scale, rather than focused on huge industrial projects, they presented few opportunities for graft. Finally, raising the status and income of women in poor societies turned out to be the single most powerful means of containing the explosive population growth that so often undermined these societies.

The Grameen bank, a microlender to women in Bangladesh, became the prototype of the successful new approach to development that focused on building capacity in a sustainable way among women in poor communities. Inspired by its example, many small grassroots women's organizations began providing services directly to local communities, often bypassing governmental institutions altogether. The small organizations tended to include many women or to be founded and run by them, whereas the governments and more orthodox development groups were almost entirely male. Thus the shift in focus from large industrial projects to "sustainable human development" was from the first associated with women. It was by means of implementing this principle that women's voices were both heard and heeded in development work.

What I see, then, is that women have played a continuing role in containing the "get while the getting's good" approach wherever it is manifest: in unmediated industrial capitalism, the wanton exploitation of natural resources, third world development, or the kind of greed and willful blindness to the long term that brought down an Enron or a WorldCom. Whether women's focus on sustainability is the result of nature or nurture doesn't matter; a concern with the long term is one of the great gifts of many women leaders. Acknowledging this is not meant to suggest that many men are not also concerned with building sustainable organizations and societies. But the dominant organizational model devised almost entirely by men has tended to encourage short-term thinking and strategies.

I believe that as the spheres and responsibilities of men and women become more similar, our model of leadership will change, dissolving boundaries between what we think of as masculine and what we think of as feminine. This is now beginning to happen, and the scandals of recent years are only making more obvious the need for change by opening us to questions about the kind of heroic go-it-alone leader whose high-profile daring garners short-term acclaim but who often leaves his organization overleveraged, overextended, a burned-out case. I believe that the focus on sustainability that has traditionally been carried by women will have a large impact on organizations in the future, creating new opportunities for extraordinary women leaders.

One of the most visionary, inspiring, articulate, and inclusive leaders I have known was Sharon Capeling-Alakija, who headed the United Nations Volunteers (UNV) until her death in late 2003. UNV's mandate is to provide and deploy highly skilled volunteers to a range of efforts, from staffing health clinics in impoverished regions to helping provide computer skills to remote communities. Sharon, who had formerly headed UNIFEM and who commissioned the original study that showed donors how investing in women's projects brought greater returns on investment, always understood the link between women and sustainable development. She sought to focus only on projects that could build long-term capacity in the regions her organization served. In addition, she worked to build greater sustainability within her own organization—supporting innovative practices and ideas that originated in the front lines, challenging staff to expand their thinking and giving them opportunities to develop their range of experience. This included using volunteers in decision making, integrating training into the work of every day, raising the profile of the organization with a range of stakeholders, and bringing in outside partners to build skills and capacity within an organization that had (like many UN agencies) looked either inward or toward headquarters for its direction.

Sharon was extraordinary, but I have seen others like her, and I believe that their legacy, and the legacy of the women whistleblowers featured in *Time*, point the way to a new model of leadership— one that sees building sustainability and capacity in organizations as the long-term goal. In effect their task will be, as the early feminist reformers put it, "making the whole world more homelike." Women leaders aim to create a place where relationships flourish and resources are held in stewardship rather than exploited for short-term gain.

Barbara Waugh is a former street activist, journalist, machinist, and campus administrator who joined Hewlett-Packard (HP) to test a simple idea: "If you can't beat 'em, join 'em and change 'em from the inside out." She went on to lead a different kind of revolution from within by helping transform the role and status of women and minority leaders in the organization. Formerly the worldwide change agent at HP Labs, Barbara recently cofounded e-inclusion, an HP group whose mission is to close the gap between technology-empowered and technology-excluded communities. In concert with other innovative HP efforts such as Digital Villages and e-government, e-inclusion is determined to invent new solutions that will increase revenues for HP while promoting economic development in emerging markets.

The chapter that follows is adapted from Barbara's book *The Soul in the Computer*. It describes three critical moments in her early leadership journey: a personal triumph in overcoming stereotypes on an individual level; an organizational triumph in delivering HP's first major women's summit; and a social triumph in leveraging her growing influence within the organization to affect an important political and societal issue.

PHOTO CREDIT: Barbara Waugh by Irene Young

24

SNAPSHOTS OF A CORPORATE RADICAL

Barbara Waugh

The Soul in the Computer: The Story of a Corporate Revolutionary is my story of seventeen years at HP. For me (but not for everybody) it has been more positive and productive to lead a revolution inside corporations than it was to lead a revolution against them. For many radicals, this is the most radical idea of all. But the facts of my life support this guiding idea in my life. What I do know is this: the cubicles of the corporate world are teeming with revolutionaries. I know because I meet us everywhere. But too many of us remain isolated, never sharing our ideas, our passions, our deep objections to "business as usual."

I believe that the future of the planet depends on the corporate sector stepping up to accept our share of stewardship of the planet and life on Earth. We can no longer leave this vital work to the religious, nonprofit, civic, and government sectors.

I believe that corporations can step up, must step up, and will step up. I believe it because I've experienced, from the inside, what can happen in a good company. I believe it because I know there are many good companies out there with a lot of people inside them who care—people who are working on orienting our companies toward "doing well by doing good." And I believe it because there are a lot of good people and organizations outside our companies— people who find it more productive to work from the outside—who are insisting on new levels of accountability and citizenship for the corporate sector. It will take all of us, working inside and out, wherever we can be most effective.

The three passages that follow are quick snapshots of my journey. In small journeys and large, we can make a difference. I hope
that you can relate to these stories. I hope that you can lean on them
and even use them as change management tools to make the corner
of your office, your organization, and your society a better place.
Most of all, I hope they inspire you to live and write your own story.
Please let me know how I can help.

The HP Way?

People at Hewlett-Packard talk a lot about the HP Way, Bill Hewlett
and Dave Packard's belief that people fundamentally want to do the
right thing and that if you give them a supportive environment and
the right tools, they will. But it seems to me that much like the "way"
of most of the religious institutions I've dealt with, the HP Way really
means "married, two kids, churchgoing"—as personified by Carol
Love, one of the people who interviewed me during my recruitment.[1]
The picture on her desk of her blond husband and two blond kids is
in a heart-shaped frame, if you can believe it. During the interviews,
I was sure she would be the one to keep me from getting the job.
Somehow this didn't happen.

Luckily, I seem to be able to do the job. I supervise all aspects of
recruiting the 110 engineers we've got to get in the door: selecting
candidates, searching through the huge HP database, phone screen-
ing, on-site interviewing, handling travel logistics, making offers,
getting new hires in place. The work is intense, and we have barely
the people we need to get it all done. Even so, it's easier than trying
to end sexism in theological education with a budget of $40,000
and fourteen volunteers, which was my job at the Graduate Theological Union in Berkeley.

I'm about four months into the job when Carol tells me that she
told the hiring manager after my interview, "If you don't hire her
I'm going to quit. She's just what we need." At morning break, we
walk outside and begin talking about our lives. She's dying inside
that heart-shaped frame. Hasn't had an evening out on her own in

years. Wants to join a group of women exploring their lives through their dreams. Can't imagine how. It would be once a month. We talk about what it could mean in her life. She makes it happen.

She wants to know about my time as the first feminist news columnist in the country (at the *Capital Times* in Madison, Wisconsin); my years as a socialist feminist hippie; the years in the peace, civil rights, and women's movements. She soaks up my story and begins to write completely new chapters in her own. In a few years I will have to call her to find out where I can do a sweat lodge and she will give me several alternatives, all with her personal assessment, along with a travel brochure of mystical journeys—personally, she's off to Machu Picchu.

So if Carol isn't the HP Way after all, at least as I'd imagined, perhaps it's a guy I'll call Bob. A total nerd—thin, pale, complete with plastic pocket protector, thick glasses, and an engineering project I can't understand. The quintessential HP employee, a man with no need to hide out. We talk now and then about nothing.

I'm just back from lunch one hot day, and Bob's sitting at my desk. Can he talk to me? Of course, I say. He has something he wants to tell me that he's never told anyone else. He looks very uncomfortable, and I ask him if we should get a meeting room where we will have some privacy. With some relief, he agrees.

Bob and I walk over to the room. And then, with great hesitation, he shares with me his great secret. He feels he doesn't fit in at all, and if HP really knew who he was, they wouldn't want him. I ask him why, imagining all kinds of things, but I'm completely unprepared for Bob's secret: he's Canadian, not American. He asks me what I think. I say I can really understand his feeling of not belonging and tell him he's the personification of HP to me. I can't imagine anyone belonging if he doesn't. He's astonished. I go on to say that I don't think being Canadian should be a reason for feeling like he doesn't belong. There are other Canadians. I name a few. And then I tell him a story that I also need to hear.

When I was directing the Center for Women and Religion, we had a retreat for the board, directors, work-study student staff, and the students we served. At some point, the question came up, "Who is at the center of the Center?" Oddly, the board thought the directors were; the directors thought the students were; the student staff thought the students were; the students thought the board of directors was. No one experienced herself at the center.

Bob and I muse on the question, What is this in us that has us always putting ourselves outside the circle of the select few that run things? Maybe the benefit of feeling "outside" is that we don't have to be responsible for what goes on. But I think a lot of us would be willing to be responsible, except at a deeper level we feel completely incapable and unable—for whatever reason. We have no sense of agency in our lives. And this leads us to collude in our own powerlessness in ways that we never examine, beginning with never sharing our fears and our dreams with the people around us.

Standing outside the circle that decides things, we become spectators to our own lives. We're watching TV, have lost the remote, and can't change the channel. At best we're bored; at worst, depressed, suicidal, or homicidal. We can never put down a stake, take a stand, act on what we care passionately about. With no stake, it becomes very difficult to feel anything at all, let alone feel something passionately.

I share with Bob some of my radical past, including the fact that my partner is a woman. He sees with great relief that there are things more strange than being Canadian. He wonders why I came to HP since I'm interested in changing the world. I tell him I think this is the place to do it, but I'm not sure how. This, he says, he can really understand. He leaves, and I am astonished: I have a new friend, Bob. Who looks like a real person to me now, not a nerd anymore. Amazing.

Strength in Numbers

The chair of the third HP Technical Women's Conference is Laurie Mittelstadt, an HP Labs engineer. She asks me to be on her advisory board and to help her put the conference together. I agree. This conference matters.

The first Technical Women's Conference (TWC), chaired by HP Labs engineer Darlene Solomon in 1988, brought together women whose voices were lost in the majority-male culture at HP. In those days, women engineers in high-tech represented a token presence, though their numbers were growing.

When women (or minorities) are distributed across a large population and isolated in departments that are otherwise all male (or any other majority), we have little influence and have a difficult time being heard or getting credit for our contributions. We are tokens. Rosabeth Moss Kanter discusses the phenomenon of tokenism in her landmark book *Men and Women of the Corporation*.[2] Tokens burn out and do not change the system. The goal of tokens who want to make a difference, then, is to aggregate and become a group, a group big enough to become a minority, because minority groups can and do change things.

With some instinctive knowledge of these truths, a steering committee of HP women organized the first TWC and created the model that would last for over a decade: workshops and papers to showcase and develop women technically, in our careers, as stewards of the planet, and as a network, all the while demonstrating the value of women employees in general and the value of this gathering in particular to the bottom line of the company. That first year, four hundred women met—on a Saturday, because the company did not regard the meeting as work related. However, CEO John Young did show up and give the keynote.

That conference, like the one we are planning now, three years later, is crucial for the women at HP. It brings together isolated women engineers and other professionals so we can scale up and see our situation from a broader perspective, see that our problems are not unique. It connects and empowers us.

The first big issue we face is that this year we want to hold the conference on company time. The TWC is clearly work related, whether or not our management sponsors see it that way. To get management to see the light, we are going to have to speak their language. And to do that, I first have to change my own mind-set—an old left-wing legacy—that says, "Of course HP doesn't want to sponsor women meeting and comparing notes about what the company is doing to us." I have to assume instead that of course HP wants to do the right thing. We just have to show them why this is the right thing.

So we reframe the context of the conference. Instead of presenting it to management as an event that benefits women, we present it as an event that benefits HP, that is in the service of company values and goals. We focus on the benefits to HP of supporting its women employees in their professional development and in their community. We point out that the conference is not only an employee-development tool but an employee-retention tool. And an excellent one, too: it's pretty cheap, it's something the target audience wants, and it works!

Luckily, we have incredibly wonderful women with a lot more credibility than I to explain this to management. There are really solid, outstanding women engineers, like Darlene Solomon—who, on any level you measure her, is your quintessential ideal employee—who really want the conference and are willing to sit down and quite reasonably make our case. It's good for me to recognize when I'm not the one who should go in and tackle the "opposition."

This is another aspect of building your cadre: sharing the opportunity to lead. When we do this, we discover that the extent to which people own a project is the extent to which they invest their time and energy to make it succeed.

Besides, I'm not real coolheaded on this particular subject. I mean, this whole notion that we shouldn't meet on company time just undoes me. Laurie and I go around ranting, "Are you kidding? Every single day here is a men's conference. We just want two days in the year for women!" Eventually, we make enough noise and win our point. We can have two work days to hold the TWC.

(Reflecting on this TWC a few years later, Laurie appears on the front page of a section of the *Wall Street Journal* saying, "Every single day at HP is a men's conference . . . we just wanted two days for women!" Oh no, I think. "You've had it," the Voice of Reason thunders in my head. I am sure someone from somewhere is going to lower the boom. But in the article, HP comes across as a company that supports people speaking their truth, even if it isn't flattering. So even this works in the service of the company.)

Laurie and I decide to invite Anne Firth Murray, founder and director of the Global Fund for Women, to be a keynote speaker. We ask her to challenge us to think about our success: "Success for what?" I am a little afraid of doing this, as I am every time I bring my radical past (or present) into work. What if "Success for what?" ticks women off? What if Anne's outspoken beliefs about patriarchy and women's oppression offend someone? But I am even more afraid of living in a world where women can't speak up.

When I prepare my remarks to introduce Anne, I remind everyone that members of the Hewlett and Packard families were founding donors of the Global Fund for Women. Compelled by the prospect of the deep and expectant listening of eight hundred women, I decide I will say that I believe global companies should define corporate citizenship not as something we do in the mile-and-a-half radius around the factories where we operate, but as something we do on the entire planet—which, for a global company, is the neighborhood. My dream of HP's raising the bar on what it means to be a corporate citizen begins to take shape with this talk.

With voice mail, working at all hours in all time zones, Laurie and I network all over the company for the self-organizing subcommittees, who invite speakers and line up the conference site. In crisis after crisis, we discover support from unexpected places all over the company.

Next crisis? We need money. A lot of it, to pay advances for the hotel and speakers. And we need it long before we can possibly collect enough conference registration fees. Will Corporate front us the money, given that the TWC is a diversity retention tool? No. No part of Corporate will fund us.

What to do? With a few days left before the hotel cancels our reservation, I pour out our woes to the HP Labs controller, Andrew Liu, already a good friend, and afterward one of my best friends in the whole company. Seeing the right thing to do, he signs for the large advances—and figures out how to do it aboveboard—even though he is risking exposure if we have a shortfall.

And one cold, dark night, it looks like a shortfall is exactly what we're going to have. Laurie comes by my office on her way out the door, stricken. Our carefully planned conference has been cancelled due to companywide expense controls. We will lose all our deposits. All our planning will be for nothing. Is there anything I can do?

I can't think of anything, but I automatically reach for the phone. I call a former boss at Corporate, now a good friend. He says, "Better believe it. It's canceled. Don't fight it. You'll just look like you're not a team player."

This isn't the answer I want, so I keep calling. I reach my current boss, the director of HP Labs, on his car phone. He's completely sympathetic. A street fighter, he kicks into action. He has a meeting the next morning with Dean Morton, the chief operating officer of the company. He'll ask Dean if they can make a special case for this conference. Frank reports back that he didn't even have to argue the case: Dean Morton declared this conference an exception. We are on!

Eight hundred people come to our two-day conference, double the number who attended the first one. Afterward, Laurie Mittel-stadt leaves me a "picture" voice mail, as she will do many more times over the next years. In these she describes all facets of her own experience of our latest kaleidoscopic event. Laurie's pictures:

> Walking into the conference room, feeling awe in the company of almost a thousand women who were kind of like me—a conference that makes insiders of outsiders, a place to fit in for those of us living in a world where we don't fit in.

> The farmer-engineer woman in overalls and boots, the techno-marketers in their red suits with bows around their necks, the feminine marketers in their high-heels and plunging necklines, the engineers like me in brand-new suits.

Dean Morton coming to the podium, sweating with nervousness, looking out at a sea of women, opening with a great sigh and the words "This must be how you feel"—and being unable to continue because of the roar of the applause.

The latticework with flowers in front of the urinals in the men's rooms that we've converted to women's rooms for the day.

Knowing that I can walk up to anyone here, describe my work, hear that it is cool, and get help if I need it.

Finding an instant network of women to call across the company [long before the Internet and posted org charts are available].

A woman who had decided not to be an R&D manager changes her mind after hearing one of the speakers. Other women also decide to take a chance, to go into management, to make that phone call.

Learning that the lessons learned are not unique to women but are human in scale.

After the conference we apply to Catalyst, a prestigious national advocacy organization for professional women, to be considered for their coveted annual award for positive change on behalf of women. We win it, making this the first time the Catalyst award has been given to a grassroots group. Our CEO flies to New York to be filmed accepting the prize. We sit in the audience for the awards ceremony. When asked how he helped make the conference happen, John Young declares, "I did nothing but get out of the way!"

Over the next decade, thousands more HP women all over the world will join to produce these conferences. Soon the TWC becomes an annual regional event that opens with meetings organized by different business sectors and attended by the sector vice president and his or her staff. At these meetings, the major business, technology, and marketing issues of the sector are discussed, and the women exchange their ideas, questions, and proposals. They are challenged to take issues back to their divisions and come up with ideas and innovations to create breakthrough solutions to them.

Besides getting a chance to meet the vice president their division reports to, women network among themselves, often recruiting each other for business and technology teams and projects. This results in cross-functional experience, job transfers, and often promotions. Retention rates increase.

The core premise and benefit of the conference is women talking business. For example, at one of these gatherings, two women start a discussion that results in developing new technology for a chemical-analysis system that involves the materials and manufacturing know-how of thermal ink jet technology.

After a decade of TWCs, HP's company culture will be radically transformed into one where women can fully contribute. HP women will become a voice, a presence, and equal partners with male colleagues for success and change.

At the same time, HP will become the first company on the Fortune 200 to be able to really "see" the best candidate for CEO—and not see just gender. Carly Fiorina will take over as HP's CEO on July 19, 1999. Coincidence that this happens in the only Fortune 200 company with a TWC? I don't think so.

So-Called Budget Reform

Later that year, one midnight as I'm doing email, my fussy baby boy finally asleep, I blink three times as my adrenaline begins to pump: I can't believe what I'm reading. It seems HP is supporting California governor Wilson's 1993 Budget Reform Initiative.

I know from my radical friends outside the company that "budget reform" is the euphemism for an initiative to reduce Aid to Families with Dependent Children (AFDC) and other benefits going to the poorest women and children in the state.

Support for this initiative seems to me absolutely contrary to HP's citizenship objective, and I am really upset. How can we be good citizens—we, the wealthiest in our communities—if we support cutting benefits for the poorest?

At the same time, I'm tired, with already too much to do. Can I really do anything that will matter when The Company has decided to go this route? I, as one employee? I fade into thinking about my favorite movie—the way I choose to remember it.

In *The Year of Living Dangerously,* a journalist in Indonesia in the 1960s is covering the downfall of the Sukarno government. He hangs around with the rest of the journalists, covering the same things they are, until he meets a nondescript "little man" played by Linda Hunt. Before long, this little man has gotten the journalist into the most important government parties, into the heart of the guerrilla movement, to the girlfriend of his dreams, and so on.

Then the journalist stumbles into the little man's digs one afternoon to discover on the man's desk an entire folder about himself, with the equivalent of a job description, performance review, and development plan. The journalist is enraged and demands that the little man tell him who he is. As I recall it, the journalist cries out, "Who do you think you are to have files on me?" And the little man replies, "Who got you all your best contacts with the government, the opposition, even your girlfriend? I am who I am."

The lesson I take from this is that being marginal can be very powerful. The little man is unimportant—he looks like a servant—so he can get into any society party or top government meeting he wants. He looks like a peasant, so the guerrillas trust him. He isn't sexually appealing, so he threatens neither women nor men and can act as the matchmaker. Being nontechnical in a high-tech company and in personnel to boot is being fairly marginal, and, relative to the line-management jobs, it's not threatening. Line managers blow us off all the time. The more marginal one is, the more one can speak truth with impunity to the powers that be. The medieval courts had their fools to round out the king's picture of reality. The contemporary corporation has me and others like me.

I come back to the phone in my hand and send voice mails to fifteen people who I think would feel the same way about HP's support for the budget reform initiative or who might have some information to bear. "Did you read this?" I ask. "What do you know about it? What does it mean? My first reaction is that it's very disappointing and in misalignment with our values as a company. What do you think?"

I get lots of responses with information, elaboration, and similar sentiments. Where once there was only my voice, I have amplified it, and there are now sixteen of us. This gives me the information and the platform and the confidence to keep going.

Then I go outside the company to amplify my own voice. I talk to activist friends and people at other companies, and I confirm that this is indeed a big thing. Groups like the local Council of Churches and children's advocacy groups, including one headed by the former president of Stanford, are saying this is a terrible thing.

Now I have a choice. I can assume that HP is the corporate bad guy my radical friends (and some part of me) think it is, or I can assume that top management must not know about this aspect of the budget reform bill. I decide on the latter. I decide to assume that HP is decent and fair, just ill informed. I assume the company wants to do the right thing.

From that stance, I can act. My next step is to contact our CEO. Do I know John Young? Not really. Our paths did cross at a recent HP Labs meeting, though, so I decide to make another positive assumption. I assume we have a relationship and approach him from that point of view.

I send John an email thanking him for his great comments at that meeting, then I add that I was quite alarmed to read that HP is supporting the Budget Reform Initiative. I summarize my research. I mention the full-page newspaper ad that's just appeared, headlined "Why Are California's Richest Citizens Conspiring to Rob Its Poorest Citizens?" The ad goes on to compare the salary of the CEO of a Bay Area company to the monthly chit of a welfare mother. I let him know what I've learned: that this ad is just the first of many that are planned. Each week will feature a different CEO. His own name and salary are already in the lineup. I remind him that it's the local Council of Churches and the local labor unions that are paying for the ads.

I tell him that the former president of Bill and Dave's alma mater, Stanford University, has called the budget reform "unspeakably cruel to children." I add that the children who will not be eating breakfast have names for me—my own kid's friends figure among the children at risk.

I ask if there isn't some alternative—perhaps a legislative solution for balancing the budget that would leave AFDC alone? (I know that HP even considered supporting a legislative solution, but chose instead to support the governor.)

Our CEO emails a response within twenty-four hours, shares his own misgivings about the company position, and tells me he's asked our head of government affairs to explore alternatives. Later I learn from friends close to the decision that my email to John has catalyzed a reversal of our support and that HP is throwing all its resources behind the legislative solution, which would leave AFDC intact.

I find myself thinking how my understanding of "the company" and "corporate" has changed since I've worked at HP. "The corporation" is not the homogenous, nefarious, unyielding monster I once thought. It's an aggregation of people who make decisions, sometimes bad ones. And we can—and will—change these decisions if the disadvantages outweigh the advantages and if people are around to make that case.

In the end, the 1993 Budget Reform Initiative dies for lack of support.

In 1984, with $350 in the bank, Eileen Fisher designed and introduced four basic pieces at the boutique show in New York City, where she received $3,000 in orders. Three months later, she expanded the line to eight pieces—and brought in $40,000 in orders. Eileen Fisher, Inc., was born. The original concept—high-quality, comfortable women's clothing that works as a "wardrobe concept"—still defines the evolving line that now fills thirty Eileen Fisher stores and is sold in department and specialty stores across the United States and Canada. Eileen remains at the helm of the company today as chief creative officer. She is surrounded by a team of talented executives, including Susan M. Schor, a former professor of organizational psychology who joined the company as vice president of people and culture because she was drawn to the company's commitment to its people and the opportunity to "practice what she had been preaching" in academia. Indeed, the story of Eileen Fisher, Inc., is remarkable not only for its business success but also for its focus on employee well-being and social responsibility.

In this interview, Eileen and Susan reveal how they maintain a focus on the triple bottom line to enhance personal, organizational, and social well-being through their leadership.

25

THE SOCIALLY RESPONSIBLE LEADER

Eileen Fisher and Susan M. Schor

Editors

Your organization serves as a model for social responsibility. When we talk to people about enlightened organizations, your company gets mentioned as an inspiration. How did your company's social responsibility focus arise?

Fisher

Part of it arose out of our involvement with the Social Venture Network, a group of global businesspeople committed to social responsibility. Our commitment to human rights originally came from my ex-husband, who was very passionate about that area. He had traveled to China, Mexico, and Guatemala and had seen the realities of the production work. He became passionate about child labor issues as a result. It resonated with what felt right to us in the company. My own earlier experiences working in the restaurant business really sensitized me to issues of decency and fair play in the workplace.

Schor

Our company is only one of three in the U. S. to comply with the workplace standards administered by Social Accountability 8000, a standard bearer in our industry. These standards cover health and safety, wages, workplace hours, and minimum working ages at factories around the globe. Last year, the company named Amy Hall as director of social consciousness to oversee corporate giving. In addition to processing some forty requests a week, Amy travels to China several times a year to visit the contractor who manufactures 60 percent of the clothes bearing the Eileen Fisher label (the other 40 percent is made in New York) and to observe that workers are treated equitably. We are a private company not publicly traded and as such can really focus on the social responsibility agenda. One example is that we were recently honored by the Trickle Up program, which provides seed money and business training for a half-million people seeking to start their own businesses in Africa, Asia, Latin America, and the United States.

Editors

In addition to your commitment to human rights and improving work conditions globally, your mission statement expresses a commitment to support women through social initiatives that address their well-being. Can you tell us more about how you do this?

Fisher

We invite every woman to express her own style, and we design clothes that give feminism back its beauty. I design clothes for the women I see and meet. None of us has a perfect body, but our bodies, a real woman's body, can be seen and shown in a comfortable way. That is what I want, for a woman to be herself. I want people to notice the woman, not the clothes.

In terms of social initiatives, we support many organizations such as the Global Fund for Women, Omega Institute, Gilda's Club, and Eve Ensler's work stopping violence against women worldwide. Women's issues are important to me. I believe women have a unique way of approaching the world. The message for me is how we change the world, very simply in our immediate lives. The way we listen, the value we place on relationships, and our instinct to connect enhance our capacity to make a difference every day—whether we are running a company or running a home (or both!).

Editors

Your mission extends to the well-being of your own employees. Can you tell us more about how this is reflected in your corporate culture?

Schor

We value individual development, well-being, collaboration, creativity, and social consciousness. We encourage employees to grow within the company and find roles they feel passionate about. We give our six hundred–plus employees a sense of ownership by sharing at least 10 percent pretax profits with them each year. Everyone gets a $1,000 personal education benefit and a $1,000 wellness benefit. The company hosts free classes in yoga, tai chi, stress reduction, and dance movement. There is also a stipend of $500 to $2,500 to spend on clothing at wholesale prices. We just want people to love this company, and we know that people's contributions are often more focused when they feel more relaxed, more centered. Living our values every day across many sites can be challenging, yet we are committed to practicing truth telling and making the values real.

Editors

Can you describe your leadership style in "making it real" every day?

Fisher

We believe in leading by example. I want the people in my company to join me in what I care about and what I want to accomplish. It is about staying with one's heart and trying to be human with others. As the company gets bigger, I am working very hard to keep it on track, to keep following my principles that guided us early on. That is part of the essence of who we are. I don't want to lose any of the good things as we continue our growth.

To make it real is tricky. It is a never-ending and ongoing dynamic. Several years ago I put out my vision of how our company could be. The minute you do that others start judging how you are falling short of ideal. We like to say we "strive for imperfection."

Editors

That is a great phrase. Can you talk more about "striving for imperfection"?

Schor

People feel very appreciative of Eileen and very privileged to be here. Many, many people say "I hope to work here until I retire." A lot of the vision relates to the way we work and what experience we want people to have. We have a turnover rate of 17 percent in the retail stores as opposed to 50.7 percent for the apparel retail industry. At the same time, we have challenges every day to deal with the cultural impact of new people who have been more oriented to the bottom line. We recently did a survey to get a sense of the challenges. We are undertaking a very exciting initiative to bring more integration of creativity, business, and culture.

Editors

You are an artist and a designer, and you're working collaboratively with Susan, chief culture officer, and Paula Bennett, chief operating officer, to lead this organization. And you also have a vision for your products, the company, and the world you live in. How does the creative energy of the artist influence your leadership practice?

Fisher

We approach things very holistically. We're always talking about the interrelationships among the things we are trying to do in the company. In the early days, we used to say that we simply make comfortable clothes. Now we talk about what we want the environment of the company to be, and how we want people to buy our clothes and be comfortable. But one thing we have experienced is that whenever we are struggling with the clothing, that's when we are often struggling with the company. It's such a metaphor.

Editors

Do you have any examples of that?

Fisher

Yes. Right now the line has gotten huge. We're working hard to sort out how it goes together. We have monthly deliveries of seasonal items, and we wonder how lines, shapes, necklines, colors, and fabrics all interrelate. What's so interesting is that we are experiencing the same struggle with the whole company. The company has reached a size that makes us wonder how it all goes together. One thing that emerged from the survey we mentioned is that people feel very connected to their immediate teams but don't feel connected to the whole company. That seems to mirror the feelings around the clothes. We like all of our designs and we like our individual pieces, but we struggle with how they go together. Does that neckline go with that, do those pants go with that top, do those two colors go together? Maybe they don't!

So the idea of interconnection is a big thing right now. I love the idea of that metaphor. There's a connection between the artistic issues and the business issues.

Schor

It comes down to a question of what are we really about? What is the line, the real message of the season? It has been a challenge to articulate that lately. And the same thing happens on an organizational level. We are asking ourselves what is our purpose, what is our vision, again and again. It evolves.

Editors

Let's talk about how they interrelate. For example, what does wellness have to do with clothing? What about yoga and work?

Fisher

We hosted an event in New York City for the Women's Network for a Sustainable Future in the Soho store. We brought a yoga teacher there, and she did yoga with everyone, and I spoke about the mission and culture of the company. And then people did some shopping! Ten percent of the proceeds from the event went to the social organization. It was all interconnected. The clothing, the yoga, the shopping, and the social issues.

Editors

Everyone seems to be experiencing a measure of stress or strain in their lives, trying to fit all the pieces together. How do your employees address that strain on a personal level?

Schor

We need for people to have boundaries. We say, we need you to go home and be the person that you are.

Fisher

It's that line between passion and obsession. There is a dark side. Sometimes I have to stop myself from going to meetings. I have trouble disengaging. We need to be clear about how we spend our time. It's not just about the five minutes or one hour that something will take. It's a question of, where does this take my consciousness? Where do I want to be?

Editors

In this book, authors such as Brady and Salvatore have been saying that the idea of *balance* isn't working as it should and that maybe *integration* is the better word to capture what we need in our lives. That sounds a little like your struggles with your clothing line.

Fisher

Yes. I think that speaks to what we are talking about at work; the wellness end, the yoga. How does doing yoga help? A lot of people say they can't take an hour out of the day to do yoga. So let's integrate it into work. We start at the beginning of a meeting and do five minutes of breathing or stretches. Susan is a much better promoter of this than I am. But integration is a word I use as well. I see that people are having a hard time separating themselves from their passion for getting it done, solving the problems, getting it right, and the artistic piece of that. To separate from it feels hard. To integrate it feels right.

Editors

On the other side of the coin, I would think that it would be very difficult for an employee to try to lead an integrated life if she didn't have leaders who hold this as important.

Fisher

Susan uses the word *permission* all the time. We need to keep giving people permission. You need to feel permission to understand and respond to urgency, to not feel like you have to suppress that and get the work done and forget about your children and husband. You need to give yourself permission to be a whole person.

Editors

And if you are not given that permission, aren't you actually being given permission to do the opposite and sacrifice family, compromise well-being and so on?

Fisher

That's true. And that's not a healthy thing.

Schor

When a few people feel permission to stop work at the end of the day or take some family time, others feel they can too. As a company, we are trying to make that happen more. Of course, there's always resistance because it interferes with work. It has to take on a life of its own, and we are committed to making it happen. We know that such an approach has its own complications, but it brings us to a new place of changing the way we think and really doing what we say we want to do. We want to help people integrate their work life and personal life.

Editors

Do you get any strange reactions to your culture from outsiders, such as customers, vendors, or partners?

Fisher

I think so. For example, we used to send people to Bloomingdale's to help support our product or work on visual presentation. Bloomingdale's thought our people were just different. There was something odd about us. We weren't there to sell clothes. But we were there to talk and listen to customers and see how people responded and understand how to make it look better. A lot of companies send people in to tell salespeople how to sell their clothes, and try to make sales. Bloomingdale's was completely baffled. How can we be one of their biggest vendors if selling isn't our biggest priority? They could tell that by the way our people are.

I got similar reactions at the event I mentioned in Soho. People came up to me and said EF people are so genuine. It's interesting to hear such things from someone who doesn't know us very well. Amy, who heads our social consciousness area, said, "I think we're going to get a lot of applications for jobs after this event." People on the outside are surprised, but they see the possibilities.

Editors

Given how differently you are seen in the industry, do you have a sense of how customers experience your company?

Fisher

We did a focus group outside the company recently. We don't really do that kind of thing. But we wanted to hear about what people think of our product. It wasn't so much about the stores as the brand loyalty. The people who ran the groups said they had never experienced such brand loyalty before. The people in the focus groups said everything they wanted to say. They wanted to tell the truth about the pieces they did and didn't like. And they wanted to tell it to me personally. That happens at our stores too. They say, "Tell Eileen this," like I am their sister or their personal designer or something. There's this inner connection.

Editors

How did your very distinctive advertising campaign, the "Women Change the World Every Day" series, come about?

Fisher

We started with the concept of photographing real people, our employees, that sort of thing. Then we went to an outside agency. Some of the women pictured in that campaign are friends of ours. You might have seen my friend Sylvia Nasar, author of A Beautiful Mind. She's a really good personal friend. Others we find through people who know someone who fits. And then we have a casting agency that is aware of the kind of people we are looking for.

We want authenticity to come through, and we want women to feel they can be who they are. Sometimes it is accomplished women, or women expressing a relaxed way of being. But we always want the reality of their authenticity to project. We want people to be who they are, and for them to know that our clothes give them permission to do that. They don't have to pretend to be anything they are not when they are in our clothes.

Editors

How about the message that "women change the world every day"?

Fisher

We struggled with that. Our internal message is to inspire women to celebrate who they are. We used to say, we want to be ourselves. When I first heard the slogan, I was terrified of it, and I thought it was too big for us. Too overreaching. But the truth is, we are a simple company, and I hope we change the world. And I hope we touch women and honor women. I think that women change the world by the little things they do as well as the big things. Sometimes it is just being kind, or writing a book. I felt a lot of pressure around the idea of "changing the world."

Editors

Are you comfortable with it now?

Fisher

I have come to a place where I like that it is there. We are changing the world. I think that it is a wonderful message, and it has inspired a lot of people. So I am proud of that. I personally feel like I am more of an artist, more of a simple person. The message for me is how we change the world simply, in our lives. My conflict about it was that we present these very accomplished women, but the point we are trying to make is that it's about how you "be" in the world rather than what you "do" in the world.

We did get responses from women who asked, "What about housewives who stay home and have babies?" Of course, we think that is hugely meaningful as well.

Editors

Let's get back to your key challenges right now of integration and interconnection. Do you see light at the end of the tunnel? Do you know what the next challenge or vision for your organization will be after this hurdle?

Fisher

That's a big one. I think we are struggling with change and with trying to move the organization forward. We call it trying to have the organization self-generate and separate itself to some extent from me. That's a lot like seeing your teenager head off to college. She's ready to create her own vision, not without me, but re-creating it in some internal way that doesn't absolutely require me. In the past, I have been called the creative inspirer, responsible for the quantum shifts in the company's direction. I feel like it is time for those things to happen independent of me. We need the vision to expand and re-create itself. Spontaneity or aliveness and the struggle about what is new are the challenges. How do we re-create the leadership of the organization so it can generate new business if I happen not to be there?

Editors

Do you have to change your leadership style when the company grows from just one location to many?

Fisher

Every time the company grows, it's hard. When we started out, we thought of ourselves as offering a new way of being in a very small organization. It was never easy, but it was easier to touch everyone. Now, it's so much harder. You have to know who those people are who are touching other people—employees and customers—and how they are doing it. Sometimes everything around you seems good, but then you go into their world and it's not the same. They say, "That is Eileen's dream, but we have to get this done. We've got to stay late. We've got to make it happen." There's pressure. I think that there are a lot of really good things going on, and I think most people feel safe to be who they are and tell the truth, even if they think that Susan, Paula or I, or their manager, isn't going to like it. We don't change what we do in essence; we just try to be more open to complexity and encourage honest conversations.

Editors

When do you have these kinds of conversations?

Fisher

It starts at the interview when they arrive. One of the first questions is, "What are you most passionate about? What do you love about this, or what do you think you love most?" Whether it is with colors you love or fabrics you love or activities that you love. It's an interconnected idea.

Editors

Going back to the artist metaphor. Sometimes artists feel very strongly that an image, an idea, or a product does not capture their voice. Does that concern you at all? If it originates from something you've begun, does that make it all right?

Fisher

Yes, as long as it's true to the real essence, the essence of what I think I am trying to do. I think it can actually be better if it is not my voice. I have already seen this so many times. In the last five years or so, I have been less engaged in design on a daily basis, and I think it has gotten better without my being there . . . in some ways. For example, I am learning how pieces can mix when I am not there. It's the interconnection theme again. I used to do that with the garments, make sure it all fit, and then I made a point of not doing it.

Editors

Does it feel like parenting in a sense? You also must see your own children as developing personalities that surprise you sometimes.

Fisher

Definitely. It's a good analogy. There are voices and personalities that don't feel like me. I tell the story about going to the warehouse and not recognizing any of the garments. Things like that happen. That was upsetting. In fact, it was terrifying.

Editors

How did you reconcile that?

Fisher

I went back into design in a different way. I shifted people around and thought a lot about it. What did I let go of too quickly? What was the essence part of it? It made me rethink.

Editors

Do you have advice for others who want to create a business that works with integrity?

Fisher

I think it's about staying with one's heart and soul, and trying to be human to others and true to yourself.

Schor

It's also about trying to be conscious of the essence.

Editors

And how do you do that? You've talked about the importance of reflection and time out, and yoga and writing in a journal. Is that the means by which you stay conscious?

Fisher

That is hugely important to me. I think the bigger way, however, is in each moment. You need to try to stay present, to stay with the heart, to listen and hear and be open to what people are really trying to say. What comes to you? What are you feeling?

Schor

I think collaboration is part of it too. When we are driven by a list of tasks, we often lose sight of the essence. But when we engage in collaborative dialogue or discussion, we are more apt to get closer to the essence. Our discussion this morning is an example. One of the questions we always ask is, Who needs to be in this room? We think of the people who are very connected to the essence of what we are doing, and who understands and can think conceptually, as well as those who can help get things done, and we try to meet that balance.

Editors

Spontaneity is a word that seems to come up a lot in your conversation. I bet you have some fun meetings that don't always stay on track.

Fisher

Track! What is track? We have people who are really excellent who help us stay on track. It's the issue of integration again. We put the trackers and the creative-conceptual peers on the same path and appreciate what both bring to the circle.

Editors

But I imagine that in your industry, that sort of capability is a strength.

Fisher

I think that is probably true. You need to be creating and re-creating all the time. You need to be receptive to what is coming to you. You cannot have it all pre-thought. You need to have backbone and heart.

 Swanee Hunt, a model of inclusion, has emerged as one of our great philanthropic and political leaders. Her work with community efforts and mental health services as leader of Hunt Alternatives Fund helped shape public policy. Then, as the American ambassador to Austria (1993–1997), Swanee forged a new path in public diplomacy, particularly in her work with women leaders throughout Eastern Europe. Her work in that arena led to the film documentary *Voices*, as well as an ongoing Vital Voices movement that has extended to other regions worldwide. Swanee's work with women in the Balkans gave rise to Inclusive Security: Women Waging Peace, a global initiative that advocates for the full participation of women in formal and informal peace processes. It is also the basis for her book *This Was Not Our War: Bosnian Women Reclaiming the Peace* (2005). Now, as director of the Women and Public Policy Program at Harvard University's John F. Kennedy School of Government, Swanee's work emphasizes women's roles in the public policy process.

In this chapter, Swanee draws on her own story to illustrate what she calls inclusive transformation. She engages us in a global dialogue that advocates for the full participation of women leaders in political and social decision making.

PHOTO CREDIT: Swanee Hunt by Rick Friedman

26

INCLUSIVE
TRANSFORMATION

A Different Power

Swanee Hunt

The need for inclusion has stoked many of America's most important social movements, including the abolition of slavery, women's
suffrage, and civil rights; it also stoked my development as seminary
student, halfway house director, civic activist, foundation president, diplomat, conflict specialist—and mother. In those roles, I've
watched lives and systems be transformed by new ideas and insights
that come with the inclusion of those who might easily have been
consigned to the margins.

Inclusive transformation is both a personal and a social quest, a
way of understanding ourselves and encountering the world with
open arms, embracing differences. It requires an ongoing reexamination of too-easy everyday assumptions and a conscious attempt to
bring opposing voices into the conversation.

This subject is worth a philosophical essay, but we also learn from
our experiences and the experiences of others. So instead of telling
you what I think, let me tell my story. You'll figure out the lessons.

Breaking the Mold

Forty years ago, Mike Wallace told his audience that my father,
H. L. Hunt, was the richest man in America. He was probably right.
A highly successful oil prospector, Dad was the largest individual

owner in the largest oil and gas field in the nation. In Texas, where I grew up, his name was a household word. Dad was an imposing figure, dominating our family life as he did his company. I was unnoticed in his shadow and developing into a strong individual in my own right was no easy task. The patriarchal structure of Dallas in the 1960s had no use for women in leadership positions.

As a teenager, I dreamed of going to Radcliffe College. My father was adamantly opposed, convinced that Ivy League schools were communist training camps. He insisted I go to Dallas's Southern Methodist University. SMU was run by communists too, but ten minutes from the house so I'd be close enough for him to keep an eye on me.

I married just after my twentieth birthday. After college my husband and I made our home in Heidelberg, West Germany, where for four years I was free of the "Hunt" (read: "money") label that had dominated my life. That time and space allowed me to develop an identity separate from Dallas. I was more than a Texan or an American. I was a citizen of the world. I returned to the United States and settled in Denver, Colorado, ready to wrestle with questions that would shape my future.

From Anger to Action

During the eight years in which I worked on my doctorate at the Iliff School of Theology, I was exposed to a danger I'd been warned about back in Dallas—the doctrine of the social gospel. Perhaps my personal, private relationship with the Lord, taught to me in a church where black people were unwelcome, was not the end-all of faith. "Inasmuch as you've done it to the least of these my brothers, you've done it unto me," I'd memorized at Southern Baptist Bible school. Who I was in the community mattered to God, whether I recognized it nor not.

I felt tormented by the discrepancy between my family's wealth and the biblical teachings of social justice. I reviewed my life options: Should I follow the compelling example of St. Francis of

Assisi, giving away all my inheritance from my father, then living a life of utmost simplicity, away from the corrupting influence of wealth? I wasn't that pure. Ultimately, I kept my inheritance, knowing it would allow me to make a difference in the lives of others. Still, a nagging voice inside warned me against the corruption inherent in money and influence. Keeping my wealth would mean walking a treacherous path, with opportunities for self-delusion and abuse at every turn. It was, at best, an imperfect decision.

My sense of myself as a woman who had been systematically excluded ran smack up against the notion of God as male. In protest, I wrote my first published piece, "The Motherhood of God," insisting that until we broaden our symbols for God, we will limit the divine to maleness, reinforcing the injustice of our society. I laid out various images of God that are classically feminine, such as giving birth and nurturing. But the logic of my theological argument flowed straight into a social cataclysm: Why did speaking of God in the feminine seem blasphemous, whereas God as male seemed appropriate? I asked. That gut reaction said more about our views of maleness and femaleness than about God, who is beyond gender. In our society, the feminine was not worthy of association with the divine. The masculine was.

This insistence on the inclusion of the female had literal application back in Dallas, where I went for board meetings at the family company. In the late 1970s, I invited a company vice president to lunch at the Petroleum Club, an institution in which the men in our family had played leadership roles. Understanding full well the significance of the act, I made a reservation in the main dining room. When the elevator opened, we faced a tall, middle-aged black man, who smiled graciously and pointed to the "Ladies' Dining Room." I smiled politely, pointed to the main dining room, and informed the maitre d', "I'd prefer a table in there." He stammered, "We have a lovely table for you in *here*," pointing to the Ladies' Dining Room. "No, our reservation is in *there*. I'm positive." Finally, the maitre d' said, "You can sit in there, but it will cost me my job." I'd made my point; the vice president and I had sandwiches delivered to his office.

But I didn't have the courage to carry the point further by writing to the club's president and launching a campaign for change. I wasn't yet transformed into an activist.

My sister June was, through her Christian ministry, exploring such issues as domestic abuse. My sister Helen was starting women-based philanthropies across the nation. I was heading up all sorts of civic projects in Colorado. I felt a profound disconnect between our lives and the company culture, where women as leaders hardly crossed the consciousness of company managers. When June, Helen, and I were invited to tour our company's elegantly renovated Fort Worth Hyatt, we were shown luxury suites, named for "leaders in Fort Worth history"—all white men. We inquired whether some women hadn't figured prominently in Fort Worth's past. The project management—all white men—dismissed this inquiry from three of the company's co-owners; their research hadn't turned up any women.

I hired my own researcher, who learned that a hundred years ago, women in Fort Worth were starting schools and hospitals instead of cattle slaughterhouses and six-lane highways. Couldn't the fountain in the lobby be dedicated to their memory? Our efforts were stonewalled, and we folded; but the incident was instructive. Fort Worth's female pioneers hadn't mattered to historians. The female owners of this hotel hadn't even been humored by the project manager. The lesson sunk in deep. "How can we be working on women's inclusion when we're pushed aside in our own company?" Helen asked. "That's *why* we do this work," I said.

I needed to turn my anger into action. Around 1980, Helen and I started a private foundation, Hunt Alternatives Fund, to push for progressive social change. After a couple of years funding soup kitchens and shelters, I realized we needed to reform the mental health care system in Denver. I was codirecting a halfway house for the chronically mentally ill, where I'd seen the effects of the mid-1960s national policy of "deinstitutionalization." The aim was right-headed: with the invention of psychotropic drugs, many people could come out of the shadow of the back wards to live in a less confined setting.

But funding to follow patients into the community was not forth-coming from either federal or state legislatures. Huge numbers of Americans with severe mental illnesses were ending up on the streets or in morgues.

Helen and I also had a personal interest in the mental health field. Our brother Hassie, the same age as my mother, was paranoid schizophrenic. After years in physical restraints, with hundreds of series of insulin and shock treatments, he was lobotomized. The procedure left Hassie less violent, but he still muttered angrily under his breath, with fists clenched, and he snarled as he warned us about "vicious killers" around him. Ten years later, he came home from the hospital to live with us.

Hassie was an embarrassment to be explained to my friends who came to spend the night. Hassie was the strong, angry man stand-ing around the corner, whom I feared. Hassie was a hounded refu-gee from pernicious, evil delusions I couldn't imagine, even in my worst nightmares. Hassie was a predictor of genetic predisposition to mental illness I might carry. Hassie was my brother, whom I loved despite precious few moments of believing my love could be returned.

For me, working on behalf of Colorado's mentally ill was a form of self-healing. Although Colorado was considered one of the more progressive states in the country, only a fraction of the chronically mentally ill was receiving help. The Hunt Alternatives Fund com-piled a directory of over seventy community-based organizations and gave grants to dozens of programs—for elderly people released after decades in mental hospitals, a social club for young adults try-ing to blend into the mainstream, sheltered workshops that helped people work even when psychotic, or long-term therapy for trau-matized refugees. I founded a coalition of nonprofits too small to at-tract funding, allowing many agencies to speak with one voice to legislators and state planners.

I was thirty-two years old, and this was my first attempt to have an impact on the world at a systemic level. With encouragement and guidance from several mentors, I designed a politicized campaign to create a mental health system with integrated services. On a yellow legal pad, I drew the system, listing key personalities, probable allies, and obstacles. Actually, the diagram resembled more a Jackson Pollock painting than an orderly system. Methodically, I called on each stakeholder to hear his or her views on what the new structure ought to be. One crotchety Kentucky-born civic leader looked at me with a scowl. "I care about all this because my family is full of drunks. How about yours?" We became instant friends.

I received a more genteel reception from an older dean of the psychiatric community in Denver, who had watched reformers come and go and knew the pitfalls. He described several reform attempts over the past twenty years—all unsuccessful. For his parting words, he offered me advice as important as any I've received in my life: "Never ascribe to maliciousness what could be explained by incompetence." Happily, I found some wonderfully competent players, with whom I conspired, consulted, and collaborated.

Over a three-year period the reform was successful, in part because I was more than an idealistic young woman out to change the world. In a field with declining resources, I was a funder. Although our grants were small, Hunt Alternatives Fund could leverage change, not just through services or products our dollars could purchase. Our coffers could also buy attention, lure untrusting participants to a meeting, and reward those willing to join in the reform. I'd discovered the bridge between the virtue of walking away from my money and the danger inherent in building up power—my wealth did, in fact, give me the wherewithal to call for change.

Perhaps our foundation's most effective mental health grant was to Colorado Outward Bound to organize a white-water rafting trip with twenty of the key players occupying boxes on my yellow pad. Many were meeting for the first time. Most had been professionally competing. Now they were plotting a course through white water, yelling out "Paddle left!" and sharing the rush of adrenaline at the base of the rapid. A few mugs of coffee by the fire, and interpersonal dynamics were permanently changed. Competitors—included rather than avoided—became partners, and our initiative moved forward.

Changing the Power Structure

Mental health work launched me into politics. To address the crisis in homelessness, the Fund sponsored a forum for Denver mayoral candidates in 1983 to elicit their commitment to improve services for persons with chronic mental illness. A little-known state legislator with a first name I couldn't pronounce called me at home, to discuss the background briefing we'd sent him. That candidate went on to become mayor of Denver, then U.S. secretary of transportation and U.S. secretary of energy in Washington. Few remembered that, far from the halls of officialdom, my friendship with Federico Peña was launched in a hot and crowded church basement, as he faced a crowd of mentally ill constituents we'd gathered so they could confront the candidates themselves.

Mayor Peña was pivotal in reforms that resulted in the formation of the Denver Community Mental Health Commission. The commission members asked me to serve as chair, as I was primarily responsible for its formation. I refused. I'd never been president of any group. "I'll stay in the wings," I insisted, and worked from the position of vice chair instead. We brought in experts to teach us about the current system, and we visited the jail to see the problems there firsthand. The commissioners represented a range of perspectives: funders, advocates, doctors, administrators. But most important were the "consumers," who had the firsthand experience. They were, after all, the real experts.

Further work in philanthropy would have been impossible without a rethinking of my position within the family company back in Dallas. Beginning in 1982, I began questioning a family power structure I considered unfair. In 1958, my father had created equal trusts for us kids. As I moved from girlhood to womanhood in a society that began taking women more seriously, I found myself at odds with the patriarchal structure behind governance of the family assets. I don't think my parents had any image of their daughters' futures, apart from being wives and mothers living in Dallas, with the corporation doling out annual allowances. But that wasn't the life my sisters and I wanted. A pivotal disagreement developed related to the nature of the company. Understandably, the leadership wanted to reinvest profits so that the company would grow as large as possible. As a beneficiary, I wanted it to distribute income, at least equivalent to a reasonable return on publicly traded stock. The strains were predictable. Several years of painful negotiations laid bare unspoken assumptions within the family ethic.

After a hugely difficult two-and-a-half years, I gained more control of my wealth. This sad battle over the business placed a great strain on the family. But the sisters now had significant financial resources to devote to goals we believed in, domestically and globally, professionally and personally, through humanitarian and political activities.

In part because of my personal struggle for respect, I put my shoulder behind the launch of the Women's Foundation of Colorado, which raised a $10 million endowment and developed an extensive grant program promoting economic self-sufficiency for women and girls. For the first time, I was reaching out across lines of class, race, and life experience, and we created a solid alliance on behalf of all women and girls. In the process, I saw firsthand the ingenuity of women living in extremely difficult circumstances. They unknowingly inspired me, motivated me, changed me.

After years of working from the sidelines, I became the fourth president of the Women's Foundation. At the first board meeting I chaired, I structured an exercise to help board members picture themselves as a group that was beautiful in its diversity. Each woman was given a flower as we stood in a circle. She was to introduce herself, then put her flower in the vase in the center. At the end, there would be a gorgeous bouquet, with every stalk different.

The exercise went according to plan, until we got to a Latina who ran a clinic for impoverished migrant workers. Staring at the alligator heels on the woman next to her, she wondered aloud how many months of birth control pills could be purchased for some indigent mother for the price of these shoes. And furthermore, she continued, she didn't particularly like rich women. "This could be a long year," I thought.

It *was* a long year, filled with ideological battles among board members—the cost of bringing together a diverse group to work toward a common goal. We'd purposely built the board with women as different from each other as possible—not just rich and poor, but Republican and Democrat, lesbian and straight, Christian and Jewish, all ethnic hues. I presided over one close vote after another. To my surprise, the split was never across class lines. Several wealthy women voted against offering incentives for big donors. They were countered by nonwealthy women insisting that the Women's Foundation was basically about getting and giving money, and, politically correct or not, our policies needed to reflect that reality.

At the same time, throughout the 1980s Hunt Alternatives Fund was evolving. We began by funding direct services, such as shelters for battered women, soup kitchens, and workshops for the chronically mentally ill. Then we moved toward systemic reforms, developing a more strategic approach to social change, addressing root causes of homelessness or illiteracy. In the role of convener, we gathered business and government players along with nonprofit organizations—and the people they served—to address such issues as public education, gay rights, or family stability with community-wide force. People who came to our meetings never knew whom they'd be sitting next to—a welfare mother, a state legislator, a high school dropout, a millionaire businessman, or a young schizophrenic. Welcome to the real world.

Going Global

In 1993, my relationships with the new U.S. president and first lady (based primarily on our mutual interest in domestic problems) led to my appointment as ambassador to Austria. The lessons I'd learned in Denver about bringing together people who were different served me well in the realm of diplomacy.

An ambassador tends to the relationship between the United States and his or her host country. But beyond that basic level, the diplomat's job is defined by individual interests. Some of my predecessors had specialized in business exchanges, others in the arts. I entered Central Europe at the dawn of an era marked by the dissolution of the Soviet empire and the abatement of the struggle between two global superpowers. My particular concern was the regional instability of the early 1990s. Postcommunist economies were devastated, corruption and organized crime were growing exponentially, and one state, Yugoslavia, had disintegrated into a bloody war. I wanted to strengthen the partnership between the United States and Europeans, whose resentment of our superpower status had kept us at a distance as Yugoslavia's power-hungry president, Slobodan Milosevic, devolved unchecked into a heinous war criminal.

Managing an embassy with five hundred employees had elements of the absurd. The Americans, half the staff, rotated every three years. Many arrived with expertise that ranged worldwide but lacked Austria-specific savvy. I discovered that before I came, the monthly "large staff meeting" had excluded our Austrian employees, many of whom had doctorates, knew the local players intimately, and had worked for the embassy more than twenty years. When I asked why, I was told there could be sensitive subjects raised. We changed that rule.

Because I was responsible for knowing not only U.S.-Austrian issues but also the U.S. position on current events worldwide, I had to let my staff become my teachers. Once I crossed the psychological line of admitting to my staff that my expertise was in domestic policy, I was free to enlist help from an extraordinary array of experts. Whether we were talking about Syria, Salvador, or Sudan, there was an American among us who had served there recently.

I hosted about a hundred events a year, some on topics of my interest but often on behalf of the embassy personnel. As a newcomer, I was amazed when my staff presented me with suggested guest lists that were 90 percent men. The lists were compiled according to the current local power structure. That meant that women were excluded from the social settings where trust was being built, ideas were being hatched, and deals were being struck. I knew that for women to be taken seriously in shaping policy, being invited into the room was an essential first step. I asked for lists with at least 30 percent women, not including spouses. "But women aren't interested in NATO expansion," my frustrated defense attaché explained. I told him to ask men who are interested for names of women, and to reach out to the nongovernmental organization (NGO) community, diplomatic academy, the media, and universities. Suddenly, women in Austria had access to male-dominated political and economic power brokers, which allowed everyone to broaden their networks. When I left the state department, Secretary of State Madeleine Albright asked me to formulate policy recommendations for our embassies worldwide on ways ambassadors could bring more women into our work.

There were plenty of other chances to promote inclusion in the conservative state department culture. Each week I led the "country team" meeting, with heads of fourteen departments. One day, after discussions of NATO and European Union expansion, I referred to plans for my first holiday party, which I was told should include employees and their spouses. "How do you handle gay partners?" I asked. My new colleagues looked at me, amazed. Finally one spoke. "There are no gay people at the embassy." I glanced at the woman on my left, who I knew was in a long-term same-sex relationship. She sat stone-faced. "I gather this isn't a safe place to be out," I observed to the group. In fact, homosexuals had been designated a poor security risk because they could be blackmailed. The argument was circular, of course. No stigma, no blackmail. Again, we changed the policy.

Crisis in Bosnia

No situation at our embassy, or in Austria, had the life-or-death drama of the nearby war in Yugoslavia as that country ruptured. In 1994, I received a request from Washington to host negotiations between two warring factions in Bosnia, due south of Vienna. Bosnia, like Serbia, was one of five republics designated when Marshall Tito created Yugoslavia after World War II. Tito died in 1980, and Slobodan Milosevic, a Serb, had moved into the political vacuum, imposing political repression against non-Serbs. His policies eventually sparked horrible devastation—first in the republic of Croatia, then in multiethnic Bosnia, which had only a poorly equipped, ragtag army to defend against the Serb onslaught. War creates heroes, but it creates devils too. With much of Croatia also seized by the Serbs, the Croats had turned on politically fragile and newly independent Bosnia, making a grab for part of the territory. The Bosnians were thus battling off Serb aggressors from their east, as well as Croat aggressors from their north and west. The secular Bosnian Muslims, remnants of Ottoman reign, were the target of a genocidal conflict that left some 150,000 dead and two million—half the Bosnian population—displaced. Our attempt was to get the Croats to reverse their position, to ally with the Muslims against the Serbs.

The state department negotiator shuttled back and forth between the Croat delegation in my private embassy dining room and the Bosnian Muslim delegation in our administrative conference room down the hall. The war-weary men were making little progress, so we decided to bring them together in a familial setting to try to ease the tension. I called my chef at the residence, saying we would have fifty for dinner. This would be the only time during the negotiations that the warring sides would be in the same room. Anticipating the scene, I realized large round tables for eight would be a prescription for awkwardness. Having learned as a therapist the importance of seating arrangements, I'd had tables made a meter in diameter, around which we could crowd six guests. I called our butler to pull out the new tables, which would require our guests to sit so close their knees would touch.

The butler called back to let me know he was setting up large tables, because we didn't have tablecloths yet and the stores had closed. "No. Use our sheets," I said. Hearing the incredulity in his voice, I went home, spread a sheet on the floor, turned a table upside-down on it, knelt down, and started cutting. This was, of course, not an original idea; Julie Andrews had inspired me with window drapes in *The Sound of Music*.

The war-weary delegates were under enormous strain until, after dinner, our six-year-old son regaled the group with his piano version of "The Pink Panther," which drew us all into the music room for what became a home concert of Bosnian folk songs. The Croats knew the same songs and joined in. Like kids at a party, the men posed for portraits, standing between the life-size Native American women on our library wall. Four years later, a United Nations (UN) employee in Geneva relayed to me a remarkably accurate description of that gathering—ensconced in diplomatic lore.

Another set of negotiations was needed the next month, to put the final touches on the agreement. The Bosnian foreign minister asked that they be held in Vienna because, he said, the ambience of our embassy was conducive to reconciliation. For those talks, I stood in a room of warmongers and peace builders and offered a toast.

> *I believe that in the mix of who we are, good and bad,*
> *there is the light of God in every person.*
> *Sometimes that light shines so bright that it dazzles young children,*
> *and makes grown-ups weep.*
> *It lights up dark memories hidden in a thousand-year-old corner,*
> *or shows the way along a treacherous path.*
> *Sometimes that light is so dim as to be imperceptible,*
> *almost drowned by heavy drops of sweat, blood, or tears.*
> *Then, just when you least expect it,*
> *the light reappears.*
> *I also believe there is within each of us a capacity for darkness*
> *that we do not willingly recognize.*
> *It casts a greed-shaped shadow over our best moments.*
> *It grows silently like a fungus in our cleanest sheets.*
> *The darkness denies life to hope,*
> *but allows seeds of doubt and suspicion to sprout into violence*
> *and cruelty.*

> *May we in this room, working here together,*
> *have the wisdom to look for the light in ourselves*
> *and in the person sitting next to us and across from us*
> *May we not be surprised when we recognize the darkness*
> *in ourselves and each other,*
> *But simply nod in understanding,*
> *then keep peering through the darkness,*
> *until finally the light reappears.*

The negotiations were successful. Croats and Bosnian Muslims joined in a tenuous military alliance, which became the first step to a lasting peace.

Vital Voices

There was always more to do for the women of Bosnia in those immediate postwar years. Fresh perspectives were desperately needed in Balkan politics, so I helped organize a three-day conference to which each of forty Bosnian political parties sent several of their most active women. One result was a mandate that three of the top ten candidates on the party lists had to be women. The number of women in parliament jumped tenfold, to nearly 30 percent.

It wasn't only in Bosnia that women were being excluded. I made some twenty trips throughout Central and Eastern Europe; I met with women leaders who described how, when communism imploded, they'd been the first laid off, even though they were as well educated as the men. Their numbers in parliaments had dropped precipitously, and an extensive organized crime ring had branched into rampant sexual trafficking of women and girls. In short, women's prospects had gone from red to rosy to raw.

My connections with women in the new European democracies came together in July 1997 at a conference we dubbed "Vital Voices: Women in Democracy." Some 320 women leaders—East and West—came to share their successes and failures and create networks. The result was not simply a conference but an ongoing initiative, and many of the leaders' strategies were replicated throughout the thirty-six countries.

The gathering was a success. Among the participants were many of the highest-ranking women in business, government, and law. Speakers included First Lady Hillary Clinton and Supreme Court Justice Sandra Day O'Connor. Our format was multifaceted: razzle-dazzle stars for inspiration, and hard-core substantive work in panels and focus groups, with experts presenting successful strategies in their fields. But in a quieter mode, a string trio played as the women lined up to register, and there were chocolates and cosmetic gifts in their rooms. To bring the group together, we had a songfest around the piano at my residence, using books made up of selections the women sent in ahead.

The day of the conference, the *International Herald Tribune* ran my op-ed calling on governments to listen to the voices of women in postcommunist Europe. Dozens of newspapers and magazines sent correspondents to cover the meeting. A journalist from Prague thanked me for "the impulse for everyday courage." An American delegate related her conversation with a Rumanian woman leader who said, with tears in her eyes, "It is for us so inspiring that the first lady of the United States and the U.S. ambassador care about women."

The relationships developed there led to replicated legislation, new organizations, further conferences, Internet relationships, and a huge boost to the spirits of women who had felt forgotten as Eastern Europe devolved into depression. The conference became a touchstone event, a turning point in the way policymakers considered women in the changing political landscape. More Vital Voices conferences were staged by the state department around the world after I left, and the movement eventually spun out into a free-standing nonprofit organization, with Hillary Clinton as the honorary chair. We had created something lasting not only for the women but also for their communities and their countries. I took the lessons with me when I left Vienna in late 1997, moving on to launch new work at Harvard and with my private foundation in Cambridge, Massachusetts.

A New Security Paradigm

The dean of Harvard's Kennedy School of Government, Joseph Nye, asked me to come and "change the culture," which was notoriously male in faculty and curriculum. Talking to friends who had attended the school and others who had made a point not to, I received more warnings about coming to Harvard than I did about going into Bosnia in the middle of the war. The Women and Public Policy Program was born with two mothers: Jane Mansbridge as faculty chair and me as director. Jane had authored *Why We Lost the ERA* and was a noted political scientist who studied collaborative democracy. She prodded me to think of ways to include not only other women faculty in this endeavor but also men faculty and women and men students and administration.

"Soft power" is the phrase Dean Nye coined, by which he meant the power to influence and persuade individuals or states without relying on military might. As a former assistant secretary of defense, he had credibility. Our ideas of including women's concerns and women actors in foreign policy discussions were compatible with his theory, which he offered as an antidote to the "clash of civilizations" notion taught by another faculty member, Sam Huntington. I knew Huntington from when I was asked to respond to his address before an illustrious Viennese audience. The distinguished professor was furious when I said his theory could become a self-fulfilling prophecy by discouraging collaboration across differences and noted that his writings were being used in the Balkans to justify ethnic cleansing.

Inclusive Security

As champion of the inclusion (as opposed to the "clash") point of view, I wondered how I might use my Harvard platform to aid women peace builders, not only in Bosnia but also around the world. I created a master's-level course to explore the possibility, inviting peace builders from Cyprus, Northern Ireland, and Serbia to speak to my students on the role of women in formal and informal peace efforts. As the women activists gathered around my kitchen table late one evening, they shared their common experiences, offering each other encouragement and advice. The potential of their synergy was unquestionable.

In 1999, the Women and Public Policy Program launched Women Waging Peace to demonstrate the power of partnership, as well as to advocate for structural changes that would bring the voices of women peace builders to those who shape public policy. The initiative was an ongoing virtual forum where women from Colombia, Kosovo, or Congo could share technical assistance, contacts, and other information; build expanding networks across conflict areas and sociopolitical sectors; and create a new paradigm for policymaking, including women's perspectives and full participation.

"Waging" brought together what I'd learned at the Women's Foundation of Colorado and with women in Bosnia, where I had seen innovative solutions devised by women working across ethnic or economic lines. As I led negotiation and media workshops with over 250 Waging network members, I became all the more convinced of the contributions women could make to the formal international security community. Watching the spectacular security failures of September 11, 2001, and subsequent terrorist bombings around the world, I developed the concept of "inclusive security"— the notion that it should be inconceivable to exclude women from security decision making if we want to achieve sustainable peace.

The damaging effects of war on women are well documented— for example, when rape is used as a tactic of war to humiliate the enemy and terrorize the population. Women lose their homes, their health, their identities. But sometimes women find that in the upheaval of war, social constructs shift, at least temporarily. With their husbands away, many have new obligations—and freedom—as the head of the family or when working in jobs formerly reserved for men. Others have unanticipated responsibilities—organizing emergency care, smuggling arms through checkpoints, mobilizing support from the diaspora, or leading a platoon. With expanded roles, women gain a new sense of themselves and their competencies.

As we examine war—with all its terror, destruction, and loss—our information comes mostly from history books, foreign policy analyses, and mass media. And what do we discover there about the roles of men and women? Men are not only making war but also negotiating peace. Women, on the other hand, are pitiable victims. These generalizations are relentlessly inculcated in the public consciousness. The White House Project reported that in the seven weeks that followed September 11, women were virtually invisible—not only behind burqas in Afghanistan but in the U.S. Sunday talk show lineup, where a paltry 6.8 percent of American guest experts were female.[1] In prestigious journals of foreign affairs, women authors rarely appear, and women's roles in shaping foreign policy are effectively ignored. Similarly, in the vast majority of UN-sponsored research, think-tank reports, and NGO publications, no reference appears to the extensive peacemaking work of women on the ground. Thus, in the critical enterprise of creating global security, important players are shut out, in large part because of widespread prejudice about what sort of work and workers are relevant to building sustainable peace. Ironically, women's advantage of knowing how to operate outside the stymied system of formal authority also renders them invisible to historians and analysts.

When policymakers buy into the notion that men are the only significant actors in the enterprise of war and peace, they fill the negotiating room with grey suits, black turbans, or their equivalent. Women Waging Peace has broken open those constructs, not only to include women alongside men but also to examine the particular advantages women may bring to confronting the greatest challenge to contemporary life: widespread terrorism and global instability.

A Matter of Efficiency

The justification for women's inclusion can be built on several platforms. *Representation* is the most obvious: women account for half the population and therefore should comprise half the decision makers. Or *compensation:* because women have been victimized, they deserve to be heard. Or *rights:* leaving women out of the peace-making process means that their concerns are likely to be ignored or bargained away at the first stage of the negotiation process.

But there's an *efficiency* argument, as well. For lasting stability, we need peace promoters, not just warriors, at the table. More often than not, those peace promoters are women. Certainly, heroic and visionary men have changed the course of history with their peace-making; likewise, belligerent women have made it to the top of the political ladder or, at the grassroots level, have joined the ranks of terrorists. But in conflict situations around the world, leaders of UN and other international peace missions have reported to me their frustration at not having access to the women in the society, whom they perceived to be the steadiest voices of moderation.

Why have we not included women in peace processes? Peace in a region must have the buy-in of millions before it is truly sustainable, and thus stakeholders from throughout the society must be involved in the informal and formal peace process. The mayor of a U.S. city wanting to address race relations would pull together not only minority leaders but also representatives from the business, religious, education, social welfare, labor, and political circles; but foreign policymakers aren't subject to the same electoral pressure to build their work on such a broad base. International negotiators have not learned to include individuals from multiple spheres who understand the dynamics of the community in which the agreement has to be lived.

Women's perspectives in formal and informal peace processes are often different from men's; their involvement in preventing conflict, stopping war, and stabilizing the country after conflict is vital for four key reasons.

Women Are Highly Invested in Preventing and Stopping Conflict. The first comment usually offered by casual observers as to why women promote peace is that women are so inclined because of their social and biological roles as nurturers. Whereas most men come to the negotiating table directly from the war room and battlefield, women's experiences usually come from caregiving professions and—hold your breath—family care.

The notion that women's contributions are linked to their being mothers (or scripted to have been mothers) has been challenged by those who see any linkage of biology and destiny as confining, dangerous, and wrongheaded. Yet the women I've interviewed in conflict areas all over the world repeatedly state that they are motivated by the need to ensure security for their families. They describe themselves as different from men with such phrases as, "After all, we bring life into the world, so we don't want to see it destroyed." That theme is picked up by many men, including Haris Silajdzic, postwar prime minister of Bosnia, who told me in 1996, "If we'd had women around the table, there would have been no war; women think long and hard before they send their children out to kill other people's children."

Women Are Adept at Bridging Ethnic, Political, and Cultural Divides. In his address to the October 24, 2000, open session of the UN Security Council on Women, Peace and Security, UN Secretary-General Kofi Annan stated, "For generations, women have served as peace educators, both in their families and in their societies. They have proved instrumental in building bridges rather than walls." In an interview with the *Slant*, Mary Robinson, former president of the Irish Republic, agreed, saying women are "instinctively . . . less hierarchical" and harness in a cooperative way the energies of those who are like-minded.[2] Scores of women have reported to me that they consider themselves generally more collaborative than men and thus more inclined toward consensus and compromise. In fact, when I asked a UN official why there were no women in several African peace talks, he said warlords refused to have women because they were concerned that the women would compromise.

Challengers note that female leaders such as Margaret Thatcher and Golda Meir have acted in a manner quite similar to men: hierarchical and power centered. The issue may be one of critical mass. In 2003, former European Commissioner Anita Gradin told me that in her Swedish homeland, when women made up 15 percent of the parliament they behaved more like the men; as their numbers increased to 45 percent, the norm changed. They advocated for more changes important to Swedish women and insisted that a woman be appointed defense minister and men be given responsibilities such as social welfare.

In *Women at the Peace Table: Making a Difference*, Sanam Naraghi Anderlini tells the story of women organizers in Northern Ireland who won the 1976 Nobel Peace Prize for their nonsectarian public demonstrations.[3] Almost two decades later, Monica McWilliams (formerly a member of the Northern Ireland Assembly) and May Blood (now a member of the House of Lords) were told that only leaders of the top ten political parties—all men—would be included in the peace talks. With only six weeks to organize, Monica and May mobilized over two hundred women's organizations to create a new party: the Northern Ireland Women's Coalition. They received ten thousand votes in the local elections, winning a place at the peace table.

The coalition is a nonsectarian, broad-based group of women of all political hues and religious traditions, with an agenda of reconciliation through dialogue, accommodation, and inclusion. Because it is composed of women on different sides of the conflict, the coalition has had credibility to work across lines. Members have helped calm the often deadly "marching season" by facilitating mediation between Protestant unionists and Catholic nationalists. They have brought together key players from each community, including released prisoners, to work with local police, maintaining twenty-four-hour contact and providing an effective extension of the limited security forces.

Women Have Their Fingers on the Pulse of the Community. Living and working close to the roots of conflict, women are well positioned to provide essential information about activities leading up to violence as well as to gather wartime evidence. Grounded in practicalities of everyday life, they also play a critical role in mobilizing their communities to begin the postconflict process of reconciliation and rebuilding.

In Kosovo, after pediatric neurologist Vjosa Dobruna was locked out of her hospital office during Milosevic's imposed apartheid, she helped create "Fe-mail," an email warning and emergency aid system. Having collected evidence from victims at massacre sites, she was targeted for murder or capture by Serb special police; she escaped by jumping out of a second-floor window into her garden. Caught up in the flood of refugees in the exodus to Macedonia, Dr. Dobruna administered trauma relief. Subsequently, she was one of three women appointed to the UN's Joint Interim Administrative Structure of Kosovo, as the minister responsible for democracy building and civil society. Her portfolio included establishment of new protocols for free elections and a system of independent news reporting to replace the mendacious media machine that contributed to the destruction of her community. She says having only her car and cell phone as an office for the first six months of her job wasn't a handicap, because she held meetings in cafes and homes, where she stayed in close touch with Kosovars' concerns.

Dobruna has won the confidence of Serb and ethnic Albanian Kosovars and has led efforts to create a women's caucus in the new assembly, the only political structure crossing party lines.

Women Are Innovative Community Leaders, With or Without Formal Authority. Women frequently outnumber men in postconflict populations; and they often drive the on-the-ground implementation of peace agreements, using innovative techniques in NGOs, popular protests, electoral referenda, and other citizen-empowering movements whose influence has grown with the spread of democracy. Precisely because they haven't been allowed full participation within power structures, women have learned to work "outside the box." For example, with no resources available to them, Sudanese women marched though their town naked to protest the abduction of their children as child soldiers. Their songs were played on radio and became popular throughout the region. Going further, during November 2000 peace talks, the women of Burundi were admonished by Nelson Mandela, mediating the civil war, to withhold "conjugal rights" ("such as cooking," he quipped) if their rebel husbands picked up arms again. *Lysistrata* revisited.

Around the world, women are overwhelmingly represented in grassroots organizing, but their work is underfunded or overlooked. The good news is that grassroots leaders can set their own agenda outside the close scrutiny of political parties or official establishments.

"After the genocide, women rolled up their sleeves and began making society work again," Paul Kagame, president of Rwanda, told me in 2001. A leader among those Rwandan women is Aloisea Inyumba, governor of Kigali-Ngali Province and former head of the Commission for Unity and Reconciliation. Born and raised in a refugee camp in neighboring Uganda, she confronted a society in crisis when she entered her parents' homeland with the Rwandan Patriotic Front in the early 1990s. Inyumba witnessed the genocide of 1994 and at age twenty-six was made minister for families and gender. Her first job: figure out how to bury some eight hundred thousand bodies from the massacres that wiped out 10 percent of the population in one hundred days.

Her second responsibility: devise a system to care for hundreds of thousands of orphans. "Each One Take One" was her motto as she urged every mother to add at least one more child to her family. Hutu women adopted Tutsi children, and Tutsi women took home Hutus. Inyumba also prepared Rwandan communities for the release of about one hundred thousand genocidaires from prison. One by one, she visited villages to ready them for the release of prisoners—mostly men—who allegedly participated in the killings but had been jailed for years without trial because the court system was completely overwhelmed by the catastrophic killing spree. Inyumba has led a daunting task: forging a peaceful society out of survivors and perpetrators of the genocide.

We don't need to argue nature or nurture to make the case that women are important agents for creating peace. Moving from collaborative community work to the policy arena is a giant leap; but in recent years, the construction of a bridge across that gap has begun. The design of the bridge is based on two fundamental principles: it's smart to try new approaches to long-standing problems, and it makes practical sense to draw on 100 percent of the population when looking for solutions. The UN Security Council and other international bodies have adopted resolutions calling for the inclusion of women throughout the peace process. But the same groups were almost exclusively male, and they've done little to walk their talk.

Through the Kaleidoscope: Life Lessons from Lillian

Inclusion is transformational, whether those included are women, children, or people living on the margins. Having been excluded from the power base in my own family, I learned early on to seek out opportunities to include others, whether in the wide-open spaces of the Women's Foundation of Colorado or in cramped negotiating rooms in the war-torn Balkans. Today I'm continuing to learn, as my private foundation supports leaders of social movements and builds a coalition of arts organizations working with disadvantaged kids.

The word *transformation* is personal and social, essential and complex. As a leader, I am changed as I perceive points of view that have been invisible to me. Those included for the first time are changed by a new sense of their own value. The problem we're working on together is changed by a process that unites a wide range of stakeholders, who together build a solid base for change.

But an internal type of inclusive transformation is possible as we embrace not only others but the whole of who we are as individuals. That lesson was taught to me by my wise and courageous teenage daughter, Lillian, who has struggled her whole life with severe bipolar illness that has led her repeatedly to the brink of self-destruction. I learned from her that life is kaleidoscopic, a turbulent and random recombination of shapes and colors constantly forming new patterns and movements. Reality isn't always beautiful; but even when distorted, it can be dazzling.

Because of Lillian, I've been transformed as I've recognized the exquisite beauty of saintly friends, family, and professionals negotiating a fragile compromise between hope and despair among mentally ill loved ones. Sometimes those helpers lay a foundation of trust and communication by day, only to have the night bring inner demons that rip apart every bridge that had been built across the abyss of madness. The next day, they begin again, holding on to the promise that failure is an event, not a person.

More than tragedy or aberration, mental illness is a reality that has added new shapes and forms to my life. Now firmly ensconced in middle age, I have settled the score with Donna Reed, that perfect mother in a perfect family who had molded my young psyche every week, courtesy of ABC. I hope I can pass on a new realism, so that my children and grandchildren won't grow up worshipping strength and beauty, banishing blemishes to shadowy margins. I want their kaleidoscopes to have hundreds of colors and shapes, including those that are not all pretty. I expect them to be confused and even frightened by some people they meet on their journeys into adulthood. That includes the person they see in the mirror.

My job is to instill in them the values, skills, and openness that will enable them to see the connection between themselves and others—whether angry, inarticulate people at the neighborhood bus stop or teenage street warriors in Serbia. After decades of struggle, I've come to terms with the fact that only as I'm willing to accept the differences in others will I be able to accept the dramatic contradictions within myself.

When I was serving as U.S. ambassador in Austria, Lillian's illness reached full-scale psychosis: angry voices screamed at her that I was dead, lava flowed around her bed, bugs crawled all over her arms and hands. On top of this, she was having wild, chaotic mood swings. Our doctors had tried every treatment they knew. Lillian was not getting better; her swollen hands trembled constantly, and she walked with a shuffle. Finally, I met with a leading researcher, who told me, with some annoyance, that I shouldn't have accepted the debilitating side effects of her medications. Her system was being poisoned. We could try a new, experimental mood stabilizer, which had produced positive response in 60 percent of his patients who were nonresponders to other drugs. My heart surged with hope. "How many have you tried it on?"

"Twelve."

I searched his eyes. "How many children?"

"None." He waited as I processed his words.

"Do you think it's safe?" I asked.

He gave me time to hear the nonsense in my words. "You've tried everything else, and your daughter has a potentially fatal illness. It's time to throw the book out the window," he counseled. He gave us a new drug, which led to an enormous improvement within only a couple of days. We were overjoyed. Never mind that Lil was now taking more than twenty pills a day, the illness had no cure, and there would still be times of high risk. At least she was able now to live in the world around her, with all its ups and downs, without swinging so often out of control.

I felt like I was watching Lazarus emerging as my daughter slowly rejoined the world around her. She continued to struggle with suicidal ideation, sleep disruption, and periodic hallucinations. But her wit, sparkle, and generous spirit were emerging from the tomb.

Ultimately, what could I hope for my daughter? I knew plenty of people with exquisitely balanced brain chemistry, extensive education, and advanced careers who were miserably unsatisfied with who they were. My life with Lillian had dramatically altered my perception of success, the value of internal strength versus external power, and the preciousness of time together.

One day, as she reviewed her progress with her gentle Viennese psychiatrist, Lil began to ruminate. "I think about all those years before my illness was diagnosed, then later as we tried to find the right medications. I imagine: if only I could have had this drug then. But I guess I really wouldn't want to go back and change anything. After all, every experience is a part of me, and I like who I am." I sat behind her, tears of admiration streaming down my face. My daughter had become my teacher—in a moment of inclusive transformation.

Rear Admiral Deborah A. Loewer has influenced and been at the forefront of remarkable change in one of our oldest and most traditional institutions—the U.S. military. In 1979, she was selected as one of the first women assigned to shipboard duty, attending Surface Warfare Officer Basic Course and graduating first in her class. Her service and her studies in the years that followed brought her recognition as a top leader. From 1993 to 2003, she commanded the *USS Mount Baker*, served as the Military Assistant to the Secretary of Defense, commanded the *USS Camden*, and returned to Washington to assume duties as The Director of the White House Situation Room. On July 7, 2003, she became Vice Commander of The Military Sealift Command.

In this chapter, Deborah recounts the unheralded yet inspiring history of women in U.S. military service. Along the way, she chronicles the changes that she has witnessed in her career. Her forthright and plainspoken tone matches the leadership qualities of perseverance, courage, and confidence that she brings to her command.

PHOTO CREDIT: Deborah A. Loewer by Barry Lake

27

PUSHING OPEN THE "DOOR OF OPPORTUNITY"

Women in Our Armed Forces

Rear Admiral Deborah A. Loewer, USN

Women have served in, with, and near the militia and the military since before our nation was founded. Our history is peppered with watershed events demonstrating the service and sacrifices made by American women for our nation. In this chapter, I tell the story of the role that women have played in our military throughout our history, and describe the tremendous strides women have made in the last twenty-five years. For those who look on the women's movement in this country as the stuff of the distant past, know that in our lifetimes we have seen and continue to witness pioneering efforts that finally open doors of opportunity to women leaders. And for those who doubt that deep social and organizational changes can happen quickly, or who question the value that women bring to our institutions when given the opportunity, the history of women in the military is instructive and inspiring.

Generations Past

During the American Revolution, George Washington employed the "Women of the Army" to help supply and provision the troops. Despite whatever images this conjures, these women were much more than just camp followers—they were contracted to provide medical, commissary, and other support services, such as sewing and repair.

You may recall the name Molly Pitcher. Although a fictional character, she was a composite of real women who served on the front lines and in combat, women like Margaret Corbin. During the battle of Ft. Washington in New York, Margaret's husband was killed. She took charge of his gun crew, was maimed in battle, received a pension from George Washington, and later became one of only a few women to be buried at West Point. Margaret Corbin and her colleagues began the push to open the "door of opportunity" for women in military service.

During the Civil War, women served honorably yet again. Some served openly, but only in restricted capacities. For example, Dr. Mary Walker was an accredited physician who wanted to serve. However, she was forced to serve as a "nurse"; back then the army would not recognize the credentials of women physicians. Proving herself on the front lines of both sides in the conflict, she eventually served as a battlefield surgeon and was awarded the Medal of Honor by President Andrew Johnson. Taken away when the rules were changed, the medal was later reinstated by President Jimmy Carter after an appeal from her family. Incidentally, she is still the only woman in history to have received the Medal of Honor.

But most women did not serve openly during the Civil War; they had to disguise themselves as men in order to serve with husbands, brothers, or sons, or "just to serve." We have no way of knowing exactly how many women served, because no records were maintained. We do know that many were buried with their identities unconfirmed.

During the Spanish-American War, women served overseas as nurses, but the next major gain for women came during World War I. With U.S. involvement in the war looming, and the United States short of personnel, Navy Secretary Josephus Daniels solved the shortage by asking, "Is there any regulation which specifies that a Navy yeoman be a man?" Eventually the answer was no.

The recruiters were flabbergasted as women flocked to their recruiting stations. They apparently had not heard the secretary of the Navy's guidance. But Bernice Duncan Smith of California had heard, and knew that the Navy was signing up women in Washington, D.C.—even if her California recruiter didn't believe her. She had to plead with him and was eventually allowed to serve; had she not been permitted to, it would have been the first time her family was not represented in an American war. She served in the Navy in World War I and went on to serve in the Army in World War II. She was too old for the Navy by then! At the same time, her son was serving as a Marine in World War II. Later, two of her grandsons served in Vietnam.

By the end of World War I in 1918, eleven thousand women had pushed open the door of opportunity a little further by serving as yeomen and as Marine reservists. In addition, French-speaking American women served as telephone operators in Europe. Many others served near the front lines with the Salvation Army, Red Cross, and YMCA and in several medical and therapeutic capacities.

During World War II, "the Greatest Generation" went to war for the Allied cause.[1] Over four hundred thousand women served— breaking many barriers simply by proving the value of "service out of necessity."

Women served in nearly every capacity, including as pilots (testing and ferrying aircraft, instructing, and towing targets), as members of the Coast Guard, as technicians and scientists (women did much of the math for the Manhattan Project), as instructors, as radio operators. Collectively, they continued to push open the door of opportunity.

Also during World War II, racial barriers were attacked head-on by very determined women. American women of Japanese descent served as translators, despite having family members interred in detention centers. And black women, still under the specter of racial bias, served proudly overseas and at home. These women showed true moral courage as they served our nation!

Many women who served in World War II as nurses were subjected to all the horrors of war. As were the men, they were bombed at Anzio, taken prisoner in the Philippines, and subjected to terrible conditions and disease in the China-Burma-India theaters.

Retrenchment After World War II

Notwithstanding all their sacrifices, women in the decades following World War II had to fight to maintain many of the gains they
had garnered during the war years. The nation was downsizing its
military. Men were returning from the war and were replacing
women factory workers and service members, and women were expected to return home obediently to their traditional role. During
the downsizing process, the number of women in military service
was limited to just 2 percent of the entire force, and very strict conditions of "employment" were established. For example, while in
military service, women were not permitted to marry or have children. If they did, their service ended.

Making Headway in the Air and in the Courts

It took twenty years, but the 2 percent ceiling on the number of
women permitted in military service was rescinded in 1967.

By the early 1970s our society began to change, and women became more readily accepted in the workforce; with this acceptance
began an evolution in the role of women in military service. In 1973
women began pilot training, and in 1974 the first woman pilot graduated. The Navy was the first service to train pilots and was the first
service to allow women to fly in fighters. Navy women were not
restricted from flying combat aircraft; they were restricted only from
flying their aircraft from the deck of a ship. From 1973 until 1993,
Air Force women were restricted to flying tankers and transport aircraft. Army women flew only combat support helicopters.

Getting women into the cockpits was a real gain; to achieve a
true measure of equality, however, military women were forced to
take their case to the courts. In 1973 American Civil Liberties
Union (ACLU) lawyer Ruth Bader Ginsburg argued successfully to
the Supreme Court (where she now sits) that policies denying on-
base housing to active-duty women with families and preventing
husbands of military women from using the base exchange and

commissary were discriminatory. In 1976 four enlisted women filed suit in U.S. District Court in Washington, D.C., asking that the federal statute prohibiting them from serving aboard almost all major Navy ships be ruled unconstitutional. The ACLU and the League of Women Voters Educational Fund offered support. Then a group of women and men junior officers joined the original plaintiffs—strengthening the suit's contention that the law discriminated against all Navy women, enlisted and officer alike. On July 27, 1978, District Judge John J. Sirica ruled that the statute in question was unconstitutional because it precluded women from "gaining access" to a wide range of opportunities for job training.

Concurrent with this litigation, important military policies were changing. By 1975 women were attending the Coast Guard Academy, and in 1976 the first women started at the Service Academies at Annapolis, West Point, and Colorado Springs. It is interesting to note that when the first women to attend the Air Force Academy marched up the ramp to the cadet assembly area on their first day, the banner that hung there read "Bring Me Men." That banner was only recently removed—in March 2003.

Experiencing a Sea Change

This brings us to a seminal point in U.S. naval history—1978. As an ensign, I was watching carefully on the sidelines as Congress modified the law, and, because of this one modification, the Navy changed its assignment policy and allowed women to serve at sea on noncombatant ships. I was very proud to be selected as one of those first women to serve our nation at sea.

In June 1979 I walked across the brow of my first ship, and a few years ago, I stepped off the quarterdeck of my last ship. Between 1979 and 2000, there were six ships, six deployments, six shipyard overhauls, and six terrific crews. In all, I served more than thirteen years at sea. During this time there were some really high highs and some very low lows. There was discrimination. There was harassment. There were many occasions on which it was clear that life was not fair and that the playing field was not level. I remember reporting on board my first ship as if it were yesterday. There were four of us (women, that is): three seagoing officers and one medical officer.

There were eleven hundred men in the enlisted crew and forty-eight male officers in the wardroom. The executive officer (second in charge behind the captain) greeted us and did his best to welcome us to the ship. He ensured that we had "running mates" to help us not get too lost on board and to get us through the first few days.

Hours later, the executive officer (XO) escorted us up several decks to the commanding officer's cabin to introduce us to the captain. To say that we were all intimidated would be an understatement!

Once we were in his cabin, the captain looked at the four of us and said only these words: "I didn't ask for women on board. I don't want women on board my ship. But you are here. XO, put them to work."

I was in shock. I couldn't believe that I had worked so hard to get to serve on board a real Navy ship, only to be met with such hostility.

On another occasion on the same ship, we were moored at Pier 23 in Norfolk, Virginia. I vividly remember walking down the pier making my way to the forward brow of my ship. As I was walking, some sailors working on the forecastle on a ship across the pier from us started shouting and making "wolf calls." I am sure you get the picture. I did a 180-degree turn and headed for the quarterdeck of that ship. When I got there I asked to speak to the executive officer—and I did. Even if I was going to be subjected to that type of behavior, I did not have to accept it.

Three-and-a-half years later I left my first ship having served in every department on board—engineering, operations, administration, repair, and supply—and having become one of the first women in naval history to earn qualification as a surface warfare officer (in August 1980) and to join the ranks with the first woman surface warrior, Ensign Roberta McIntyre (who earned this distinction on the destroyer tender *USS Dixon*, in 1979).

Even though I was disappointed with the "less than equal" reception I received on that first ship, I left as a more confident, better person. I acquired extensive leadership and management skills and was much more secure in my role as a naval officer.

I've mentioned the lows, but during my seagoing years there were some really high highs. Sailing every ocean, visiting exotic ports of call, overcoming new and unexpected challenges, and, most important, working with my teams to accomplish seemingly impossible tasks, made every day at sea worthwhile.

A thousand sea stories later, in July 2000 I stepped off the brow of my last ship for the last time. Instead of hearing wolf calls, I heard the "ding-ding, ding-ding," of the ship's bell and the sound of the bosn's pipe, signifying my departure from the ship as the commanding officer.

Measuring Progress

What happened to the other three women who reported on board with me on that very first ship? The medical officer separated after four years of service and is a highly respected psychiatrist practicing in Norfolk, Virginia. One of the seagoing officers separated after her four years of service, attended Wharton Business School and is earning serious money on Wall Street. The other seagoing officer and I continue to serve in today's Navy as surface warfare admirals.

Twenty-five years have passed since women began serving at sea in 1978. And our Navy has truly come a long way—in assignment and personnel policies, in acceptance, and in expectations.

In 1979, there were more than 600,000 personnel in our Navy, and there were only eighteen women officers serving on board four ships. In today's Navy (March 2004), there are 391,000 personnel. Of those, 57,000, nearly 15 percent of the total force, are women; 8,000 of them are officers. Nineteen thousand women now serve at sea on 164 ships; women may now serve on any ship type in the Navy, with the exception of submarines and coastal patrol craft.

And I would submit that those two exceptions will change in my lifetime.

Honoring Those Who Serve

In twenty-first-century America the service of women in, with, and near the military has changed dramatically. On the ground, in the air, and on the seas bordering Iraq and Afghanistan, military women represent greater than 15 percent of the several hundred thousand American forces in the region. It is the largest and most significant deployment of American military women in U.S. history.

Military women serve an integral role in the ongoing global war on terrorism. They bear arms and are using them. They have won medals for valor and Purple Hearts for combat wounds. They have been captured as prisoners of war, killed by enemy fire, and buried as heroes in Arlington National Cemetery.

They have participated more extensively in combat in Iraq and Afghanistan on the ground, in the air, and on the high seas than in any previous war. They serve side by side and under the exact same conditions (and risks) as men. They continue to assume combat roles that were nearly inconceivable just two decades ago. American military women patrol the streets of Baghdad armed with automatic weapons; they fly fighters and assault helicopters and attack the enemy on call; and they command guided missile destroyers and launch missile raids at the direction of the National Command Authority. In all the military services, women command units composed primarily of men.

The global war on terrorism has blurred the line that once existed between combat and noncombat units and removed from our lexicon the concept of "front lines" and "rear support areas." On September 11, 2001, this point became real to us all.

Any history of women in service to our nation should also honor and remember a special group of women whose patriotism, bravery, and determination must not go unnoticed. These are the women who went to work at the Pentagon on September 11, 2001, and lost their lives when terrorists struck. Of the 125 Pentagon military and defense department civilian workers who died that day, 51 were women: 38 from the Army, 9 from the Navy, and 4 from the Defense Intelligence Agency.

These women became a part of history not by being "first" at anything—they became a part of history because they believed that serving the nation was the right thing to do. They lost their lives because of the honorable profession they had chosen, and they died because of how they lived.

If we look into the proud pages of our history, we realize that not all heroic acts in war were performed by men—many women have performed acts just as heroically and made the ultimate sacrifice. We recognize that standing up for fair and equitable treatment is as honorable and as worthy of remembrance as serving in the nation's armed forces. We remember that women who served with honor in World War I—who could travel overseas to work in the mud and grime as nurses, entertainers, or switchboard operators—could not exercise the right to vote. And just prior to my own time of service, women could serve and die in Vietnam, but they could not serve as seagoing officers in ships or as pilots in combat aircraft.

Throughout our history, each generation of women has pushed open the door of opportunity just a little bit farther, allowing each successive generation to pass more freely through the door and to open the door even farther themselves.

Marilyn King was a two-time Olympian (Munich 1972 and Montreal 1976) in the grueling pentathlon. When an automobile accident in 1979 rendered her unable to train physically for her third Olympic team, Marilyn used only mental training techniques to place second at the Olympic trials for the 1980 Moscow games. This extraordinary experience led to Marilyn's twenty-four-year career as an expert in the field of exceptional human performance. As the founder of Beyond Sports, a peak performance consulting practice, Marilyn provides business leaders at Fortune 500 companies and other leading organizations with keynote speeches, training, consulting, and thinking tools that will serve them for a lifetime. Marilyn is also the creator of an inner-city youth empowerment program called Dare to Imagine. Her most pioneering work, a joint Russian-American venture called the Peace Team, prompted two invitations to speak at the United Nations.

In this chapter, Marilyn discusses how we can employ her Olympian Thinking approach in our everyday work as leaders to help align passion, vision, and action among the people around us. Marilyn also outlines why women leaders must help create the necessary (and lacking) vision of peace in the world today.

28

OLYMPIAN THINKING

Producing Extraordinary
Results in Our World

Marilyn King

In 1980, while preparing for my third Olympic team, I had an extraordinary experience that led me to think of my friend Bruce Jenner. I'd come to know Bruce while training for the 1976 Montreal games. I was proud to place sixteenth in Montreal, and Bruce went on to win the gold medal in the decathlon. And the group of track and field athletes we'd trained with won more medals than many countries. An auto accident in November 1979 resulted in a bulging disc in my lower back. The injury made it impossible even to jog, much less train six to eight hours a day in preparation for my final opportunity to compete in Moscow in the five-event pentathlon. Unable to train physically, I trained mentally, watching films of the world-record holders in all five of my events. I would then stand on the tracks for hours, envisioning each of my performances.

Placing second at the 1980 Olympic trials using only mental training was a pivotal moment. To better understand what happened, I quit my head coaching position at UC Berkeley and began a twenty-four-year exploration of the field of exceptional human performance. What I discovered led to working with groups as diverse as inner-city Oakland youth, professional athletes, corporate executives, and social activists working at the global level.

In working with many of these groups, I found that Bruce's story was a great example of what I came to call *Olympian Thinking*. This powerful way of thinking dramatically affects personal lives, super-charges professional goals, and has far-reaching implications for our aspirations to live in a world at peace. For those in leadership, Bruce's story indicates that our most important function in times of rapid change and high anxiety is to ensure that the desired goal remains crystal clear and to inspire and support our best thinking. What and how we think affect what we do. It is what we think and do, our daily mental and physical practices, that determine whether we win the gold or even make the team.

The Bruce Jenner Story

Bruce's story began at the Munich Olympic Games in 1972. The Russian, Victor Avilov, was the favorite and went on to win the gold medal in the decathlon. Bruce went to the stadium that evening, sitting in the athletes' section of the stands to watch the medal ceremony. As he sat there, almost close enough to reach out and touch the medal as it was placed around Avilov's neck, Bruce was seized by a feeling. As the Soviet anthem filled the stadium, he realized that next time it could be him standing there on the top step, gold medal gleaming. He knew in an instant that for him it would have to be at the next Olympic Games. He knew he did not have eight or twelve years to achieve his goal; it would have to be in Montreal.

Bruce committed himself to using every moment to ensure that in four years it would be he on the victory stand. That same night in his room in the Olympic village he was so excited about the next chapter of his life that he could not sleep—so he went for a training run! Over the next four years, every decision he made was with his goal in mind. Of all the activities Bruce employed, there is one that was pivotal to his endeavor.

Back in San Jose, the multievent athletes ran together every morning at the golf course. Bruce took his five-mile morning run solo with a very specific mental movie in his head. As his feet pounded out the rhythm on the ground, in his head he imagined being in Montreal at the Olympic Games winning the gold medal, setting the world record, and retiring. Although I had often told this part of his story, I had not known about his "moment of truth" in Munich, nor did I know that in the evening he ended his training day with a cool-down run, often in the dark, envisioning Victor Avilov two steps behind him. Every single day for four years, Bruce pursued the dream that was born in Munich. He envisioned winning the gold medal, setting the world record, and retiring.

At the Montreal Olympic Games four years later, Bruce was not the most naturally gifted nor the best-trained athlete in the event. After two days of fierce competition for the title of "world's best athlete," it came down to the last event. The Olympic decathletes stood at the starting line of the dreaded 1,500 meters. The athletes all knew that after two days of competition in nine events, this final event would demand every ounce of mental capability and physical endurance that they possessed. As they stood there, most of them dreading the last one-and-a-half laps of the four-lap event, Bruce was beaming inside. Just as he had for every day of the last four years, he was envisioning himself winning the gold medal, setting the world record, and retiring. As the race unfolded, Bruce ran propelled by an energy source that came from deep within. The results played out exactly as he had envisioned. That evening Bruce Jenner stood at the top of the victory stand and listened to the "Star Spangled Banner" fill the air as they placed the gold medal around his neck.

Bruce's story is a dramatic example of what we now know about how ordinary people do extraordinary things. The framework I call Olympian Thinking demystifies exceptional human performance and assists us in achieving extraordinary results in important areas outside the athletic arena.

Olympian Thinking

After my own experience in 1980, I began my exploration in the field of exceptional human performance and discovered that most extraordinary things in the world are done by ordinary people who have three things in common. If any one of these elements is missing, there is no chance of moving into realms of previously unimaginable performance. Most exciting to me was that these three elements are innate abilities that can be identified and developed in each and every one of us.

Vision Guided

First, my mental training, sometimes called visualization or mental rehearsal, was being taught to astronauts and salespeople, to executives and cancer patients. It is a naturally occurring human capability that we all use, usually unconsciously. It is not only a visual phenomenon but a multisensory one. During mental practice, our nervous systems fire in ways that are similar to what occurs when we physically execute a task. Athletes can feel the movement as they envision it in their minds. Musicians hear the music in their imaginations, cooks smell the herbs and can taste how they will flavor the sauce, artists see the statue inside the block of stone. Dreams, memory, fantasy, and imagination are all forms of imagery. What is important is to recognize that these multisensory images that are naturally occurring and constantly streaming day and night through our minds have a profound impact on us.

These multisensory images affect every cell of our bodies. Cancer and AIDS patients are taught specific types of imagery to increase their white blood cell and T-cell counts. The field of psychoneuro-immunology, pioneered by Drs. Carl and Stephanie Simonton in the 1980s, has led to similar breakthroughs in the areas of stress reduction and pain control using imagery methods. We know that the mind-set of the patient influences her health, even if we don't completely understand how or why. We will see a significant improvement in societal health when we teach young people the natural body-mind connection to affect their physical well-being.

The images that we create day and night also affect our professional performance. Successful artists and actors, athletes and astronauts, salespeople and executives all mentally rehearse, whether naturally or through specific training, the important moments in their careers. Envisioning a performance filled with tension and anxiety will often produce those undesirable results. Envisioning a flawless performance with moments of transcending with ease a challenging aspect of that performance will increase the chances of producing the desired result.

Although the process of creating images is natural and universal, most people are unaware of the profound impact their images have on their health, their performance, and their future. The challenge is to become conscious of the images we create and to determine if those images are moving us toward our goal or inhibiting our progress. Then we can consciously create images that effectively guide our daily action in alignment with that goal.

Most people are not aware that our genus-species name is not homo sapiens, "one who thinks." It is homo sapiens-sapiens, "one who thinks about his (or her) thinking." So when we notice our thinking and make conscious decisions to ensure that our thinking is in alignment with our values and goals, we are in fact experiencing life through our uniquely human capability.

At this point in my exploration of exceptional human performance, I thought I had discovered the "holy grail" and that if everyone knew how her mind worked she would become a high achiever, positively affecting her health, her performance, and her future. After receiving a grant to learn how to teach mental rehearsal effectively, I discovered that the conscious application of these skills did not produce high achievers. Working with a group of Olympians from Northern California, I learned that these traits clustered and became the categories of passion, vision, and action.

Passion Powered

I found myself asking the question, "Given that we are born with such great capabilities, why aren't we all performing at a much higher level?" I discovered a simple but profound answer. Although what we envision guides our actions, passion is the rocket fuel for exceptional human performance. When you are engaged in something that really matters to you, you have access to a high level of energy, and creativity soars as you envision your desired goal. When you truly care about something, your entire system shifts into high gear, and you access energy and skills that are unavailable when you are only mildly interested in an activity. It is truly a heady and physically exhilarating state of being.

For me, life changed dramatically when the Olympic Committee invited someone I had previously beaten to be part of the Olympic training camp for the 1968 Olympic Games. I was seized by the notion that if the Olympic Committee thought this person could be in the Olympics, that meant that I could be in the Olympics. It was an audacious thought for someone of average ability like me, but it would not go away. Every morning from that day on, I awoke with the notion that I could be in the Olympics, and I began to change my behavior and act like a future Olympian. Just the thought of walking into the Olympic stadium was so exciting that I began to make daily choices and major life decisions with that in mind. My actions became aligned with my passionate goal of being an Olympian.

When you are connected to something that matters, major obstacles become minor details and you access the creativity to find new resources and solutions. Teams, organizations, and even countries can function in the same way. The idea of putting a man on the moon and returning him safely to the earth energized and aligned powerful minds. That passionate vision prompted the development of new resources and new inventions, and took humankind where it had never been before.

Action Oriented

Being passion powered and vision guided are two essential elements required for exceptional human performance, but without action, you are just a vivid dreamer. What we envision and hold dear must have a way to come into being. Effective daily action requires a strategy and feedback to let us know if we are on the right track. Most of all, we create daily mental and physical practices that keep the vision alive and our actions aligned as we move closer to our goal each day.

Athletes rely on game plans and coaches. The *Apollo* scientists had a meticulous plan of action because they knew there were too many variables to leave to chance. Although the lunar landing module was off course 98 percent of the time, it was designed with a feedback system for constant course correction. So too in our individual and collective endeavors, we must have an effective plan and a feedback system that assist us in guiding our daily actions.

Applying Olympian Thinking to Leadership

Each of these three components—passion, vision, and action—is powerful and indispensable. Vision and action will bring only mediocre results if the team does not care about the outcome. Although financial rewards and prestige can motivate some for a time, they do not bring out the best people or the best in people. Tapping into what matters to people at a deeper level provides access to an unending source of energy and creativity. Some people are motivated by service to others, others by doing something new, and still others by the challenge of becoming one's best self or being part of a winning team. Effective leadership recognizes that each team comprises many types of people, and the leader provides structures and activities that remind each of them about the deeper reasons she has come to work.

Likewise, a passionate team with an action plan but with an unclear vision, misinformation, or negative beliefs cannot be effective or achieve meaningful results. Leaders must provide not just a clear goal but also the perspective and information people need to set priorities and understand the big picture. Leaders who communicate in this way demonstrate respect and trust, and enable everyone to make good decisions and contribute their best to a high-performance team.

Finally, passion and vision without action get you nowhere. Passionate, visionary people are very exciting to be around because of their energy and conviction, but they are not the high achievers. Passion and vision without a plan or effective daily practices make you a dreamer.

Most people have experienced a time when all three elements have fallen into place, often by accident. The role of a leader is to align these elements by design. It is easy to identify the moment when Bruce became passion powered at the Munich games: when Avilov won the gold. Bruce's five-mile run each morning was the vision-guided component. As he ran each morning envisioning the goal, he quite naturally and spontaneously envisioned his day, and it was easy to determine what behaviors and activities were most effective in leading him to his goal that day and what activities and behaviors were detrimental. From there he committed to effective daily action, eliminating the negative or time-wasting activities and emphasizing the positive ones with the best chance of moving him closer to his goal.

Stop for a moment and remember the last time you "set your mind" to something. It probably was something that really mattered to you, that you envisioned in very particular ways, and that motivated you to follow through with action. You were passion powered, vision guided, and action oriented. Likewise, leaders know that for a team to sustain long-term high performance, they need to keep the team connected to why the goal matters, provide complete and accurate information to guide the team's thinking, and support effective daily practices. In these times, however, the pressing challenge is to find ways to apply Olympian Thinking on a global scale.

Applying Olympian Thinking to the Ultimate Human Challenge: A Personal Commitment

My own evolution in the field of high performance led me to apply Olympian Thinking to the most pressing challenge on the planet: to live in a world at peace. The Olympian Thinking framework tells us that all three elements—passion, vision, and action—must be present for a new level of performance or achievement to occur. It appears, however, that most people have only two out of the three elements required to contribute to the global desire for peace.

We are living in a time when people in the United States and around the world are much more concerned about and engaged in thinking and talking about peace than perhaps any time since World War II or the Vietnam War. Clearly the desire or passion to live in a world at peace is nearly universal. It also has become clear to me that most people are willing to act when they know what to do and believe that their actions will make a difference. When people have a goal they care about and have specific actions that they see will help achieve the goal, they respond.

If we allow that most people want to live in peace and are willing to act, we have to ask ourselves how clear we are in terms of our *vision* regarding peace. Are we as clear as Bruce was about his goal? Do we know the history of peace and how close are we to the goal now? What are the critical success factors, and how do we rate on them? Just how effective is our thinking about peace? These are questions any effective leader would ask about a desired outcome.

Because so few are asking such questions, most people lack a clear and compelling vision of peace. It lives as a vague feeling, a longing for something that we cannot quite envision. When you engage people in a conversation about the prospects of living in peace, you hear a litany of explanations of why it is not possible. People cite human nature, poverty, corporate greed, government corruption, and a host of other "reasons" why we cannot live in peace. You cannot chart a course to a goal that is not clear, and the negative beliefs held by most people will never lead to the creative solutions necessary to achieve the global dream of peace.

Leaders must do two things. First, we must inspire people to envision clearly what our goal—a world at peace—looks like, and second, we must clarify where we are relative to that goal. As leaders, our most important contribution is to inspire and support the kind of thinking that leads to effective action and to begin with ourselves.

Olympian Thinking and World Peace

What Does the Goal Look Like?

Ask yourself, "How clear am I about the goal of peace?" Our role as leaders is to inspire others to create and hold fast to a clear vision of that which they hold dear. It is also vitally important that each person who truly cares about peace and wants to be part of seeing it become a reality has her own very personal, powerful image of what peace means to her. As Bruce Jenner demonstrated, the clearer you are, the more effective you can be with your time and energy in bringing your goal to fruition. I invite you as a leader and as someone who wants to engage your best thinking for peace to stop reading at this time and answer the question, "What do I mean by peace? What does it look like and feel like? How close am I to living in peace in my family, in my community, at work, and in the world?" The simple act of focusing on this image will begin to shift your actions into alignment with your desire to live in a world at peace.

As an Olympian I was fortunate to have had a profound experience of living in peace in the Olympic village with people of every race, religion, and political persuasion. I know now that what we had in common and what allowed us to transcend our differences was respect. Every Olympian there had respect for herself or himself and respect for the other athletes who had earned the right to be there among the best in the world. When I talk about peace I recall that feeling of being in the village, and I envision people everywhere having that same feeling of respect.

At other times I recall when Dr. Martin Luther King received the Noble Peace Prize and said, "I have the audacity to believe that people everywhere can have three meals a day for their bodies, education and culture for their minds, freedom and dignity for their spirits." That is a vision of a world at peace. In these trying times, I implore you to make it a part of your daily practice as a leader to begin each day with an image of the world you intend to live in and would like to pass on to your children. The simple act of reminding yourself each day of this goal will tap into a deeper source of energy and creativity, and it will effectively guide your daily actions. Holding that image of peace will have a positive influence at home, at work, and in the world.

How Leaders Make a Difference

In challenging times, leaders also must provide information that will assist people in making good decisions regarding their goal. At this time it is our responsibility to let people know that passionate, committed people have laid a foundation for living in a world at peace. Consider some little-known facts pertaining to peace:

- Despite earlier predictions that world population would reach between ten and fourteen billion people at the turn of the twenty-first century, we have only six billion people. The current prediction is that population will stabilize in the next fifty years at about nine billion, which we know is sustainable.
- Experts are expanding successful strategies and predicting when hunger will be history.
- Democracy is becoming the dominant form of governance and fully informed, participatory democracy is the emerging next step.
- Technology and communication capabilities have dramatically accelerated the level of international cooperation in fields as diverse as genome mapping and space exploration.
- Transparency and accountability are changing the practices of corporate executives and government leaders in ways unimagined just ten years ago.

Many of these trends are converging and creating new possibilities for living in a just and sustainable world. If those in leadership do not provide access to this kind of information, people persist in their negative beliefs and do not engage their most creative capabilities to participate effectively in creating the world they so deeply desire.

Ordinary people—informed, passionate, connected, and aligned—are an emerging powerful, positive force. As leaders we must inform and inspire people to engage their best thinking and be part of the team creating the new story with a practical agenda for how to create a world that works.

The Gold Medal

As Bruce Jenner stood at the starting line of the final event of the decathlon, he beamed as his competitors trembled. He took a deep breath and envisioned his goal, confident that all his hard work and his vision would carry him through. As leaders we too must take a deep breath. We must be role models; we must demonstrate our awareness and faith in the work of all those who have gone before us and trust that our common vision will produce the effective action that will carry us through to the ultimate gold.

In the end, it is what we and our teams do each day that determines whether we win the gold. I would like to suggest a powerful daily practice that aligns your passion, your vision, and your actions, increasing the effectiveness of all that you do each day. Whether your goal is harmony at home, productivity at work, or peace in the world, I recommend what Bruce has allowed me to call the Bruce Jenner Technique. To apply this kind of Olympian Thinking in your life, I recommend that instead of running five miles each morning as Bruce did, set your alarm clock five minutes early and run a mental movie of your goal, your gold medal. See it clearly and in great detail. Through this practice you will quite naturally begin to look at your day and notice what actions and behaviors are moving you toward that goal and what actions are inhibiting your progress. You will begin to focus more attention on the behaviors that contribute and move away from the behaviors that detract. Like Bruce envisioning the victory stand in Montreal, you will find yourself energized by these images. Using this simple daily practice, you will align the three elements common to all high achievers: passion, vision, and action.

The question is, will you engage as fully as Bruce Jenner did in envisioning the real gold?

 Marian L. Heard is one of our most distinguished leaders from the nonprofit world. During her twelve-and-a-half-year tenure as the president and CEO of the United Way of Massachusetts Bay, Marian transformed her organization into the number one United Way chapter in the United States, receiving the greatest amount of donor funds at the $10,000 and above level along the way. She also has earned two Presidential appointments: President George H. W. Bush appointed Marian as founding president and CEO of the Points of Light Foundation in 1990, and President Clinton appointed her to run the Summit for America's Future in 1997. Although Marian retired from her position of CEO of the United Way of Massachusetts Bay in July 2004, she has remained a member of a number of corporate and non-profit boards including MENTOR, a national mentoring partnership program active in twenty-seven states, where she serves as the National Spokesperson.

In this chapter, Marian relates her personal journey as a leader. She emphasizes the importance of listening, inclusion, and mentoring to the overall (and critical) process of lifelong learning.

29

BEING A LEADER
OF LEADERS

Marian L. Heard

My parents always told us that life was not an event
where you could call in sick. So I learned by doing.
I also learned how to be bold.

I could not have been born at a better time—a time when being
willing and able to keep learning has become central to personal
and professional success. For leaders in my parents' generation and,
in fact, for many peers in my generation, the path to success was
quite different than the path I have traveled.

There was a day when success was pretty much a straight march
up the ladder. There was a prescription for leadership. You excelled
in your early years as a learner, went to the right university, and went
to work for a solid company, where you planned to stay for much, if
not all, of your life. If you kept your head down and worked hard, you
could expect to begin the sometimes slow but steady climb up. Once
you reached a certain point you became a manager; one hopes you
learned how to be a leader along the way. And then . . . ? Well, you
have heard all the old adages: "Life stops at forty" and "Can't teach
an old dog new tricks," among others. It may seem silly today, but
there was a pervasive belief that once you reached a certain age there
was no need to continue learning. Most organizations didn't provide
the incentive or opportunity for further growth because by the time
you were forty it was clear that either you were a leader or you were
not destined to lead.

Not so today! Careers now are more dynamic, less linear. Out of necessity, organizations are forced to reinvent themselves constantly and so too are the individuals who work there. Some skills become obsolete almost as soon as they are mastered. As the world around us changes, leaders today can't just emerge from the traditional corporate experience with management skills and expertise in a narrowly defined field. Rather, leaders *develop,* personally and professionally, because they simply refuse to stop learning. You can be thankful that if you set high standards, stay relentlessly focused, and *never* close your mind to new ideas or new opportunities, you can lead long after you celebrate your fortieth birthday. I for one am looking forward to new leadership challenges well into my "retirement" years.

My Leadership Edge: Trusted to Take Risks

Now as I look back, I think I was given an edge. The quest to continually learn was fostered throughout my childhood. Life in my parents' home was meant to unfold day by day, each one reflected on for what was gained and lost, each morning to be started with a renewed quest for learning. My parents had high standards. They set ambitious goals for our family, and together we created a real sense of mission. For me, that mission was education. My family was prepared to take on the hard task of leaving this world a better place than we found it. However, I was not given an instruction manual to follow. There were no quick fixes or shortcuts. I learned from their examples.

I remember the year I was turning sixteen—who doesn't? I was finally going to learn to drive. Most of my friends had already turned sixteen, so they, of course, shared their learning experience with me. It was by the book. They learned how the car operated, they attended driver's education classes, and they ventured out slowly and cautiously. I was preparing myself for the same experience. The morning I was going to be taught, I envisioned heading out to the parking lot of my high school. After all, it was Saturday, and a nice empty parking lot felt just about right to me. My father, it seemed, had a different idea. He backed the family's brand-new, two-tone green DeSoto to the curb and motioned for me to hop into the driver's seat. He calmly took his place next to me, opened the window, lit up his Lucky Strike, and sat back to enjoy the ride. I was terrified. But I did it. Later I asked him why we didn't go to the high school as I had expected, and he replied, "Do you want to spend the rest of your life driving around a parking lot?"

I learned that day that taking personal risks allows you to open yourself to new experiences.

I didn't expect to get in the car that morning and simply take off. I didn't expect my father to have that much confidence in my abilities. I certainly didn't expect to be entrusted with the brand-new family car. It wasn't until much later that I realized that day he had taught me much more than how to drive. The experience taught me very clearly that my father trusted *me*, and not with the old Dodge but with his prized new DeSoto. His trust allowed me to take risks— to go outside my comfort zone and to believe that I am capable of accepting any challenge. Indeed, life has presented its share of hurdles. I don't dwell on them. They are simply there to be experienced and, more important, as a place to learn.

Accept Only Candor

When I came to the United Way of Massachusetts Bay in 1992, we were in a far different place than we are today. It was a low period for United Way in what otherwise is a long history of exemplary service. We had a reputation for being passive, for not making things happen. I knew I had to shake things up. But for the first few months my primary task was to prepare the board and the staff to address issues at United Way of America headquarters in Alexandria, Virginia. My secondary task was to listen. And listen I did. Much of the feedback about our local and national organization was hard to hear at times, but I accepted nothing but total candor.

Then I went out in the community, and I listened some more. Even if I didn't totally agree with what people were telling me, I was not defensive. I realized that people needed to feel that this organization cared, and needed to know I was going to make a difference. Three months into my tenure with the organization, I was invited to an annual meeting with one of our larger agencies. I hadn't yet met them, but I was in the audience observing, listening, and waiting for my turn to speak. They went on at great length criticizing the work of my organization. When I was finally introduced, I practically ran to the podium. When the people in the audience realized who I was, they were hushed. I took the microphone and turned to the audience and thanked them. I praised the work their agency does. I told a story about how I was a long-time supporter of their agency, and I thanked each of them for their commitment. Then I told them about my agency and how the work we were about to embark on would forever change the lives of the children of this community. I told them I hoped they would join with us and, if not, return the money! And then I left. By the time I made it to my car, the phone was ringing. They knew change was afoot. They knew I listened, that I cared, and that I was going to make things happen. And I did.

People often tell me that I must have the words "Talk to me" emblazoned on my chest. This is only because I have learned how to watch closely and listen attentively, how to hear what people are really telling me, not what they think I want to hear. I have had long conversations with many of our donors and many of my staff members. We talk about everything from social problems to personal philosophies to families. Sometimes what they are telling me isn't immediately obvious, but I can sense when they need help. And I do what I can to give them the support they need. That is why I am here.

"What Do You Dream About?"

If you are going to listen to others, you must be open to new ideas. There is one thought I keep with me always—good ideas can come from the most unlikely places.

Early on in my career I sensed an unwritten code of behavior: "Good ideas belonged to those in management." And you needed to earn your place there before it was okay to contribute ideas. I never accepted this.

Others fear that if someone presents an idea that they hadn't thought of, it will make them appear less competent. In fact I have found the exact opposite to be true. It is actually quite liberating to accept that in an ever-changing world you can never know it all. You have to be willing to let go of old notions, to "know when to hold 'em and know when to fold 'em"—in effect, to "know what you don't know."

One of our greatest success stories was born out of an idea that didn't come up through the ranks. Instead it was offered casually in a meeting. It could have been missed. I simply asked a person whom we were interviewing for a job, "What do you dream about?" "License plates" was the answer. But not just any license plate—one that would help support our most vulnerable citizens, the children under six. It seemed crazy at the time; this was long before the idea of a specialized plate became commonplace. But it wasn't crazy; it was a big, big idea. And we jumped on it. Before you knew it, we launched the plates that today have raised over $1 million to support statewide school readiness programs designed to ensure that young children enter kindergarten with the skills they need in order to learn. That's over $30,000 each month in renewal fees, all from a simple question, "What do you dream about?"

Endow Others with Dignity and Respect

Good ideas really are everywhere. I have always accepted people for who they are, and I have always believed that everyone has something unique to contribute—that everyone deserves to be treated with dignity and respect. I never assume I have all the answers. No one does. I believe that I can learn from everyone, that there is not a person on this earth who cannot make a contribution to the idea bank!

Last year we launched a new ad campaign. We were all very happy with the work—the ads were really smart, and the campaign embodied great strategy. The basic premise was to turn the camera on our donors, to make them the heroes. In so doing we hoped to help others see themselves and envision how they too can be donors. Lots of companies participated in the campaign. Late one evening I was waiting for the elevator outside my office. I struck up a conversation with Peter Doherty of UPS, the firm that delivers packages to the office. He motioned to a poster of our campaign and remarked, "I don't like it." Instead of dismissing his comments, I probed. "Why not?" He responded, "These donors, they have only been supporters for a few years; it makes it look like you just arrived. Where are the folks like me who have been donors for twenty years?" And he was right. We immediately arranged to get him in an ad, and we made sure to better represent donors of all types. It just made the work better.

Yes, our organization faced challenges. Through it all—the press conferences, the endless meetings, the agency visits—I had to make some tough and, at times, unpopular decisions. However, bad times don't wear me down. Instead they become a source of learning and growth. I have found that if you listen carefully and approach issues with an open mind you can survive the most difficult experiences. This is especially true in my work with young people.

Mentoring: An Exchange of Learning

Studies confirm what many of us intuitively know—the single most important influence in a young person's life is the relationship with a caring adult. This is the cornerstone of mentoring. I have long been a mentor, both formally as the director and national spokesperson for MENTOR—National Mentoring Partnership and informally throughout my life. I was a mentor for a young woman for seven years. During this time, I learned at least as much from her as she learned from me. The usual expectation for a mentoring relationship is that the mentor is going to be the only one on the giving end. Sometimes, though, we stumble into learning, and we receive unexpected gifts when we are open to what a relationship or a situation can bring. I hadn't known Keisha long. I met her at a time in her life when she was having difficulty coping. Her mother was ill. She had a limited support system. I knew I could help her. But what I didn't know was how much she could help me. I saw a strength and resiliency in her that made me stronger. Her perseverance gave me renewed focus and commitment to my mission—to ensure that every person has the opportunity to reach his or her dreams. I must relentlessly remind people that we can't afford to let even one child go hungry, for that little person just may have the cure for cancer in his or her head. Keisha wasn't going to let go of her dreams despite significant obstacles. And together we created a new future full of promise. Keisha has now graduated from college. She is working and moving in the right direction. There are thousands more Keishas out there; I know it. You must listen. And you might learn something in the process.

Assess Failure and Success Honestly

Three times in the last ten years, we have taken a hard look at our business and made big strategic changes. Each time, the shifts were far reaching, affecting all operations of our business. We didn't have to undergo this intense level of self-scrutiny. After all, by many objective measures we were doing okay. But I have never been one to be comfortable with the status quo. The opportunity cost of sitting still is just too great.

When I first arrived in Boston I was informed that it was not a generous town. In fact our United Way ranked eighty-seventh among all United Ways across the country for the number of individuals who give $10,000 or more each year. I refused to believe that the citizens of this region didn't care. I set out to prove all the naysayers and all the surveys wrong. I believed that there were many in our community with the means to get things done and the desire to do so. I simply asked them if they wanted to be remembered as a group of people that could, but didn't. I called on them to come together and show the community they care.

When Life Is Most Rewarding

In response, a group of real estate executives gathered together members of their industry to demonstrate their collective support by raising money for the community. At the same time, a handful of ambitious donors in the venture capital industry treated their colleagues to an informal breakfast focusing on United Way of Massachusetts Bay and our mission. The idea rapidly caught fire. Over the next few years, meetings and events targeting leaders across all major industries were convened. We even focused on specific demography through our special women's initiative. With almost 50,000 individuals attending these events and other special meetings over the years, the leadership series has become a powerful means of uniting the local leaders representing Boston's business community. These events have raised over $25 million in just nine years. And today Boston ranks first in America among *The Alexis de Tocqueville Society* donors and *The Women's Leadership* donors as well. A leap of faith rewarded.

What spurs me on is my commitment to the goals I have set and the dreams I aspire to. Those goals and dreams give me the strength to endure the short-term pain that often comes with growth. When we were growing up, my parents always taught us that "the shame is not in failing but in not trying." If you have set your goals and are clear on your aspirations, setbacks can facilitate the development of learning. That is when life is most rewarding.

A Sense of Purpose Every Day

These days I get up at 4:30 in the morning. That is my time, a time when I can read or exercise. It helps me prepare for the day ahead. Often I spend my days in constant motion. There are meetings to sit in on, speeches to deliver, programs to visit, calls to make, dinners to attend. People often ask me, "How do you do it?" For me the question is "How could I not?" It is about stamina and much more. I was born with a competitive drive. The word *can't* just isn't in my vocabulary. When I was in the third grade, there was another student in my class named Marion. She did good work, but I worked harder. I didn't want my efforts to be confused with hers, so I changed the spelling of my name to Marian so there could be no confusion. But it is really more than simply being competitive, I was infused with a sense of purpose—and it has been the catalyst for all I have done in my life.

I have many plans for the next phase of my life. I am lucky. I have a wonderful husband and strong family. I have grandchildren to spoil. I have so many opportunities. I will continue as a board member for the Points of Light Foundation, which was established to perpetuate former president George H. W. Bush's call for volunteers to address social problems. I will continue to serve on the boards of several of my country's major corporations as well as continue to be trustee for institutions dedicated to education and cancer research treatment. I will also remain as the director of MENTOR, a national mentoring partnership program active in twenty-six states. When asked to serve in these activities, I am told, "Marian, we have so much to learn from you." It makes me laugh. I have so much to learn from them as well.

As a school teacher at an inner-city high school in Long Beach, California, Erin Gruwell helped 150 of her students, many of whom were written off by the education system, write a book, graduate from high school, and attend college. Erin's tenacity and dedication to her students is chronicled in the book *Freedom Writers' Diary: How a Teacher and 150 Teens Used Writing to Change Themselves and the World Around Them*. Her inspiring story is currently being developed into a major motion picture.

In this chapter, Erin draws on her experiences with her students to remind us of the importance of dreaming big, defying odds, making a difference, and doing the right thing because it is the right thing to do. As the voice of the next generation of women leaders, she calls for us to create a renaissance of hope and possibility for our children.

PHOTO CREDIT: Erin Gruwell by Glenn Zucman

30

AREN'T WE THE DREAM?

Erin Gruwell

This story is not mine alone; it belongs to 150 "at-risk" students in an inner-city high school who managed to transform their lives and the expectations of everyone around them. The story begins, though, because of the choice I made to become a teacher. I took that path for a simple reason. My father had been active in the civil rights and antiwar movements in the 1960s, and I went to college with those ideals in mind. Instead of burning bras, however, I wound up selling them at Nordstrom's, at prices that ensured that no one would ever burn them for any cause. As an idealist, I felt cheated because there was nothing galvanizing my generation. Then one day in 1992, something happened that changed my mind and my life forever.

I was watching TV because the Rodney King verdict—in which four white policemen were acquitted of beating an African American motorist in Los Angeles—was about to be announced. On screen, I saw an outraged father pick up a Molotov cocktail and throw it at a Circuit City store. The father walked with his young son into the store and took away a television and some stereo equipment. The little boy was not an instigator or an accomplice; he was just following a parent's lead. But when I saw the way he looked up at his father, I realized that education starts at home. In my life, I wanted to join a worthy cause because my father had been part of one and had told me stories around the dinner table about Martin Luther King, among others.

If I wanted to fight the good fight because of what my father taught me, what kind of fight was this little boy on television going to learn from his father? At that moment, I decided I didn't want to fight battles in a courtroom, but I would rather fight battles in a classroom.

In my excitement, I called my father, who ironically was on the golf course. He did not take my revelation as great news. Instead, he made proverbial jokes that teachers don't make any money and that they no longer get apples from their students. They lead difficult lives. To prove him wrong, I enrolled in graduate school, where I encountered what would turn out to be a vast gap between theory and practice. My professor, with her tinted blue hair and $95 text-books, probably hadn't been in a classroom since *Leave It to Beaver*, but her message—that we were not a melting pot but a salad bowl, coexisting together in harmony—sounded wonderful to me, like a refrain from "Kumbaya." When I finished my program I went forth, eager for the challenge of educating young minds in the most eclectic setting I could find. It was a challenge all right, but not the one I expected.

Woodrow Wilson High School is in Long Beach, California. It is not in a terrible area, and in fact it is a desirable school, but thanks to MTV and gangster rap videos it had experienced "white flight." My friends from my gated community thought I should wear a bulletproof vest, but on my first day as a teacher, I showed up in a polka-dot dress with pearls and a Coach attaché case. My classroom was bare. In one corner, there was an Apple 2E computer. I looked around and saw I had no chalk, no textbooks, and for a disconcerting length of time, no students. After the tardy bell rang, a security officer finally escorted my students inside. They took their seats in corners of the room as if selecting designated comfort zones. In one corner there were African Americans, in another Latinos. The Asians sat in another corner. Front and center sat the only Caucasian, and because he was extremely dyslexic, he wondered if he was in the wrong room.

Without missing a beat, I passed out my syllabus. Fifteen seconds later, a student named Andre threw it back at me in paper airplane form. Still stunned, I watched as crumpled-up versions followed the airplane. Then Andre spoke for everyone when he said, "Why do we have to read books by dead white guys wearing tights?" Sure enough, I looked at my syllabus and discovered he was right. On the page, I saw Homer and Shakespeare. At that moment, I realized I had no idea what I was doing. Had I made the wrong decision? These kids were going to eat me alive. They hated reading, and they hated each other. But at least I had succeeded in uniting them in one common cause: they now all hated me.

Demoralized, I barely made it through the day. When I got home, I could not pick up the phone to call my father. I didn't want to hear an "I told you so." My primary urge was to go back to university and consult with my professors to figure out where I went wrong. But then I reconsidered. Instead of searching for the answers through traditional authority figures and textbooks, what if I treated my students as if they were the ones with the Ph.D.s? I looked at my syllabus to try to understand what they had been telling me. How could I make a connection between what I was supposed to be teaching them and their immediate reality? I started thinking about Homer and the *Odyssey*. Weren't my students on a journey themselves? They had their own Cyclops, their own sirens. So the next day, I went into the classroom determined to give voice to the voiceless by asking them questions and finding out what they knew that I didn't.

What was their world like? Andre raised his hand and said, "I feel like I live in an undeclared war zone." This took me aback. When I thought of a war zone, I thought of tanks and battle fatigues, not Long Beach, which is only thirty minutes from Disneyland and Beverly Hills. But as I continued to listen, I learned that by the age of fifteen this young man had already lost dozens of friends and family to gang violence. Every time a lowered Chevy passed him on the street, he worried that another drive-by shooting was about to take place. Maria raised her hand next. She had been to more funerals than birthday parties, she said. It was unbelievable and chilling. Listening to them one after another, I began to understand. No wonder they reacted to the world in such a way. With their backs up against the wall, they felt nothing but a fight-or-flight instinct, an urge to pick up a spray can or a gun and fight back, or to run away.

There had to be other, nonviolent means by which they could respond to life that wouldn't help perpetuate the cycle in which they were trapped. Over the next few weeks, I began to think about what I could do to introduce them to the larger issues of the world and show them that they were not alone.

At one point in my early teaching career, I intercepted a note when it was being passed through the room. Scribbled on the page was an ugly racial caricature, a cartoonish drawing of one of the toughest students in the class. Despite his toughness, he was really hurt by the image, and tears came to his eyes. Although I had no action plan in place to respond to the note, it galvanized me nevertheless. Everything I'd been thinking and feeling erupted, and I told the class that this was an example of the kind of racial insensitivity that had been at the root of the Holocaust. When I looked around at the faces in the room to see the effect of my outburst, I realized that no one knew what I was talking about. The Holocaust? The worst atrocity mankind had ever known? They had never heard of it.

I wondered how to deal with that. An opportunity seemed to be presenting itself, if only I could seize it. Perhaps I could use the example of the Holocaust and other incidents of racial intolerance throughout history to help these students look in the mirror and evaluate their own lives. I realized that there were books about such matters written for and by children—children who had been in real wars with extermination camps and ethnic cleansing campaigns. I went to my principal and said that I wanted to use three books in my class: *The Diary of Anne Frank*, by Anne Frank; *Night*, by Elie Wiesel; and *Zlata's Diary: A Child's Life in Sarajevo*, by Zlata Filipovic, a young girl who had written about her family's experiences with ethnic cleansing in Bosnia. My principal said that it was too late to fill out the requisition forms and that I would have to wait for another year. So I went to my English Department head and asked her for advice. She said, "Your kids are too stupid! They won't appreciate the books anyway." But she had magazines from Scholastic with abridged versions of Anne Frank's diary for me to use.

Her comments stunned me. She thought my students were too stupid to read a book. As I considered the implications, I realized that although we can deflect a certain amount of negativity in our lives, when we hear the same things, over and over, it becomes a self-fulfilling prophecy. My students had probably heard that they were too stupid to read since before they were even old enough to read. I knew I had to get copies of those books and figure out a way to change those perceptions.

I didn't have tenure, I didn't have a substantial paycheck, but I had my dad. I told him I needed money, without really explaining why, and he FedExed me a check. Then I went to the Yellow Pages and found a bookstore that would feel sorry for a poor teacher and her 150 students. My anxiety began to rise as soon as I'd placed the order. What if my students didn't read the books and simply threw them away? I considered the old adage from Mary Poppins that "a spoonful of sugar helps the medicine go down." The books were medicine, but Anne Frank, Elie Wiesel, and Zlata Filipovic were the real teachers. I needed to make my students excited about their stories.

What would motivate them? A clean break. A fresh start. Some hope and opportunity. In my life, every time I have experienced some sort of symbolic change, my family celebrated with a toast. So I went out at midnight the night before class and bought plastic champagne glasses and sparkling apple cider. Tomorrow we would start our new rite of passage. Maybe my students would realize that even though they had scored straight F's all their lives or lived in homes with generations of violent gang members, they could wipe the slate clean and start anew.

I got everything set up the next morning. Each student took a glass of cider, and we stood in a circle. Maria started us off with the toast. In her mind, a fresh start was not about grades; it was more philosophical. She raised her glass and said, "I don't want to be pregnant when I'm fifteen years old, like my mother. I don't want to be in jail for the rest of my life, like my father. I don't want to be six feet under when I'm eighteen, like my cousin. I want to change."

The more I knew about Maria, the more amazed I was by her. This fifteen-year-old who appeared so tough and feisty had already seen more drama and tragedy in her life than most of us see in movie theaters. At five years old, on her way to kindergarten, she had seen her role model shot five times in the back by police officers. Shortly thereafter, she'd watched her father get handcuffed and hauled off to San Quentin. Throughout her formative years, she hadn't been primed to go to Yale; she'd expected to go to jail. Every weekend, growing up, she'd sit in the back of a beat-up Chevy Impala and drive to San Quentin to see her daddy. She and her brother would cover their heads with blankets during this eight-hour trip and try to guess the upcoming forks in the road. No matter how many times they took the journey, she was always wrong. And she believed that this feeling of being in the backseat in the dark was an analogy for her life. The road was always going to be a mystery. Someone else was always going to be in charge of her life. Now, standing in our circle, she was talking openly about the concept of change.

When she finished talking, I handed her a copy of the *Diary of Anne Frank*. She looked at it and became upset with me. "What does this mean?" she asked. She didn't think that real change was going to come from a three hundred–page book. She flipped through it and commented, "I don't look like her, I don't talk like her, and I don't pray to the same God." I told her to give it a try and suggested that she might just find herself inside the pages of this book.

Disgruntled, Maria went home. Determined to prove me wrong, she crawled into bed and gave the book a try. The electricity had been turned off. She felt that there was no way she could relate to this girl in a far-off land. But as she read, she came across this sentence: "Sometimes I feel like a bird in a cage and I wish I could fly away." The line was like a light bulb for her. She felt as though Anne Frank, sitting in her attic all those years ago, had written it just for her.

Each day, until she finished the book, Maria came to class excited by what she had read the night before. One day, she asked me if Anne was going to "smoke" Hitler. To her, Anne Frank was like one of Charlie's Angels in stiletto heels. I told her to just keep reading. Another day, she asked me if Anne and her friend Peter were going to do a little "something, something." Just keep reading, I said. Then one day she came into class screaming at me in Spanish. "Why didn't you tell me Anne dies?" she cried. She was furious at me, and I realized that in Maria's mind Anne was a symbol of innocence and escape. What was I telling Maria about her own chances? She told me that she hated me and was never going to read another book again. Then Andre stood up and said "Maria. Anne is going to live on after death because she wrote about her life. None of our friends ever show up in an obituary in the paper or on the cover of a magazine. But because Anne wrote a book, she is alive."

Andre's words seemed to connect Anne's life to our world. All of a sudden, my students were debating among themselves vigorously. The next day, Andre came to class with more books. I don't think he checked them out of the library, but that's OK. He and his associates had discovered that the woman who hid Anne Frank in the attic was still alive. Her name was Miep Gies. She was eighty-seven years old and lived in Amsterdam. Like the movie *Field of Dreams*, Andre was convinced that if we were to build it, she would come. In other words, if we wrote to her, Miep Gies would visit us and talk about the real Anne Frank.

There was no way in the world I thought we could pull that off. At the very least, I hoped that we would write letters to Miep Gies and move on to the next book. If we managed that much, at least my students would be reading and discussing books. But the next day, Andre came to class with a huge jug, the kind that sits on top of a water cooler. I knew that Andre didn't have a water cooler at home, but he was very proud of his jug. He set it down on the desk and said, "This is what we are going to use to raise money and get Miep Gies to come to our classroom." He reached in his pocket and pulled out a little fuzz, a meal ticket, and seven coins. He dropped the coins in the jug and told everyone else to ante up.

Within a few weeks our letters were written. Andre asked me, "What happens if we raise enough money and she doesn't come?" In Hebrew, the number eighteen means life, and we had eighteen dollars in our jug. I didn't realize the symbolism at the time, but as I looked around the room, I saw that my students weren't sitting in their respective corners anymore. They were sitting together, debating among themselves, engaged. I said, "Don't worry. If Miep Gies doesn't come, we'll either buy more books or go on a field trip together, so it's a win-win. If she does come, our lives will never be the same." We took our letters to Kinko's and mailed them off to Amsterdam like a message in a bottle. Luckily, she answered our pleas and agreed to come visit us.

We chose a dilapidated community center to host Miep where we could all stay at the same time. What could we do to decorate the space and make it nice? I had about every "tagger" in the school in my class, so I got them paper and paint, and for one day they worked like Matisse, Picasso, or Diego Rivera, transforming the room with its peeling ceiling into the Metropolitan Museum of Art. Then we started thinking about how we would feed Miep Gies. Maria's mom made sensational tamales. Andre's grandma made some sweet potato pie. Lucy's grandma made a Cambodian rice dish.

The morning Miep Gies was scheduled to arrive, I noticed another change. On most days, students like Andre wore baggy pants that hung below their boxers. On this occasion, however, Andre came in wearing a belt. He even had a crease in his shirt, as though he were attending church. When you get dressed up for a special event, the kids call it "flossing," and Andre was as proud as a peacock.

Miep Gies walked into the room. You would have thought Michael Jordan himself was making an appearance. She was no more than four feet tall, but to my students she was cooler than P. Diddy or J-Lo or anyone else you could imagine. She stood before us and talked about a little girl named Anne and her diary. We sat there transfixed. Miep told us that the going rate for turning someone in to the Gestapo was $2 per person. She would never forget August 4, 1944, the day someone made $16 for turning in Anne

Frank, her family, and four other people. As a secretary in her twenties, Miep felt so vulnerable and afraid when the Gestapo entered the attic that there was nothing she could do to stop them.

Andre stood up and lost it. He told us all about a similar day when his best friend was given $25 to go to Target and buy some school supplies. Instead of purchasing a backpack and some folders, the friend bought a used .38 special from the streets. He wanted to teach Andre a game called Russian Roulette. Andre was thirteen at the time, and his friend went first. With one cock of the trigger, he blew his brains out all over Andre. Andre had shared with the class in the past that even if he took Comet and a Brillo pad and scrubbed himself raw, he would always be able to feel his friend and smell him. Crying, he said, "I've never had a hero in my entire life, but you are my hero."

Miep Gies became very upset when Andre said this to her. She pounded her fist on the podium and said, "No. I am not a hero. I simply did what I had to do because it was the right thing to do." She looked at Andre, Maria, and 148 other kids who had been told they were dumb and stupid. In her eyes, they were brilliant and beautiful. They were not a gathering of rejects or dangerous teenagers, but a wonderful chorus of shattered stereotypes. Looking straight at Andre, she said, "Please make sure that Anne's death was not in vain."

That was the moment that changed everything for my students and opened their entire lives. They went home and began to write. They wrote about the men sitting on stoops, about the mothers that would steal the gold chain off their children's necks to sell it for crack, about the grandfather who did bad things to them but whom they weren't supposed to tell on because he loved them. When they started writing, they were afraid and desperate. But when they came back to class, they were hopeful and triumphant. They shared beautiful stories about desperation and despair and tiny little victories. As their English teacher, I didn't care about dangling modifiers, I just wanted to give my students an opportunity to share their stories with anyone who would listen. It didn't matter if I was the only one who ever read them. I wanted them to feel as though there were no boundaries holding them back and that they had resounding voices.

I never imagined how far our pens would take us. Together, we traveled around the world on our "field trips," doing what we could to prompt change and learn about others. We visited Anne Frank's attic, and we testified before Congress. It was difficult at times. I continued to sell bras, work at the Marriott, and teach night school in addition to the regular classes. But we picked up friends along the way. When I was driven to distraction about money, a CEO called me out of the blue and said, "I don't live in your neighborhood or have kids at your school, but what can I do to help?" I needed to buy books, so he wrote me a check. And then I wanted to take my students on a field trip, so he came with us. He was hooked. The involvement was very fulfilling to him, and he became our consigliore, helping us to pull off whatever new idea came up. As we expanded our network of friends and contacts, we learned how to ask others for help. Our needs were never very big. In fact, I learned that it is always the simple things that a teacher and a student can really use. Sometimes it is just your involvement, a simple gesture like joining us on the bus and bringing along some bagels or juice.

My students needed love, support, and safety. At first, they didn't want to be at school, and no wonder. When I sat in the teachers' lounge and heard the horrible things that people would say about them, it was depressing to me, too. I did not believe that education was about making derogatory generalizations; I believed that it was about being optimistic. I tried to create that kind of atmosphere in my classroom. We turned that messy, dirty room into a home. We put pictures up on the walls, a bit like Anne Frank did in her attic. We stuck together. We brought food into the classroom at lunch so that everyone would have something to eat. The students who were dyslexic worked with the students who were great writers. We became a family. It didn't matter what negative things anyone said about us or to us because the issues were bigger than all of us together. In fact, the harder things became, the more meaningful they felt.

On one of our field trips, while standing on the steps of the Lincoln Memorial in Washington, D.C., Andre looked at me. "So, this is where he said it, huh, Ms. G?" He was talking about Martin Luther King. It was raining that night, and for this English teacher, the rain seemed like a metaphor. Andre continued, "Look, aren't we the dream? Aren't we what Dr. King was talking about?" I realized that these students believed for the first time that they could be judged for the content of their character, not the color of their skin. My students had many dreams, and one of them was about change and a new beginning. Every one of them wanted a "Get out of Jail Free" card, not from a parole officer or a judge but from the power of a high school diploma. As things turned out, every one of them graduated from high school and went on to college.

Now, I am their teacher again at the university level. Although I am now their "professor," I feel more like their student. I have 150 different teachers who show me how to color outside the lines, how to be humble and gracious, how to dream big and stand up to bullies. We continue to do our work for other "at-risk" students. A major studio bought our story and is bringing it to the big screen. I can only imagine what it will be like to be a kid from a bad neighborhood sitting in a corner of the theater, watching Andre and Maria and the others. I hope that child thinks, "I look like them. I talk like them. I don't have to sing or hit a baseball over a fence to get out of here. Maybe education is the real answer."

We are not heroes, but we can make a difference. Miep Gies really did understand the answer. It is not about leaping over buildings, it's about doing the right thing because it is the right thing to do. At the end of the day, that's what's important. It doesn't matter how much money you get in your paycheck. It's the psychic income that is truly worth making.

Pat Mitchell is the first woman president and CEO of the Public Broadcasting Service (PBS), a $2 billion national enterprise. Before assuming senior leadership at PBS, Pat was president of Time Warner's CNN Productions and Time Inc. Television, where she was responsible for developing, commissioning, and supervising original nonfiction programming projects for CNN, TBS, and other Turner and Time Warner networks and businesses. Under her direction, the division produced more than five hundred hours of documentaries and received more than one hundred major awards, including forty-one Emmys, seven Peabodys, and thirty-five CableACEs. Pat began her television career in Boston, after five years as a college teacher. During her twenty-five years in television, she has worked for three major broadcast networks as well as cable. She has produced and reported news, current affairs, and documentaries; been an independent producer; and created and managed her own production company. In 2003, PBS was listed on the Forbes Magnetic 40 Companies and Pat was named Woman of the Year by *Women in Cable and Communications*. She has also earned nationwide respect for her deep involvement in global concerns such as women's rights and environmental protection.

In this Afterword, Pat Mitchell reiterates the importance of changing the nature of power and using it wisely in addressing the compelling and urgent global challenges we face.

Afterword

CHANGING THE NATURE OF POWER

Pat Mitchell

When I speak with other leaders who are women, I often think of something my friend Bella Abzug, that trailblazing, hat-wearing New York congresswoman, once said: "In the twenty-first century, women will change the nature of power rather than power changing the nature of women." In reading this book, which evolved from the Linkage, Inc.'s annual Women in Leadership Summit, Bella's words come to life for me.

Bella was absolutely right. Women are changing the nature of power: the way we get power, the way we use it. The people in this book are examples of that. Through their personal power, they have made their world a more equitable place to live and work. The currents of their personal journeys, and the understanding they have brought to the workplace and to society, resonate with all of us. They understand what it's like to be a woman in today's world, that it's necessary to take risks, break barriers, and create change. This book is a celebration of the changes that such power has been able to bring about and a recognition of the need to ensure that we pass along those changes to a future generation of young women and men. We should not forget that, as has been noted throughout this book, every successful woman helps empower others.

Nor can we forget how much power we've obtained. It wasn't even possible for women to own companies and pursue their dreams one hundred years ago. Women didn't have rights then; they had a lot of wrongs. It was wrong to speak out in public or to take a leadership stand as a role model of another way.

And clearly, women leaders have established a new standard of rights in this country that *has* forever changed the world. In the United States, more than nine million women own their own businesses today. They employ more women than all of the Fortune 500 companies combined. Women make up 45 percent of the executives and managers in this country. By 2010, women will account for 65 percent of the labor force. There are more women graduates in every discipline you can name, more women voters, more women elected to office than at any time in history. Our progress has been tremendous, and that progress is felt in other countries too.

To be sure, we've broken through a lot of barriers and crashed a lot of glass ceilings. But we also need to remember that there are still many rooms at the top that are not open to qualified women. From media to politics to Fortune 500 companies, women are seriously underrepresented in boardrooms and executive offices. This represents a terrible loss of brainpower. Much has been made of the fact that I am the first woman president of a broadcast network, for instance. But what really concerns me is that in my thirty years in the television business, I never worked for a woman leader. Many of you have been there too. You have been, are now, or will be the first or only woman in a position in your field. We need to change that. It is up to all of us who have achieved positions of influence to use that power (not just for ourselves alone, but for all the others who will be watching us closely). They will see how we define power and use it. What we do now will affect them more than we can know.

As is true of many of the journeys you've read of in this book, my own journey to leadership was largely improvised. It began in a rural town in South Georgia. Growing up, I didn't see many role models of powerful or successful women. I never even thought of my mother as a working woman, but that's all she did. She cooked and cleaned and took care of the family, and never sat down. I see her now more clearly as the force that held our family together. She was a caring, giving, powerful woman who drew her power from the way she gave of herself to her family, neighbors, friends, and community.

My father encouraged my dreams and made it clear that there was only one way to pursue them, and that was through education. I became the first person on either side of my family to go to college. I started on a drama scholarship, but my practical side told me to get a teaching degree as well, so that I would be prepared to make a living.

On the day I received my master's degree in English, my son was born, putting into place a balancing act that continues throughout my life as a working mother. Teaching at the college level offered a better work-life balance than many careers, but after five years at the University of Georgia and one on the faculty of Virginia Commonwealth University, I was offered a job at *Look* magazine in New York.

Leaving the South and the security of teaching, I moved with my young son to the big city and was loving my new life and career. But nine months later, *Look* suddenly went bankrupt. There's nothing like unemployment to make you reassess your dreams and your journey. I was encouraged by a friend to try television. Along with many other unemployed writers, I sat outside an NBC executive's office all day with a story I had written for *Look*. When he finally saw me, he said, "Let's do this story for television." I said yes quickly before he realized that I had absolutely no idea what "doing the story for NBC" really meant. Fortunately for me, the early 1970s was a time when doors were opening for women in television. The government had created something called the Equal Employment Opportunity Commission, which began requiring media companies to make the hiring of women and minorities a priority so that the news programs would look a bit more like the communities they were serving. Even so, I just couldn't find the right open door.

I was twenty-six, which is considered old for television, and had no experience outside of the few freelance assignments I was picking up to learn-by-doing. But it seemed to me that the combination of my teaching skills and my brief experience in magazine journalism with media was good preparation for television. I thought of the newsroom as a larger classroom, and writing was key to telling a story succinctly and with impact. It took a while to convince television networks of this, but eventually, after dozens of auditions and interviews all over the country, I was offered a job as a producer at the NBC affiliate in Boston.

In those early days of television, the few women in newsrooms were still pioneers, and we had to prove ourselves every day. Many executives weren't sure what to do with us, realizing that we were supposed to make a difference by being there, but not sure what that difference was.

We were encouraged to lower our voices, wear ugly suits, and stay away from any subject having to do with women. We were told never to mention children, our own or someone else's. It was difficult to find allies, much less women mentors. It was even more difficult to find an authentic voice among us—a voice that was unafraid to go against the powers that be and speak out when there was need for reform. Fortunately, some of us were able to reassess the game being played.

If the goal really was to make a difference, we realized we couldn't do that by merely participating in the game. We needed to speak with a different voice, to bring a different perspective to the news and the stories that got covered. We needed to bring a different approach to work practices and management strategies. We needed to get and use our power differently. And we did.

Over the course of my time in Boston, my female colleagues and I realized that we could use the power of television to bring issues of importance to women to the TV screens and homes of America. Looking back on the incredible strides we made in those days makes me even more aware of the ways today in which we are failing to use the power of television effectively.

In the media, we have turned away from stories that matter for women and children, not only in this country but around the world. In Afghanistan, for example, women were dying underneath the burqa, unable to live or work with any sense of freedom. But in America, there were few stories about this until after September 11. Now that the Taliban has been banished from power, women are no longer required to wear the burqa, even though many still do out of fear. Women are now able to return to their careers (it may surprise you to know that 40 percent of the doctors and lawyers in Afghanistan were women), and they have reopened the schools. If only you could see the eyes of the girls who were denied education and the eagerness they have to learn and read, you would be committed to making sure those schools stay open forever.

Much has changed in the world, but much has to be done to ensure that those changes are lasting. I worry that when the press leaves Afghanistan, we will turn our attention away from those women and children, and they will find themselves fighting for basic rights again. It is part of our responsibility as leaders, as women who have come to positions of power through our own challenges, to help others in America and around the world find their way. If women's voices are engaged during conflicts, lives are changed. If women's voices are more fully recognized when decisions are made, history is changed. When women speak up, they help all of the generations to follow.

Imagine what would be different if women's voices and women's power were more fully engaged in finding solutions to problems of poverty, disease, and peace. Imagine what the world would be like if half of its nations' leaders were women. Imagine what America would be like if half of the governors, senators, and city council members were women. Would the schools be better, worse, or just the same? Would there be support for childcare? If half the insurance companies were run by women, would legislation be required so that women could see a gynecologist? If half the entertainment companies were run by women, would there be a different kind of reality television? Perhaps, instead of the Bachelorette choosing her suitor, we might have Madame President choosing her cabinet. Imagine if half our academic institutions were run by women. Would women still make up two-thirds of the world's illiterate population? If half the Fortune 500 companies were run by women, would men find it easier to take paternity leave?

The leadership of women does make a difference. We are moving toward the critical mass necessary for major change in the world. Sociologists put the number to achieve a tipping point at 30 percent of a population, and we are nearing that in many avenues of

American life. The time will come when it will not be news when we have a new CEO or president who happens to be a woman. But until that time, we need to be vigilant about breaking new ground.

Coming into my job as the first woman president of PBS, I knew there would be an additional spotlight on me, a different judgment about the decisions I made and the leadership skills I deployed. So one of the first things I did was to make sure I had enough women's voices represented on the senior management team. Eventually, the spotlight will not be on a leader just because she is a woman. But while the spotlight is on us, let's use its power—inclusively—to illuminate the great needs that still exist for women and children in America and around the world.

Women ask different kinds of questions. Women are less invested in the status quo. Women are willing to take risks. On our climb to power, with each step up the ladder we make, let's be sure to become the kinds of leaders who reach down and give a helping hand to those behind us. That's real power—power that can dispel fear and promote freedom and equality. The challenge today is the same challenge that the suffragists faced. We need to spread the light of freedom that has illuminated our journeys and made it possible for us to accomplish so much.

One of the themes of this book is bringing an authentic voice to power. We need to speak power in a woman's voice. When we do, as Bella Abzug predicted, we really do change the nature of power, rather than allowing power to change the nature of women. The voices here call on us to look beyond ourselves, to focus our power on positive change for our organizations, for our communities, and for the world. For when we speak with enlightened power, we will truly be heard.

Notes

Foreword

1. Helgesen, S. (1990). *The female advantage: Women's ways of leadership*. New York: Doubleday.
2. Tischler, L. (2004, February). Where are the women? *Fast Company*, p. 52ff.
3. Wilson, M. (2004). *Closing the leadership gap: Why women can and must help run the world*. New York: Viking, p. 4.
4. Wilson, *Closing the leadership gap*, p. 4.
5. The 2004 Fortune 500. (2004). *Fortune Magazine*. Available at http://www.fortune.com/fortune/fortune500?promoid=cnn money.
6. Wilson, *Closing the leadership gap*, p. xii.
7. Wilson, *Closing the leadership gap*, p. 4.
8. Catalyst. (2004). *The bottom line: Connecting corporate performance and gender diversity*. Available at http://www. catalystwomen.org/knowledge/titles/files/full/financial performancereport.pdf.
9. Jamieson, K. H. (1995). *Beyond the double bind: Women and leadership*. New York: Oxford University Press, p. 5.

Introduction

1. Sellers, P. (2003, October 13). Power: Do women really want it? *Fortune*, pp. 80–100.
2. Tischler, L. (2004, February). Where are the women? *Fast Company*, pp. 52–60.

3. Belkin, L. (2003, October 26). The opt-out revolution. *New York Times Magazine*, pp. 7 et. seq.

4. Adler, R. D. (2001). *Women in the executive suite correlate to high profits*. Glass Ceiling Research Center. Available at http://glassceiling.org/InTheNewsFolder/HBRArticle PrintablePage.html.

5. Catalyst. (2004). *The bottom line: Connecting corporate performance and gender diversity*, p. 2. Available at http://www. catalystwomen.org/knowledge/titles/files/full/financial performancereport.pdf.

6. Catalyst. (2002). *Women in leadership and learning*, cited in *Women and diversity: WOW! facts 2002*. Washington, DC: The Business Women's Network, p. 91.

7. McCracken, D. (2002, November–December). Winning the talent war for women: Sometimes it takes a revolution. *Harvard Business Review*, pp. 159–167.

8. U. S. Department of Labor, Bureau of Labor Statistics (February 2004). *Monthly labor review*, pp. 37–57.

9. Catalyst. (2003). Cited in *Women and diversity: WOW! facts 2003*. Washington, DC: The Business Women's Network and Diversity Best Practices, p. 51.

10. Catalyst. (2003). Available at http://www.catalystwomen.org/knowledge/titles/title.php? page=cen_WBD03; The Committee of 200 (2004). *The C200 business leadership index 2004: Annual report on women's clout in business*, p. 6. The Committee of 200 is a membership organization of the world's most successful women entrepreneurs and corporate leaders dedicated to fostering growth and opportunity for the next generation of women business leaders. Its most recent annual report reveals that the benchmark for the number of women ascending to board positions increased a mere 6 percent between 2003 and 2004. The C200 also estimates that equal representation of women on the boards of America's biggest companies could take another fifty years.

11. Catalyst. (2003). Cited in *Women and diversity: WOW! facts 2003*, p. 51; The Committee of 200. (2004). *The C200 business leadership index 2004: Annual report on women's clout in business*, p. 6. The C200 report shows that the pace of women moving into high-level positions slowed to a 4 percent increase between 2003 and 2004 (compared with a 25 percent increase between 2002 and 2003).

12. Statistics available from the Center for American Women and Politics at http://www.cawp.rutgers.edu.

13. Merrill-Sands, D. M., & Kolb, D. M. (2001, April). Women as leaders: The paradox for success. *CGO Insights* (Briefing Note No. 9), pp. 1–4.

14. Merrill-Sands & Kolb. *CGO Insights* (Briefing Note No. 9), pp. 1–4. *Note:* The Cochran study was reported on in the Merrill-Sands article.

15. Merrill-Sands & Kolb. *CGO Insights* (Briefing Note No. 9), pp. 1–4.

16. Merrill-Sands & Kolb. *CGO Insights* (Briefing Note No. 9), pp. 1–4. *Note:* The Kabacoff study was reported on in the Merrill-Sands article.

Chapter One

1. Greenhalgh, Leonard. (1987). The case against winning in negotiations. 3 *Negotiation Journal* 167.

2. Naisbitt, John, & Aburdene, Patricia. (1985). *Re-inventing the corporation: Transforming your job and your company for the new information society*. New York: Warner Books.

3. Sargent, Alice, & Stupak, Ronald. (1993). Managing in the 90s: The androgynous manager. *Training and Development Journal*, 8(3), 13.

4. Eisler, Riane, Loye, David, & Norgaard, Kari. (1995). *Women, men, and the global quality of life*. Pacific Grove, CA: Center for Partnership Studies. The nine measures we used to assess the degree of gender equity were (1) number of literate

females for every hundred literate males; (2) female life expectancy as a percentage of male life expectancy; (3) number of women for every hundred men in parliaments and other governing bodies; (4) number of females in secondary education for every hundred males; (5) maternal mortality; (6) contraceptive prevalence; (7) access to abortion; (8) social equality for women; and (9) economic equality for women. The thirteen measures used to assess quality of life were (1) overall life expectancy; (2) human rights ratings; (3) access to health care; (4) access to clean water; (5) literacy; (6) infant mortality; (7) number of refugees fleeing the country; (8) percentage of daily caloric requirements consumed; (9) gross domestic product (GDP) as a measure of wealth; (10) percentage of GDP distributed to the poorest 40 percent of households; (11) ratio of GDP going to the wealthiest versus the poorest 20 percent of the population; and as measures of environmental sensitivity, (12) the percentage of forest habitat remaining; and (13) compliance with the Convention on International Trade in Endangered Species. When we explored the relation between the gender equity and quality of life variables with descriptive, correlational, factor, and multiple regression analyses, we found a strong systemic correlation between these two measures. These findings were consistent with our hypothesis that increased equity for women is central to a higher quality of life for a country as a whole and that gender inequity reduces the opportunities and capabilities not only of women but of the entire population. The link between gender equity and quality of life was confirmed at a very high level of statistical significance for correlational analysis, with a total of seventy-nine significant correlations in the predicted direction. This link was further confirmed by factor analysis. High factor loadings for gender equity and quality of life variables accounted for 87.8 percent of the variance. Regression analysis also yielded significant results.

An R-square of .84, with statistical significance at the .0001 level, provided support for the hypothesis that gender equity is a strong indicator of the quality of life.

5. See Pietila, Hilkka. (2001, February). Nordic welfare society—a strategy to eradicate poverty and build up equality: Finland as a case study. *Journal Cooperation South*, pp. 79–96. For a more detailed discussion of these social and economic dynamics, see Eisler, Riane. (1987). *The chalice and the blade*. New York: HarperCollins; Eisler, Riane. (2002). *The power of partnership*. Novato, CA: New World Library.

6. For more information about the Global Competitiveness Programme and Global Competitiveness Report of the World Economic Forum, see http://www.weforum.org.

7. Naisbitt & Aburdene, *Re-inventing the corporation*.

8. Butruille, Susan G. (1990, April). Corporate caretaking. *Training and Development Journal*, 44(4), 48–55.

9. http://www.city.toronto.on.ca/health/baby.htm.

10. See Eisler, Riane, & Levine, Daniel S. (2002). Nurture, nature, and caring: We are not prisoners of our genes. *Brain and Mind*, 3(1), 9–52.

11. For more information on the Alliance for a Caring Economy, see Eisler, Riane. (2004). *Changing the rules of the game: Work, values, and caring*. Available at the Center for Partnership Studies website: http://www.partnershipway.org. (Go to Library, Articles and Interviews, Partnership Economics.)

Chapter Three

1. *Merriam-Webster's collegiate dictionary* (9th ed.). (1985). Springfield, MA: Merriam-Webster, p. 922.

2. Jamieson, D. (2003). *The heart and mind of the practitioner: Remembering Bob Tannenbaum*. Retrieved Feb. 14, 2004, from http://www.odnetwork.org/odponline/vol35n4.

3. United Nations Association of Utah. Retrieved Feb. 10, 2004, from http://unau.org.

4. Lorde, A. Quote available at http://www.lambda.net/ ~maximum/lorde.html. For a more complete collection of Audre Lorde's work and views, see Lorde, A. (1984). *Sister outsider: Essays and speeches*. Trumansburg, NY: Crossing Press.

Chapter Four

1. Personal story recounted in Corcoran, B. (2003). *Use what you've got & other business lessons I learned from my mom*. New York: Portfolio, pp. 1–6, 31–38, and 207 and in Corcoran, B. (2004). *If you don't have big breasts, put ribbons on your pigtails & other lessons I learned from my mom*. New York: Portfolio, pp. 1–6, 31–38, and 206.

Chapter Five

1. Gibran, K. (1976). *The prophet*. New York: Alfred A. Knopf, pp. 27–31.
2. Norris, G. (2004). *Inviting silence: Universal principles of meditation*. New York: BlueBridge, p. 9.
3. Kabir. (2004). *The Kabir book*. (Robert Bly, Trans.). Boston: Beacon Press, pp. 8–9.
4. Oliver, M. (1997). *West wind: Poems and prose poems*. New York: Houghton Mifflin, p. 40.
5. Cameron, J. (1992). *The artist's way: A spiritual path to higher creativity*. New York: Putnam.
6. Rumi, J. (1997). *The essential Rumi*. (C. Banks, Trans.). San Francisco: HarperSanFrancisco, p. 36.
7. Ker-Conway, J. (2001). *A woman's education*. New York: Knopf, p. 90.
8. Ker-Conway, *A woman's education*, p. 90.

Chapter Six

1. This poem can be found in Chapman, A. (1968). *Black voices: An anthology of Afro-American literature*. New York: Mentor Books, p. 355. Original work: Dunbar, P. L. (1913).

The complete poems of Paul Lawrence Dunbar. New York: Dodd Mead and Co.

2. Collins, P. H. (1986). Learning from the outsider within: The sociological significance of black feminist thought. *Social Problems, 33*(6), 14–32.

3. Guinier, L., Fine, M., & Balin, J. (1997). *Becoming gentlemen: Women, law school and institutional change.* Boston: Beacon Press, p. 85.

4. For additional information on the challenges and benefits of mentoring for women managers, see Blake-Beard, S. (2003, January). Critical trends and shifts in the mentoring experiences of professional women. *CGO Insights, 15.* Boston: Center for Gender in Organizations, Simmons School of Management. Available at www.simmons.edu/som/cgo/insights15.pdf.

5. Wellington, S., & Catalyst. (2001). *Be your own mentor: Strategies from top women on the secrets of success.* New York: Random House; Catalyst. (1996). *Women in corporate leadership: Progress and prospects.* New York: Catalyst.

6. Information about Procter & Gamble's Mentor Up program can be found in Zielinski, D. (2000, October). Mentoring up. *Training,* pp. 136–140.

7. For a detailed description of the work done by Deloitte & Touche, see Kanter, R. M., & Roessner, J. (1999). *Deloitte & Touche (A): A hole in the pipeline.* (Case 9-300-012). Boston: Harvard Business School Press.

8. Kanter & Roessner, *Deloitte & Touche (A),* p. 6.

9. Wells, S. (2001, June). Smoothing the way. *HRMagazine, 46*(6), 52–58.

10. Wells, *Smoothing the way,* pp. 54–55.

11. Murray, M., with Owen, M. A. (1991). *Beyond the myths and magic of mentoring: How to facilitate an effective mentoring program.* San Francisco: Jossey-Bass; Forret, M., Turban, D. B., & Dougherty, T. W. (1997). Making the most of mentoring: How five firms managed the issues that arise. *Training & Management Development Methods, 11*(2), 917–921.

12. Reisz, S. (2004). Mentoring: A cost-effective retention tool. *Catalyst*, May/June, 42–43; Pettit, L. (2004, April 13). Mentoring will motivate. *Personnel Today*, pp. 20–21; Dreher, G. F., & Cox, T. H. (1996). Race, gender and opportunity: A study of compensation attainment and the establishment of mentoring relationships. *Journal of Applied Psychology*, 81(3), 297–308; Heery, W. (1994). Corporate mentoring can break the glass ceiling. *HR Focus*, 71(5), 17–18; Bahniuk, M. H., & Hill, S. K. (1998). Promoting career success through mentoring. *Review of Business*, 19(3), 4–7.

13. O'Reilly, D. (2001, July–September). The mentoring of employees: Is your organization taking advantage of this professional development tool? *Ohio CPA Journal*, 60(3), 63–67; Blake-Beard, S. D. (2001). Taking a hard look at formal mentoring programs: A consideration of potential challenges facing women. *The Journal of Management Development*, 20(4), 331–345; Hegstad, C. D. (1999, Winter). Formal mentoring as a strategy for human resource development: A review of research. *Human Resource Development Quarterly*, 10(4), 383–393; Heimann, B., & Khushwant, K. S. (1996). The impact of formal mentoring on socialization and commitment of newcomers. *Journal of Managerial Issues*, 8(1), 108–117.

14. Cited in Guinier, Fine, & Balin, *Becoming gentlemen*, p. 27.

Chapter Seven

1. Lewis, J. J. (n.d.). Audre Lorde quotations. *About women's history*. Available at http://womenshistory.about.com/library/qu/blqulord.htm.

2. Morris, W. (Ed.). (1981). *The American heritage dictionary of the English language*. Boston: Houghton Mifflin.

3. Sellers, P. (2003, October 13). Power: Do women really want it? *Fortune*, pp. 80–100.

4. Sellers, P. Power: Do women really want it? *Fortune*, p. 82.

5. *Women and diversity: WOW! facts 2003.* (2003). Washington, DC: The Business Women's Network and Diversity Best Practices.
6. Kanter, R. M. (1977). *Men and women of the corporation.* New York: Basic Books.
7. Langford, J., & Clance, P. R. (1993, Fall). The imposter phenomenon: Recent research findings regarding dynamics, personality, and family patterns and their implications for treatment. *Psychotherapy, 30*(3), 1–8.
8. Mehrabian, A. (1981). *Silent messages: Implicit communication of emotions and attitudes.* Belmont, CA: Wadsworth.
9. Tannen, D. (1990). *You just don't understand: Women and men in conversation.* New York: Ballantine, p. 25.
10. Gilligan, C. (1993). *In a different voice: Psychological theory and women's development.* Cambridge, MA: Harvard University Press; Miller, J. B., & Stiver, I. P. (1997). *The healing connection: How women form relationships in therapy and life.* Boston, MA: Beacon Press.
11. Meyerson, D. (2001). *Tempered radicals: How people use difference to inspire change at work.* Boston: Harvard Business School Press.
12. Tannen, D. (1994). *Talking from 9 to 5.* New York: HarperCollins.
13. Tannen, *Talking from 9 to 5.*
14. Tannen, *Talking from 9 to 5.*
15. Jamieson, K. H. (1995). *Beyond the double bind.* New York: Oxford University Press, p. 5.
16. Jamieson, K. H. *Beyond the double bind,* p. 13.
17. Simmons, A. (2001). *The story factor.* Cambridge, MA: Perseus.
18. Meyerson, *Tempered radicals.*
19. Kotter, J. (1996). *Leading change.* Boston: Harvard Business School Press.
20. Gottman, J., & Silver, N. (1999). *The seven principles for making marriage work.* New York: Three Rivers Press.
21. Rubin, H. (1998). *The princessa: Machiavelli for women.* London: Bloomsbury.

22. Blake-Beard, S. (2003, January). Critical trends and shifts in the mentoring experiences of professional women. *CGO Insights* (Briefing Note 15). Boston: Center for Gender in Organizations, Simmons School of Management. Available at http://www.simmons.edu/som/cgo/insights15.pdf.

23. Catalyst. (2004, January). *The bottom line: Connecting corporate performance and gender diversity.* Available at http://www.catalystwomen.org/knowledge/titles/title.php?page=lead_finperf_04.

24. Catalyst. (2003). *Women in U.S. corporate leadership* (Pub. Code D36). Available at http://www.catalystwomen.org/knowledge/titles/title.php?page=lead_wuscl_03.

Chapter Eight

1. For an in-depth analysis of women's and men's biological aptitudes and their impact on modern business and social life, as well as all references for factual data cited in this article, please see Fisher, H. (1999). *The first sex: The natural talents of women and how they are changing the world.* New York: Random House.

2. Wilson, M., and Daly, M. (2004). Do pretty women inspire men to discount the future? *Proceedings of the Royal Society of London.* B (Suppl.) 271; S177–S179.

3. Moskal, B. S. (1997, February 3). Women make better managers. *Industry Week,* p. 17.

Chapter Eleven

1. The Center for Mindfulness, Healthcare and Society has compiled a descriptive research bibliography based on their twenty-five years of research into mindfulness and related practices. To access this bibliography along with research abstracts, please visit http://www.umassmed.edu/cfm.

2. Kobasa, S. (1979). Stressful life events, personality, and health: An inquiry into hardiness. *Journal of Personality and Social Psychology, 37*, 1–11.

3. Lewis, T., Amini, F., & Lannon, R. (2001). *A general theory of love*. New York: Vintage Books.

4. Kabat-Zinn, J. (1990). *Full catastrophe living: Using the wisdom of your body and mind to face stress, pain and illness*. New York: Delacorte.

5. Goleman, D., Boyatzis, R., & McKee, A. (2002). *Primal leadership: Learning to lead with emotional intelligence*. Boston: Harvard Business School Press.

6. Borysenko, J. (2001). *Inner peace for busy people*. Carlsbad, CA: Hay House; Rosch, E., Varela, F., & Thompson, E. T. (1991). *The embodied mind: Cognitive science and human experience*. Cambridge, MA: MIT Press.

7. Davidson, R. J., & Kabat-Zinn, J. (in press). Alterations in brain and immune functions produced by mindfulness meditation. *Psychosomatic Medicine*.

8. Schwartz, J. (2004, September 5). Always on the job: Employees pay with health. *New York Times*, p. A1.

9. Schwartz, Always on the job. *New York Times*.

10. Leslie, J. B., & Van Velsor, E. (1996, February). *A look at derailment today: North America and Europe*. Greensboro, NC: Center for Creative Leadership, no. 196.

11. O'Neill, J. (1993/2004). *The paradox of success*. New York: Tarcher/Penguin; Zweig, C., & Wolf, S. (1999). *Romancing the shadow: Guide to soul work for a vital, authentic life*. New York: Ballantine.

12. This list is based on an adaptation of the Enneagram system. Recommended reading: Lapid-Bogda, G. (2004). *Bringing out the best in yourself at work: How to use the enneagram*. New York: McGraw-Hill.

13. Bennett-Goleman, T. (2001). *Emotional alchemy: How the mind can heal the heart*. New York: Harmony Books, p. 111.

14. If symptoms become debilitating in terms of depression or addictive behaviors, it is important to seek professional guidance. Mindfulness has been shown to be extremely effective in treating depression when combined with cognitive therapy (called MBCT). See work of J. D. Teasdale, et al. (2000), *Journal of Counseling and Clinical Psychology*, 68(4), p. 622.

15. Childre, D., & Cryer, B. (2000). From chaos to coherence: The power to change performance. *Heartmath*. Boulder Creek, CA: Planetery.

16. Halpern, B. L., & Lubar, K. (2003). *Leadership presence: Dramatic techniques to reach out, motivate and inspire*. New York: Gotham Books.

17. Personal communication with Peter Bubriski, stage actor and corporate communications coach, June 2004.

18. As cited in Heim, P., & Murphy, S. (2001). *In the company of women: Turning workplace conflict into powerful alliances*. New York: Tarcher/Putnam, p. 82.

19. Personal communication with Susan Ray, August 2004.

20. Smith, A. D. (2004, July 30). Show and tell. *New York Times*, Section A, p. 19.

Chapter Twelve

1. My research, reported in *Working Identity: Unconventional Strategies for Reinventing Your Career* (Harvard Business School Press, 2003), is an in-depth study of thirty-nine managers and professionals who changed careers or were in the process of trying to change careers. Most made significant changes in both what they do and where they do it, but most important, all experienced a subjective feeling of reaching a crossroad, one that would require significant personal change. My sample ranged in age from thirty-two to fifty-one, with an average of forty-one; 65 percent of the study participants are men, and 35 percent are women. Almost half live and work outside the

United States. All have college degrees, and about three-fourths have graduate degrees (for example, business, science, or law). My methodology consisted of clinical interviews. The research was longitudinal: I conducted an average of three open-ended interviews over a period of two to three years. Between the interviews, I had email exchanges and telephone conversations with participants to keep track of their progress.

2. Markus, H., & Nurius, P. (1986). Possible selves. *American Psychologist, 41,* 954–969.

3. McKenna, E. (1998). *When work does not work anymore: Women, work and identity.* New York: Dell, pp. 161–162.

Chapter Thirteen

1. U.S. Census Bureau estimates.

2. American Demographics, 2002, and Ken Dychtwald, AgeWave.

3. Quotation available at http://www.borntomotivate.com/Soul.html.

4. Center for Women's Business Research, 2004.

5. Center for Women's Business Research, 2004.

6. Center for Women's Business Research, 2004.

7. Center for Women's Business Research, 2004.

8. Old Girl's Network, 2003.

Chapter Sixteen

1. The concept of balancing advocacy with inquiry was developed by professors Chris Argyris and Don Schön and refined by the partners of Action Design. See Argyris, C., Putnam, R., & Smith, D. M. (1985). *Action science.* San Francisco: Jossey-Bass.

2. The Ladder of Inference was developed by Chris Argyris and Don Schön, elaborating on an idea first put forward by S. I. Hayakawa. See Argyris et al., *Action science,* for a more in-depth discussion of it.

3. The social psychologist Lee Ross calls this phenomenon *naïve realism* and has written extensively about it. See, for example, Ross, L., & Ward, A. (1996). *Naïve realism in everyday life: Implications for social conflict and misunderstanding.* Stanford, CA: Stanford Center on Conflict and Negotiation.

4. This "two-column case" format originated with professor Chris Argyris. See Argyris, C., & Schön, D. A. (1974). *Theory in practice: Increasing professional effectiveness.* San Francisco: Jossey-Bass.

Chapter Seventeen

1. As quoted in Kravitz, L., & Olitzky, K. M. (Eds.). (1993). *Pirke Avot: A modern commentary on Jewish ethics.*Feldman Library UAHC Press.

Chapter Eighteen

1. In 1998, Management Research Group (MRG) began research that explored the ways men and women approach leadership differently and similarly. Our initial gender study (Rabacoff, R. (1998). *Gender differences in organizational leadership*) included nine hundred women and nine hundred men in middle management positions matched for company, management level, management function, and years of management experience. The data came from our extensive database of North American leaders who have completed MRG's 360-degree assessment instrument while participating in leadership development programs sponsored by their organizations.

Chapter Nineteen

1. Annis, B. (2003). *Same words different language: Why men and women don't understand each other and what to do about it.* London, England: Judy Piatkus Publishers, Ltd.

2. *Women and diversity: WOW! facts 2003*. Washington, D.C.: The Business Women's Network and Diversity Best Practices, pp. 59–60.

Chapter Twenty

1. Klaus, P. (2003). *BRAG! The art of tooting your own horn without blowing it*. New York: Warner Books.

Chapter Twenty-One

1. Bossidy, L., & Charan, R. (2002). *Execution: The discipline of getting things done*. New York: Crown Business.
2. The white paper referenced by Tracey Warson is available at http://www.nettps.com/press/whitepapers/wp06.html.

Chapter Twenty-Two

1. Rourke, M. (2002). His faith in peace endures. *Los Angeles Times*.
2. Based on Joan Chittister's statement "To be human is to give yourself for things far greater than yourself," as cited in Franck, F., Roze, J., & Connolly, R. (Eds.). (1998). *What does it mean to be human?* Nyack, NY: Circumstantial Productions Publishing, p. 194.
3. Whyte, D. (1994). *The heart aroused*. New York: Currency Doubleday, p. 27.
4. Carly Fiorini's Commencement address at the Massachusetts Institute of Technology (MIT) on June 2, 2000, available at http://www.hp.com/ghp/ceo/speeches/mit.html.
5. See Adler, N. J. (1994). Competitive frontiers: Women managing across borders. In N. J. Adler & D. N. Izraeli (Eds.), *Competitive frontiers: Women managers in a global economy* (pp. 22–40). Cambridge, MA: Blackwell. Also see Adler, N. J. (1984). Women in international management: Where are they? *California Management Review, 26*(4), 78–89.

6. Adler, N. J. (1984). Women do not want international careers: And other myths about international management. *Organizational Dynamics, 13*(2), 66–79.

7. See Adler, N. J. (1987). Pacific basin managers: A gaijin, not a woman. *Human Resource Management, 26*(2), 169–192.

8. Rosabeth Moss-Kanter, comment on Nichols, N. A. (1994). *Reach for the top: Women and the changing facts of work life.* Cambridge, MA: Harvard Business School Press, as cited in Hook, J. R. (1994). *Academy of Management Executive, 8*(2), 87–89.

9. Adler, N. J. (1998). Did you hear? Global leadership in charity's world. *Journal of Management Inquiry, 7*(2), 135–143.

10. From Mary Robinson's presidential acceptance speech, November 9, 1990, Dublin, as reported by Finlay, F. (1990). *Mary Robinson: A president with a purpose.* Dublin, Ireland: The O'Brien Press, p. 1.

11. Adler, N. J. (in press). Shaping history: Global leadership in the twenty-first century. In H. Scullion & M. Linehan (Eds.), *International human resource management.* London: Palgrave/Macmillan.

12. Eagley, A. H., & Johnson, B. T. (1990). Gender and leadership style: A meta-analysis. *Psychological Bulletin, 8*(2), 233–256, as cited in Vinnicombe, S., & Colwill, N. (1995). *The essence of women in management.* London: Prentice Hall, p. 32.

13. Roddick, A. (1991). *Body and soul.* New York: Crown, p. 226.

14. For a broader discussion of the ideas in this section, see Adler, N. J. (2001). Leading globally: Giving oneself for things far greater than oneself. *Insights: Journal of the Academy of International Business, 1*(2), 13–15.
For a discussion of predicted differences between women's and men's leadership, see Adler, Shaping history.

15. Adler, N. J. (2005). The art of leadership: Coaching in the twenty-first century. In H. Morgan, P. Harkins, & M. Goldsmith (Eds.), *The art and practice of leadership coaching: 50 top executive coaches reveal their secrets.* Hoboken, NJ: Wiley, 2005. Also see Nancy J. Adler's description (2003) of the seminar

"Leadership, Power, and Influence: The Art of Leadership,"
Faculty of Management, McGill University, Montreal, Que-
bec, Canada. (nancy.adler@mcgill.ca)

16. The term *dehydrated management vocabulary* comes from the
poet David Whyte.

17. From the videotape *The Next Industrial Revolution: William
McDonough, Michael Braungart and the Birth of the Sustainable Economy*. Videotape available from http://www.
mcdonough.com or contact: William McDonough, 700 East
Jefferson Street, Charlottesville, Virginia 22902; tel: 434-
979-1111, fax: 434-979-1112. See McDonough, W. (2001,
July/August). William McDonough on designing the next
industrial revolution. *Timeline*, pp. 12–16.

18. For a discussion of "collusion against illusion," see Palmer,
P. J. (1990). *The active life: A spirituality of work, creativity,
and caring*. New York: HarperCollins.

19. Pogacik regularly combines his music with profound
leadership messages for executive audiences worldwide.

Reference Information for Quotes on p. 355

Joseph Rotblat, as cited in Franck, F., Roze, J., & Connolly,
R. (Eds.). (1998). *What does it mean to be human?* Nyack,
New York: Circumstantial Productions Publishing, p. 67.

Alan Riding, from Riding, A. (2003). Anxiety and hope
in a mystical fusion: Paris show offers Chagall's intense
humanism beyond the *joie de vivre*. *New York Times*, April
22, 2003, p. B5.

David Krieger, as cited in Franck, F., Roze, J., & Connolly,
R. (Eds.). (1998). *What does it mean to be human?* Nyack,
New York: Circumstantial Productions Publishing, p. 273.

Carman Moore, as cited in Franck, F., Roze, J., & Connolly,
R. (Eds.). (1998). *What does it mean to be human?* Nyack,
New York: Circumstantial Productions Publishing, p. 119.

Ramon Munoz Soler, as cited in Franck, F., Roze, J., &
Connolly, R. (Eds.). (1998). *What does it mean to be human?*

Nyack, New York: Circumstantial Productions Publishing, p. 295.

Abraham Joshua Heschel, as cited in Dresner, S. H. (Ed.). (2001). *I asked for wonder*. New York: Crossroad.

Donella Meadows, as cited in Franck, F., Roze, J., & Connolly, R. (Eds.). (1998). *What does it mean to be human?* Nyack, New York: Circumstantial Productions Publishing, p. 96.

Chapter Twenty-Four

1. Stories in this chapter concerning my interactions with Carol Love and Laurie Mittelstadt are printed here with their permission.
2. Kanter, R. M. (1977). *Men and women of the corporation*. New York: Basic Books.

Chapter Twenty-Six

1. *Who's talking? An analysis of Sunday morning talk shows*. (2001, December 1). *The White House Project*. New York, Appendix B, 30, available at http://www.thewhitehouse project.org/research/who_talking_full-report.
2. *Voices of women leaders*. (1997, Spring). New York: SLANT. Available at http://www.Columbia.edu/cu/sipa/PUBS/ SLANT/SPRING/quotes/html.
3. Anderlini, S. N. (2000). *Women at the peace table: Making a difference*. U.N. Development Fund for Women, pp. 16–17. Available at http://www.unifem.undp.org/resources/ peacebk.pdf.

Chapter Twenty-Seven

1. Brokaw, T. (1998). *The greatest generation*. New York: Random House.

Acknowledgments

Our acknowledgments reflect the power of community past and present—as this book is truly a reflection of the contributions of so many.

First we thank Phil Harkins, CEO of Linkage, Inc., for listening to our customers and lending his guidance to the annual Women in Leadership Summit. We also thank longtime Linkage friend Warren Bennis for supporting the first summit and giving it an impetus that has carried far.

Rayona Sharpnack proposed the original idea for a gathering of women leaders. She has been an unwavering champion to transform the women-in-leadership landscape, helping so many to shift power from the personal to the global level. Susan Brady was a significant trailblazer and natural leader who served as "coconspirator" with many at Linkage, Inc., in making the first summit a breakthrough success.

Jenn DeVan Troutman, our first program director, envisioned and grew the renowned summit to reach thousands of emerging and senior leaders and exhibited a true depth of commitment and capability to impact the women's leadership field. Rich Rosier provided oversight over the years, and Jen Rosier and Pamela Bowne delivered a stellar fifth anniversary program.

Jacqueline Lewis has carried the torch forward and sustains the momentum with boundless intellect, passion, and energy, as well as the personality of a woman leader at home in the world. She and co-director Robin Pedrelli, a true partner in creating change, continue to exceed customer expectations in providing a transformational learning experience. Jim Laughlin and Nina Coil, senior consultants and experts in the latest theories of leadership, lent intellectual support and their skill at the written word as they translated critically important leadership principles offered at the summits to the pages of this book. Kira Hower provided much of the research that helped shape our ideas and supports our conclusions. Carol Anderson facilitated our early planning efforts with pictorial brilliance.

We also thank Marnie D'Uva, Angeline Alexakos, and Robin Craig, who have contributed their enthusiasm, design ideas, skills, and personal experiences to helping us develop a book that reaches leaders of younger generations.

We are particularly grateful to our Linkage colleagues for taking the time to read the final collection and provide their invaluable editorial insights and suggestions for refinement: Angeline Alexakos, Dan Cohen, Erica Colonero, Debbi Coppins, Sarah Dayton, Dick Gauthier, Gustavo Garcia, Jasmine Green, Christine Hizny, Jacqueline Lewis, Aruna Joglekar, Muriel Jones, Tracy McLaughlin, Stacey Roberts, Angela Stanhope, Madeline Tarquinio, Meghan Tranos, Katie Whatmore, and Karina Wilhelms.

Anne Taylor, as always, creates an exceptional learning space. Meghan Tranos contributed her marketing efforts. Tracy McLaughlin has provided tremendous support with our proposal and marketing efforts. Erica Colonero, Sarah Dayton, Jim Foster, Scott Gavriel, and Jennifer Principe provided topflight support in qualifying individuals that make up Linkage's customer base. Angela Stanhope provided design and photographs, while Lynda Jemson gave us her invaluable design expertise and her artistic eye. Lori Hart helped shape our collage into a coherent package.

We thank Tulani Kinard, performance artist and social activist, who has lifted our audiences to new heights of expression and energy in knowing "we've got the power." Kathe Sweeney, our editor at Jossey-Bass, believed in the book and saw its potential in redefining power for women and men. We owe much gratitude for her leadership in bringing this work into the world. Paul Cohen lent us his superior talents as reviewer and editor. Mary Garrett,

Rob Brandt, and Tamara Keller—all from Jossey-Bass—graciously lent their talents and efforts to this book.

We would like to thank all of the many people supporting our extraordinary contributors, whose behind-the-scenes efforts we can't even imagine. A special thank you, in particular to Anne Marie Piazza, Molly Hamaker, Susan Neris, Sheryl Martinelli, Pat Murphy, Susan Bash, Ann-Marie Brennan, Laura Peeling, and Sylvie Losie for their critical efforts.

Most significantly, we wish to thank two individuals at Linkage, Inc., without whose leadership this book would never have made the journey from dream to reality. Jasmine Green's dedication, hard work, and commitment have carried us to the finish line—again and again! She has always been there when we needed her, even-keeled, overly effective, and always generous. Rusty Sullivan—senior vice president, general counsel, proposal shaper, market assessor, savvy advocate, contract negotiator, project manager, professional author, writing coach, Red Sox fan, tireless friend and in-house humorist— need we say more? As overseer and steward in making *Enlightened Power* happen, he is owed our deep gratitude and thanks.

I, Lin Coughlin, want to express my deep appreciation to my three extraordinary children—Brooke, Emily, and John—for supporting my passion and eccentricities and for coming full circle. I also thank Debbi, my sister and global travel companion, who brings such a positive, upbeat tone and constantly reminds me that anything is possible, and Janina Fisher for her masterful analytical brilliance in perspective taking. I thank Carol Anderson for her abundant wisdom, insights, and generosity of spirit in spurring me to reflect, frame, and articulate years of critically important leadership lessons. And thanks to the leaders of the Committee of 200, the Women's Leadership Board at Harvard University's Kennedy School, The Commonwealth Institute, The Belizean Grove, and the Institute for Women's Leadership for providing me with the space to develop my voice as a change-oriented leader, committed to the realization of the full partnership of men and women leaders. To Phil Harkins, for suggesting the idea of this book, for pushing me to have the courage of my convictions, and for his pioneering work in developing enlightened, high-performing teams of men and women leaders.

I, Ellen Wingard, wish to thank my extraordinary clients, who exemplify the principles and practices of enlightened power every-day. My deepest gratitude is in memory of Elizabeth Rose Campbell, who offered her brilliant, imaginative counsel in early drafts and continues to provide inspiration through the life that she lived. My appreciation goes to many colleagues who graciously offered support on this book: Rusty Sullivan, for his heroic call above and beyond duty all along the way; Peter Bubriski for his magnanimous spirit and outstanding collaboration; Carol Franco and Kent Lineback for their generosity of time and seasoned expertise; Catherine Fitz-gerald for her rigorous editorial eye and generative perspective; Caroline Pincus for finding new language; Pamela Ashe, Sunny Bain, Linda Benoit, Bonnie Kippen, and Laura Peeling for being an exceptional support team; Jon Kabat-Zinn, Saki Santorelli, Elana Rosenbaum, Ferris Urbanowski, Kacey Karmichael, and the won-derful teachers at the original UMass Memorial Stress Reduction Clinic; David Whyte and John O'Donohue for their encourage-ment to write; Oriah Mountain Dreamer for her care and eloquence in defining a new power; Cheryl Richardson, Pat Adler, and Nanna Aida Svenson for graceful early support; Mark Hyman, MD for enlightened medical care; The Helix Group (Danit Fried, Ro King, Gunilla Norris, Gail Straub) for exemplifying women supporting women for 20 years; and my dear friends and sources of inspiration over the years, including Riki Alexander, Joanna Brown, Mary Tess Crotty, Carole Ireland, Tulani Kinard, David and Ronit Kreger, Bill Kueppers, and Pamela Putney. Special thanks to the Smith family for their love and support. My contribution to the book is dedicated to Andy Carroll, a beloved and enlightened man passionate to bring a new power for good into the world.

I, Keith Hollihan, would like to thank my son, Garrett Graham Hollihan, for making his timely entrance into the world on the night of our first scheduled book meeting, and for learning how to walk before the project was finished!

About Linkage, Inc.

The development of this book was sponsored by Linkage, Inc., a global organizational development company that specializes in leadership development.

At the core of our work is a passion for developing great organizations led by great men *and* women leaders. The research here is clear and conclusive: those organizations with the best track record of promoting women leaders are decidedly more profitable vis-à-vis other organizations. Developing great organizations and developing great women leaders go hand in hand.

The leadership development needs of women leaders are unique, however. Linkage meets those needs so that we can help connect aspiring and high-performing women leaders to the futures they want to create. Specifically, we equip women leaders with the strategies, confidence, and skills they need to catalyze change, accelerate their development, gain visibility, and achieve breakthrough results—individually and as part of inclusive leadership teams and organizations.

To this end, Linkage has developed a full suite of integrated programs, products, and services that we call Women in Leadership. The centerpiece of this portfolio is Linkage's annual Women in Leadership Summit, a program that addresses the unique challenges and opportunities facing women leaders. Since 1999, this program has provided more than 5,000 participants with the knowledge, network, and impetus necessary to thrive as individuals and within their organizations. Along the way, the summit has spawned a vibrant community of women who are, as the title of this book indicates, transforming the practice of leadership.

The following are other Women in Leadership offerings that Linkage provides clients:

- Regional forums that address emerging issues and special functional challenges facing women leaders
- Targeted skill-building workshops that develop the capabilities that are critical to women leaders, including communications, risk taking, and decision making
- Customized on-site development experiences that resonate among women leaders within an organization's unique culture
- Assessment and coaching services that help women leaders forge concrete plans for positioning, advancement, and success

All of these offerings grew out of Linkage's commitment to the subject of women in leadership. And that commitment continues to deepen. After all, without a commitment and a passion for developing women leaders, how else could you possibly develop great organizations?

If you are interested in finding out more about our company and our array of Women in Leadership programs, products, and services, please call 781-402-5555 or visit www.linkageinc.com.

Name Index

Subject Index

A

ABC, 435
Accountability, 459
Accuracy, influence and, 127–128
Achievement: bragging about, 331–337, 348; high-, in job-sharing arrangement, 236; high orientation to, 177–178, 184; as motivation for working mothers, 155
Acknowledgment, in communication, 273–276
Action orientation, for exceptional human performance, 454–456
Activism: corporate, 380, 381–393; inclusive, 411–434. *See also* Global change; Social change
Actualization, hierarchies of, 29–31
Advancement, career. *See* Career advancement; Career paths
Advocacy, in communication, 273–276
Affinity groups, in corporation, 326
Affirmation, 1–2
Affirmative action, 147
Afghanistan, 26; media coverage of, 428, 488–489; U.S. military women in, 446; women in, 428, 488–489
Africa, women in, 430
African American women, 102, 441
Aggressive style. *See* Masculine or aggressive style
Aging baby boomers: characteristics of, 220–221; online lifestage company for, 216, 218–221, 224–226, 229
Agrarian societies, 23, 26
Aid to Families with Dependent Children (AFDC), 390–393
AIDS patients, mental imagery for, 452
Air Force Academy, 443

Al Qaeda, 263
Alchemical Studies (Jung), 183
Alexis de Tocqueville Society, 470
Alliance for a Caring Economy, 20, 35
Alliance for Strategic Leadership, 288
Ambiguity tolerance, 135
Ambition, reflection on, 183–187
American Civil Liberties Union (ACLU), 442–443
American Express Company, *xxxii*
American Field Service, 79
American Heritage Dictionary, 112
American Revolution, 439–440, *xxix*
American West, 374
Americas Mutual Funds Group, *xxxii*
Angel's advocate, 119
Anima and animus, *xxii*
Annapolis Service Academy, 443
Annapurna: A Woman's Place (Blum), *xv*
Anthropology, corporate, 244, 258–263
Anxiety: authenticity and, 61; stress and, 176–177
Apollo, 455
Apprenticeship, 206
Art and artistic processes: global leadership and, 353–355, 363–366; holistic leadership and, 398–400, 406–407, 408–409; human imagination and hope in, 353–355
Articulation ability, 137
Artist's Way, The (Cameron), 93
"At-risk" students, teaching, 472, 473–483
"At the Shore" (Oliver), 91–92
Athena, 129
AT&T, 172
Attributions, exploring, 281–282
Attrition, of women in corporations, 7–8, 112–113